WARFARE IN HISTORY

Chivalry and Violence in Late Medieval Castile

WARFARE IN HISTORY
ISSN 1358-779X

Series editors
Matthew Bennett, Royal Military Academy, Sandhurst, UK
Anne Curry, University of Southampton, UK
Stephen Morillo, Wabash College, Crawfordsville, USA

This series aims to provide a wide-ranging and scholarly approach to military history, offering both individual studies of topics or wars, and volumes giving a selection of contemporary and later accounts of particular battles; its scope ranges from the early medieval to the early modern period.

New proposals for the series are welcomed; they should be sent to the publisher at the address below.

Boydell & Brewer Limited, PO Box 9, Woodbridge, Suffolk IP12 3DF

Previously published volumes in this series are listed at the back of this volume

Chivalry and Violence in Late Medieval Castile

Samuel A. Claussen

THE BOYDELL PRESS

© Samuel A. Claussen 2020

All rights reserved. Except as permitted under current legislation no part of this work may be photocopied, stored in a retrieval system, published, performed in public, adapted, broadcast, transmitted, recorded or reproduced in any form or by any means, without the prior permission of the copyright owner

The right of Samuel A. Claussen to be identified as the author of this work has been asserted in accordance with sections 77 and 78 of the Copyright, Designs and Patents Act 1988

First published 2020
The Boydell Press, Woodbridge

ISBN 978-1-78327-546-5

The Boydell Press is an imprint of Boydell & Brewer Ltd
PO Box 9, Woodbridge, Suffolk IP12 3DF, UK
and of Boydell & Brewer Inc.
668 Mt Hope Avenue, Rochester, NY 14620–2731, USA
website: www.boydellandbrewer.com

A CIP catalogue record for this book is available
from the British Library

The publisher has no responsibility for the continued existence or accuracy of URLs for external or third-party internet websites referred to in this book, and does not guarantee that any content on such websites is, or will remain, accurate or appropriate

This publication is printed on acid-free paper

To Sarah
Dreaming an impossible little dream.

Contents

Acknowledgements	viii
Map: The Kingdom of Castile, ca. 1400	ix
Genealogical Table: Royal House of Castile, 1311–1504	x
Introduction	1
1 Knights and Kings	29
2 Knights and Commoners	69
3 Holy War	104
4 War Against Christians	145
5 Chivalry, Men, and Women	174
Conclusions	208
Timeline of Major Events	212
Bibliography	214
Index	227

Acknowledgements

The present volume is the culmination of my own work, but it could not have been completed without the advice, support, and criticism of others. I am most grateful to Professor Richard W. Kaeuper, who challenged me intellectually, supported me as a young academic, and shared a lifetime of experience as a medieval historian. Without his advice and support, this book would not have been possible. I am also grateful to Professor Peter W. Sposato for his constant support and advice. He has read more drafts of this book than a polite person would have asked him to. Long discussions at Kalamazoo, St. Louis, and elsewhere have sharpened my thinking about my topic.

The library staff at Rush Rhees Library have also made this project possible in a very real way. Alan Unsworth has assisted me in my search for medieval Spanish sources and aided me in finding digital sources. Kristen Totleben helped me find the resources to develop my linguistic abilities in medieval Castilian. The Interlibrary Loan staff dealt with my numerous requests for obscure sources with saintly patience and made possible both the primary and secondary research necessary for this project. I am also indebted to the staff at the Biblioteca Nacional de España in Madrid, who assisted me in archival research in medieval documents on multiple occasions. To all the librarians, archivists, and staff who made this project possible, I am sincerely grateful. My research was also made possible due to several grants from California Lutheran University which allowed me to travel to Madrid and Toledo in 2016 and which supported my attendance and presentation at conferences over the last five years. The financial support from my university was crucial in completing this project.

Sincere thanks go to Caroline Palmer, who listened with patience and interest to my proposals about this book and who provided expert guidance as the book made its way to print. She was instrumental in seeing this project through to completion. My thanks also go to the readers at various stages who offered critical feedback on various aspects of the work.

Finally, I would like to thank those close to me, the people who did not provide academic expertise in the discipline of history but without whom I never would have completed this book. I am thankful to my parents, who supported me in very concrete and very abstract ways throughout my academic career. Deep thanks go to my wife, who tolerated the many late nights working and the weeks away in Spain, Michigan, Missouri, and elsewhere. Her patience and support are endless.

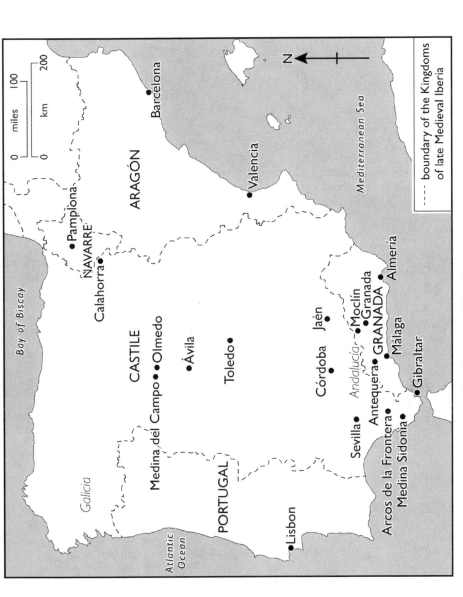

The Kingdom of Castile, ca. 1400

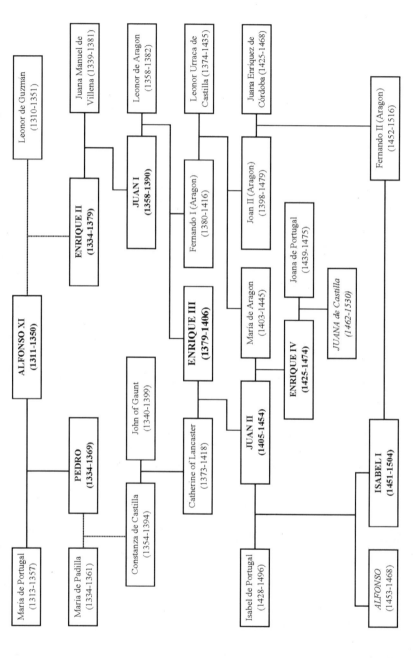

Introduction

The medieval knight Rodrigo Díaz de Vivar, better known as El Cid, died over a thousand years ago as the ruler of the minor state of Valencia on the Mediterranean coast of the Iberian Peninsula; his historical significance is debatable. The values he represented, though, long outlived him. The ideals of medieval chivalry – the guiding principles of medieval knights – with which El Cid was familiar, would also have been familiar to knights at the end of the Middle Ages. The great 15th-century knight Rodrigo Ponce de León, for example, thought of himself as a "new Cid" and, if the two men could have sat down and chatted, they would have found much that they had in common.[1] El Cid himself was animated by an early manifestation of medieval chivalry and later medieval knights of Iberia transformed him into a chivalric hero, even as they edited the facts of his life in order to mold him into an image of themselves. They told stories and sang songs of him, highlighting his valor in battle, his defense of his honor, and his loyalty to his king. Late medieval Iberians were *imagining* El Cid in a way that served their own needs, achieved their own social and political ends, and confirmed their own cultural values. Medieval chivalry in the Iberian Peninsula focused strongly on valor in battle, violence against one's enemies, and service to God on the battlefield, and these values were projected onto the hero who had died hundreds of years before they were born. The legend of El Cid was important to late medieval knights because it allowed them to place themselves in a long line of powerful heroes, and to see their own virtues and values become timeless.

Although medieval chivalry slowly began to wane in the 16th century, remembrances of it continued to animate key moments in the Spanish Golden Age and the Age of Exploration. Conquistadors, noblemen, and explorers imagined themselves as medieval knights going forth in service of God and the lord king, augmenting and defending their honor, and pursuing violence against their enemies. They imagined themselves as living versions of the great romances of medieval Iberia, discovering fantastic new lands and slaughtering non-Christians. After the empire fell by the 19th century, Spain sought to reinvent itself as a nation. Artists, politicians, and writers turned to the ideals of the Middle Ages to create a national identity for Spain, and they placed chivalry in their service in order to do so.

---

[1] *Historia de los hechos del marqués de Cádiz*, ed. Juan Luis Carriazo Rubio (Granada: Editorial Universidad de Granada, 2003), 28.

From the earliest times, medieval chivalry has been imagined and reimagined in the service of contemporary goals, whether those pertained to an individual knight of the Middle Ages, a monarch seeking power and glory, or a conquering warrior in Mexico or Peru. The ideas of chivalry have been immensely powerful throughout Iberian history, even as they have been modified, edited, or even abused.

The image that graces the cover of this book is one such piece of reimagined chivalry. Created by the Spanish painter Juan Vicens Cots in 1864, the painting is titled *Primera hazaña del Cid*, or *The First Deed of El Cid*. El Cid's first act as a young man, according to some medieval and early modern stories, was taking vengeance on Count Lozano, a man who had insulted El Cid's father. El Cid beheaded the count and presented the head to his father – the scene depicted in Cots' work. The young hero stands proudly in the light in full chain mail, with his bloody sword in one hand and the head of his enemy in the other. An invisible wind seems to nobly tussle his hair and tunic. El Cid's father leans in to gaze at the head with incredulity, perhaps at his son's bold deed, even as the other young men at the table recoil in horror at the grotesque scene. Aside from being an arresting image, *Primera hazaña del Cid* is remarkable because it represents the appropriation of the violent medieval past in the service of the modern world. Cots operated in a romantic and nationalist world that idealized the medieval past. For 19th-century romantics and nationalists the medieval world was exciting and honorable, even if it could be frightening and mysterious. But most importantly, it was the period in which national identities were truly formed. From the perspective of nationalists in the 1800s, Spain became Spain as a result of its experience in the Middle Ages. The animating force of that medieval nativity was chivalry and all that went with it – honor, nobility, holy war, and violence.

To be sure, this was partly an imagined history, but the realities of the Middle Ages loomed large for the modern world. Nationalist thinkers needed an ideology and a worldview that ennobled Spain as a nation, held its various peoples together, and gave Spain and Spanishness meaning. The selection of medieval chivalry and war as a defining feature of 19th- and 20th-century Spanish nationalism would matter a great deal as Spanish people debated who they wanted to be in the modern world. Indeed, the idea that Spain had been formed as a result of heroic medieval knights fighting for God and for Spain would be a particularly virulent component of certain strains of Spanish nationalism. Francisco Franco imagined himself as a latter-day El Cid, serving God by destroying godless communists and anarchists and building Spain into a powerful state worthy of its historical legacy. One relic of this attitude was the title page of an essay written by Darío Fernández Flórez in 1939. Below the title, "Dos Claves Históricas: Mio Cid y Roldán" [Two Historical Keys: El Cid and Roland], is typed "MADRID 1939 AÑO DE LA VICTORIA" – The year of victory (Franco's victory in the Spanish civil war). On the following page, the essay is dedicated to "the caudillo": Franco.[2] The medieval past was an essential part of Franco's self-fashioning. Though Franco has been dead for almost fifty years, the Spanish world is not done with medieval chivalry. In an election in Andalucía in 2018, eighteen seats went to the relatively new political party, Vox, which advocates for a powerful Spanish nationalism, rejecting Basque and Catalonian separatist movements. Similarly, in the general election in November of 2019, Vox placed third in the polls, capturing 10% of the vote and securing 24 seats of the 350 in the Congress of Deputies. Vox envisions a fundamentally Catholic Spain, railing against Muslim immigration, and after the electoral victory in 2018, a Vox social media account tweeted "The *Reconquista* will begin in Andalucían lands", accompanied by a video of men riding horses, overlaid with music from *Lord of the Rings* (another artifact of medievalism).[3] The *reconquista*, a modern historiographical term referring to the effort by Christians to rid the Iberian Peninsula of Islam, was a key part of medieval Iberian chivalric ideas. Even today, then, medieval ideas are used very loosely but very powerfully by people with strong political agendas.

One wonders if Cots, Franco, and the leaders of Vox understood the implications of medieval chivalry, particularly as it pertains to violence. To be sure, the idea of *reconquista* or holy war was not just understood, but actively incorporated into the political programs of modern nationalists. But violence pervaded medieval chivalry at an even deeper level than simply a drive to exterminate non-Christians. As citizens of the modern world, if we hope to speak intelligently about how history ought to be used in our politics and society, we need to try to understand ideas such as chivalry and violence on the terms in which they existed in their own time. This book seeks an understanding of medieval chivalry in the Kingdom of Castile during the Trastámara period, and chivalry's relationship with violence.

The Trastámara Period

Most readers of this book, even if unfamiliar with late medieval Spanish history, will know the basic story of the Catholic Monarchs: Isabella, the queen of Castile (r. 1474–1504), married Ferdinand, the king of Aragon (r. 1479–1516), and together they unified Spain into a single country, ejected Islam from the peninsula, introduced the Inquisition, and sent Christopher Columbus off to the New World, thus ushering in the Golden Age of Spanish history. Readers may be familiar with some of the figures of that Golden Age as well: the great painter Diego de Velázquez, the powerful

---

[2] Darío Fernández Flórez, *Dos claves históricas: Mío Cid y Roldán* (Madrid: Signo, 1939).
[3] https://twitter.com/voxnoticias_es/status/1061917901031129088?lang=en.

emperor Charles V (r. 1519–1556), or, most likely, the world-renowned playwright Miguel de Cervantes. Even if we accept such a specious and facetious summary of the "glory" of Spain at the dawn of the early modern period, we should be left wanting more. The supposed political, religious, cultural, and ideological unification of Spain – the beginning of the Spanish Golden Age – was remarkable precisely because of the period that preceded it. The Catholic Monarchs did not peacefully inherit their thrones and casually choose to send Spain into the world more aggressively. Instead, the success of the Catholic Monarchs and their Habsburg heirs in the late 15th and 16th centuries grew out of intense disorder and chaos in Iberia in the 14th and early 15th centuries. It was the ability of such rulers to overcome chaos and disorder that allowed for their successes. The chaotic period that predated the 16th century was that of the Trastámara dynasty.

The chapters of this book are organized thematically rather than chronologically. As such, a brief chronology is included here in order to help orient the non-specialist.[4] When King Alfonso XI (r. 1312–1350) died in 1350, he was initially succeeded on the Castilian throne by his son, Pedro (r. 1350–1369). For a variety of reasons, some of which will be discussed in Chapter 1, Pedro was challenged for the throne almost immediately by his bastard half-brother, Enrique de Trastámara. Between 1351 and 1369, the brothers fought, seeking support not only from the various noble families of Castile but also from foreign powers. Enrique found support from France and Aragon, while Pedro was championed primarily by England. As such, this Castilian civil war became one more theater of the ongoing Hundred Years' War which ravaged much of western Europe in the 14th and 15th centuries.[5] At the end of the war in 1369, Pedro was defeated and killed by Enrique and his supporters. King Enrique II (r. 1369–1379) established a new dynasty, which would rule Castile for the next century and a half: the Trastámara dynasty.

Enrique and his two immediate successors (his son, Juan I (r. 1379–1390), and his grandson, Enrique III (r. 1390–1406)) set about consolidating the Trastámara ascendancy by rewarding their supporters and punishing those Castilian noblemen who had resisted them. Part of this process entailed granting lands, titles, and latitude of action to some of the most powerful lords in Castile. As such, despite their success in securing the throne of Castile for themselves, the early Trastámaras also weakened their own

---

[4] One of the best surveys of the period is Teofilo F. Ruiz, *Spain's Centuries of Crisis: 1300–1474* (Oxford: Blackwell Publishing, Ltd., 2011). For a dated but more comprehensive survey of the long stretch of medieval Spanish history, see Joseph F. O'Callaghan, *A History of Medieval Spain* (Ithaca, NY: Cornell University Press, 1975).

[5] For an assessment of Castile during the Hundred Years War see L.J.A. Villalon and D.J. Kagay, eds., *History of Warfare: The Hundred Years War (part II): Different Vistas* (Boston: Brill, 2008).

authority in the kingdom, allowing the knights and nobles of the realm to assert themselves more independently and aggressively in Castilian war and politics. This slow process of the weakening of Castilian royal authority was dramatically accelerated in late 1406, when Enrique III died unexpectedly and was succeeded on the throne by his infant son, Juan II (r. 1406–1454).

A joint regency by Juan's mother, Queen Catalina (of Lancaster), and his uncle Fernando (later Fernando de Antequera and Fernando I of Aragon (r. 1412–1416)) preserved some of the Crown's authority, but the long minority, unsurprisingly, resulted in the young King Juan being dominated by the powerful men surrounding him. Upon attaining his majority, Juan relied heavily on powerful court favorites – men such as the Constable Álvaro de Luna. As a result of such favoritism and of Juan's own political weakness, the kingdom devolved into multiple periods of civil discord, precipitated by the nobles of the realm and by Juan's own relatives, who hoped to secure wealth and power for themselves. When Juan died in 1454, his son, Enrique IV (r. 1454–1474), succeeded him. Enrique relied on favorites just as his father did, but he was more assertive than his father in trying to reclaim royal authority. In response to the Crown's attempt to rein in unruly nobles, those very nobles rebelled against Enrique and proclaimed first his half-brother Alfonso and then his half-sister Isabel as the legitimate ruler of Castile. The end of Enrique's reign was occupied with civil war for the throne. When Enrique died in 1474, his supporters continued fighting against Isabel's claim by supporting Enrique's daughter, Juana. By 1476, the civil war came to a close with Isabel (r. 1474–1504) as the victor.

Alongside such internal problems, Castile's foreign wars, entanglements, and adventures were critical to the disorder of the period. As part of the ongoing Hundred Years' War, Castile sent knights and retinues to France to fight against the English on multiple occasions. Similarly, Castile and Portugal were at war frequently over questions of territory, dynastic successions, and segments of the Hundred Years' War. Wars with Navarre and the princes of Aragon were also ubiquitous, and frequently led to the formation of factions within Castile who took to fighting one another and sometimes fighting against the king himself. While these wars against the other Christian kingdoms of western Europe were significant, the intermittent wars against the Islamic Kingdom of Granada would leave a stronger mark in the Castilian (and Spanish) psyche over the centuries. Castile's southern neighbor was sometimes imagined as a vassal state of Castile, sometimes as a territorial rival, and sometimes as a religious enemy which must be exterminated. As a result, war with Granada was often – though not always – tinged with religious or even crusading overtones. As we will see in Chapter 3, different approaches to this holy war played an outsized role in the success or failure of various kings and nobles. As Castilian policymakers wavered over how vigorously to prosecute the war against Granada, some knights and nobles undertook their own wars against Iberian Islam and even fought against fellow Christians when the intricacies of the holy war became too complicated. External wars contributed to the chaos of the Trastámara Period.

It is no understatement to suggest that most of the Trastámara Period was a troubled time for the Kingdom of Castile. Political, social, religious, martial, and socioeconomic conflict and violence were commonplace, leading to instability and disruption throughout the kingdom. This book examines the turbulent Trastámara Period and seeks to explain *why* there was such trouble, violence, and disorder in Castile. Ultimately, those individuals who undertook the violence, war, and disruption, together with the ideology that informed their actions, were responsible for much of Castile's difficulty in the late Middle Ages. Knights and chivalry were the chief causes of the problems of the Trastámara Period.

Chivalry and Violence in Trastámara Castile

The years between 1369 and 1474 represent a formative period in Castilian history, marking the dominance of the Trastámara family over Castile (as well as Aragon and Navarre), and laying the foundation for the reign of Isabel I, which witnessed the unification of Spain and the establishment of the global Spanish empire. Yet the period is one of the most chaotic and disruptive in Castilian history. The first century of Trastámara rule witnessed a more powerful nobility arrayed vis-à-vis the Crown, regular civil strife and civil war, foreign wars and invasions of Castilian territory, and destruction in the cities and towns of the kingdom. How can this transition have occurred? How is it possible that in the century leading to Castile's preeminence among the states and kingdoms of Europe and the world, Castile was wracked with such disorder? John Edwards has argued that Isabel and her husband, Fernando II of Aragon, consolidated their rule after Isabel came to power in Castile by leveraging a more effective central government in order to maintain internal peace. He points to the establishment of the *Santa Hermandad* as a means of doing so. This was a body designed to enforce law, maintain peace, pursue offenders, and mete out royal justice. Edwards notes that the *Hermandad* also helped the Catholic Monarchs to recruit a national army under royal control and allowed the central government to collect taxes without recourse to a consultative body. In short, Edwards identifies the slow development of the apparatus of central government, which finally came to fruition in the late 15th century.[6] Certainly the tools of an early modern state were necessary for Isabel and her husband to restore order in Castile and then expand their joint kingdoms into a global empire.

---

[6] John Edwards, *The Spain of the Catholic Monarchs, 1474–1520* (Oxford: Blackwell Publishers Ltd, 2000), Chapter 2. See also Edwards' *Ferdinand and Isabella* (Harlow, England: Pearson Longman, 2005).

But tools of state alone cannot explain the change in Castile's fortunes. We must understand and analyze the dominant lay ideology of late medieval Castile in order to understand how to arrive at the success of the Catholic Monarchs. Ideas about violence permeated the thoughts and identity of the Castilian lay elite – the knights, nobles, and men-at-arms. Throughout this period of demonstrably intense violence in thought and deed, Trastámara Castile was at the mercy of such individuals whose first impulse in nearly all aspects of life was to resort to violence.

The argument at the center of this book has several components. Firstly, the book will argue that knights lived a violent lifestyle. Late medieval Castilian knights were not simply refined courtiers and gentle poets. They may have played both of these roles, but they were first and foremost warriors whose primary activity in life was violence. Secondly, late medieval warriors defined themselves by their capacity for violence. Their very identity revolved around the furiously blazing star of vigorous and violent action – on the battlefield, as Christians, as a social elite, and as political actors. Thirdly, the chivalric elite actively thought about their relationship with violence and discussed important issues concerning that violence. They were concerned about how their violence affected their rewards in this life and the next. They wondered if they ought to listen more closely to clerical strictures, even as they generally chose to disregard them. They discussed how they ought to serve the king and the common good, though they usually decided that their own interests shaped the royal interest and the interest of the realm. Knights, like most people in most times and most places, spent time thinking about their world as their thoughts informed their actions and their actions informed their ideas. Finally, knightly violence often presented a considerable challenge to other actors or segments of society. The Trastámara kings often found it difficult to reconcile their own interests with knightly violence and with the ideology which informed it. Bishops and clerics pleaded for knights to stop killing fellow Christians. Commoners formally objected as knights violently tore down their homes, destroyed their crops and spilled their blood, explicitly recognizing that chivalric ideology was helping to fuel such destruction. The late 14th and 15th centuries were a period of crisis for the kingdom of Castile, and chivalric violence was at the heart of this crisis.

Three powerful themes ran through the violent ideology of late medieval Castilian knights. The first was the powerful and abstract concept of honor, sitting at the root of chivalric violence. More than any other force, the drive to accumulate and defend personal honor drove knights to violent action and helped to construct a knightly identity. The second was that a knight's *linaje* (family status and ancestry) was closely connected to his sense of honor. The concept of family honor and family achievement magnified the knightly commitment to honor and, as a result, magnified knightly violence beyond the personal. The third was a conception of chivalric violence as part of a divine plan. Over and over again, knights expressed their belief not only that their brutal actions were not evil or immoral, but that they pleased God.[7]

In advancing this multilayered argument, this book will engage with historians of chivalry and violence in the general European context and in the specifically Castilian context. Nearly a century ago, Johan Huizinga helped to open a new field of inquiry in medieval studies when he examined the ideas and cultural expressions of the late Middle Ages. Huizinga's argument revolved around the idea that the late Middle Ages was marked by a "violent tenor of life" which was hidden with "ideal forms, gilded by chivalrous romanticism, a world disguised in the fantastic gear of the Round Table."[8] This description of the relationship between a violent reality and a pleasant cultural veneer atop it serves as the starting point for this book's historiographical engagement, because it takes seriously the possibility of the study of knightly culture and knightly ideas. In short, Huizinga allowed that expressions of chivalry and knighthood were a worthwhile area of study. Through the 20th and 21st centuries, historians of chivalry and knightly ideas owe a debt to Huizinga for pioneering the field, and some have continued to advance his thesis. José Luis Corral, writing more than ninety years after Huzinga's pioneering *Autumn of the Middle Ages*, similarly argued that knights in the High Middle Ages may well have lived a chivalric life, but that by the late Middle Ages the nature of such a life had changed. Because, Corral argued, knights and nobles had become less relevant due to powerful national governments and the march of military technology, chivalry in the late Middle Ages was no longer an attainable reality. Instead, chivalry was simply a "disguise," and the forms and symbols were an empty and melancholic echo of past glories.[9]

Yet most of those who followed in Huizinga's footsteps have moved in directions that he might not have anticipated. Instead of accepting his argument that chivalric ideas and cultural expressions were a soft veneer hiding the true and frightening tenor of late medieval life, scholars have more recently insisted that a more direct connection existed between ideas and reality. In the mid-20th century, the Spanish historian and philologist Martín de Riquer expanded on Huizinga's thesis, looking specifically at late medieval Spain. Riquer sought to connect life and art more fully, suggesting that the two regularly influenced one another and that, as a result, the lives of knights in the late Middle Ages were at times adventurous, bellicose, or full of showy heraldic flourishes and colorful adornments. For Riquer, knights

---

[7] Richard W. Kaeuper, *Holy Warriors: The Religious Ideology of Chivalry* (Philadelphia: University of Pennsylvania Press, 2009), 68–87.

[8] Johan Huizinga, *The Autumn of the Middle Ages*, trans. Rodney J. Payton and Ulrich Mammitzch (Chicago: University of Chicago Press, 1996), 39.

[9] José Luis Corral, *La torre y el caballero: el ocaso de los feudales* (Barcelona: Edhasa, 2002), 67.

actively aspired to the chivalric life, imitating the tropes of chivalric literature even as their thoughts and deeds shaped chivalric ideology.[10] Riquer's methodology is a useful one which has been underutilized by historians in the late 20th and early 21st centuries.

Where Riquer operated at a fairly broad level, making general arguments about ideas, art, and behavior, other historians have articulated more specific arguments concerning exactly how knights understood chivalric ideology and their relationship to it. Maurice Keen, in his magisterial treatment of chivalry, suggested that the ideals of the chivalric ethos were very real for medieval knights and that, as a result, they served to change knightly behavior. For Keen, chivalry was a softening and ennobling force that helped to restrain the violence of the Middle Ages and produced a society in which knights were moral exemplars.[11] Similarly, David Crouch has argued that knightly literature as early as the 12th century produced chivalric courtiers who were as concerned with the peaceful exercise of good government as they were with a violent lifestyle.[12] In the Iberian context, Joseph O'Callaghan has employed a similar approach. In a trio of monographs, O'Callaghan has worked diligently to assert that Iberian knights fighting the religious enemy in al-Andalus were the western equivalent of knights on crusade in the eastern Mediterranean. Papal blessings, the preaching of holy war, the forgiveness of sins, and the larger conflict between Christendom and Islam, O'Callaghan argues, meant that holy Iberian warriors were no less Christian warriors than their crusading counterparts.[13] Lying at the heart of O'Callaghan's argument is an assertion not only that Iberian knights existed in the same intellectual plain as their trans-Pyrenean counterparts, but that they were morally equals as well. As good knights fighting for Christendom, Iberian knights contributed as much as French, English, and German knights did.

In connecting ideas and reality, other historians have highlighted less positive aspects of the influence of medieval chivalry. Richard Kaeuper, focusing on the question of public order in the Middle Ages, has argued that knightly violence was responsible for a good deal of public disorder throughout the medieval period. In contrast to Keen and Crouch, Kaeuper has insisted that chivalric ideas expressed in literature, chronicles, and other

---

[10] Martín de Riquer, *Caballeros andantes españoles* (Madrid: Espasa-Calpe, 1967), 11–12.
[11] Maurice Keen, *Chivalry* (New Haven, CT: Yale University Press, 1984), 249–253.
[12] David Crouch, *The English Aristocracy, 1070–1272: A Social Transformation* (New Haven, CT: Yale University Press, 2011).
[13] Joseph F. O'Callaghan, *Reconquest and Crusade in Medieval Spain* (Philadelphia: University of Pennsylvania Press, 2003), 17–22. See also O'Callaghan, *The Gibraltar Crusade* (Philadelphia: University of Pennsylvania Press, 2011); and O'Callaghan, *The Last Crusade in the West: Castile and the Conquest of Granada* (Philadelphia: University of Pennsylvania Press, 2014).

sources acted as an impulse for disruptive knightly violence. For Kaeuper, chivalric ideas and reality were closely connected, and the most powerful component of chivalric ideology was the worship of prowess. To be sure, Kaeuper acknowledges that a great deal of chivalric literature sought to make knights into good Christian warriors, defenders of the public good, and even gentle courtiers. However, he argues that such reform-minded efforts were ubiquitous throughout the Middle Ages, strongly suggesting that the problems of knightly violence and chivalry persisted throughout the period.[14] Kaeuper's methodology and argument seem particularly productive for an examination of chivalry and violence in late medieval Castile.

The historiography of chivalry and medieval Castile has centered on similar issues. Teofilo Ruiz has highlighted the same destructive tendencies of the knightly class. Ruiz tends to approach the question using the tools of social history, acknowledging a high degree of knightly violence while focusing more on its impact on the Castilian peasantry. Marking knightly violence as one characteristic of "Spain's century of crisis," he has suggested that the violence of the elites from about 1300 to about 1500 brought the kingdoms of Iberia close to complete fragmentation. As a result, in the late 15th and 16th centuries, there would be religious, institutional, political, and cultural responses to noble violence.[15] Ruiz' observations are apt here and this book seeks to expand on his work through an interrogation of the ideology that sustained, informed, produced, and was produced by knightly violence.

Ruiz' position, though, has not always been embraced by other historians of medieval Castile. Jesús Rodríguez-Velasco, in his 2010 work aptly titled *Chivalry and Order*, argued that by the 14th century we can see clerical, royal, and urban influences on chivalric ideology that resulted in a chivalric ideology which actively restrained violent action on the part of knights and nobles.[16] Identifying the creeping influence of humanism, Rodríguez-Velasco suggests that "the creation of knighthood is a process that transforms disorderly violence into institutionally regulated violence, and sets a structure that buttresses the civic values of a peaceful society."[17] He goes on to argue that through the 14th century, efforts of Alfonso XI to institute and control a royal order of chivalry, the economic interests of the rising class of urban knights, and the peaceful ideology of clerics, "chivalry emerges

---

[14] Richard W. Kaeuper, *Chivalry and Violence in Medieval Europe* (Oxford: Oxford University Press, 1999), Chapters 4, 11, and 13.

[15] Teofilo Ruiz, *Spain's Centuries of Crisis, 1300–1474* (Oxford: Wiley-Blackwell, 2011). See especially pp. 37–52.

[16] Jesús Rodríguez-Velasco, *Order and Chivalry: Knighthood and Citizenship in Late Medieval Castile*, trans. Eunice Rodríguez Ferguson (Philadelphia: University of Pennsylvania Press, 2010), 1.

[17] Ibid.

from a system of institutional violence to become a substantial component in a discourse of peace."[18] The implication carried in this argument is that because there were powerful actors in late medieval Castile who ostensibly desired a gentle and peaceful chivalry, such behavior was produced.

Also disagreeing with Ruiz' assessment of late medieval violence, but approaching the question from a different direction, Cecilia Devia acknowledges the violence of the chivalric elite in late medieval Castile, while emphasizing that it was primarily a constructive force in society. Devia's approach draws on anthropological methods which assume that violence in pre-modern societies was a carefully balanced and calculated means of resolving disputes. In her most recent work, she has not only sought to examine how knightly violence created hierarchies in late medieval Castile, but has analyzed violence "in its constructive, positive aspect," improving society through social interactions and exchanges, economic interactions, the building of power structures, the construction of apparatuses of justice, and laying the foundations for the cultural expressions of late medieval Castile.[19] For Devia, late medieval violence was primarily a positive force, building the structures of society that produced the modern age.

The argument of this book will be much closer to Kaeuper's and Ruiz' than to Rodríguez-Velasco's or Devia's. Based on the evidence from the Trastámara period, we must acknowledge that knights were especially violent, that they thought about their violence and incorporated it into their identity, and that their violence presented serious challenges to the stability of the central government, to the people of Castile, to their Christian and Muslim neighbors, and complicated their relationship with powerful theological ideas articulated by clerics. At a certain level, both Rodríguez-Velasco and Devia are correct in their assessments. For the former, we cannot doubt that kings asserted their supremacy over knights and chivalric ideology, just as clerics claimed to direct knights and feed them their religious ideas. We must recognize, though, that knights had their own ideas; the evidence of this book will demonstrate that knights regularly diverged from royal or clerical initiatives. For the latter, we might acknowledge that the potency of knightly violence would eventually be coopted by the Crown in the early modern period and helped to fuel the rise of the Spanish empire. Such an acknowledgement, though, does not guarantee that knightly violence in the period from 1369 to 1474 was productive and creative for this outcome. This book will refute Devia's articulation of a progressive characteristic of knightly violence. Castilian knights in the late Middle Ages were not usually concerned with building a better government, with laying the foundations of a global economy, or ensuring that the king's justice functioned according

---

[18] Ibid., 5.
[19] Cecilia Devia, "Violencia y dominación" (Phd diss, Universidad de Buenos Aires, 2013), 13–14.

to grand ideals. For the most part, they were concerned with wielding their swords to protect their honor. If there were results of knightly violence that had other effects, we should not imagine that it was by design.

Concepts

In the modern world, "chivalry" often suggests a code of behavior, especially of men towards women. The mind conjures visions of Sir Walter Raleigh laying his coat in a puddle so that Queen Elizabeth's feet would not get wet, or men holding the door open for women – surely evidence that chivalry is not dead. Chivalry in this modern sense is seen as a prescriptive set of rules by which boorish males become gentlemen. Such a conception of chivalry has a certain link to the medieval world, but it is created from a romantic Victorian reading of medieval texts. The Victorian misreading comes from the prescriptive nature of much of our medieval chivalric literature. Such literature instructed knights how they *ought* to behave rather than describing how they *did* behave. In other words, chivalric literature often recognized problems such as violence against women, destruction of peasants, or damages to churches. The literature would be written to show that a model fictional knight (such as El Cid, or, in the broader European tradition, Sir Galahad) would avoid such nasty behavior. Historians in the 19th and early 20th centuries accepted such prescriptive works as accurate descriptions of medieval knighthood. Instead of accepting that chivalric literature was attempting to address a problem in society, romantic historians saw medieval knights as the *actual* embodiment of the virtues described in the literature. In short, the reformative element of medieval chivalry has come in the modern world to define the entirety of chivalry.[20]

The term "chivalry" (*caballería*) was typically used in medieval Europe in three interconnected ways. Firstly, it could refer to a body of knights or warriors. A nobleman might bring his chivalry with him to the battlefield, suggesting that he had a retinue of armed (and likely mounted) men with him. This definition could be used much more broadly as well. The chronicler Diego de Valera noted that King Enrique IV had "so many and such great means to recover the land which the Moors in Spain had usurped … and with such noble chivalry such as he had in his kingdoms, his proposition in wanting to make war was holy and good."[21] Enrique's advantage consisted of the number and quality of knights and men-at-arms in his service. Secondly, the term "chivalry" could refer to deeds committed by a

---

[20] Richard W. Kaeuper, *Medieval Chivalry* (Cambridge: Cambridge University Press, 2016), 12–22.
[21] Diego de Valera, "Memorial de diversas hazañas," in *Biblioteca de Autores Españoles* (*BAE*) (Madrid: M. Rivadeneyra, 1876), vol. 70, 4.

knight or man-at-arms, typically on the battlefield. The word is used with this connotation much less frequently in the Castilian world than in other parts of Europe, but it does appear from time to time. As a boy, the famous knight Pero Niño was told by his tutor that "[h]e who is to understand and use the art of chivalry is not suited to spend a long time in the school of letters."[22] Fernando del Pulgar claims that the count of Alva, "was raised in the martial discipline, and always from his youth desired to perform in the habit of chivalry worthy things of laudable memory".[23] Finally, chivalry could refer to the ideas and values of the lay elite of medieval Europe; in this sense, we can speak of the ideology or worldview that was chivalry.[24] Medieval writers deployed the term in this sense occasionally, as when the writer Pedro de Corral lamented the death of a prince of the 8th century, asking God "how it should please you that I should see the death of the mirror of chivalry of all the world,"[25] or when the reforming cleric Alfonso de Cartagena wrote that fighting "in jousts or tournaments … [was] a game or rehearsal [for warfare], but not a principal act of chivalry."[26] But more often, they simply discuss the ideas and values that were at the heart of the ideology of the knightly elite of their world without specifically designating everything as a component of the abstract concept of chivalry. Nevertheless, they are certainly describing the larger set of values and ideas that they call chivalry. Chivalry as a more abstract idea is the main focus of the present book, and its various components, such as honor, prowess, status, largesse, and piety, will be discussed at length in the chapters that follow.

In the past several decades, historians of late medieval Castile have sought to identify the various grades of knighthood. First of all, we must observe that all nobles were referred to by the term *hidalgo*. A man of *hidalgo* status had special legal privileges and, in theory, a close relationship with the Crown. Both *hidalgos* and non-noble knights existed in a loose hierarchy which distinguished between the various ranks of the *caballería*. At the top were the

---

[22] Gutierre Díez de Games, *El Victorial*, ed. Juan de Mata Carriazo (Madrid: Espasa-Calpe, S.A., 1940), 64. "El que á de aprender e vsar arte de cavallería, non cobiene despender luengo tiempo en esquela de letras."

[23] Fernando de Pulgar, *Claros Varones de Castilla* (Buenos Aires: Espasa-Calpe Argentina, S.A., 1948), 50–51. "Fué criado en la disciplina military, é siempre desde su mocedad deseó facer en el habito de la Caballería cosas dignas de loable memoria."

[24] Richard Kaeuper's work over the last several decades has plainly laid out the existence of the ideology of chivalry in the European Middle Ages. See especially Kaeuper, *Chivalry and Violence* and Kaeuper, *Holy Warriors*. See also Keen, *Chivalry*.

[25] Pedro de Corral, *Crónica del Rey don Rodrigo (Crónica sarracina)*, ed. James Donald Fogelquist (Madrid: Editorial Castalia, S.A., 2001), vol. II, 519. "¿cómo … que te plaze que yo vea morir el espejo de cavallería de todo el mundo?"

[26] Noel Fallows, *The Chivalric Vision of Alfonso de Cartagena: Study and Edition of the Doctrinal de los caualleros* (Newark, DE: Linguatext, Ltd., 1995), 255. "en justas o en torneos … vn juego o ensaye mas non prinçipal acto de la caualleria."

títulos, or *grandes*, men who had been granted lands and titles by the Crown.[27] These men were few in number but were often the most visible and powerful nobles in society. In the 15th century, the number of *títulos* began to grow significantly, reflecting the larger number of men who were raised to nobility by the Trastámara kings. Below the titled nobility was the widely defined group of noble knights, the *caballeros hidalgos*. These were the traditional knights of medieval Europe. They were defined by a military profession and were members of a family of some significance. Below the noble knights were *escuderos*, or squires, men who were not dubbed knights but attended knights and embraced warfare as their profession. These three divisions (*títulos*, *caballeros hidalgos*, and *escuderos*) are the easiest to define as the chivalric elite, the subject of this book. They were men who subscribed to chivalric ideals, who usually fought for a living, who most likely owned horses and arms, and who belonged to noble families. Enrique de Villena, a Master of Calatrava in the early 15th century, summed up this approach, saying

> The estate of knights I understand to be *rico hombres* [the higher nobility], the noble vassal, the *infanzon* [a member of the lower nobility], the armed knight, gentleman, and all the others who are *hidalgos* to whom it is appropriate to undertake martial exercises and to multiply the virtuous and good customs of the conservation and defending of the common good.[28]

For Villena, nobility itself had a necessary martial component and, as a result, all who were nobles and carried arms (as they all ought to), should be considered knights.

Other members of late medieval society who do not fit into this tidy schema but whom we still must consider in this book are those men who embraced war as their profession but were either not nobles, not knights, and sometimes neither nobles nor knights. When medieval writers referred to this large and poorly defined group, they sometimes used the term *gentes de armas* – men-at-arms – and other times simply referred to them as *gentes*, with context showing that they were soldiers, horsemen, archers, etc. At times the voices of these men can be harder to hear, but they were a large and significant group that almost certainly embraced most of the ideals analyzed in this book.

We can surmise as much through several means. Firstly, we have cases such as Gutierre Díez de Games, a chronicler of the famous knight Pero

---

[27] We will occasionally see in this book the term *ricos hombres*, lit. "rich men," which referred essentially to the high nobility. John Edwards, *Christian Córdoba: The City and Its Region in the late Middle Ages* (Cambridge: Cambridge University Press, 1982).

[28] Enrique de Villena, a Master of Calatrava in his early 15th-century *Doce Trabaxos de Ercules*, wrote "Por el estado de caballeros entiendo rico hombres, noble vasuero, infanzon, cavallero armado, gentil hombre, et todos los otros son fidalgos a quien pertenece usar exercicio (militar) y multiplica las costumbres virtuosas y buenas aconservaciones y defendimiento del bien comun." BNE MSS/6526.

Niño. We have no evidence that Díez was ever knighted, nor that he was of noble lineage. But we do know that he was a soldier and that when he wrote he enthusiastically expressed chivalric ideas. Sometimes, to be sure, he was simply expressing his lord's ideals, but other times, he makes fairly clear that he is expressing his own opinions. Those opinions are almost always in line with concepts of honor, violence, and divine sanction. Secondly, chroniclers describe the actions of men-at-arms or "men" alongside the actions of knights and nobles, seeking honor and glory on the battlefield, wreaking havoc among the enemy, and discussing questions of right behavior. As Andrew Cowell has argued, while lords and noble knights themselves are more prominent in primary sources, "those mounted warriors supported by the lords or linked to them in relationships of a fundamentally military nature" ought to be included in an analysis of the chivalric elite.[29] Thirdly, we know that the late Middle Ages represents a broadening of the social pyramid in a general sense, and we know that this includes the expansion of chivalric influence as well. Richard Kaeuper, examining England and France from the 13th century, has argued that "the chivalric ethos in fact generalized to all who lived by arms, whether of noble family or not ... it touched all men-at-arms."[30] Kaeuper's evidence is drawn both from treatises of late medieval writers and the reality that many warriors could not afford the costs and obligations of legal knighthood.[31] For Castile, our evidence is most plentiful in the latter case – that there were poorer men who aspired to knighthood in their actions – but also in the evidence of the language used by chroniclers and the records of central government. The records of the *cortes*, for example, regularly refer to formal categories – *caballeros* and *hidalgos* – and add generic third categories such as "powerful men" or "companies." What we ought to draw from this is that knights were regularly accompanied by men who acted and lived a chivalric lifestyle, even if they were not formally acknowledged as such.

Just as there were non-noble and non-knightly members of the chivalric elite, so there were knights who are not included in this definition. Because there were advantages to knighthood – tax breaks, social status, economic benefits – the late Middle Ages, in Castile as in other parts of Europe, saw a growing number of men taking up knighthood who had little or no desire to actually carry out the martial and violent functions of that profession. These men, often wealthy merchants, became known as *caballeros de premia* or *caballeros de cuantía*. Often, they were descended from urban frontier knights, known as *caballeros villanos*, and they sometimes retained that designation as well. By the Trastámara period, though, as the frontier

---

[29] Andrew Cowell, *The Medieval Warrior Aristocracy: Gifts, Violence, Performance, and the Sacred* (Cambridge: D.S. Brewer, 2007), 3.
[30] Kaeuper, *Chivalry and Violence*, 191–193.
[31] Ibid., 192.

had moved away from these cities, the martial role of these knights began to disappear.[32] Legally, they were still required to fight or provide the arms and armor for another man to fight in their place, but there was a fairly widespread perception that many of these men were shirking their responsibilities.[33] Between this process and the desire of wealthy men to claim the benefits of knighthood, an entire class of knights developed that were not strenuous fighters and often not fighters at all. The *caballeros de premia* were criticized in their own time for claiming the benefits of knighthood without fulfilling the martial functions that knighthood entailed. This book will not include these knights as part of the chivalric elite. It seems clear that they were not animated by nor had any desire to accept fundamentally chivalric ideas. They were largely knights in name only – certainly not in practice, and probably not in thought.

Finally, we have a very exclusive group of men who are partially included in this group: the kings of Castile themselves. Kings were certainly members of the chivalric community – they had generally been knighted themselves and the exercise of arms on the battlefield was a key part of their identity. As kings, though, they had one foot outside of the chivalric world. In addition to being knights, they were also rulers and statesmen, and at times we see them acting differently from typical knights. Instead of resolving whether they belong inside or outside of this group, this book will consider the issue of the relationship between kings and chivalry at key moments when complications in that relationship arose.

The chivalric elite that this book deals with, then, is broadly defined. In the most general sense, any man whose actual profession was the exercise of arms is included. Naturally, this does not include all men who ever fought – peasant levies, Muslim mercenaries, and others who were not regular members of elite Castilian society or who did not bear arms as their profession are excluded. All of the other categories described above had some amount of fluidity. Membership in any legally defined group in Castile, as in Europe more broadly, was constantly shifting.[34] Ultimately, sorting out whether a given author, knight, nobleman, or man-at-arms had sufficient

---

[32] For a complete study of what he calls these bourgeois knights, see Rodríguez-Velasco, *Order and Chivalry*.

[33] The problem was significant enough that Juan II received petitions at a *cortes* held in Burgos in 1453 asking that the legal components of knighthood be better regulated. The petitioners asked that only those who actually pay the *pechero* – essentially a tax on the honor of knighthood – be allowed to actually be legal knights. In the same *cortes* Juan received a petition insisting that knights maintain themselves as armed and mounted men if they wished to continue enjoying privileges, franchises, and exemptions from legal processes. *Cortes* held at Burgos in 1453. *Cortes de los antiguos reinos de León y de Castilla*, ed. Real Academia de la Historia (Madrid: M. Rivadeneyra, 1861–1866), vol. 3, 643–650 and 666–667.

[34] Kaeuper, *Medieval Chivalry*, 121–136.

legal or social standing to qualify as part of a narrowly defined chivalric elite becomes not only impossible but unnecessary. Given the various and overlapping grades of knights, nobles, and fighting men in late medieval Castile, it may be helpful to move past strict legal definitions or precise questions of privilege and title when defining the chivalric elite. Rather, we ought to understand them as constituting a cultural community – a diffuse group of individuals who shared social, religious, and personal values. One did not necessarily have to be knighted to be a part of the community that consumed chivalric literature, embraced the ideals of knighthood, and saw themselves as part of the chivalric community.[35]

The beating heart of the chivalric elite was honor, an abstract concept dealing with one's reputation and abilities. We can define honor, drawing on other theorists, as a man's public persona, identity, worth, and ability, as perceived by his peers through his actions and his reputation. Julian Pitt-Rivers defined honor similarly as "the value of a person in his own eye, but also in the eyes of his society. It is his estimation of his own worth, his *claim* to pride, but it is also the acknowledgement of that claim, his excellence recognized by society, his *right* to pride."[36] In short, a man of appropriate social status was born with a certain amount of honor to his name which reflected what people expected of him. As an adult he would be expected to defend his honor against those who would diminish it through insults, physical attacks on his person or holdings, attacks on his family, counterclaims against his titles or possessions, or any other action that would make him seem a less important or powerful man than he claimed to be. At the same time, a good knight would seek to increase his honor above and beyond his birthright. Honor could be increased through good service to the king, through the awarding of new titles, and through taking new land from his enemies, among other means. The purpose of defending and seeking honor was the social value that honor carried – it functioned as social currency throughout the Middle Ages. A man who was seen as very honorable was well respected by his friends and enemies, could expect to be favored by his king, and, in the most general sense, was a leading member of his family, community, realm, and the order of chivalry. As Pitt-Rivers argues, the abstract concept of honor in Mediterranean history provided "a nexus between the ideals of society and their reproduction in the actions of

---

[35] For the concept of cultural or emotional communities, see Barbara H. Rosenwein, *Emotional Communities in the Early Middle Ages* (Ithaca, NY: Cornell University Press, 2006).

[36] Julian Pitt-Rivers, "Honour and Social Status," in *Honour and Shame: The Values of Mediterranean Society*, ed. Jean G. Peristiany (London: Weidenfeld and Nicolson, 1965), 21. See also Nancy Shields Kolman, *By Honor Bound: State and Society in Early Modern Russia*.

individuals," linking the expectations of chivalric society to the desires and actions of the knight himself.[37]

In late medieval Castile, as in much of the rest of late medieval Europe, the primary means of accumulating and defending honor was through violent action. David Gilmore has argued for a broader theoretical concept of honor, which would include means for cooperation, a sense of honesty, hospitality, and mutual respect.[38] What we see in late medieval Europe is likely a relatively extreme case of honor being fundamentally connected to violence. In the 15th century, there *were* other means for accumulating and defending honor, but they were less reliable. In medieval Castilian sources, no method was so highly valued as putting one's hand to his sword to vindicate himself. By the very nature of their abilities, knights resorted first to violent action to expand their honor, often at the expense of another, and had little choice but to defend their honor violently as well. The logic works itself out easily enough. If a knight made a violent attack on his chivalric neighbor, the neighbor's only real choice was to defend himself and his honor violently. If he failed to do so, his honor would have been called into question and the only means of making up his honor deficit would be through positive violent action equivalent to the negative violent actions he had suffered. A reciprocal economy of honor formed the most crucial sociocultural framework of late medieval Castile for the chivalric elite.

Honor by its very nature was not a private affair. Simply resolving one's conflicts or perceived slights to one's honor behind closed doors was not and could not be sufficient. Because honor was a *public* representation of a man's reputation and ability, slights to and vindications of honor had to be dealt with in a very public way.[39] In practice this meant a clear statement of a knight's *intent* to revenge himself for a perceived insult, followed by a verifiable follow-through on the stated intent.[40] The public character of honor violence implied a showy act of violence and a concern that other knights and nobles would be aware of the action. As a result, our sources are riddled with the evidence of violence based on honor. Far from simply a distortion of the evidence, honor violence was a regular and important part of life. As we will see, knights' concern for the public vindication of their honor resulted in discussions amongst themselves, reported by chroniclers, premised on how their peers would react to their choice to perform violence or not. Fear of their honor being publicly called into question resulted in

---

[37] Pitt-Rivers, "Honour and Social Status," 38.
[38] David D. Gilmore, "Honor, Honesty, Shame: Male Status in Contemporary Andalusia," in *Honor and Shame and the Unity of the Mediterranean*, ed. David D. Gilmore (Arlington, VA: American Anthropological Association, 1987), 90–103.
[39] Craig Taylor, *Chivalry and the Ideals of Knighthood in France during the Hundred Years War* (Cambridge: Cambridge University Press, 2013), 56–57.
[40] Pitt-Rivers, "Honour and Social Status," 21.

skirmishes and, in several cases, open warfare within and outside of Castile. Perhaps most significantly, the extreme love of honor and fear of shame led knights and men-at-arms to take outsized vengeance for any possible slight to their honor. If a man was insulted, shamed, or defeated in battle, the appropriate chivalric response was to violently seek vengeance on the perpetrator, preferably in greater proportion than the injury done to him.

A key component related to knightly honor and violence is the concept of *linaje*. Literally "lineage" in English, the term *linaje* encompasses much more than a man's genealogical predecessors. *Linaje* encompasses a man's ancestry as well as his living family, their titles and holdings, their family history and accomplishments, and their failures. In short, as Faustino Menéndez Pidal de Navascués, puts it, "The honor – and also dishonor, of course – thus reaches from each of the past and present components of the *linaje* and falls onto each and every one of its members."[41] There was a corporate character to *linaje* in the Middle Ages, as no man existed outside of his family, his ancestry, and their reputation. A man's advantages and disadvantages were tied up with the deeds of his relatives past and present. Rafael Sanchez Saus has articulated this point more vigorously than perhaps any other historian, arguing that *linaje* was "a community of affections and interests, a receptacle of a familiar past without which the medieval man would not be able to conceive of himself, and a projection made into the future of his set of values and his aspirations."[42] When we spoke above of a man being born with a certain amount of honor, it was through his *linaje* that his endowment was determined. Birth into a great *linaje* implied that a knight's ancestors had worked vigilantly to preserve and augment their personal and familial honor and placed the burden of that family history on the young knight's shoulders. Incumbent upon him was the duty to preserve the accomplishments and honor of his family through his words and deeds.

Linaje and the development or invention of an honorable family history was valuable to knights because it provided automatic entry into the chivalric elite.[43] A man born into a respected *linaje* certainly had the responsibilities of belonging to a great family, but he did not have to preemptively prove himself as a member of the chivalric elite. As importantly, his foundational honor was already higher than that of a man who sought to rise from lower origins. From the beginning of his knightly career, he could rely on the reputation that his family had provided him as he sought to build his

---

[41] Faustino Menéndez Pidal de Navascués, "El linaje y sus signos de identidad," *En la España medieval*, Extra no. 1 (2006), 14.

[42] Rafael Sanchez Saus, *Caballeria y linaje en la Sevilla medieval: studio genealogico y social* (Cádiz, Spain: Universidad de Cádiz, 1989), 39.

[43] Carlos Heusch, "La pluma al servicio del linaje: El desarrollo de los nobilarios en la Castilla trastámara," *e-Spania: Revue interdisciplinaire d'études hispaniques médiévales et modernes*, no. 11 (Jun. 2011), 1.

own public persona. At the dawn of the Trastámara age in the late 1360s, much of the new nobility would lack clear family histories, as they were often either junior branches of greater families or, in some cases, new families altogether.[44] Thus, *linajes* of the Trastámara period worked diligently to assert the strength and history of their families, providing their sons with an automatic claim to nobility, membership in the chivalric elite, and an advantage over those who could not claim a *linaje*.[45]

Indeed, the creation of a family history was also a purposefully ideological act. Carlos Heusch asserted in no uncertain terms that the creations of family histories in the Trastámara period represented "the idea of a '*linajistic* fiction', that is to say the manipulation of history with specific ends which proves that it is a propagandistic literature."[46] As Heusch has observed, the writers of these *linaje* histories often compared and contrasted the subject *linaje* to another in order to demonstrate preeminence in a particular region. By making the hero of a given *linaje* a great knight (sometimes the greatest knight), genealogical authors implied that the family itself had inherited the glory and honor of the *linaje*'s forebears. The historical accuracy of the work was less important than that it should plausibly lay out the great deeds of arms and the honorable words and actions of the historically important members of the *linaje*. These sources, then, not only created the foundational honor for their knightly scions but also broadcast models of ideal behavior for knights of the family.

Sources

The ideology of chivalry helped to direct the actions and behavior of the social group which both produced and embraced it. Ideology was articulated, modified, and changed by members of the chivalric elite while at the same time knightly behavior was informed, influenced, and guided by chivalric ideology which involved the projection of ideals into an analysis of the present and an understanding of the past. In short, chivalry was often prescriptive – it articulated ideals about how knights and men-at-arms *ought* to behave. We must be careful here because the ideology itself could be influential enough that it might also end up describing knightly action even as it prescribed. A methodology that attempts to sift out prescriptions from descriptions must inform our engagement with various classes of sources. The three main classes of sources used in this book are examined below. A variety of other kinds of sources will be dealt with individually as they appear throughout the book.

[44] Ruiz, *Spain's Centuries of Crisis*, 81.
[45] Heusch, "La pluma al servicio del linaje," 9–17.
[46] Ibid., 33.

Many chivalric ideas come from imaginative literature. In late medieval Castile, this includes a few epic poems, a few romances, a body of folk ballads called *romances*, and a few other odds and ends. Kaeuper has argued convincingly that literature represents the ideals, fears, and hopes of the knightly elite, and his methodology applies to Castile as much as to France and England.[47] Angus MacKay has similarly suggested that "the ballad audience – like society itself – was dominated by the ethos of the *caballeros*."[48] As such, we can read the *romances* as representing the ideas and desires of frontier chivalric society. The fantastic or unrealistic nature of imaginative literature undoubtedly excited and inspired knightly audiences, offering them a superlative vision of all that of which they were capable. Importantly, all of the imaginative literature used in this study contains ideas relating to the practice of violence. When, in the late medieval epic poem *Mocedades de Rodrigo*, Rodrigo Díaz de Vivar enters his first battle as a pre-teen and gloriously slaughters dozens of his enemies, we understand that the author was positing prescriptive ideals about knightly masculinity, namely that it was expressed through violence.[49] When the Arthurian knight Tristan fights an enemy count in single combat, lowering his lance and spurring his horse forward, we understand that the author was articulating an ideal of knighthood, namely that knights ought to know the tools of their trade (the lance and horse, in this case) in order to win honor and glory.

Not only were writers articulating these ideas, but readers were consuming them. Evidence of knightly readership (or at least listenership) exists in scattered references in other sources. The family history of the Ponce de Leones, for example, described the deeds of Rodrigo Ponce de León, saying that "Roland in his time could not do more."[50] Similarly, Gutierre Díez de Games warned his readers to "make sure that you do not believe false prophecies … such as are those of Merlin and others."[51] In Aragon, in the late 14th century, Prince Juan named his three mastiffs Amadís, Ogier, and Merlin, for the legendary knights of Spain, France, and Britain, respectively.[52] All of

---

[47] For a succinct and convincing articulation of Kaeuper's methodology concerning imaginative literature, see Richard W. Kaeuper, "Literature as Essential Evidence for Understanding Chivalry," *The Journal of Medieval Military History*, ed. Clifford J. Rogers, Kelly DeVries, and John France (2007): 1–15.
[48] Angus MacKay, "The Ballad and the Frontier in Late Mediaeval Spain," *Bulletin of Hispanic Studies*, LIII (1976): 16–17.
[49] *Las Mocedades de Rodrigo: The Youthful Deeds of Rodrigo, the Cid*, ed. and trans. Matthew Bailey (Toronto: University of Toronto Press, 2007), 40.
[50] *Historia de los hechos del marqués de Cádiz*, 175. "que Roldán en su tiempo non pudo más fazer."
[51] Díez de Games, *El Victorial*, 68. "Guardadvos non creades falsas profezías … como son las de Merlín e otras."
[52] William J. Entwistle, *The Arthurian Legend in the Literatures of the Spanish Peninsula* (New York: Phaeton Press, 1975), 53–54.

these writers casually mention figures from imaginative literature, suggesting that they were familiar with the romances and epics in which these figures appeared and, more importantly, that their readers would find them immediately accessible. After all, a medieval author would have little reason to make a cultural reference that his readers would find incomprehensible. For knightly readers, imaginative literature was not only accessible, but probably quite popular. Noel Fallows has shown that Alfonso de Cartagena, bishop of Burgos, in several of his works, entreated Castilian knights to *stop* reading of the deeds of Lancelot and Tristan, and instead look to the deeds of historical figures as exemplars of chivalry.[53] If Cartagena was encouraging knights to stop reading imaginative literature, it stands to reason that knights were reading imaginative literature.

The final question concerning imaginative literature is whether or not it had any impact on knightly action. Certainly the ideas articulated in imaginative literature were incorporated into the turbulent currents of chivalric thought, but did these ideas find expression in real life? The simple question of whether knights became violent as a result of their imaginative literature is the wrong question to ask. Knights, as part of the dominant lay elite of medieval Europe, already lived in a violent society and operated under certain assumptions concerning violence, as evidenced by their very role in society as warriors. In other words, they did not need imaginative literature to spur them to violence. Imaginative literature functioned to influence the way they thought about the exercise of violence and could augment or modify knightly violence. In much the same way that a modern television series dealing with political culture might color viewers' understanding of the democratic process because we already operate in a democratic society, medieval imaginative literature colored the knightly understanding of the appropriate and inappropriate use of violence within a society where violence was a regular part of life.[54] One excellent example of the tropes of knightly literature directly influencing knightly action is the *passo honrosso* of Suero de Quiñones. This Castilian knight appeared at the court of Juan II and requested and received permission from the king to hold a month-long tournament at a bridge in northern Castile. He swore to wear a chain around his neck, claiming that he had been imprisoned by the love of a lady. The goal was ostensibly to free him from his prison through deeds of arms which, presumably, would lead his lady to return his love. The tournament sounds like something out of Arthurian romance, or perhaps an episode from *Amadís de Gaula* or *Tirant lo Blanch*. Any knight who crossed the bridge where Quiñones and his nine companions were

---

[53] Noel Fallows, *The Chivalric Vision of Alfonso de Cartagena: Study and Edition of the Doctrinal de los caualleros* (Newark, DE: Linguatext, Ltd., 1995), 13–16.
[54] Noel Fallows, *Jousting in Medieval and Renaissance Iberia* (Woodbridge: Boydell Press, 2010), 14.

waiting was required to joust with Quiñones and his companions until the company broke 300 lances.[55] This seemingly ridiculous arrangement echoes older forms of chivalric literature so well that it is difficult to imagine that art and life were not interacting with one another. Chivalric imaginative literature must be taken as having some bearing on the thoughts and behavior of real historical knights.

Much of the historical evidence of medieval Castile comes from the major chronicles written throughout the period. These often serve as baseline accounts of the major events of medieval Castile and were typically written by men close to the king or queen. As such, they were often written with a sympathetic approach to the monarch, yet they provide historians with key information about the grand narrative of Castilian history. For example, Pedro López de Ayala, eventually the Grand Chancellor of Castile, wrote chronicles of the reigns of Pedro, Enrique II, Juan I, and Enrique III. As a partisan of the Trastámara cause, a soldier who had participated actively in the wars of the Trastámara monarchs, and a diplomat who had represented their interests abroad, Ayala obviously presents a biased account of the events of his day.[56] If, however, we want to learn about the worldview of a leading Castilian knight and the political, social, and military circles in which he operated, Ayala's work presents an excellent account. Chronicles hostile to the monarch, though, are equally valuable. While Ayala and other monarch-friendly chroniclers like him (e.g. Fernán Pérez de Guzmán for Juan II, Diego Enríquez de Castillo for Enrique IV, or Andrés Bernáldez for Isabel) may offer praise for a monarch and justify his actions from a chivalric point of view, chroniclers who were hostile to the monarch, as Diego de Valera and Alfonso de Palencia were toward Enrique IV, help to present a vision of how knights and the chivalric elite might condemn the leaders of their day. In a sense, though, the political persuasions of the various chroniclers do not matter as much as the way that they talk about specific individuals, events, ideas, and behaviors. Such "minor" incidents comprise a significant part of the chronicles of late medieval Castile. Almost all of the chroniclers consider knightly behaviors on the battlefield, questions of loyalty or disloyalty to the king or queen, moments of intense violence against all members of society, religious warfare, etc. In other words, the chroniclers help us to build a cohesive narrative of Castilian history, but they are more useful in presenting chivalric ideas, both explicitly and implicitly.

This is partly because, unlike earlier periods in the Castilian and European Middle Ages, many of the chronicles of the Trastámara period were

---

[55] Pedro Rodríguez de Lena, *El passo honroso de Suero de Quiñones*, ed. Amancio Labandeira Fernández (Madrid: Fundación Universitaria Española, 1977).

[56] For the life of Ayala, see Michel García. *Obra y personalidad del Canciller Ayala* (Madrid: Editorial Alhambra, 1983) and, Constane L. Wilkins *Pero López de Ayala* (Boston: G.K. Hall & Co., 1989).

written by members of the chivalric elite. Ayala actively participated as a knight in the wars of the late 14th century. Similarly, his nephew, the chronicler Fernán Pérez de Guzmán, fought at the battle of Higueruela, a clash between Castile and Granada in 1431.[57] The chronicler Diego de Valera fought on the battlefields of the war with Granada as well as in other theaters across Europe, balancing a life of the mind with a life of arms.[58] Even the scholarly Alfonso de Palencia helped to organize the logistical arrangements for the Catholic Monarchs' assault on Gran Canaria in the late 1470s.[59] The chronicles, in other words, can also serve as a somewhat reliable account of the events of the Trastámara period, even as they encompass the thoughts and viewpoints of members of the chivalric elite. The apparent problems of using the chronicles as evidence are easily transformed into advantages in gaining insights into the chivalric mind. For example, in Chapter 2, we will see that chivalric chronicles do not always discuss how many peasants or agricultural workers perished when orchards and vineyards were destroyed. We lose crucial evidence about the lives of common people, but we gain an understanding that chivalric writers thought of such people as fundamentally unimportant. Chronicle evidence is therefore key in accessing some core assumptions of chivalric ideology.

Just as kings sought supporters to write the histories of their reigns, elite warriors commissioned their own biographies or family chronicles, a group of sources which we might define broadly as "chivalric biographies." This class of documents includes works such as Gutierre Díez de Games' *El Victorial*, an encomiastic account of the chivalric deeds of his lord, Pero Niño; the anonymous *Coronica del yllustre y muy magnifico cauallero don Alonso Pérez de Guzmán el Bueno*, which glorifies the martial life of one of the most powerful Andalucian family's forebears; the anonymous *Hechos del condestable Don Miguel Lucas de Iranzo*, which seeks to justify the eponymous hero's noble status through a recounting of his chivalric activity; and *Historia de los hechos del marqués de Cádiz*, which establishes the Marquis of Cádiz as a knightly hero in the mold of Roland or El Cid. Each of these biographies, naturally, is heavily biased in favor of its subject. This is precisely what makes them so valuable in understanding the chivalric mindset. Pero Niño was a great knight because he fought so vigorously in battle, according to his chronicler. Alonso Pérez de Guzmán was a model of chivalry because he was willing to sacrifice his family for military victory.

---

[57] Mercedes Vaquero, "Cultura nobiliaria y biblioteca de Fernán Pérez de Guzmán," *Lemir: Revista de Literatura Española Medieval y del Rancimiento*, 7 (2003).

[58] For a dated but still useful account of Valera's life, see Hipólito Sancho de Sopranis, "Sobre Mosen Diego de Valera," *Hispania: Revista Española de historia*, 29 (1947): 531–553.

[59] Juan Álvarez Delgado, "Alonso de Palencia (1423–1492) y la Historia de Canarias," *Anuario de Estudios Atlánticos*, vol. 1, no. 9 (1963): 51–79.

Miguel Lucas de Iranzo presented himself as worthy of noble status because he was willing to prosecute a holy war against Islam. The chivalric biographies are often fanciful, frequently formulaic, and sometimes dubious in their historical accuracy, but they represent the mindset of powerful and respected Castilian knights and they therefore offer us a window into the medieval chivalric mind.

Chapter 1 will examine the origins of the Trastámara nobility and the development of their political identity and ideology. Born of a bloody conflict between two claimants to the Castilian throne, the Trastámara nobility would be defined through violent political action, beginning with their rebellion against King Pedro the Cruel, the last member of the ruling Borgoña dynasty, and their support for Enrique de Trastámara, the founder of the new dynasty. Through military support of the Trastámara kings, knights found economic, social, and political reward. More than any other action they could take, knights understood that good fighting on the battlefield was the surest way to advance their political position. The favorites of the 15th century – Juan Furtado de Mendoza, Álvaro de Luna, Juan Pacheco, and Beltrán de la Cueva – all conceived of themselves first and foremost as vigorous knights and only secondly as courtiers or politicians. Where we have their words or ideas expressed, they argued that their privileged positions near the king were a result of their good military service to him.

The Trastámara nobility also claimed a political right to advise the king and share in the government of the realm. To attain a position of influence near the king and to remove rivals from such positions, knights and nobles regularly resorted to violent action. Declaring themselves to be acting in the service of the king, knights would take up arms against the king and his advisors in order to secure their own political positions. Chivalric ideology on this point was remarkably flexible. Knights sought to define for themselves what good service to the king entailed and, as a result, knights on opposite ends of a given political crisis could both claim to be performing loyal service. A central component behind the chivalric political identity of late medieval Castile was a jealously guarded autonomy. The Trastámara nobility was happy to serve the king when it advanced their interests, but for decades they resisted royal encroachment on their traditional right to fight when and where they pleased.

Chapter 2 takes up the question of the social position of the Trastámara nobility. The knightly class relied on their legal and cultural right to honor won through deeds of arms to set themselves apart from the rest of the people of Castile, specifically the peasants and urban dwellers. The common folk could not accumulate honor in the same way or to the same degree that knights and nobles could and, as such, existed in a separate conceptual category. Most knights and nobles found that they began life with a certain amount of honor inherited from their chivalric ancestors. Peasants and merchants could rarely make such grand claims, and this cemented their existence as a fundamentally inferior social cohort. From a social standpoint, knightly ideology clearly demarcated the difference between the chivalric world and the non-chivalric world.

Because knights could accumulate honor in a way that was not feasible for peasants, they had a right to commit violence as well, and they did not hesitate to do so. A great deal of the violence committed by the Trastámara nobility was aimed not directly at fellow knights, but at the peasants and urban dwellers who made up the bedrock of the medieval economy. In theory, knights preferred to exercise their sword arms against the greatest warriors in the land, but in practice, plenty of honor could be won in any martial activity. Knightly ideology allowed for and even valorized the destruction of commoners and their goods. Indeed, knights could rest assured that the God of the Old Testament had long blessed destruction against the subchivalric segment of society. Our sources record a constant and bitter reaction on the part of commoners against knightly violence. For the most part, the complaints of the common people were unsuccessful in their attempts to redirect chivalric bloodshed.

Chapters 3 and 4 deal with the violent activity for which knights most lived: warfare. Chapter 3 examines the ideology surrounding holy war, the superlative knightly activity in late medieval Castile. Although the *reconquista* had largely sat idle since the late 13th century, knights in the late 14th and 15th centuries continued to hold up the ideal of holy war as a crucial expression of their identity. Looking to the deeds of their ancestors, Trastámara nobles emphasized the deeds of arms they had accomplished against the infidels and sought to defend and augment the honor of their *linajes* by protecting their gains and seeking to win more territory from the Nasrid Kingdom of Granada. For the Trastámara nobility, the honor to be won in the holy war existed at an individual level, at a familial level, and even at a kingdom level. There was a real sense that, as subjects of Castile, Castilian knights needed to seek vengeance on the Muslim enemy for the dishonor done to Spain in the 8th century. Divine sanction, multiple opportunities for honor, and a historical imperative all fed the ideology of holy war in late medieval Castile.

The ideology of holy war became so powerful in this period that it had an impact on the stability and order of the kingdom itself. Fernando de Antequera, one of the regents during the minority of Juan II, enjoyed widespread love and support among the nobility for his successful resumption of the holy war. During Juan's majority and the reign of his son, Enrique IV, a slow royal response to the knightly clamor for holy war contributed to the problems experienced by both of those kings. In other words, the idea of holy war manifested through real chivalric actions and helped to steer the course of Castilian history.

As important as holy war was, though, it was not the only means for a knight to win honor. Chapter 4 explores the reality that much, if not most, of the battlefield experience that most knights would see occurred in war against fellow Christians. Castilian knights in the late Middle Ages fought against their Portuguese, Navarrese, and Aragonese neighbors and served as allies of the Kingdom of France against England during the Hundred Years' War. In addition, there was ample opportunity to fight against their Christian neighbors in Castile during the civil wars, rebellions, and infighting that marked the Trastámara period. Even when there was not a kingdom-wide civil war, knights found opportunities to fight against their Castilian neighbors, fellow vassals of the king of Castile. Inter-Christian warfare was a regular and lauded activity among late medieval Castilian knights and nobles.

Just as there was an ideology of holy war, there was an ideology of inter-Christian warfare, though it was not often expressed in a succinct and organized fashion. Instead, it existed in the cultural ether of late medieval Castile. In literature, in historical writing, and in the records of central government, there existed a firm belief that fighting against fellow Christians was a way to win honor and a way to please God. At the same time, knights and nobles intellectually and emotionally saturated with the deeds of their ancestors sought to defend and augment the honor passed down to them. Because so many noble *linajes* understood their family honor to be bound up with the holy war, the war against Islam itself contributed to violence against fellow Christians. In other words, competing Christian claims to lands and cities previously held by Muslims could and did spur Castilian knights to fight one another. To maintain their families' ancient achievements against the religious enemy, late medieval knights often found it necessary to fight Christians even when the opportunity to fight Muslims existed.

Chapter 5 examines chivalric violence and identity as it pertained to gender. The masculinity of medieval knights was envisioned through violence. Chivalric men were men largely because they fought. Manly violence was perpetrated not just against peasants or fellow knights, but also sometimes against women in acts of rape and sexual violence. Chivalric prescriptions largely proscribed such violence, which attests to the reality that it occurred. Men, though, were not the only participants in chivalry; elite women also embraced chivalric ideology. At times elite women served a very passive and submissive chivalric role, encouraging men's deeds of arms, praying to God for their success, and, importantly, producing male heirs to continue a man's *linaje*. At other times, women took a more active role that has largely been passed over in traditional understandings of the Middle Ages. Women could and did direct and incite violence on behalf of themselves, their families, and their families' honor. While they rarely took up arms themselves, they clearly understood chivalry as an animating force. Prime among such women was Queen Isabel, who understood chivalric ideology better than most of her predecessors on the throne of Castile. She was especially committed to prosecuting the holy war more actively, thus shaping a very active female chivalric role for herself.

The late Middle Ages represent a violent period in Spanish history. Not only was violence being performed on a regular basis, but it was being performed in various ways and against diverse individuals and groups: men and women, the king himself and the peasant in the field, the fiendish religious enemy and pious Christian warriors. If we want to take the endemic violence of the late Middle Ages seriously, we must acknowledge that that violence took place and we must attempt to comprehend the ideas that informed and directed that violence. Bloodshed was not undertaken by medieval knights because they were brainwashed by the holy church or directed by a perfect prince. Knights developed an ideology of violence – chivalry – and embraced it on their own terms. As offensive as modern people might find the idea, violence was important to medieval knights, forming a core part of their identity in political, social, religious, familial, and professional terms. To understand the dominant figures in Castilian society at the cusp of Spain's union, empire, and march into the modern world, we must grasp their ideas about themselves and their world. Violence was the linch-pin of chivalry.

1

Knights and Kings

Pedro had problems. As the king of Castile since 1350, he had endeavored to conquer the region of Valencia from his neighbor, Pere IV of Aragon (r. 1336–1387). In waging this War of the Two Pedros against Aragon, Pedro had concluded an alliance with England and won the hostility of France. With these international political developments, Pedro found that Castile had become a new theater of operations in the Hundred Years' War. Meanwhile, Pere IV had given financial and political support to a claimant to the Castilian throne, Pedro's half-brother Fadrique. A paranoid man, perhaps rightly so, Pedro worked to secure his place on the throne throughout his reign by destroying his enemies wherever he found them. During his nineteen years on the throne, Pedro was rumored to have discovered among his enemies some leading nobles of the realm, royal advisors, his half-brother, an archbishop, and even the French princess who was his wife; he had them all murdered.[1] In this atmosphere of hostility and suspicion, many noblemen rose against Pedro, finding an alternative claimant to the throne in another of his half-brothers, Enrique de Trastámara. In 1366, the realm had erupted into full-blown civil war. It seems that Pedro's violent actions had returned violence upon him.

Indeed, Pedro's problems were about to get much worse. In 1369 the king found himself besieged by Enrique's army in the castle of Montiel in south-central Castile. Desperately, Pedro contacted a French mercenary in Enrique's army, a knight named Bertrand du Guesclin, and offered him a handsome payment and future lordship if the French knight would help him to escape his predicament. Bertrand, ever the opportunist, went to Enrique and asked him to beat his half-brother's offer. Enrique was all too happy to participate and Bertrand agreed to betray Pedro. On the evening of March 23, 1369, King Pedro snuck out of the castle of Montiel, and Bertrand led the monarch to his tent in the besiegers' camp. Bertrand stepped out, ostensibly to prepare horses for Pedro's flight, and in stepped Enrique de Trastámara. The half-brothers took a moment to recognize one another,

---

[1] Clara Estow, *Pedro the Cruel of Castile, 1350–1369* (Leiden, Netherlands: E.J. Brill, 1995), 190–195.

perhaps cursed at each other, and then lunged, each hoping to end the civil war then and there. The two men tumbled to the ground in the tent and when the dust settled, Pedro lay dead on the earth, a dagger protruding from his face.[2] Thus was born the Trastámara dynasty, baptized in a font of blood and christened in the name of vicious fratricide.

This chapter will argue that the political identity of the Trastámara nobility, as well as non-noble knights and men-at-arms, was founded on chivalric violence. This was particularly true of the relationship between the knights and the Crown. Chivalric identity was comprised of two main components. Firstly, the protection of traditional knightly autonomy – which, in the Trastámara period, meant regular resistance to the king himself – was a key component in allowing knights the latitude to defend and augment their personal and familial honor through great deeds on the battlefield, an important part of chivalric behavior. Secondly, an innate knightly belief in the right to wield political power derived from their chivalric military function and yielded honor and wealth. The latter component included the right of knights to have a voice in the government of the kingdom as advisors in the king's council and at his court. Both components of the knightly political identity led to constant conflict with the Crown. Additionally, kings tended to have more success as rulers when they embraced the violent impulses of chivalry, modeling honor and violence themselves while encouraging knights to fight and deflecting the chivalric hunger for violence from devouring the Crown's power and stability. When kings violated principles of accepted violence or when they seemed disconnected from the virtues of chivalry altogether, they faced serious trouble from the knights and nobility of the realm.

Late medieval Castile might appear to be a highly centralized polity, but in reality there was a constant tension between the king and the knights of the realm. At times king and knights worked in concert to achieve mutually beneficial ends. At other times, the two were at odds. The efforts and determination of knights to defend their autonomy led to conflict between the nobility and the Crown through violent action on the part of both knights and the king.[3] Richard W. Kaeuper has examined this tension in the High Middle Ages, primarily in England and France, and rightly noted that while kings cooperated with and embraced knightly violence in many cases – especially during war – kings as the heads of states often found knightly independence and chivalric violence truly challenging from the perspective of stability and public order. As for the chivalric right to wield political power, we see in the Trastámara period a pattern of individual

---

[2] Pedro López de Ayala, "Crónica del rey don Pedro," in *Biblioteca Autores Españoles*, ed. M. Rivadeneyra (Madrid: Impresores de Camara de S.M., 1876), vol. 66, 556.
[3] Richard W. Kaeuper, *Chivalry and Violence* (Oxford: Oxford University Press, 1999), 93–100.

knights pursuing this ideal to a breaking point, wherein one advisor would come to dominate the king and essentially rule in his name. While this may have been a fulfillment of the chivalric will to power for one individual, other knights and nobles naturally resented political power being concentrated in the hands of one of their peers and generally sought to remove overpowerful advisors. The chivalric claim to political power encouraged violence from others in the chivalric world.

Jesús Rodríguez-Velasco has described the Trastámara period as a neat progression from royal control to noble initiative.[4] From a legal perspective, his schema is insightful, with laws and legal treatises moving in the direction he articulates. Rodríguez-Velasco's outline may require adjustment, though, if we wish to consider the question of political ideology and culture expressed more broadly by knights themselves, both through their imaginative literature and through their understandings of their own actions. We ought to see the whole Trastámara period as one of intense and rarely resolved debate. Just as Craig Taylor has emphasized that the challenges of late medieval France generated intense debate among knights and chivalric writers, so too did the Trastámara period produce discussion and disagreement among Castilian knights.[5] More recently, Rodríguez-Velasco examined knighthood and chivalry, asserting that chivalric ideology in the late Middle Ages became "a substantial component in a discourse of peace."[6] He identifies bourgeois knights – the rising middle class – as the driving force behind the peaceful impulses of chivalry. This chapter will argue that while chivalry may have provided a certain amount of intellectual stability through its framing of violent issues, it rarely checked actual violence in any serious way. Instead, chivalric ideology actually encouraged violent behavior, due to its valorization of personal and familial honor and the need to defend that honor physically.

The brutality at the heart of the Trastámara noble identity was not fundamentally new; knights had been violent men for centuries. But from the mid-14th century onward, Castilian knights and nobles seized a unique opportunity to define themselves in the political world *primarily* through violence. The accession of the Trastámaras did not erase what had come before but allowed for an augmentation of knightly violence by confirming it as part of the character of the dynasty. As we will see, Enrique de Trastámara faced questions about his legitimacy on the throne. After all, he had seized power from the rightful ruler and asserted a weaker claim to rule.

---

[4] Jesús D. Rodríguez-Velasco, *El Debate Sobre la caballería en el Siglo XV* (Salamanca: Europa Artes Graficas, S.A., 1996), 375–376.
[5] Craig Taylor, *Chivalry and the Ideals of Knighthood in France during the Hundred Years War* (Cambridge: Cambridge University Press, 2013), x–xii.
[6] Jesús D. Rodríguez-Velasco, *Order and Chivalry*, trans. Eunice Rodríguez Ferguson (Philadelphia: University of Pennsylvania Press, 2010), 1–5.

His justification was founded in the use of extreme and vengeful violence to silence his critics and defeat his enemies. In this, Enrique modeled for the new nobility what would be the standard operating procedure in his brave new world. Given the existing tension between the Crown and knights, the Trastámara nobility followed Enrique's lead and embraced chivalric violence as the core of their own political identity. Late medieval chivalry was not a set of unattainable ideals or flowery and nostalgic ornamentations. In Trastámara Castile, as in much of Europe, it was a powerfully violent ideology that imbued the nobility with a bellicose political identity.

This violent and rebellious political identity was cloaked in the language of loyalty and service to the king, drawing on prescriptive ideals of generations past. Almost without exception, knights claimed that their violent political actions were done for the love and service of their king, even when they made war without the king's consent or rose up against the Crown itself. Kings insisted on their subjects' complete loyalty and understood loyalty to imply clear obedience. Debates over the meaning of loyalty to the sovereign served as a means for knights to make sense of and engage with one another and with the monarch concerning their ideas and actions. In short, the *language* of loyalty in Trastámara Castile was constant and unchanging. The *definition* was inconstant and could cover a wide array of actions. Indeed, some knights were probably sincerely concerned about staying loyal to their king, while others likely used the dominant discourse as cover for their own personal ambitions.

We will see the establishment and parameters of this ideological flashpoint first through the very establishment of the Trastámara nobility, when nobles, knights, and kings embraced violence as part of their political identity. From there we will examine how this political concept functioned to allow for debate and latitude for the Trastámara nobility. Finally, we will see how this politically violent impulse played out in the late 14th and 15th centuries, with knights and nobles routinely causing disruption to the Kingdom of Castile through their violent initiatives.

Chivalry, Violence, and the Early Trastámara State

The men who would ultimately become the Trastámara nobility had their origins in acts of political violence. By the middle of the 14th century, the Castilian nobility had a number of grievances concerning their monarch. Some were religious in nature, such as anger over Pedro's tolerant treatment of Castilian Muslims and Jews. Others were economic – many nobles saw their rents decline as a result of economic disruptions in the 14th century and Pedro did little to relieve their financial difficulties.[7] In the tumultuous

---

[7] Julio Valdeón Baruque, *Pedro I, el Cruel y Enrique de Tastámara: la primera guerra civil española?* (Madrid: Santillana Ediciones Generales, S.L., 2002), 11–16.

1350s and 1360s, these various issues bubbled in the background, forming a general discontent with Pedro and his rule. Less evident from the sources, but perhaps more significant in the long run, was a desire on the part of the nobility to assert themselves more forcefully in the political sphere vis-à-vis the king. Julio Valdeón Baruque has rightly suggested that most of the other complaints of the nobility were more ephemeral, coming and going with little relevance, but that "[i]n truth, the high nobility sought to play a decisive role in the government of the kingdoms."[8] The nobility would indeed come to play a decisive role in Castilian politics, first through violent rebellion and then, over the next hundred years, through the expression of the violent political identity embraced in the context of the Castilian civil war.

The tipping point for the Castilian nobility's discontent with Pedro came through a series of political actions, which turned violent first on the part of Pedro and then on the part of the nobles. In 1353, Juan Alfonso de Alburquerque, a noble of Portuguese extraction who was Pedro's favorite, arranged a marriage between the king and Blanche de Bourbon, a French princess. Three days after the marriage was celebrated, Pedro abandoned his young bride in favor of his mistress, leaving Blanche humiliated, France scandalized, and Alburquerque shamed. The latter returned to Portugal, fearing the growing division between himself and the king as Pedro purged the Castilian court and government of all of Alburquerque's allies.[9] From his exile in Portugal, Alburquerque entered into league with the Trastámara brothers, Enrique and Fadrique, and together they brought an army into Castile to make war against Pedro. By mid-1354, a serious rebellion was under way, led by the Trastámaras and Alburquerque, who were sympathetic to the travails of the poor Queen Blanche and aimed to reconstitute the government of Castile. On September 28, the political world of Castile was shaken by news of the death of the Señor de Alburquerque. Rumors swirled that King Pedro had had him poisoned.[10] The rebel army seized the moment to make a symbolic and grotesque political statement. They carried Alburquerque's body as their new standard, refusing to have him buried until they were victorious against Pedro. The death of Alburquerque would remain powerfully embedded in the minds of the rebellious nobility and of the future King Enrique II. Other murders, too, were important in Pedro's attempts to secure his rule and as propaganda items for his enemies. In 1358, Pedro had captured Fadrique, the Trastámara claimant, and had him executed. The king's enemies claimed that Pedro had not simply executed his half-brother, but had him marched into a courtyard where Pedro was feasting. At a signal from the king, Pedro's men clubbed

---

[8] Ibid., 70. "En verdad, la alta nobleza pretendía desempeñar un papel decisivo en el gobierno de los reinos …"
[9] Estow, *Pedro the Cruel*, 143–145.
[10] Valdeon Baruque, *Pedro I, el Cruel*, 71; Estow, *Pedro the Cruel*, 150.

Fadrique in the back of his head with a mace, killing him. Pedro, the story claimed, went ahead and ate his meal with Fadrique's bloody corpse in a heap on the same table.[11] Pedro had used violence as a political tool, a policy against which his opponents railed. Yet, in opening the Pandora's box of violence as a political tool, Pedro had set a standard; his enemies would utilize the very same tool, though they clothed it in the justifying garments of honor and chivalry.

The Trastámaras and their supporters explicitly acknowledged that their own political violence was founded and legitimated by Pedro's violent actions.[12] The royal chronicler Pedro López de Ayala justified Enrique's actions by describing Pedro as a tyrant and asserting that Enrique acted as a tool of God in deposing and killing his half-brother.[13] To be sure, Ayala was relying on an ancient argument concerning limits on the right of kings to rule. But Enrique II, when he had killed his half-brother and secured the throne for himself, articulated a new ideological defense of his violent actions against his half-brother, the legitimate king of Castile. Sometime after the bloody coup of 1369, Edward III of England wrote to Enrique. The letter from Edward is no longer extant but we can fairly speculate that Edward lambasted Enrique for his dishonorable deposal of a legitimate king.[14] In Enrique's response, he acknowledges that he did use unorthodox violence in order to gain the throne, but he explains that his violence was justified because of Pedro's own violence. Enrique provides a detailed and yet incomplete list of Pedro's political murders:

> [King Pedro] killed in this kingdom the Queen Doña Blanca de Borbon, who was his legitimate wife and he killed the Queen of Aragon Doña Leonor, who was his aunt ... And he killed Doña Juana de Acuña and Isabel de Lara, daughters of Don Juan Nuñez, Señor de Vizcaya, who were his cousins ... and he killed three of his brothers, Don Fadrique, Master of Santiago and Don Juan and Don Pedro, and he killed Don Juan, Señor de Alburquerque. He killed the Infante of Aragon Don Juan, his cousin. He killed many knights and squires of the great men of the kingdom ... and in order to

---

[11] López de Ayala, *don Pedro*, 481–483.

[12] Cecilia Devia has argued that the violence of Enrique and his supporters was a constructive force in society. Cecilia Devia, "Pedro I y Enrique II de Castilla: la construcción de un rey monstruoso y la legitimación de un usurpador en la Crónica del canciller Ayala," *Mirabilia*, 13, ed. Ricardo da Costa (Jun.–Dec. 2011), 68.

[13] Carlos Estepa Díez, "Rebelión y rey legítimo en las luchas entre Pedro I y Enrique II," in *Lucha política: condena y legitimación en la España medieval*, ed. Isabel Alfonso, et. al. (Lyon, France: ENS Éditions, 2004), 43–61.

[14] Edward had supported Pedro during the civil war. In the years to come, Edward would also support his son, John of Gaunt's pretensions to the Castilian throne. P.E. Russell, *Portugal, Spain and the African Atlantic, 1343–1490: Chivalry and Crusade from John of Gaunt to Henry the Navigator* (Aldershot, England: Ashgate Publishing Limited, 1995), 173–185.

defend the said kingdom [of Castile], God gave his sentence against [Pedro], who of his own will abandoned the kingdom …[15]

For Enrique, the case was clear. Although he was concerned about the optics of having killed a sitting king, he and the rest of the kingdom could rest assured that Pedro's death was not only deserved, but ordained by God.[16] The actions of the last king of the House of Borgoña left a powerful legacy for the House of Trastámara. The theoretical legal justification for the deposing of Pedro was rooted in the idea that he was a tyrant king who had abused royal power and cruelly punished his Castilian subjects.[17] Enrique was breathing life into the theory that a bad king ought to be resisted, violently if necessary. Just as importantly, though, Enrique was taking vengeance against Pedro for his transgressive violence against their shared family. The violence with which Enrique inaugurated the Trastámara dynasty was chivalric in nature, with Enrique protecting his family and its honor from a dishonorable and wicked relative. The message of the new Trastámara monarch set a chivalric tone for the new nobility. Violence tied to honor and chivalric virtue would not only be tolerated, but lauded.

At the top of this new nobility, naturally, were the relatives of the new monarch. Enrique's brother, Sancho, was rewarded with the county of Alburquerque, the holding on the Portuguese frontier that had previously belonged to Pedro's favorite. Other relatives would also be rewarded, though few fraternal lineages would survive for more than a generation or so. In similar fashion, Enrique was quick to reward the foreign mercenaries with whom he had spent much of his adult life in Portugal, Aragon, and France. The famous Bertrand du Guesclin was granted significant holdings in Castile in exchange for betraying Pedro, though he ultimately abandoned them to return to France. In the longer term, Bernal de Foix, the bastard son of a French lord, found his fortune in Enrique's service, aiding him throughout the civil war, and was rewarded in 1368 with the county of Medinaceli and a marriage to one of Enrique's distant cousins, Isabel de la Cerda. The Aragonese nobleman Felipe de Castro, who fought with Enrique at the Battle of Nájera, was similarly granted the lordship of Paredes de Nava, though he would be killed by the locals shortly after the civil war ended.[18] Although they did not last long as the cream of the new nobility, Enrique's family and his foreign mercenaries were all rewarded for their rejection of Pedro and martial support of Enrique. The new king was simultaneously rewarding his supporters and demonstrating largesse, a key chivalric quality.

---

[15] Biblioteca Nacional de España, MSS.MICRO/2063.
[16] Valdeón Baruque, *Pedro I, el Cruel*, 241–242.
[17] Ibid., 234–235.
[18] Ibid., 256–257.

The pre-Trastámara nobility found a more permanent life as the new Trastámara nobility and, just like the more ephemeral winners mentioned above, they too found their political identity in the Trastámara order through violent support of Enrique against Pedro. The old powerful nobility were often quick to support Enrique and were showered with rewards in return. Juan Alfonso de Guzmán, the fourth in a line of Señores de Sanlúcar in Andalucía, was made the first Count of Niebla in 1369, expanding his already impressive holdings near the Granadan frontier. Lesser families found even greater reward, coming from small means and ending up with powerful holdings and political influence. The Mendoza *linaje*, an old but minor family in the 14th century, eagerly supported Enrique during the civil war and found themselves rewarded with land and titles. The Mendozas parlayed their early rewards from Enrique II into such grand fiscal and political capital that one of their number would become the most powerful man in the kingdom in the 15th century. Indeed, the Mendozas are one of several families known to historians as a "nobility of service," precisely because they were initially loyal servants of the Trastámara dynasty.[19] Our narrative sources confirm that the rewarding of prowess with lands and titles was recognized at the time, with Gutierre Díez de Games noting that "The king Don Enrique, to reward and pay those who helped him win the kingdom, shared it out with them …"[20] In the 1360s, this meant that they had rebelled against the legitimate Pedro in order to support Enrique's vengeful rising.

Some of the old nobility, though, were never able to make their peace with the new monarch. In particular, the lords and knights of northwestern Castile and Galicia were reluctant to acknowledge the legitimacy of Enrique, and pockets of resistance to the Trastámara dynasty remained in parts of Andalucía as well. For several years after killing his half-brother, King Enrique was occupied with the pacification of these territories, besieging his enemies, and violently establishing his new political order. He had hope, certainly, that the partisans of Pedro, known as the *petristas*, would seek reconciliation and come into his service. Two of the last lords to resist the Trastámara dynasty were Martín López de Córdoba, the Master of the Order of Calatrava, and Matheos Ferrandez de Cáceres, Pedro's chancellor and the keeper of his royal seal. The Master of Calatrava was apparently a great and worthy

---

[19] For a very brief overview of the establishment of a *nobleza de servicio*, see Julio Valdeón Baruque, "Enrique II, King of Castile," in *Medieval Iberia: An Encyclopedia*, ed. E. Michael Gerli (New York: Routledge, 2003), 303–304. We can compare this nobility with the nobility of service that existed in other parts of medieval Europe. For one example, see Kaeuper, *Chivalry and Violence*, 107–110.

[20] Gutierre Díez de Games, *El Victorial*, ed. Juan de Mata Carriazo (Madrid: Espasa-Calpe, S.A., 1940), 58. "El rey don Enrique, por galardonar e pagar aquellos que le ayudaron a cobrar el reyno, partió con ellos …"

knight. Ayala wrote that "the King Don Enrique had earlier yearned greatly to bring Don Martín López to his mercy and service, for he was a good knight,"[21] just as the monarch had done with so many of the old nobility. As part of this effort, the king and his knights and men-at-arms besieged the two *petristas* in the castle of Carmona in Andalucía in 1371. During this siege, the Master made a critical error: he resisted Enrique too vigorously. The king had sent some forty of his loyal men to scale the walls of Carmona, and they had entered into one of the towers. The defenders of Carmona rushed to defend the tower, causing some of the attackers to fall from the fortification, breaking the ladders, and leaving their comrades in the tower trapped. Then, in a brutal act of defiance, "Don Martín López de Córdoba, the so-called Master of Calatrava, then came, making prisoners of all those who had climbed up the ladders, and ordered them to be killed in an evil manner, in a pen with sword and lance blows."[22] In killing Enrique's men, Martín López de Córdoba was violently acting out a political statement – resistance to the Trastámara monarchy. At the same time, the chronicler's scorn for the Master's behavior is evident in his refusal to dignify him with the title he held. Ayala seems to have objected to the Master's behavior as unbecoming of a knight and nobleman.

Enrique's response to Martín's brutal act would be some time in coming, but as soon as the king heard of Martín's actions, "he swore that [Martín] would never do homage to him, but that [the king] would kill [Martín]; by many oaths he swore this."[23] Enrique had seen his honor slighted by Martín's brutality toward his loyal knights and would have his vengeance. Several months after the incident, the Master of Calatrava realized that he would have to surrender Carmona to Enrique. The terms of the surrender were that the Master would hand over to Enrique the town and castle of Carmona, all of King Pedro's remaining treasure, and Matheos Ferrandez de Cáceres, Pedro's chancellor. In return, Enrique would grant the Master of Calatrava safety, either granting him mercy and forgiveness, or exiling him to another kingdom. The king happily agreed to these terms, swore an oath before the Master of Santiago that he would uphold the agreement, and allowed Martín to fulfill his end of the bargain. As soon as Martín had made good on the terms, King Enrique had him arrested and taken to Sevilla as a prisoner. On a Thursday in June of 1371, Enrique ordered

---

[21] López de Ayala, "Don Enrique Segundo," in *Biblioteca Autores Españoles*, vol. 66, 8. "el Rey Don Enrique, que cobdicia mucho antes atraer á su merced é servicio á Don Martin Lopez, por ser buen Caballero …"
[22] Ibid. "E Don Martin Lopez de Cordoba, Maestre que se decia de Calatraba, desque llegó, fallólos presos á todos los que subieron por el escala, é fizolos á todos matar de malas maneras en un corral á espadadas é lanzadas."
[23] Ibid. "é juró que nunca faria otra pleytesia con él, si non quél muriese, por muchas juras quél ficiese …"

Matheos to be dragged through the streets of Sevilla before his hands and feet were cut off and he was beheaded. On a hot afternoon the following Monday, Enrique had the Master of Calatrava dragged through the streets of Sevilla and paraded into the Plaza de San Francisco, the main public space in the city. The peaceful nature of that plaza's eponymous saint was absent that day as Martín López de Córdoba had his hands and feet cut off before he was burned to death.[24] Such was the fate for refusing to serve the new Trastámara monarch. Enrique's wrath, Ayala claims, was fueled not only by the Master's refusal to swear allegiance to the new monarch, but "especially for the death which [Martín] had caused of those men-at-arms, the servants of the King, who had climbed the ladders at Carmona."[25] If we take Ayala's chronicle as the voice of the king, his anger was simultaneously over the Master's continued resistance to Enrique and over the Master's assault on those who had displayed their loyalty and service to the new monarch. The Master had challenged Enrique's honor by slaughtering his martial followers, and Enrique furiously nursed a grudge that blossomed into a bouquet of vengeance. Enrique II would be a violent and chivalric king who would exact vengeance on any who challenged his authority or his honor.

The vengeance visited by Enrique on these men was a pointed opening to the Trastámara period, and its very public nature helped to set the tone for the new regime. Supporters and dissidents alike could hardly miss the theatrics of violence which the new monarch put on display in 1371.[26] The killings were not neat judicial affairs designed to emphasize the rule of law. Enrique destroyed his enemies in a moment of showy brutality, designed to emphasize his leadership of the new chivalry of Castile and as a warning to any who might rebel. For possible dissidents, the chilling message would have been clear: insult or offend Enrique's honor or royal dignity and suffer a frightening public death. For his supporters, perhaps a different message was understood. If the king himself vindicated his honor and protected his dignity through showy violence, a good knight or noble ought to do the same. Enrique may not have been innovating in his violence, but he was certainly embracing the chivalric honor involved in it and signaling such virtues to his knights and men-at-arms.

The torture and execution of Ferrandez and López were probably the most extreme and the most public punishment of *petristas*, but we know that Enrique similarly hunted others down, besieging their strongholds and

---

[24] Ibid., 9.
[25] Ibid. "especialmente por la muerte que ficiera de aquellos omes de armas sus criados del Rey que avian subido por el escala en Carmona ..."
[26] Thomas Devaney has modeled a useful methodology for examining acts of public spectacle and public theatrics. See Thomas Devaney, *Enemies in the Plaza* (Philadelphia: University of Pennsylvania Press, 2014).

killing those who continued to resist him.[27] We do have one significant case of a *petrista* who managed to survive the dynastic change without being eliminated. The forebears of Pero Niño, a famous knight of the late 14th and 15th centuries, were apparently themselves supporters of Pedro, though the Niños were not a powerful or ancient *linaje*. Pero Niño's biographer, Gutierre Díez de Games, is careful when he discusses this heritage. He notes that Pero Niño's grandfather, Pero Fernández Niño, "was always with the king Don Pedro until [Pedro] died; and after his death, he never wanted to obey the king Don Enrique."[28] Indeed, Pero Fernández was Pedro's *adelantado mayor* – effectively a royal governor – of the Kingdom of Murcia and fought vigorously for Pedro during the civil war.[29] Many of Pero Fernández Niño's like-minded comrades left Castile after Enrique's success and Díez claims that "although [Pero Fernández] did not flee the kingdom, always it remained his intention, and he labored to do so, until the day he died."[30] We do not know much more about the grandfather, only that he remained a *petrista* for some time after the establishment of the Trastámara dynasty. Pero Niño's father, Juan Niño, was also a *petrista* during the civil war. In fact, Díez claims that Juan Niño was present in the castle of Montiel on that fateful day in 1369 when Pedro was killed, serving as a page in the king's household and as a crossbowman.[31]

Juan Niño did eventually switch his loyalty from Pedro to Enrique, but Díez unfortunately never reveals what the transition from Pedro's service to the Trastámaras' service looked like. The only hint that Díez provides in his chivalric biography is that Juan Niño had made some political enemies for himself during the reign of Juan I (r. 1379–1390). Some of his knightly neighbors, who were "favorites as much of the intimates of the king as of

---

[27] Gutierre Díez de Games gives a brief account of Enrique's pacification of Castile after the civil war, naming some of the *petristas* defeated by Enrique as well as a few of the more significant battles and sieges. See Díez de Games, *El Victorial*, 58–61.

[28] Ibid., 61. "Pero Fernández fué sienpre con el rey don Pedro hasta que murió; e después de su muerte nunca quiso oveteçer al rey don Enrrique."

[29] In a letter from King Pedro to Enrique Enríquez, another of his *adelantado mayores*, the king writes: "Know that Pero Fernandez el Niño, my Adelantado in the kingdom of Murcia and my *alcaide* [castellan] of Alicante sends to tell me that he has sent to buy food and other things which are necessary for the provisioning of the said castle of Alicante …" This letter was included in an appendix to Angel Luis Molina, "Repercusiones de la guerra castellano-aragonesa en la economía murciana (1364–1365)," *Miscelánea Medieval Murciana*, no. 3 (1977), 132. "Fago vos saber que Pero Fernandez el Niño, mio Adelantado en el regno de Murçia e mio Alcayde de Alicante, me enbio dezir que enbiaua conprar viandas e otras cosas que auia mester para basteçimiento del dicho castiello de Alicante …"

[30] Díez de Games, *El Victorial*, 61. "avnque él no salió del reyno, sienpre duró e tovo en su yntençión, e puso sus trauaxos, hasta que murió."

[31] Ibid., 57.

other great knights of the kingdom,"[32] came to Juan's house one day, where he was dining with some twenty or more of his own men. The two groups of knights took to fighting and Juan Niño "killed by his own hand Juan Gonçález de Valdolmos, a stout knight, with powerful relatives, who was the chief figure of those with whom [Juan Niño] had enmity."[33] We would expect that such behavior would earn Juan the vicious punishment of the Trastámara monarch; after all, he was from a *petrista* family and had actively fought with men who could count on the favor of the king's inner circle. Yet Díez has nothing more to say on the matter, instead moving in the next sentence to discuss King Juan's war in Portugal and the great service and deeds of arms that Juan Niño performed for him at the siege of Lisbon.[34] Juan Niño had made a bold political statement: he refused to endure the aggression of his political rivals and he responded with his sword to slights against his honor. Such action was eminently chivalric, fitting well with the violence that Enrique II had committed against his enemies. When his honor was challenged in any way, he had to respond with force. Moreover, Juan Niño would find political favor with King Juan during the war against Portugal, through his powerful deeds on the battlefield. For Juan Niño, like his fellow nobles, his political actions were joined with chivalric violence and he was rewarded for it by the Trastámara king.

Enrique II's policies and the behavior of what was becoming the new Trastámara nobility were indelibly imprinted with chivalric violence. For Enrique himself, his original core of Castilian and foreign supporters, the nobles who joined Enrique's side after the war began, and the *petristas* who attempted to resist Enrique, violence was the *modus operandi*. In order to express their political identity at the birth of the Trastámara dynasty, all major parties resorted to violent means. For much of the Trastámara period, this political violence would manifest primarily around the question of loyalty and service to the king, counterbalanced with the noble and knightly drive for political autonomy.

The Loyalty Debate

The question of loyalty to the Crown was at the heart of the violence of many of the major political actors in Trastámara Castile. For the *petristas*, their devoted loyalty to the old dynasty and their tenacious refusal to discover a loyalty to Enrique II placed them outside the new nobility. For

---

[32] Ibid., 61. "los quales heran favoresçidos, ansí de priuados del rey como de otros caualleros grandes del reyno."
[33] Ibid., 62. "mató él por su mano dél a el Juan Gonçález de Valdolmos, vn reçio cavallero, e muy enparentado, que hera el más prençipal de los con quien él avía henemistad."
[34] Ibid.

Enrique, loyal behavior provided the standard by which he could judge who would suffer his wrath and who would fall under his protection. For Enrique's supporters, new and old, their loyalty to the new dynasty motivated their violent actions. Loyalty and service became the buzzwords of the Trastámara nobility at the time of its founding, even as knights and nobles sought greater latitude for independent action.

The question of loyalty and service to the king was the Gordian knot of the Trastámara nobility – fundamentally important, yet fraught with tension. In the largest sense, the very nature of the Trastámara dynasty raises the question of loyalty; Pedro, for all his problems, was the legitimate king of Castile, while Enrique de Trastámara was not. Yet a majority of Castile's nobility rose up against Pedro and served Enrique instead. Loyalty and service to Pedro disappeared in order to place Enrique on the throne. For decades, royal chroniclers and knightly authors struggled with the very foundation of the Trastámara dynasty and what it meant for the chivalric ideal of loyalty.[35] Given the punishment visited on Enrique's enemies, Castilian knights had little appetite to disserve him and a keen willingness to embrace the appearance of perpetual service and loyalty. Knights and chivalric authors would labor diligently to ensure that they were always described as doing good and loyal service to the king. Therein lay both a critical challenge and a unique opportunity for the Trastámara nobility. Often they were doing good service, fighting the king's wars or serving in his household. Often, though, they were in open rebellion against the monarch or his agents. In either case they assured themselves and their peers that they served the king loyally. Casting nearly every violent political action as a service to the king, often with an effort to explain *how* such actions were a service, created a space wherein the chivalric elite could debate what service and loyalty actually meant. The gnarled nature of the knightly virtue of loyalty allowed for a wide variety of actions to be called good and loyal service, even as the nobility preserved and augmented their traditional autonomy.[36]

The chivalric ideal of autonomous knightly action and that of loyalty, especially to the monarch, had long been a part of Castilian culture. Indeed, the earliest piece of Castilian chivalric literature, *Cantar del Mio Cid*, dating from around the turn of the 13th century, was primarily occupied with the question of loyalty to the king. In the 14th and 15th centuries, the story of

---

[35] Cecilia Devia has argued that Pedro López de Ayala would be responsible for converting Pedro into a monster, thereby making Enrique not a fratricide and usurper, but an agent of God. Devia argues, rightly, that Ayala ideologically converted Pedro from a legitimate king into an illegitimate king. Cecilia Devia, "Pedro I y Enrique II," 60–78.

[36] For a summary of this traditional understanding of Enrique's success see Julio Valdeón Baruque, "La revolución Trastámara," in *Historia de España de la Edad Media*, ed. Vicente Ángel Álvarez Palenzuela (Barcelona: Editorial Ariel, S.A., 2002), 679–680.

Rodrigo Díaz de Vivar, better known as El Cid, remained a popular literary subject and the original poem was well known. The extant fragment of the great Castilian epic opens with a powerful knight and vassal weeping as he rides his horse into exile from the Kingdom of Castile, having run afoul of King Alfonso's good graces.[37] We no longer know how the poem once began, but we do know that the author was convinced that El Cid was deeply dismayed at having his loyalty and service called into question. As a result, El Cid works throughout the poem to do good service for his king even while he is exiled, sending Alfonso captured treasure and slaves, conquering lands, and generally spreading fame for himself and his lord. Developments in the story add layers of complication to the simple ideal of knightly service to the king. For example, King Alfonso is dominated by his nephews, evil advisors who vilely work to separate the loyal Cid from his king.[38] It cannot, therefore, be El Cid's fault that he has fallen out with Alfonso; it must be the work of the wicked royal official. Beyond nefarious advisors, King Alfonso himself is problematic in the proper relationship of knight and king. Alfonso was understood in the Middle Ages as unworthy of El Cid's vassalage. This is largely because the king fails to fully comprehend the concept of chivalric honor. He fails to honor El Cid as he ought and, as Alan Deyermond has pointed out, seems to have little grasp of the appropriate behavior of a vassal toward his lord.[39] The king's misunderstanding of El Cid's honor and his inability to cooperate with his vassal, even bringing *dishonor* to the great knight, help to drive the story. Geoffrey West has compared the historical relationship between Alfonso VI and El Cid with the imagined relationship in *Mio Cid*, concluding that the poem evolved out of historical facts, passed down through an oral tradition before being written into the work we know today. The links of oral history suggest that individuals were interested in hearing the history of El Cid told in different ways and in discussing the details of the story. The theme of king, knight, and chivalric honor in *Mio Cid* would have served as a jumping-off point for discussion and debate in medieval Castile.[40]

---

[37] For ease of access, I have chosen to cite a modern translation into English alongside the original language, see *The Song of the Cid*, trans. Burton Raffel (New York: Penguin Group, 2009), 3–4.

[38] Ibid., 98.

[39] Alan Deyermond, *El "Cantar de mio Cid" y la épica medieval española* (Barcelona: Simio, 1987), 26–29.

[40] Geoffrey West, "King and Vassal in History and Poetry: A Contrast Between the 'Historica Roderici' and the 'Poema de Mio Cid'," in *"Mio Cid" Studies*, ed. A.D. Deyermond (London: Tamesis Books Limited, 1977), 195–208. For a recent analysis of this theme in the poem, see Luis Galván, "'A todos alcança ondra': consideraciones sobre el honor y la relación del Cid y el rey en el 'Cantar de mio Cid'," in *"Sonando van sus nuevas allent parte del mar". El Cantar de mio Cid y el mundo de la épica*, ed. Alberto Montaner Frutos (Toulouse, France: Presses université de Toulouse, 2013), 19–34.

The tensions and conflicting viewpoints presented in *Mio Cid* help to frame Trastámara political ideals, broaching the large questions that would dominate the troubled politics of the late 14th and 15th centuries. On the one hand, we can imagine how a newly established king of Castile might have read *Mio Cid*. Even if a vassal should run afoul of the king, the vassal ought to work tirelessly to freshly ingratiate himself with the monarch, keeping in mind that all of his actions ought to be taken with the ideal of returning the political world to its proper order. From the royal perspective, a properly ordered political world meant that loyal knights served their monarch. Knights might have read this same message, recognizing the emotional trauma that El Cid felt when he was separated from the loyal service of his king, but they likely would have gleaned other meaning as well. Rodrigo Díaz de Vivar – the greatest knight in Castilian history – operated largely independently from his king. He fought with the Muslims and with other Christians as he pleased, winning an incredible amount of booty to distribute among his men. By the end of the story, Rodrigo's independent violence won him his own state, centered on the city of Valencia, which was effectively independent of Castile. How appealing this must have been for the new Trastámara nobility! If El Cid could act as a traditional knight, fighting when and against whom he pleased, and still claim to be a devoted servant of his king, why could 15th-century knights not do the same? Prowess on the battlefield, with or without the king's approval, was a characteristic of a great knight. If that prowess led to political glory, so much the better.

The key to understanding the political ideal of loyalty in chivalric ideology lies in the absence of a clearly defined and agreed upon prescription about *how* service to the king ought to manifest itself; the ideal of service to the king served as a fulcrum upon which different authors and thinkers could debate. Such debate spanned a wide spectrum, from those who articulated strict theories of royal supremacy, to those who were much more willing to allow for independent knightly action.[41] At one end of the spectrum of loyalty, authors and thinkers articulated positions which asserted in no uncertain terms that a knight's first and most important duty was to serve his lord the king in all cases and to recognize that evil things arise from ignoring that service. Going beyond simply couching knightly activity in the *language* of loyalty and service, this ideological position held that service to the king was simply the highest chivalric ideal and that deviance from that service was frighteningly destructive. The *Siete Partidas*, the great 13th-century law code reconfirmed by kings throughout the 14th and 15th centuries, deals directly

---

[41] Rodríguez-Velasco, *Order and Chivalry*, 230. Rodríguez-Velasco also offers insights into the debate over chivalry and its values and tensions in the 15th century but unfortunately leaves out what he calls "fictional" literature. Rodríguez-Velasco, *El Debate*, 25–26.

with the question of knightly loyalty and, unsurprisingly, takes a strongly "royalist" position. Without mincing words, Law IX of Title XXI of the second *partida* is titled "Knights Should be Very Loyal."[42] Because loyalty was "the mother of all good practices," Law IX declares loyalty a necessity for knights if they are to defend society (their primary purpose, according to the *Partidas*), to preserve the honor of their lineage, and to prevent them from doing anything which would bring shame to them.[43] Each of these points speaks to the dominant elements of chivalric ideology – prowess, lineage, honor – and all are subsumed to the greater ideal of knightly loyalty to the king.[44] As a statement of royal initiative, the *Partidas* also claimed for the Crown the role of arbiter of knighthood and chivalry. Law XII of the same title asserts that the Crown has the authority to decide what qualifies a man as a knight. Among other things, "We also decree that a man should not be created a knight ... known to be a traitor; nor one who has been guilty of perfidy, or has been condemned as such."[45] Even the accusation of disloyalty or treason was enough, in the mind of the royal lawyers behind the *Partidas*, to ban a man from the honor of knighthood.

As much in the cultural as in the legal world, there existed a "royalist" position. *The Book of the Knight Zifar*, a consciously didactic 14th-century chivalric romance whose popularity continued into the 15th century, overflows with episodes and lessons emphasizing that ignoring one's loyalty to the king or acting against his service results in death, destruction, and damnation. A superlative and supernatural example highlights the problems with disloyalty or revolt, the vices corresponding to the virtues of loyalty and service. A certain Count Nason has broken his oath of fealty to his king (the titular Zifar), ravaged his lord's lands, and attacked the king's other vassals. After he is defeated in battle and captured, the count asks the king for forgiveness but unintentionally admits that he *knowingly* broke the bonds of loyalty that bound him to the king. In response, Zifar orders an incredibly violent and symbolic punishment on the count, saying:

> [F]or all the other things which you did against the faith and loyalty to me which you promised to keep and which you did not keep ... And so that you will not infect other lands with your treason wherever you go, I do not want to throw you out of my kingdom, but I order your tongue to be torn out through your neck for the words you spoke against me and your head cut off ... and that you be burned to ashes ... so that neither the dogs nor

---

[42] *Las Siete Partidas*, trans. Samuel Parsons Scott and ed. Robert I. Burns, S.J., vol. 5 (Philadelphia: University of Pennsylvania Press, 2001), 421.
[43] Ibid.
[44] Keen, *Chivalry*, 9, 68. Kaeuper, *Chivalry and Violence*, 8.
[45] *Partidas*, 423.

the birds may eat you, for they would be infected with your treason; I order your ashes thrown into that lake ... which they say is a sulfuric lake.[46]

Disloyalty and rebellion against the king result not only in specific and horrifying physical dismemberment, but also permanent destruction. A personal pollution on the part of Nason, disloyalty also creeps through society like a disease, poisoning any who come into contact with it. A pestilence so dangerous that it might infect even the beasts of the earth and sky, rebellion against one's rightful lord must be snuffed out with the fires of a burning lake. In this life, according to *Zifar*, incredible punishment must be doled out for disloyalty or rebellion.

The author of *Zifar*, though, was not content to leave his lesson on treachery in the temporal world and extended Nason's punishment into the next life. In an otherworldy adventure, a knight known simply as the Bold Knight, at the beckoning of a beautiful woman, travels beneath the sulfuric lake where Nason's ashes were interred. He finds that the woman is the mistress of a strange city under the lake, and he is her guest for several days. One day, while exploring the city and its environs, the Bold Knight encounters the mistress of the city, with her arm around Count Nason. Sitting next to Nason is his great-grandfather, who in life had also betrayed the loyalty of his king. Instead of seeing the mistress as a beautiful woman, though, the Bold Knight sees a "very ugly and very frightening devil" inflicting a Promethean punishment on the count and his ancestor, tearing out their hearts from their chests and devouring them.[47] Seeing the Bold Knight watching her, the horrifying demon looks up at him and screeches "You reckless and daring knight ... I am the Mistress of Treason!" The demon then causes an earthquake, convulsing the land under the lake and destroying much of the city.[48] The Bold Knight is magically ejected from the lake and returns to the court of King Zifar, who remarks on the religious nature of the story he has just heard: "Friends, I truly believe that place is accursed by our Lord and therefore, all those who fall into that sin of treason ought to be thrown into that place."[49] From a "royalist" perspective, disloyal

---

[46] *El Libro del Cauallero Zifar*, ed. Charles Philip Wagner (Norwood, MA: The Plimpton Press, 1929), 224–225. "e por todas las otras cosas que feziestes contra la fialdat e la lealtad que me prometistes guardar e las non guardastes ... E porque non enconedes la otra tierra por do fuerdes con la vuestra trayçion, non vos quiero echar de mio regno, mas mando que vos saquen la lengua por el pescueço por las palabras que dixistes contra mi, e que vos corten la cabeça ... e que vos quemen e vos fagan poluos ... porque nin vos coman canes nin aues, ca fincarian enconadas de la vuestra trayçion; mas que cojan los poluos e los echen en aquel lago que es en cabo del mi regno, a que dizen lago solfareo..."

[47] Ibid., 240.

[48] Ibid.

[49] Ibid., 242. "Amigos, çiertamente creo que aquel lugar es maldito de Nuestro Señor,

knights suffered punishments not only in this life, but in eternal life as well. Treachery was a sin, its reward eternal damnation. Personal honor was important, but obedient service to the king was a better definition of loyalty.

Appropriately, some of the best material dealing with the chivalric ideal of loyalty comes from the late medieval continuation of the legend of El Cid. The mid-14th-century epic poem *Mocedades de Rodrigo* (The Youthful Deeds of Rodrigo, The Cid) is primarily concerned with Rodrigo's activities in war, both within Castile and against Muslims and Frenchmen; most of his political activity is conducted through prowess on the battlefield. Rodrigo is always ready to serve his king (sometimes angrily), even when he has sworn no formal oath of loyalty. He acts as a champion in battle for King Fernando against the king of Aragon, and when he conquers Aragonese territory, the reader is told that "Rodrigo the Castilian won Calahorra, for the good king Don Fernando [of Castile]."[50] In another episode, Rodrigo pursues a count who had rebelled against the king, pulls him out of a church, where he had sought refuge, and says to him in what can be heard only as a sardonic sneer, "Come out here, vile criminal, and go betray Christians … and kill your honourable lord."[51] Finally, Rodrigo, heading into battle, kisses the hands of the king and asks that he be allowed to enter into the battle ahead of others in order to "strike [the enemy] with my own hands, and … open the way through which you may pass."[52] In each case, Rodrigo is serving the king and attacking those who do him a disservice. Loyalty to the king is once again paramount and it is performed through violent action.

An intellectual commitment to the ideal of loyalty to the king was expressed not only in imaginative literature but also in chivalric biographies. In *El Victorial*, Gutierre Díez de Games describes Pero Niño's actions while simultaneously suffusing them with idealistic explanation or moralization. One might expect that Pero Niño, a man raised in the royal household, was always a loyal servant of the king, and Díez confirms this for us when he describes the abstract ideals of his model knight. Like those exemplars of chivalric goodness, El Cid (both young and old) and Zifar, Pero Niño

> was constant and true; never was he untrue to those to whom he had given his word. He was always loyal to the king; never did he make treaty nor league with any man whom he knew disserved the king, as much outside the kingdom as within it. He always moved to defend the will of the king; he always hated and went against those who disserved his King.[53]

---

e por eso todos los que caen en aquel pecado de trayçion deuen ser echados en aquel logar."
[50] *Las Mocedades de Rodrigo, The Youthful Deeds of Rodrigo, the Cid*, trans. Matthew Bailey (Toronto: University of Toronto Press, Inc., 2007) (*Mocedades*), 84.
[51] Ibid., 85–86.
[52] Ibid., 90.
[53] Díez de Games, *El Victorial*, 88. "Hera constante e verdadero; nunca pasó la berdad

Díez' choice of terminology is significant; he is ultimately concerned with the question of the king's service or disservice, language which appears in a wide range of sources. The author surely wants his reader to know that one reason why Pero Niño is such a worthy knight and worth emulating is because the service of the king was always foremost in his mind. Given the troublesome loyalties of Pero Niño's father and grandfather, we might wonder if Díez was protesting too much when it came to his lord's loyalty.

El Victorial, *Zifar*, the stories of El Cid, and the *Siete Partidas* all assure their readers that knights and nobles in the late Middle Ages were always loyal to their lord and that everything they did, they did it for the king, building an image of a nice, neat, feudal world. Indeed, the Trastámara kings would very much have appreciated the kind of devoted loyalty which these texts prescribe. But all of these works were propagandistic, articulating *prescriptions* about loyalty and royal service for their chivalric audience. The very saturation of these texts with episodes showing how good knights truly loved their lord king reveals that this was an issue worth discussing, and one that numerous writers thought they needed to emphasize. In other words, the amount of time authors spent articulating this point suggests that there was something worth arguing about – there was something at stake for them. Such authors were willing to invest intellectual activity in the creation of good and loyal knights precisely because they saw the question of loyalty contested in the real world. Medieval authors debated crucial points even when no debate was explicitly acknowledged.

Another viewpoint in that debate, often articulated in the very same pieces of literature, questioned the "royalist" premise that the dictates of the king should be recognized before all else. Quite the contrary, this position held that a good knight could and should follow his own inclination, even if it conflicted with what a king might want. The loss of the opening of *Mio Cid* is unfortunate, to say the least. In a poem clothed in language insisting that Rodrigo was truly a loyal vassal of his lord the king, it would satisfy so much intellectual curiosity to know how the author dealt with the hero's exile from Castile. Even so, we can surmise from the rest of the poem that the author would have laid no blame on the king himself, for Alfonso is described as a good king throughout the work. Instead, the author assures the reader that both before and after El Cid's exile, the king was counseled and even dominated by evil advisors, out to increase their own fame and

---

a aquel con quien la pusiese. Fué siempre leal al rey; nunca fizo trato ni liga con honbre que él supiese que deseruiese al rey, ansi fuera del reyno como en el reyno. Siempre punó en defender la uoz de su rey; sienpre desamó e fué contra los deseruidores de su rey." Indeed, Rodríguez-Velasco describes the biography as a "very conservative" conception of chivalry, which tends to favor the idea that the king is someone to whom a good knight always renders good service. Rodríguez-Velasco, *El Debate*, 185.

glory at the expense of the great knight.[54] As we will see, the question of overmighty advisors and favorites dominating the royal court regularly incited chivalric violence against the king's household throughout the 15th century. The concern was undoubtedly realistic, but it could also serve as a convenient cloak for knightly action independent from the royal will.[55]

While the burden of evil advisors was a useful component of chivalric ideology, it was not the linch-pin for independent knightly behavior. Much of the knightly literature of late medieval Castile considered the possibility that kings themselves were a dangerous sort of creature, who needed to be dealt with very carefully. Literary kings were liable to seize vassals' properties or rights without justice, to imprison vassals without cause, or to give in to furious fits of anger during which they made regrettable decisions. One of the major episodes of the *Mocedades* begins with a private war between El Cid's father, Diego Laínez, and Count Gómez de Gormaz. Rodrigo, a boy of twelve years who has never seen battle, rides into the melee and kills Count Gómez, among others.[56] Seeking to maintain peace in his realm, the king sends messengers to summon Rodrigo and Diego to his court. Don Diego's reaction to the letters hints at the complex way a knight might have viewed his relationship with the king.

> Don Diego looked over the letters and his colour changed, he suspected that for the death of the count the king wanted to kill him. "Hear me," he said, "my son, take a look at this, I am fearful of these letters that are full of lies, for in these matters kings have very evil ways. Any king you serve, serve him without trickery, and be wary of him as of a mortal enemy."[57]

The ideal of service to the king is not challenged; Rodrigo is simply warned that such service can be dangerous. At its most benign, knightly reluctance to heed royal authority is simply caution.

As Rodrigo travels to the king's court, though, he gives orders to his vassals clearly outlining a more independent approach to the relationship between king and knight.

> "If you see that the constable wants to capture [Don Diego], kill him immediately. May the king have as dark a day as the others that are there. They cannot call you traitors because you kill the king ... For the king would be more of a traitor if he were to kill my father because I killed my enemy in fair battle on the field."[58]

---

[54] For example, *Song of the Cid*, 131.

[55] For literary archetypes of the powerful Jew and the *privado* see David Nirenberg, "Deviant politics and Jewish love: Alfonso VIII and the Jewess of Toledo," *Jewish History*, vol. 21 (2007): 15–41.

[56] *Mocedades*, 75.

[57] Ibid., 77.

[58] Ibid., 78.

Such words are not simply arbitrary opposition to royal authority but an independence rooted in violent chivalric ideals, especially the values of honor and *linaje*. Rodrigo was performing admirable deeds of arms on the battlefield, the surest way for knights to accumulate personal honor. Particularly for such a young man to destroy his enemies so effectively, the reward of honor and renown would have been immense. A king had no right to impinge on the ideological center of chivalric life. Rodrigo's honor, won on the battlefield, should allow him to violently resist the king's political actions against him. Similarly, there is an undertone of the importance of *linaje* here. In this case, Rodrigo relies on the importance of his family heritage to defy the king. Not only is Rodrigo defending his father's life against an encroaching royal government, he is also fighting against Count Gómez on his father's behalf. In other words, it is not only Rodrigo's personal honor at stake in the battle, but the honor of his family, of his *linaje*. When the king threatens to arrest his father (another assault on the *linaje* rather than the individual), Rodrigo sees his most natural and useful option as violent political resistance. The chivalric concepts of personal honor and protection of *linaje* saturated the literary Rodrigo's political relationship with his lord the king. Because his chivalric identity was rooted in prowess, his political relationship with the king was characterized by violence.

Knights combined the language of service with two of the premier values of Castilian knighthood – namely honor and *linaje* – in much the same way that the author of *Mocedades de Rodrigo* did. In 1435, as the royal government reviewed the privileges and franchises of the *hidalgo* class, King Juan II received a petition in the *cortes* from representatives of the *hidalgos*, asking that these legal privileges endure. As evidence in support of their political advantages, the representatives insisted that they "and their fathers and grandfathers and their other ancestors of the *linajes* from which they descend in service of the said past kings and of you lord, endured many toils and travails and spilled much blood and many of them died as loyal vassals."[59] As a result, the knights held that they ought to maintain their political privileges in remuneration for their long service.[60] The knights of the 15th century were expressly reminding their monarch that their political status was won through prowess exercised on the battlefield in pursuit of honor. Not only they themselves, but their ancestors – the building blocks of their proud *linajes* – had fought and died in loyal service to the king.

---

[59] *Cortes* held at Madrid in 1435. *Cortes de los antiguos reinos de León y de Castilla*, ed. Real Academia de la Historia (Madrid: M. Rivadeneyra, 1861–1866), vol. 3, p. 212. "los quales ellos e sus padres e abuelos e otros sus anteçesores delos linajes donde ellos dezienden en seruiçio delos dichos rreyes pasados e do vos sennor, soportaron muchos afanes e trabajos e derramaron mucha sangre e murieron muchos dellos asi commo leales vasallos …"

[60] Ibid.

What should we make of this messy and apparently inconsistent ideological corpus of evidence? Jesús Rodríguez-Velasco has suggested that we can untangle the question by assigning certain texts to either "royalist" or "anti-royalist" intellectual factions throughout late medieval Castilian history.[61] But, instead of examining this as a grand clash between two sides, it might be productive simply to acknowledge that imaginative chivalric literature intentionally left open the question of service to the king. Indeed, many chivalric sources contained both "royalist" and "anti-royalist" viewpoints simultaneously. This much is clear: all sources value service to the king and deploy the concept in a positive way, suggesting that a good knight ought to perform service to his king. The waters become murky in an attempt to definitively identify what that service entailed. Leaving the particulars open to debate would have preserved the traditional independent impulses of the chivalric elite. Just as El Cid made his own decisions at the risk of offending the king, so would other knights, all the while attempting to convince their peers that their actions were done in the king's service, even if the king himself refused to recognize them as such. Indeed, several late medieval knights insisted (or had their biographers insist) that they were modern-day El Cids themselves, for their loyalty, for their honor, or for their being spurned by the king.[62] It would be a remarkably powerful and flexible approach, giving great latitude of action to knights vis-à-vis the king. The violent political identity of the Trastámara nobility could be worked out with sword and lance while still toeing an ideological line of loyalty. The nature of this debate provided the intellectual space necessary to marry violence and political identity.

Juan II and the Loyalty Debate in Action

The theoretical articulation of loyalty and service to the king – and the violence bound up with it – played out in both the minds and the actions of historical knights. The language of biographers, chroniclers, and, indeed, of government itself is deeply infused with the concept of "service to the king." As in chivalric literature, the concept is a flexible one – sundry actions are attributed to the universally good concept of service of the king, even when those actions directly contradict the king's explicit interests. The primary political relationship between knights and kings was founded on violence, both when the relationship was mutually beneficial and when it was more complicated. In nearly every case, knights and their authorial allies believed

---

[61] Rodríguez-Velasco *Order and Chivalry*, 29.
[62] See *Hechos de condestable Don Miguel Lucas de Iranzo*, ed. Juan de Mata Carriazo (Madrid: Espasa-Calpe, S.A., 1940) and *Historia de los hechos del marqués de Cádiz*, ed. Juan Luis Carriazo Rubio (Granada, Spain: Editorial Universidad de Granada, 2003).

(or wished others to believe) that these chivalric actions were taken because of loyal impulses to serve the king. Only toward the end of the Trastámara period, during the reign of Enrique IV, did this political relationship change – a chivalric and violent political identity remained but, during the reign of Enrique IV, the language of service and loyalty was stripped away as many knights saw a king who no longer fit with a chivalric standard. The disappearance of this language signaled a crisis for the fragile political arrangement of Trastámara Castile.

Ernst Kantorowicz argued that a distinction existed in the Middle Ages between the man who occupied the throne and the institution of kingship itself. That is to say that the person who wore the crown was a separate entity from the abstract concept of the Crown itself.[63] The logic of Kantorowicz' argument in the context of loyalty and rebellion in late medieval Castile is that it was theoretically possible to resist the king's imperatives, to disobey his orders, and even to rebel against him, all while claiming to defend the public good and tender good service to the Crown. In other words, in Kantorowicz' schematic, knights could resist the *man* who occupied the throne without being disloyal or rebelling against the abstract idea of the king. This approach serves us well, but cannot explain all of the nuance and particularities of the Trastámara case.[64] As we observe knights acting against the interests of the king while claiming that they were doing good service, we might add to Kantorowicz' theory a chivalric component, namely that knightly ideology was eminently practical. Knights sought to bend and modify chivalric ideas to fit the situation at hand. At times, they likely did think that they were serving the abstract concept of the Crown even as they fought against an individual such as Juan II or Enrique IV. At other times, though, it seems that they were using the language of knightly ideology as justification, apology, or explanation of their actions.

In so many cases, knights and chivalric authors never claim to have a problem with the man occupying the throne. As we will see, opposition to Juan II or his advisors was almost never premised on knightly problems with Juan the man or Juan the king. Instead, knights found that in pursuing their violent political interests they needed a sound ideological logic. They found that logic in the language of loyalty and service. In short, the idea of the king's two bodies helps to explain armed resistance to a king such as Enrique IV. Rebels against Enrique described the man as unfit to wear the crown and claimed that his unfitness contributed to corruption of the common

---

[63] Ernst H. Kantorowicz, *The King's Two Bodies: A Study in Mediaeval Political Theology* (Princeton, NJ: Princeton University Press, 1957).
[64] Kantorowicz himself would likely agree that the theory he describes is but one piece of the intricate system of medieval government and political theory. Kantorowicz, *King's Two Bodies*, ix.

good.⁶⁵ While the rebels may have found justification in a Kantorowiczian way, this was the exception rather than the rule for the Trastámara period. Most knights resisting the royal will did not seek to condemn the man who occupied the throne, instead finding less legalistic or canonical justification for their actions. They looked first to chivalric ideology and the ideals of loyalty and service.

El Victorial provides an excellent example of the effusive language of loyalty and service. According to his biography, Pero Niño took manifold actions directly in the service of the king or against his disservice. As a youth, he assisted the king in putting down rebellious vassals, "strik[ing] signal blows in which he shed the blood of those who disserved his lord the king."⁶⁶ At sea, the great knight fought corsairs who had troubled the king and he raided the African coast on the king's orders, even refusing bribes and gifts from the king of Tunis because "I do not go about to receive gifts … but to fulfill the order of my lord the king."⁶⁷ Assisting in the war against England at the order of his king, Pero Niño encountered the captain of a Castilian fleet who, instead of fighting vigorously for the king, spent his time employing merchants and trading with the French; Pero Niño upbraided him because he "cared little for the service of the king" and had therefore "not acted as a good knight."⁶⁸ Pero Niño, as a good knight, was constantly in the service of the king himself and attacking those who did the king disservice.

One can imagine the biographer, Díez, his eyes wide with excitement, excitedly recalling one instance when his young lord did battle with some rebellious vassals of the king. First Pero Niño took an arrow to the neck but, "as a wolf does among the sheep when there is no shepherd to defend them," he continued fighting.⁶⁹ As he continued slaughtering his enemies – those who disserved his lord, the king – he took a crossbow bolt to the face, a wound which only spurred him on to greater deeds. Ultimately Pero Niño won this battle, even as his enemies continued smacking the bolt protruding from his nostrils. Díez can hardly contain himself in praising Pero Niño's great prowess on the battlefield and suggests that such a bloody battle was finally able to satisfy his lord's bloodlust, for "until that day, never did such satisfaction come to Pero Niño in an hour with that need which he desired

---

⁶⁵ See especially Alfonso de Palencia, "Crónica de Enrique IV," ed. and trans. Antonio Paz y Meliá in *Biblioteca de Autores Españoles* (Madrid: Ediciones Atlas, 1973), vol. 257.
⁶⁶ Díez de Games, *El Victorial*, 74. "E dió allí muchos golpes señalados, en los quales sacó sangre de los deservidores de su señor el rey …"
⁶⁷ Ibid., 119. "yo non ando a reçevir dones … mas a cumplir mandado de mi señor el rey."
⁶⁸ Ibid., 216. "diziéndole que curaba poco del servicio del rey … non abía fecho como buen caballero."
⁶⁹ Ibid., 82. "como faze el lobo entre las ovejas, quando no an pastor que las defienda …"

so much."[70] Pero Niño's skills and calling undoubtedly rested in the exercise of arms, and Díez is sure that this is what made him a great knight. The bloody and grotesque actions were a source of incredible honor for Díez' lord. That he was performing these great deeds of arms in the service of the king was an added bonus and an expression of his political identity.

Pero Niño was certainly not the only knight loyally performing violence for his Trastámara king. Álvaro de Luna, Master of Santiago, Constable of Castile, and the favorite of Juan II understood his meteoric political rise as a story of exemplary and loyal military service to the king. Luna's first major political activity was simultaneously violent and performed in the king's service. In 1420 Juan II had effectively been taken prisoner by his cousins, the infantes of Aragon, who sought to dominate the young king for their own benefit. Luna responded, gathering knights and lords to join him in forcefully freeing the king from the power of his cousins. Luna's chronicler claimed that the Constable did this "seeing that all the factions of men were in disservice of his King and damaged his kingdoms, and diminished his crown."[71] The Constable acted not for bald-faced political ambition, nor for personal calculations, but only because he loved his king and abhorred the thought of others disserving and damaging his lord. To be sure, Luna was successful in freeing the king from the infantes and, according to his chronicler, he was lauded and praised throughout the kingdom, even throughout Iberia, for his noble and loyal violence. As gratitude for Luna's actions, the king, "with the agreement of his council, gave that ville and castle [of San Esteban de Gormaz], with its land, to Don Álvaro de Luna, and made him count of it ... and the King gave the ville of Ayllón with its land to the Count Álvaro de Luna, not asking anything from him [in return]."[72] For Luna, these political rewards were founded on his chivalric behavior, fighting in battle for honor and reputation.

Over the next decade, there would be regular war with the infantes. Because two of the infantes were the kings of Aragon and Navarre, the troubles simultaneously entailed dynastic intrigue and war with these two neighboring kingdoms. Throughout the 1420s, Luna was always eager to loyally lead the king's knights against the infantes in order to protect Juan's throne and defend Castile. Time after time, Luna's chronicler notes that

---

[70] Ibid., 83. "fasta aquel día nunca tan farto fué Pero Niño en vna ora de aquel menester que él mucho deseaua."

[71] *Crónica de Don Álvaro de Luna, Condestable de Castilla, Maestre de Santiago*, ed. Juan de Mata Carriazo (Madrid: Espasa-Calpe, S.A., 1940), 39. "viendo que todos quellos ayuntamientos de gentes eran en deseruicio de su Rey e daño de sus reynos, y mengua de su corona ..."

[72] Ibid., 48–49. "E yendo el Rey la vía de allá, pasó por Sant Estevan de Gormaz, e con acuerdo de los de su Consejo dió aquella villa e castillo, con su tierra, a don Álvaro de Luna, e fízolo conde de ella ... e el Rey dió la villa de Ayllón con su tierra al conde Álvaro de Luna, no procurando él nunguna cosa."

the Constable stepped forward as the king's cousins invaded his realm or worked to control the monarch. In 1429, the war with the infantes reached its apex, and so did Luna's service to the king. As the Castilian court heard news that the infantes were once again invading the kingdom, Álvaro de Luna eagerly offered to lead the king's men in war. He not only defeated the invading forces, but then led an army to the Aragonese frontier and invaded the Kingdom of Aragon, precisely because, we are assured, "he never refused any travails, nor feared danger, and went ever onward in service with great loyalty to his King, and furnished him great honor to his crown."[73] Having made such destruction in Aragon, the Castilian king and his court agreed that someone needed to stay behind at the Aragonese frontier in order to protect the kingdom against another attack. None of the knights and lords of the court stepped forward to offer their service, complaining that their men had been fighting all summer in the king's war and that they were craving a long winter break. The Constable, a paragon of honor and loyalty, stepped forward, seeing that none of the other great men would serve the king on the eastern frontier. He addressed the king, saying

> "Lord, if ever my service was worthy to you in any way, I beg you that in this case it should be now, by your giving to me alone the charge of all these frontiers, especially between your kingdoms and that of Aragon. And with the aid of God and you, and with the knights and squires of my house, I understand to give to you, lord, a good account of it ... and my men are so tired and have worked so much, but my true heart is not tiring of serving you in this, and in all the other things which fulfill your service."[74]

Moreover, according to Luna's chronicler, "the king thanked [Luna], and valued very much the great will and good heart that the Constable always showed in that which fulfilled his service" before refusing Luna's request, because the king needed his service elsewhere.[75]

We can, on the one hand, read the example of Álvaro de Luna first of all as a sincere embodiment of the political identity of late medieval Castilian knights. Time after time, Luna expressed his political identity through his loyalty to the king. Given the course of Luna's career as the "greatest man

---

[73] Ibid., 90. "Don Álvaro de Luna, Condestable de Castilla, que nunca refusó los trabajos, nin temió los peligros, e por fallarse siempre adelante en servir con grand lealtad a su Rey, e allegarle grand honrra a la su corona ..."

[74] Ibid., 97. "Señor, si el mi serbiçio en algúnd tiempo vos vino en grado, e fué bien resçebido de vos, yo vos suplico que en este caso lo sea agora, dándome a mí sólo el cargo de todas estas fronteras, espeçialmente entre vuestros reynos e los de Aragón. E con al ayuda de Dios e vuestra, e con los caballeros y escuderos de mi casa, y oentiendo de dar a vos, señor, buena cuenta dello ... e mi gente esté asaz cansada e trabajada, pero mi corazón çierto no está cansado para vos servir en esto, y en todas las otras cosas que a vuestro serbiçio cunplan."

[75] Ibid. "E el Rey ge lo agradesçió, e le presçió mucho la grand voluntad suya e buen corazón que el Condestable sienpre mostraba en lo que a su serbiçio cunplía."

uncrowned," historians sometimes forget that the Constable did indeed have a most storied career as a vigorous knight – he was not *only* a figure at court. In his chronicle – a perception of himself – Luna saw his career as founded on martial service to the king. Every grant of land, every title, every mercy granted him by Juan II was as a reward for violent acts performed on the battlefield. Whether King Juan honored him because of these acts or because of some other fascination with Luna, the Constable projected a public persona in which his political identity was inseparable from his loyal service and prowess as a knight of the king. Björn Weiler has argued that "[p]olitics were a public affair, and this public nature permeated the source." Weiler rightly notes that chroniclers were not always aiming to speak to an audience that constituted the entire "political community of the realm." Chronicles, especially when dealing with a particular individual such as Álvaro de Luna, were more likely tailored to be read to or by a specific audience; in this case, the knights of the realm. Luna's chronicler was not necessarily attempting to speak to all the political actors in Castile, only the chivalric and royal political actors.[76] Luna's identity as a vigorous knight was wedded with the chivalric and political language of loyalty and service to the Crown.

On the other hand, we can imagine how Luna's fellow knights and lords might have imagined his behavior. Far from an ideal and glorious knight, they saw a man who leveraged every opportunity in his own favor. When all the knights of Juan II's court refused to serve as a captain of the frontier, Luna's speech offering his loyal service likely seemed sycophantic. Luna was not simply trying to serve his king to the best of his abilities, but was seizing an opportunity to make himself look good, implicitly criticizing all the knights and lords who had refused and undermining their traditional fondness for independent action. Simultaneously, Luna was embarrassing or even emasculating them, calling into question their own bravery and therefore their own honor. Indeed, chivalric writers voiced this concern. Fernán Pérez de Guzmán, a contemporary of Luna's, described him as "somewhat doubted in his words, very discreet, a great dissimulator, deceptive and stealthy, and one who much delighted in the use of such arts and sleights."[77] Guzmán goes on to call into question essentially all of Luna's actions and rewards, suggesting that the man simply had no worthy virtues. Is it possible that Luna's rivals and political enemies were simply jealous of his firm grasp of what the Castilian knightly political identity looked like? Was he not

---

[76] Björn Weiler, *Kingship, Rebellion and Political Culture: England and Germany, c. 1215–c. 1250* (New York: Palgrave Macmillan, 2007), 105–107.

[77] Fernán Pérez de Guzmán, *Generaciones y semblanzas* (Buenos Aires: Espasa-Calpe Argentina, S.A., 1947), 84–85. "[C]omo quier que algo dubdase en la palabra, muy discreto, grant disimulador, fingido e cabteloso e que mucho se deleytaua en usar de tales artes e cabtelas …"

simply the man in the 15th century who best understood the links between chivalry, violence, politics, and royal favor? Answers to these questions are elusive, but they may be clearer when we see the same language of loyalty and service articulated by knights and lords who took military action *against* the king or his agents. In other words, the *concept* of loyal service to the king was not predicated wholly on the sorts of material incentives achieved by Álvaro de Luna. Even under the very real and dangerous threat of disfavor, imprisonment, or violent retaliatory action from the king, late medieval Castilian knights understood their independently minded actions as perpetually in the loyal service of their lord, the king.

In 1419, for example, a few years before Álvaro de Luna began his breathtaking ascent to the pinnacle of Castilian political society, Juan II had fallen under the influence of another advisor, Juan Furtado de Mendoza. As was often the case in the late Middle Ages, some of the leading nobles of the realm expressed serious concern about a king being unduly influenced by any one advisor and they sought to remedy the situation.[78] In response to Mendoza's influence, a faction of Castilian noblemen called Pero Niño to them and discussed a possible rectification.[79] They began by addressing him as "a servant of our lord the king … and one of those who love the service of the king,"[80] then devised a plan to arrest Mendoza and remove him from the king's presence. Pero Niño agreed "because he was in such service of the king … but he swore that it was very much for the fulfillment of the service of the king."[81] The very terms of discussion among knights centered on fulfilling the service of the king or disserving him. Indeed, the great knight made an explicit point of casting his actions as serving the king. Despite Pero Niño's dedication to the loyal service of Juan II, these discussions culminated with Pero Niño leading armed men to Mendoza and arresting him. Entering Mendoza's chamber in the king's palace at night, Pero Niño was prepared to act violently to achieve his political goals. Only when Mendoza saw that he was outgunned by Pero Niño and his men did he give himself up. Gutierre Díez de Games says that other men then entered the chamber where the king was sleeping and explained the situation. The king agreed that they had acted well in removing a bad advisor and that they had fulfilled his service.[82] What in modern political terms

---

[78] For a comparison to England see Claire Valente, *The Theory and Practice of Revolt in Medieval England* (Burlington, VT: Ashgate Publishing Company, 2003), 130–138.
[79] Fernán Pérez de Guzmán, "La crónica del serenísimo príncipe Don Juan, segundo Rey deste nombre en Castilla y en Leon," in *Biblioteca de Autores Españoles*, vol. 68, 381.
[80] Díez de Games, *El Victorial*, 321. "servidor de nuestro señor el rey … e vno de los que aman serviçio del rey."
[81] Ibid., 322. "e por quanto hera ansí serviçio del rey … mas que le jurasen que cunplía ansí a serbiçio del rey."
[82] Ibid., 323.

might be called a palace coup is instead a good and loyal action, with even the king himself agreeing that his knights had loyalty in their hearts.

Neither was this language wholly an invention of an overenthusiastic biographer. When Fernán Pérez de Guzmán deals with the removal of Mendoza from political power in his chronicle of the period, he describes it in terms similar to those of Gutierre Díez de Games. Guzmán emphasizes Pero Niño's readiness for bloodshed, noting that "Pero Niño entered [Mendoza's chamber] with his naked sword in his hand, and found Juan Furtado naked in bed with Doña María de Luna, his wife, and told him that he was a prisoner of the King, and Juan Furtado was very confused and wanted to put hand to his sword which he had at the head of the bed."[83] Guzmán also describes what happened in the king's chamber in greater detail. The first man to enter the king's chamber was his cousin, the Infante Enrique, who found the king sleeping (with Álvaro de Luna at his feet!). Enrique woke the king, who was naturally

> quite confused and angry, and he said "What is this!?" And the Infante responded "Lord, I am come here for your service, and to take and drive from your house some persons who do ugly and dishonest things much against your service, and to remove you from the subjection which you are in."[84]

The question at hand was about the honor of the king and the role of knights in upholding that honor. Guzmán is less certain that the king was instantly pleased with the actions of his knights and nobles, and claims that the king asked Enrique, "How is it, cousin, that you have to do this?"[85] In response to the king's indignant confusion, a number of lords and bishops of the kingdom, who had been involved with the coup, described all the reasons why Mendoza had been a vile and ugly influence on the king, "and each one of them gave as many reasons as they could to show that the deed was done for the service of the King and the common good of his Kingdoms."[86] Just as Pero Niño had acted only after working through the logic of how his violent actions would be in the service of the king, so his co-conspirators diligently worked through a similar logic for the king himself. All were sure that their actions were – *had to be* – in the service of

---

[83] Pérez de Guzmán, "don Juan, segundo," 381. "é Pero Niño entró su espada desnuda en la mano, é halló á Juan Hurtado desnudo en la cama con Doña María de Luna, su muger, é díxole que fuese preso por el Rey, é Juan Hurtado fué mucho turbado, é quisiera poner mano á la espada que tenia á la cabecera."

[84] Ibid. "[Y] el Rey fué dello muy turbado y enojado, é dixo: *¿Qué es esto?* y el Infante le respondió: 'Señor, yo soy aquí venido por vuestro servicio, é por echar é arredrar de vuestra casa algunas personas que hacen cosas feas é deshonestas é mucho contra vuestro servicio, é por vos sacar de la subjecion en que estais …'"

[85] Ibid. "é dixo al Infante: *cómo, primo, ¿esto habíades vos de hacer?*"

[86] Ibid. "é cada uno dellos daba las mas razones que podia para mostrar que lo hecho se hacia por servicio del Rey é bien universal de sus Reynos."

the king. It was simply a matter of figuring out how they could be cast as such. Political action was often violent action; indeed it was typically chivalric action, which depended on the exercise of the sword or lance. It was justified through the ideal of loyalty and service to the Crown.

Juan II's personal reign was turbulent, and the removal of Juan Furtado de Mendoza was only the opening act. The most famous period of intrigue and disorder, as we saw above, was the period of Álvaro de Luna's influence. In response to what was seen as Luna's undue power, a league of knights and nobles banded together to remove Luna from his position. The removal of Álvaro de Luna from power was even more brutal than that of Mendoza. Indeed, this period might even be called a minor civil war, complete with battles and sieges. Even as the Kingdom of Castile was disturbed by great bands of knights and men-at-arms fighting one another throughout the country, all participants claimed that they were serving the king.

Pedro Carrillo de Huete's *Chronicle of the Falconer of Juan II* records the struggles of the period, often through the reproduction of letters and records of royal government.[87] The chronicler was, as the title suggests, the king's falconer and was therefore close to the king. Despite his own personal bias, most of Carrillo's chronicle involves little intervention on the part of the author, instead manifesting a fairly sterile and neutral account of the events and the related documents. He reproduced a letter sent by two leaders of the rebellion to the king as the troubles began in 1439. Even as they were gathering an army to fight against the king, Don Álvaro, and the king's other allies, the rebels spoke in the language of service, opening the letter with the proper diplomatic: "Most excellent lord and most powerful King: We your humble servants … humbly kiss your feet and hands, and speaking with that reverence and humility which we should …" The rebels insist throughout the letter that they are acting only in the interest of serving the king, claiming that their intentions "are to your true service" and that their actions are done "in that which fulfills your service," contrasting their actions with the king's supporters.[88] Echoing El Cid, the leaders of the rebellion claimed that they would do great service to the king in removing from him those whom they saw as evil advisors. Just as in the case of the removal of Mendoza from Juan's household, the rebels against Juan and

---

[87] For the fullest narrative account of the troubles of Juan II's reign, see Luis Suárez Fernández, *Nobleza y Monarquía, Entendimiento y Rivalidad* (Madrid: La Esfera de los Libros, S.L., 2003). For a compelling analysis of Alvaro de Luna and his role in Castilian history that has held up remarkably well over several decades, see Nicholas Round, *The Greatest Man Uncrowned, A Study of the Fall of Don Alvaro de Luna* (London: Tamesis Books Limited, 1986).

[88] Pedro Carrillo de Huete, *Crónica del Halconero de Juan II*, ed. Juan de Mata Carriazo. 257. "Muy exçelente señor e muy poderoso Rey: Vuestros omildes seruidores … omilmente besamos vuestros pies e manos, e fablando con aquella rreberencia e omildad que devemos," 259. "son a verdadero seruiçio vuestro … lo que cunple a vuestro seruicio."

Luna were worried about their actions being perceived as treasonous or disloyal. Their letter to the king was designed precisely to preempt any such criticism – they knew that they needed to use the framework of loyal service to the king. Because the Castilian chivalric identity – expressed here, as so often, through violence – was so deeply connected to the concept of loyalty and service, the rebels worked from the very beginning to claim that ideological position for themselves.

The rebels of 1439 were not alone in claiming this ideological position. Pedro Carillo de Huete left a great gift to historians when he preserved not only the letter of the rebels to the king, but also Juan's lengthy response to them in which he systematically rejects the rebel claims about service and loyalty. Juan begins by telling his recalcitrant knights that "I marveled that you used such words" in claiming to be good vassals when it was so clear to the king that they were not serving him well.[89] Instead, the monarch articulates his belief that his once loyal vassals have betrayed him and have brought disorders, scandals, and troubles to his kingdom. The king explains to his misguided vassals that if they wish to truly fulfill his service, they ought to cease all the scandals and troubles and evils and damages which they are causing.[90]

Juan did recognize someone else, though, who very much fulfilled his obligations and duties to the Crown: Álvaro de Luna, the Constable of Castile. As an example of how the rebels ought to behave, the king lauds his Constable, "considering his great loyalty and the good and loyal services" which he provides to the king."[91] Luna's chronicle does not mention this letter specifically and the entries for the late 1430s are quite sparse, probably because Luna's enemies succeeded by the end of 1439 in having the Constable expelled from the royal court. That the king agreed with Luna's behavior in this moment is perhaps no surprise. That all parties were debating the specific qualities that fell under the umbrella concept of loyalty to the king is more interesting. At a moment of political crisis in the Kingdom of Castile, the king, his favorite, and discontented knights were all preparing for a violent conflict by attempting to monopolize the chivalric virtue of loyalty. The debate would continue as chaos erupted in the kingdom.

Within months of the ideological encounter between Juan and the rebellious knights, the factions were at war. The question of who was properly in the king's service could apparently not be decided by the king, neither could it be resolved through discussion; both sides could legitimately claim the virtue of serving the king. The political resolution would come only through warfare, the appropriate means to resolve chivalric differences. In

---

[89] Ibid., 263. "yo maravillado de vosotros en usar de tales palabras..."
[90] Ibid., 271.
[91] Ibid., 268. "[C]onsidereada su gran lealtad e los seruicios buenos e leales."

the ensuing civil war, Gutierre Díez de Games relates that Pero Niño and a collection of nobles went to the castle of Montalbán wherein the king had ensconced himself. A tense situation ensued:

> Pero Niño came to the foot of the castle, and greeted the king, and those who were with him. And the Count of Benabente [inside the castle] spoke, and said "Pero Niño, does it seem good to you that you have surrounded the king here and given aid to those who are here against his service?" And Pero Niño said "You do not speak the truth; and those of whom you speak – and I with them – are here together for the service of the king, and we are his servants, as much as you are ..." Then Pero Niño spoke to the king, and said "Lord, is there something which I can do, by your order, in your service? Command; I am ready ..." Then Pero Niño put his hand on his sword and turned his face against the others and said "Lord, I do that which I ought; if it fulfills your service, command me, for I am ready ..."[92]

Even in a standoff between two factions in the developing civil war where Pero Niño had besieged his lord king, he apparently chose to debate with his opponents about who was truly doing loyal service to the king. The incongruity of this situation to a modern reader would have appeared less of a vexing situation to a medieval Castilian knight and more a pivotal political moment. Who would succeed in doing the best and most loyal service to the king? How could one determine which service was the best? In the short term, the anti-Luna faction would succeed. As Pero Niño placed his hand on his sword, the larger significance was clear: the means of determining the best service was violence. At the Battle of Medina del Campo in May of 1441, the rebels captured King Juan, removed Luna's political allies from their offices, exiled Luna from the kingdom, and instituted a new royal council under which Juan II essentially became a puppet of the infantes of Aragon. In response, over the next four years, Luna would gather an army to challenge the infantes, finally defeating them on the field at the Battle of Olmedo in May of 1445.

Although Luna was an eminently political figure who is often remembered, as Fernán Pérez de Guzmán did, as a figure primarily of the court, it is crucial for our understanding of the political component of chivalric ideology to observe Luna's self-perception.[93] Both battles – Medina del

---

[92] Díez de Games, *El Victorial*, 325–236. "Pero Niño llegó al pié del castillo, e saludó al rey, e a los que con él estauan. E fabló el conde de Benabente, e dixo: – Pero Niño, ¿parésçevos agora bien tener vosotros çercado aquí todos contra su serviçio? E dixo Pero Niño: – Vos non dezides berdad; que aquellos que vos dezides, e yo con ellos, somos aquí juntados por serviçio al rey, e somos sus servidores, tanto como vosotros ... Estonze fabló Pero Niño al rey, e díxole: – Señor, ¿ay alguna cosa en que vos yo pueda fazer serviçio e mandado? Mandad, que yo soy presto ... Estonze Pero Niño puso mano a su espada, e volvióse el rostro contra los de fuera, e dixo: – Señor, yo fago aquello que debo; si ál cunple a vuestro serviçio, mandadme, que yo soy presto ...'"

[93] Luna himself did not write his own chronicle and so, in one sense, we are a step

Campo in 1441 and Olmedo in 1445 – were defining moments in Luna's understanding of himself, and in both battles the Constable fashioned himself as a man whose service to the king was best performed through violence. As Luna's chronicler recalls the Battle of Medina del Campo, he opens a chapter describing the Constable's chief virtues, writing "Most clear and manifest was the great loyalty and pure love which the Constable Don Álvaro de Luna always had for the King, and how at all times he served the King his lord."[94] The chronicler assures his audience that the Constable fought most forcefully and struck signal blows and that even as Juan II saw the writing on the wall and ordered Luna to stand down, Luna tenaciously continued fighting. In language that echoes epic poems, the chronicler writes: "The Constable went blazing in the fight, his sword bloodied, wounding his enemies, not fearing anything, throwing himself amongst them all."[95] The chronicle then skips ahead four years, ignoring Luna's period of exile and resuming with his preparations for Olmedo. The chronicler ends this long hiatus with the rhetorical question, "Who, for trying, could count the continuous travails that the Constable received, to serve the King his lord, and to exalt his crown, and for the public good of his kingdoms?"[96] This language is explicitly joined with the fighting at the Battle of Olmedo itself. The Constable and his men, as they strike against their enemies, are "those of the King of Castile, [who much desired] to serve him, and to die for him." Meanwhile, the men of the infantes are "those [who much desired] to err and offend against [the king]."[97] Álvaro de Luna thought of himself first and foremost as a knight of the king of Castile. He expressed his political identity through violence and always couched his actions in the language of service to his king. As a good

---

removed from Luna's self-perception. Carriazo has reasonably suggested that the chronicle was begun while the constable still lived and was likely written by someone close to Luna. It was not completed until after Luna's death and so he could not have had a final editorial hand in the content of the chronicle. Due to the likely closeness of the chronicler to Luna's life (evidence suggests he was an eyewitness, and perhaps a member of Luna's household), it is fair to say that the chronicle either represents Luna's own ideals or the ideals of someone who thought very highly of him. See *Crónica de Don Álvaro de Luna*, xxi–xlvii.

[94] *Crónica de Don Álvaro de Luna*, 152. "Muy claro e manifiesto fué la grand lealtad e puro amor que el Condestable don Álvaro de Luna tovo sienpre al Rey, e de cómo en todo tienpo sirvió al Rey su señor …"

[95] Ibid., 154. "El Condestable andava ençendido en la pelea, el espada ensangrentada, firiendo por los enemigos, no temiendo a ninguno, lançándose enmedio de todos."

[96] Ibid., 155. "Quién por menudo podría contar los continuos trabajos que el Condestable resçibía, por seruir al Rey su señor, e ensalçar la su corona, e por el bien público de los sus reynos?"

[97] Ibid., 170. "muy deseosos, los del Rey de Castilla de le servir, e de tomar la muerte por él, e los de la otra parte de le errar e ofender …"

Castilian knight, it was nearly impossible for him to imagine himself being disloyal to his king.

We have seen in the reign of Juan II these ideas in action over and over. The knights of late medieval Castile, even when they disagreed with one another, all believed (or at least claimed that they believed) that they were always working in the service of the king. Through the late 14th and much of the 15th centuries, the concept of loyal service to the king operated as an arena for debate among the chivalric elite. Although they rarely expressed it explicitly, Castilians at the time recognized that this was a reality. At a *cortes* held in 1440, amid the civil strife in the kingdom, the representatives of the cities of Castile formally requested that King Juan put armed guards on the gates of the cities by day and on the walls and towers by night, in order to ensure that the armed men who were causing scandals and uproars "against the king's service" could not enter the cities and cause destruction therein. These representatives may have had their own ideas about what constituted the king's service, but they were also aware of the differences of opinion. Observing that all the lords and knights thought they were serving the king through their violent action, the townspeople protested that they could not figure out, and had no intention of doing so, which lords and knights were *actually* doing the king good service. They simply wanted these armed men to stop attacking the cities. Chivalric political identity was simply too violent for the townsfolk.

Enrique IV and the Crisis of Loyalty

If the Trastámara nobility had learned during the reign of Juan II that their violent action could result in political rewards or concessions from the king, up to and including the effective usurpation of the royal prerogative, they carried this lesson to its next iteration during the reign of Juan's son, Enrique IV. A decade after Enrique took the throne, a powerful faction of Castilian nobles would attempt to depose the king through dynastic civil war. Enrique suffered from complaints similar to those levied against his father, as well as new complaints about his conduct, his religious inclinations, and his sexuality. But at the heart of all accusations were the political ambitions of the nobility, their aspirations to greater political power expressed through chivalric violence throughout the 1460s and 1470s.

As the heir to the throne of Castile, Enrique had built his household in imitation of his father's. The prince even established a favorite as the most prominent man in his household: the future Marquis de Villena, Juan Pacheco, a man of noble lineage and modest wealth. Pacheco's father served in the court of Juan II and became close with Álvaro de Luna, leading his son, a careful observer at court, to set out to imitate Luna in his own career.[98] Indeed, when Enrique became king of Castile, Pacheco continued in loyal service and retained his position as a favorite of the king. Unlike Luna, though, Pacheco faced stiff competition for the position of favorite in Enrique's household. Very quickly other rising men found favor with King Enrique, among them Miguel Lucas de Iranzo, who would become Constable; Juan de Valenzuela, the prior of the Order of San Juan; and, most significantly, Beltrán de la Cueva, who held the Mastership of the Order of Santiago and would eventually become duke of Alburquerque.[99] In this crowded atmosphere, each of these men rose temporarily to be the favorite of the king and, consequently, most of them fell from favor or left the court as well. By 1462, the clear favorite was Beltrán de la Cueva.[100]

Juan Pacheco, finding himself removed from his privileged place as the king's sole favorite, began to conspire with other nobles of the realm against la Cueva and, more often, against Enrique himself. In 1464, Pacheco gathered leading knights of the realm and formed a league against King Enrique and Beltrán de la Cueva. In the city of Burgos, Pacheco's league drew up a manifesto guised as a letter to the king in which they demanded that the king remedy four errors he had made. First, they insisted that he stop insulting the holy Catholic faith by keeping Muslim captains in his retinue. The knights insisted that these captains attacked Christians and insulted their faith. Second, they declared that the offices of the realm had been given to incapable men and they demanded that these men be removed from office and replaced with capable men. It is difficult to read this as anything but a demand for la Cueva to be removed from his positions and replaced with Pacheco. Third, they insisted that the Mastership of Santiago, recently granted to la Cueva, needed to be granted instead to the king's brother, the Infante Alfonso. The Mastership was a political and military position coveted by Pacheco, and Enrique's granting of this position to la Cueva had been the catalyst that moved Pacheco to leave the king's

---

[98] The links between Pacheco and Luna as well as the similarities of their careers is skillfully examined by María del Pilar Carceller Ceviño, "Alvaro de Luna, Juan Pacheco y Beltrán de la Cueva: un estudio comparativo del privado regio a fines de la Edad Media," *En la España Medieval*, no. 32 (2009), 98. She insightfully observes that "Juan Pacheco imitated the model of Don Álvaro and applied it to ascendancy around the future heir to the throne, anticipating, perhaps, that when [Enrique] was the king himself, he would reach the same level of influence and power as his mentor."

[99] The Masterships of the military orders in Castile became very similar to a lay title. While there were differences, such as the requirement to formally become a member of the order, nobles who served as Masters attempted to establish the title as hereditary possessions of their *linajes* and participated in Castilian politics just as any other titled nobility. See Enrique Rodríguez-Picavea Matilla, "Linaje y poder en la Castilla Trastámara. El ejemplo de la Orden de Calatrava," *Anuario de Estudios Medievales*, 35/1 (2005), 91–130.

[100] Carceller Ceviño, "Alvaro de Luna, Juan Pacheco y Beltrán de la Cueva," 109–111.

service. Finally, the knights and lords claimed that the king's daughter, the Infanta Juana, had been fathered not by the king but by Beltrán de la Cueva himself, and they took to calling the princess "La Beltraneja." They demanded that Enrique disinherit his daughter and name his brother Alfonso as heir to the throne instead.[101] These last two demands were calculated political moves. The nobles likely believed that it would be easier to control Alfonso as king than it would be Juana, and they wanted to make a political statement to the king that the nobility had the power to determine the succession to the throne. At the same time, it was a clear attack on the political power of Beltrán de la Cueva. The fierce political appetites of the Trastámara nobility, whetted during the troubled decades of Juan II's reign, were becoming more ravenous.

Unlike his father, though, Enrique IV was less willing to submit to noble demands for power or privilege. Enrique ultimately refused the demands of Pacheco's league, and civil war erupted once again in Castile in 1465. At the onset of the war, one of the most famous political performances in Castilian history played out. That summer, in the city of Ávila in central Castile, a great assembly of leading knights and lords came together. Among them were the eleven-year-old Infante Alfonso, the king's half-brother; Alfonso Carillo, the archbishop of Toledo; Juan Pacheco himself; Álvaro de Zúñiga, the count of Plasencia and his brother, Diego López de Zúñiga; Gómez de Cáceres, the Master of the Order of Alcántara; Rodrigo Pimentel, the count of Benavente; and many other knights of great and small estate and renown.[102] In short, a wide cross-section of the chivalric elite were present for what the supporters of King Enrique would derisively refer to as the Farce of Ávila.[103] The rebels wheeled in an effigy of King Enrique, seated on his throne, wearing his crown, and carrying the symbols of his authority. Bit by bit, the effigy was symbolically dishonored. The archbishop of Toledo removed the crown, and with it, Enrique's royal dignity. The count of Plasencia removed the sword, representing Enrique's ability to administer justice. The count of Benavente removed the staff, because Enrique did not deserve to have the government of the kingdom. Finally, Diego López de Zúñiga knocked the effigy off the throne and into the dirt, famously shouting "¡A tierra, puto!"[104]

---

[101] Diego Enríquez del Castillo, "La historia del rey Don Enrique el Cuarto," in *Biblioteca de Autores Españoles*, vol. 70, 137–138.

[102] Ibid., 144.

[103] Also present was a great crowd of the people of Ávila. As Weiler has argued, a public assembly was crucial in asserting political legitimacy. Weiler, *Kingship, Rebellion and Political Culture*, 113 and 133. For a thorough analysis of the Farce of Ávila and a comparison with other works that treat the Farce symbolically, see Angus MacKay, "Ritual and Propaganda in Fifteenth-Century Castile," *Past and Present*, no. 107 (May, 1985), 3–43.

[104] Barbara Weissberger, "'¡A tierra, puto!': Alfonso de Palencia's Discourse of Effiminacy," in *Queer Iberia: Sexualities, Cultures, and Crossings from the Middle Ages to the*

Barbara Weissberger translates this famous phrase as "Eat dirt, faggot!", a reasonable if not literal translation. For Weissberger, the Farce of Ávila is imbued with the symbolism of gendered objects – the sword and the staff. Indeed, Weissberger has argued that Enrique's troubles were fundamentally concerned with acts of sexual violence. Her argument revolves around the obsession with gendering history and politics in medieval Castile, feminizing political enemies who invaded the masculine body politic. In questioning Enrique's sexuality and masculinity, as we will see in Chapter 5, the rebels had questioned his ability to lead and his identity as a chivalric man. All of the bits of identity that came together in a knight, among them masculinity, violence, honor, and Christianity, were symbolically removed from the king. Having declared Enrique unfit to rule, the rebels proclaimed the Infante Alfonso the rightful king of Castile and swore allegiance to the boy.[105] The civil war was no longer formally concerned with the demands presented to Enrique, but instead sought to replace him altogether.

A political earthquake for Trastámara Castile had occurred that summer. Historians have examined the Farce of Ávila and its immediate effects on the civil war, as well as the politically theatrical nature of the dethroning of Enrique.[106] But something else happened as well. The events at Ávila represented the culmination of a growing sense on the part of the rebels that they no longer owed allegiance to King Enrique – their political language had changed from what Castilian knights and nobles had been claiming for the last hundred years. To be sure, the supporters of the king continued to speak in the language of service and loyalty. Miguel Lucas de Iranzo's chronicler contrasted the actions of the rebels at Ávila with his own actions at the same time. Noting first that Iranzo "in all things conformed with that which was the service of God and of the said lord king," Iranzo's chronicler goes on to say that the participants in the Farce, "to whom his highness had done many and signal favors, with a blind and sinister course, they agreed to put themselves in all disobedience and rebellion against the king our lord."[107] Diego Enríquez del Castillo, the king's chaplain, fervently chastised Pacheco and the others at Ávila, naturally returning to the language of loyalty and service (or, in this case, disloyalty and treason):

Renaissance, ed. Josiah Blackmore and Gregory S. Hutcheson (Durham, NC: Duke University Press, 1999), 301.

[105] I have taken the basic account from Castillo, "Don Enrique el Cuarto," 144.

[106] See McKay, "Ritual and Propaganda" and Weissberger, "'¡A tierra puto!'".

[107] *Hechos del condestable*, 266–267. "[C]omo el señor Condestable en todas cosas se conformase con lo que era serviçio de Dios y del dicho señor rey ... [D]on Juan Pacheco [etc.] y otros muchos cauvalleros a quien su alteza avía fecho muchas y señaladas mercedes, con çiego e siniestro camino, se acordaron de poner en toda desobidiençia y rebilión contra el rey nuestro señor."

O ungrateful servant! O evil creature! That after you are placed in such prosperity, you are lifted to high peaks and estates, with such ingratitude you forget the benefices which you have received from the King. O perverse servants who shape yourselves so as to dishonor he who honors you! What new perversity have you devised and demonstrated to the people? Why without fear have you opened the doors of treason, and dropped the veil of shame for disloyalty? What have you cherished that loyalty should be treason and treason crowned as loyalty?[108]

These two men, invested in supporting the king, accepted the paradigm of the late medieval Castilian chivalric political identity. A good knight always ought to serve his king. In the century-long tradition of debating what was in the king's service, Iranzo and Castillo were making the first claim – that the rebels were not acting in the king's service.

But the rebels did not rebut this claim with the language of service and loyalty. Both Diego de Valera and Alfonso de Palencia, two chroniclers who tended to favor Pacheco's party, were silent on the question of loyalty and service to the king. Instead, they described the participants at Ávila discussing how they ought to explain and justify their actions. Both chroniclers note that the rebels accused the king of abandoning Holy Mother Church and destroying the true faith in Castile, with Palencia suggesting that the king had secretly converted to Islam.[109] They suggested that Enrique had homosexual relationships and was therefore unfit to rule. Never did they return to the intellectual gymnastics of showing that the rebels were actually serving the king by forcing him to come to terms with them. Instead, when the rebels sought justification for their actions, they found it in ancient principles of elective kingship. Both sympathetic chroniclers record nearly identical arguments for dethroning Enrique and crowning Alfonso. The rebels made vague claims that it had always been the right of the people and the nobles to dethrone a king who was acting as a tyrant and to elect a new king in his stead. They noted the case of Alfonso X of Castile, who was elected emperor by the nobility.[110] In other words, there was historical precedent for

---

[108] Enríquez del Castillo, "Don Enrique el Cuarto," 145. "¡O crianza desagradecida! ¡O fechura sin bondad! que despues de puestos en tanta prosperidad, subidos en alta cumbre y estados, con tanta ingratitud olvidasteis los beneficios que del Rey recebisteis. ¡O servidores perversos que así vos conformasteis, para deshonrar á quien vos honró! ¿Por qué tan nueva perversidad aveis devisado é demostrado á las gentes? ¿Por qué tan sin miedo abristeis las puertas de la traycion, é quitasteis el velo se vergüenza á la deslealtad? ¿Por qué aveis querido que la lealtad sea traycion, é la traycion por lealtad coronada?"

[109] Diego de Valera, "Memorial de diversas hazañas," in *Biblioteca de Autores Españoles*, vol. 70, 33. Palencia, "Enrique IV," 167.

[110] Palencia, "Enrique IV," 167; Valera, "Memorial de diversas hazañas," 33. The rebels were technically incorrect on this point, as Alfonso X was only ever elected King of the Romans, never Emperor. His election was also decided not by Castilian nobles but

their rebellious actions in general, and particular reasons to remove Enrique IV specifically. The rebels did not need to speak of loyalty and service – they were right in their violent actions, regardless. The beating heart of chivalric ideology was honor and violence. At Ávila, this had been divorced from the loftier ideals of loyalty and service.

Remarkably, the rebels of the 1460s were not speaking the same political language as the nobility of the 1380s. Nor were they acting like the rebels of the 1440s, claiming to rebel against the king in his service. When the supporters of Enrique IV challenged the loyal service of Pacheco and his supporters, the latter simply refused to respond in the same terms. The chivalric discourse on service and loyalty was broken. Without the umbrella of this concept to allow for debate and discourse between competing parties, the ideological justification for knightly political violence evaporated. Pacheco's rebellion was founded on the loss of his jealously guarded place of privilege near the king. When he initiated a civil war, it was predicated on reclaiming that position, not on his loyalty to the king. With the rebels of the 1460s abandoning the argument, it meant that the eventual winners of the long civil war would devise a new foundation for political violence and political action. Isabel I and her supporters, emerging victorious in the 1470s, would remake the concept of loyalty and service to the monarch and would struggle to find new ways to check or redirect the traditional violence that marked knightly political independence.

Conclusions

The political identity of the Trastámara nobility was fundamentally violent. Knights found reward and advancement from their king primarily through vigorous service on the battlefield. When they failed to gain such recognition, violence against the king or others was the default method of making a political statement or achieving political goals. From the very origins of the Trastámara dynasty in the Castilian civil war, political objectives were achieved through vigorous deeds of arms and through bloody rebellion and fratricide. There simply was no viable alternative political identity for the late medieval Castilian chivalric elite. From El Cid to Pero Niño to Álvaro de Luna, violence was the answer to political questions because violence was at the heart of the chivalric identity. Knights expressed themselves politically using the language and actions of chivalry, vindicating their honor, seeking augmented honor in battle, and defending themselves and their families against attack.

---

by German princes. Even so, the rebels had evidence of elective kingship in Castilian history.

Given the politically violent origins of the Trastámara dynasty and nobility, the question of loyalty and service to the Crown was always a tense and contradictory component of Castilian chivalry. For a nobility that had found its political identity through violent rebellion against a legitimate king, the idea that obedience and loyalty to their monarch was an essential part of their political lexicon appears somewhat incongruous to modern eyes. Looking at this time span, we may savor the irony that the rebels at Ávila in 1465 took as an example of legitimate rebellion not only Alfonso X, but also Enrique II. Pedro, they said, had been a cruel and unjust king, and had to be unmade by Enrique. Therefore, they were simply imitating the first Trastámara dynast in removing his descendant from the throne. In one sense, they were correct – they objected to Enrique IV's rule just as Enrique de Trastámara and his supporters had objected to Pedro's rule. But the ideological justifications had changed. The charges leveled at Pedro had been his immense cruelty and unjustified acts of violence, while those leveled at Enrique IV involved his religious commitment, his indulgence of favorites, his sexuality, and, as we will see in Chapter 3, his failure to commit greater violence on the southern frontier. Where Pedro's chivalry had faltered due to his wicked and unjust violence, Enrique IV's had faltered because he was not committed to chivalric violence and chivalric ideals. The Trastámara dynasty and its noble supporters, born in bloodshed to check the brutality of a bad king, had cultivated an ideology of political violence that inverted the stakes by the late 15th century. Pedro had been a monster who could not control his love of bloodshed. Enrique had become a *puto* – feminine, weak, and possibly Muslim. Perhaps Enrique IV was not violent enough for his noblemen.

The very tension between loyal service to the king and the violently jealous guarding of knightly privilege and honor counter-intuitively functioned as something of a pressure-release valve. Knights and men-at-arms could find justification in the political language of their day for a wide variety of violent actions. That powerful men could debate with one another about what was or was not in the appropriate service of the king allowed a certain amount of independent knightly violence without destroying the whole delicate political structure of Trastámara Castile. When this ideological superstructure finally fell apart in the 1460s, Castile experienced a crisis unlike any it had seen in the last hundred years, and a crisis that could be resolved only with the reordering of Castilian politics under the Catholic Monarchs.

2

Knights and Commoners

In 1824 the French romantic artist Eugène Delacroix painted two knights fighting in the countryside.[1] On the left side of his painting is a knight clad in gold armor wielding a sword and shield and mounted on a beautiful white steed with golden mane and tail. On the right is his opponent, a knight wearing black armor, wielding a mace and mounted on a brown and black horse. The painting represents a fine romantic view of medieval knights: proud, noble men engaged in single combat, with clearly delineated "good guys" and "bad guys." We can imagine the great golden knight protecting the weak, guarding the virtue of women, and fighting for God in holy wars. In embracing Delacroix's painting, we would of course be embracing a romantic rather than a historical understanding of knighthood. Medieval knights were morally and intellectually complex and did not always attain to their own high ideals. It is a wonderful thing, perhaps, that the 21st century allows us to enjoy fantasies of medieval knighthood at the same time that we can recognize that the reality might be significantly different from our (and Delacroix's) fantasies.

Yet Delacroix's method of accepting medieval prescriptive literature as historical reality continues to inform historical writing even in the 21st century. The modern military historian Michael Howard, in his general history of European warfare, argued that in most war in the Middle Ages knights would try as hard as they could to ease the damage to the community and would avoid targeting peasants or clerics, who were not legitimate targets. For Howard, it was a rare and extreme case that peasants, women, and children might be killed in war.[2] Certainly, medieval clerics and some lawyers and knights argued for such a proposition. Medievalists as well have taken a fairly generous and forgiving view of medieval knightly violence. While Cecilia Devia acknowledges that violence occurred in the late Middle Ages, she argues that "violence has ambivalent functions: although it sows destruction, it also serves as an element of social cohesion, and it is this

---

[1] The painting, titled *Combat de chevaliers dans la campagne*, resides today in the Louvre Museum.
[2] Michael Howard, *War in European History* (Oxford: Oxford University Press, 2009), 6–7.

latter point that [she] emphasize[s]."[3] This anthropological approach holds that much violence in human history functions as a sort of social ritual wherein different agendas are put forth and different segments of society can resolve their differences. David Gilmore, in studying modern rural Andalucía, offered a theoretical framework for this approach, suggesting that "[a]ggression is the human motive underlying the action of a normative framework, a cultural superstructure, a shared frame of mind ... which holds the group together by disallowing deviance ... The force of hate, writ large, becomes ... a force that binds."[4] Gilmore's framework proposes to offer historians a means to explain aggressive tendencies in human history and to emphasize their positive contributions.

But late medieval warfare was not a kinder, gentler form of warfare governed by pleasant and gentlemanly rules. Neither was it a particularly cohesive force in society at large. Indeed, violence served to separate the knightly class from other segments of society. Knights perpetrated violence against others in society – what we might call social violence – in order to win honor and demonstrate their social superiority. Salustiano Moreta published his work on social violence in Castile in the 13th and 14th centuries in 1978, and his argument is still central to the historiographical debate precisely because of the historiographical move toward diminishing the serious and destructive violence performed by medieval knights. Moreta's argument was essentially that *malhechores feudales* – feudal evildoers, which consisted primarily of knights, *hidalgos*, and other powerful men – preyed on the poor, the weak, the peasants, and their children.[5]

This chapter will argue that the chivalric elite of the late 14th and 15th centuries caused intense disruption to the common folk of Castile – peasants and urban dwellers. Knights fought one another with regularity, but often the immediate losers in any dispute were those who farmed, served, and only barely subsisted. This violence was founded on a chivalric ideology which held that knights had a *right* to commit violence by virtue of their unique ability to possess, defend, and augment honor. Importantly, the right to violence did not extend to the non-chivalric classes. Violence was a marker of social status. The exercise of violence was an exclusive right exercised by the chivalric elite and one that was intimately connected to the concept of honor. The exercise of violence either in defense of a man's

---

[3] Cecilia Devia, *La violencia en la Edad Media: la rebelión irmandiña* (Vigo, Spain: Editorial Academia del Hispanismo, 2009), 21. "La violencia tiene funciones ambivalentes: si bien siembra destrucción, también sirve como elemento de cohesión social, y es en este último punto en el que hace hincapié el autor."

[4] David D. Gilmore, *Aggression and Community: Paradoxes of Andalusian Culture* (New Haven, CT: Yale University Press, 1987), 10–11.

[5] Salustiano Moreta, *Malhechores-Feudales: Violencia, antagonismos y alianzas de clases en Castilla, siglos XIII–XIV* (Madrid: Ediciones Cátedra, S.A., 1978), 54–55.

personal or familial honor or in an effort to accumulate greater honor was not simply a function of his position or a perk that he gained, but was a significant factor in determining his social identity. Similarly, the inability of the commoner to accumulate honor and, therefore, to exercise violence helped to mark his own social identity. Indeed, where Nicholas Wright has noted "the unwillingness of the men-at-arms who fought in the wars of the 14th and 15th centuries to give serious consideration in their code of honour to their relationship with the other, non-combatant, classes of society," I suggest that the chivalric elite *had* thought about their relationship with commoners and decided that their code of honor positively did not extend that far down the social scale. Knights were not ignorant of their relationship with peasants, but actively chose how to interact with them. Violence, in other words, was a key factor in the theoretical construction of the social hierarchy of late medieval Castile.[6]

Evidence of Social Violence: Chivalric Voices and Silence

The evidence of social violence can be difficult to access. For the chivalric elite of late medieval Castile, there is almost a sense that the lowest members of society were irrelevant to their daily activities. While chronicles and chivalric biographies regularly record the deaths and wounds suffered by knights and men-at-arms, they less frequently attempt to assess the actual suffering of the poor and weak.[7] On this point, in other words, the descriptive chronicle evidence is very weak; chroniclers simply did not typically find it remarkable or noteworthy when peasants or city folk were killed or harmed by chivalric warfare. We must therefore seize on the few instances of chronicle evidence and examine government records in order to rest assured that social violence was a regular part of life in the Trastámara period.

---

[6] Nicholas Wright, *Knights and Peasants: The Hundred Years War in the French Countryside* (Woodbridge: Boydell Press, 1998), 44.
[7] Knights and men-at-arms were indeed being wounded and dying regularly in battle. Pedro López de Ayala names 23 Castilian knights and *señores* who died at a battle at Santarém during the war with Portugal. He names another 10 who were not Castilian but who fought and died for King Juan at the battle. Additionally, he suggests that there were many other knights who died; presumably Ayala either did not know their names or is simply speculating. Whatever the case, plenty of knights were dying in battle. Pedro López de Ayala, "Don Juan Primero," in *Biblioteca Autores de Españoles*, ed. M. Rivadeneyra (Madrid: Impresore de Camara de S.M., 1876), vol. 66, 105. This evidence stands in contrast to Maria Concepción Quintanilla Raso's suggestion that late medieval encounters were much less violent and deadly than historians have recently argued. See Maria Concepción Quintanilla Raso, *Nobleza y caballería en la Edad Media*, 60. See also Craig Taylor, *Chivalry and the Ideals of Knighthood in France during the Hundred Years War* (Cambridge: Cambridge University Press, 2013), 72–73.

The mode of warfare practiced by knights in the 14th and 15th centuries typically took the form of raids through an enemy's territory rather than engagements in great pitched battles, the goal being to disrupt an enemy's economic bases.[8] This form of warfare was acknowledged by kings, lords, and chroniclers, who fumed at these tactics when perpetrated on their own lands and holdings but resorted to them immediately when they went to war themselves. When, in 1378, the king of Navarre decided to invade Castile, King Enrique II of Castile sent his twenty-year-old son, the future Juan I, to the Navarrese frontier to respond. Juan, together with numerous lords and knights of Castile, entered into Navarre "[a]nd came to Pamplona, and made to burn and destroy all the country around the city."[9] As king in 1385, Juan called a council of his leading knights and vassals and proposed that they "ought to enter into Portugal to cut down crops and vines, and make all the damage that they could … and they did so."[10] This language of burning, chopping, and destruction appears ubiquitously throughout the chronicles as they describe warfare, strongly suggesting that chivalric warfare in Castile often targeted agriculture and its infrastructure, including peasant workers. When Castile was invaded by its neighbors, the chroniclers reported similar events, but colored them as glorious or tragic based on who was invading whose territory. The violence of late medieval Castile was indeed vigorous, even when knights were not engaging one another directly. And how could it be otherwise? Staking one's life, possessions, and fortune on a single pitched battle too regularly would surely lead to catastrophe before long. The method of warfare was certainly informed

---

[8] In the late Middle Ages, these are most famously known by the French term *chevauchée*, used to describe the tactics of both French and English armies during the Hundred Years' War. The Castilian term *cavalgada* described a similar tactic. See Philippe Contamine, *War in the Middle Ages*, trans. Michael Jones (Oxford: Basil Blackwell, 1984), 31. Matthew Bennett has placed the *chevauchée* as a central component of the English strategy to disrupt and demoralize the France even as he recognizes that raids were not the *only* strategy deployed. Matthew Bennett, "The Development of Battle Tactics in the Hundred Years War," in *Arms, Armies and Fortifications in the Hundred Years War*, ed. Anne Curry and Michael Hughes (Woodbridge: Boydell Press, 1994), 1–20. L.J. Andrew Villalon aptly observes the rarity of major encounters on land in the War of the Two Pedros. L.J. Andrew Villalon, "'Cut Off Their Heads, or I'll Cut Off Yours': Castilian Strategy and Tactics in the War of the Two Pedros and the Supporting Evidence from Murcia," in *History of Warfare: The Hundred Years War (part II): Different Vistas*, ed. L.J.A. Villalon and D.J. Kagay (Boston: Brill, 2008), 161. Nicholas Wright has noted that the *chevauchée*, ubiquitously employed by English armies, was in fact the norm for late medieval warfare, whether directed by the English and French crowns or by local lords in private wars. Wright, *Knights and Peasants*, 68–70.

[9] López de Ayala, "Don Enrique Segundo," in *Biblioteca Autores de Españoles*, vol. 66, 34. "E llegó á Pamplona, é fizo quemar é destroir toda la comarca que el alli enderredor de la cibdad."

[10] López de Ayala, "Don Juan Primero," 98. "é que dende entrasen en Portugal á facer talar los panes é viñas, é facer todo el daño que pudiesen … é ellos ficieronlo asi."

by a desire to perform violence, but the violence was not always directed against other men-at-arms.[11]

For the medieval knight and standard bearer Gutierre Díez de Games, nothing was more certain than that his lord, the great and famous Castilian knight Pero Niño, was a good knight. In the service of his king during the Hundred Years' War, Pero Niño set out to raid the English coast and the Channel Islands and, as Díez recalls this series of events, we are given a glimpse into an issue around which he strove to portray his lord in the best possible light: the treatment of the poor English peasants and city-dwellers by Castilian knights and men-at-arms. Díez begins by pointing out that the Castilians refused to burn down peasant homes in Portland because, unlike their French counterparts, they took pity on the poor folk of the town. Their compassionate actions followed the sentiments of their captain, Pero Niño, who was "tender to the weak and strong against the strong."[12] Díez, at pains to make his lord's tenderness to the poor perfectly clear, lays out four rules which any man must observe while at war, even in contravention of his orders. Firstly, he must not kill another man whom he has taken prisoner. Secondly, he must not do evil or damage to churches, taking from them only enough to feed himself and his horse. Thirdly, he must not bring any women with him on campaign, for indulging in wine or (sexual) luxury will sap him of his strength and sense. Finally, he must not burn crops or houses because "that damage and evil reaches to the innocents and the children," who are not responsible for war. Díez ends the chapter by assuring his reader that "all these things the captain [Pero Niño] ordered always to be kept, in all places …"[13] According to Díez, Pero Niño was a great man and a great knight, not only upholding strong values himself but ordering his men to behave themselves as well. If we take the chronicle at face value, we would conclude that Castilian knights did not damage the poor and humble members of society.

It seems unlikely that Pero Niño held as true to Díez' chivalric program as the author would have us believe. Shortly after explaining how tender his lord was to the poor, Díez opens a chapter titled "How the men of Pero Niño burned down the town of Poole; and of the fight which they had with the English."[14] The Castilians had gone ashore and set fire to Poole and were then driven back by English men-at-arms. Pero Niño then drove forward

---

[11] Nicholas Wright has examined the French peasant as the main victim of the Hunderd Years War even as he moves to complicate the simplistic picture of knights as victimizers and peasants as victims. Wright, *Knights and Peasants*, 62–67.
[12] Gutierre Díez de Games, *El Victorial*, ed. Juan de Mata Carriazo (Madrid: Espasa-Calpe, S.A., 1940), 204. "fué blando a lo flaco, e fuerte contra lo fuerte."
[13] Ibid., 215. "todas estas cosas mandó guardar sienpre el capitán, en todas las partes …"
[14] Ibid., 206. "Cómo la gente de Pero Niño quemaron al villa de Pola; e de la pelea que ovieron con los yngleses."

again – his goal through the whole expedition not being the defeat of an English army, but holding them off for long enough to destroy the town in order to punish its lord. In this he was successful.[15] The burning of Poole no doubt would have been a stinging assault on the honor of the English lord and thus a success for Pero Niño and his knights. But it would have been much more painful to the inhabitants of the town, who, if they were not killed during the town's destruction, would have been left with no home, food, or means of survival. Díez is not explicit about this sort of damage to the common folk, but his account confirms that Castilian knights perpetrated violence against them.

If peasants were a target of warfare, then surely the protection of one's own peasants was also a worthy endeavor for medieval knights. Yet such defensive actions appear less ubiquitously in the sources. Lords and knights did labor to protect their economic resources, as demonstrated at Poole when Pero Niño encountered armed resistance to his attack. There was honor to be gained from defending the common folk, just as there was honor to be gained from defending a herd of cattle from the enemy's predations. But a knight sitting at home, guarding his peasants as if he were a shepherd keeping watch over his flock, demonstrates little initiative and perhaps little desire to actually engage the enemy. Boldly seeking an attack on his enemy was a greater calling than guaranteeing that his honor was never slighted in the first place by diligently defending Castilian peasants. This is not to say that knights and nobles did not vigorously defend the peasants of their lands against the predations of fellow knights. But waging a daring attack on an enemy would yield more honor than waiting for an enemy's attack.

Indeed, the knightly emphasis on offensive rather than defensive action hints at the complex place of revenge in chivalric ideology. Pero Niño would have won honor attacking English peasants in essentially all cases – prowess on the battlefield won honor. That he attacked the inhabitants at Poole as an act of *vengeance* for the English attack on his own lord's peasants suggests that his bold and dangerous aggressive move was more highly regarded than simply sitting at home, waiting for a new English attack to come. Would it be worth allowing an enemy to attack one's peasants in order justify a reciprocal and perhaps disproportionate counterattack on the enemy's peasants? Was an aggressive initiative so central to knightly identity that

---

[15] Díez asserts that the town was fired while English evidence suggests that the Castilian case was overstated and that the Castilians and French set fire to only a single large building. This would appear to be a case of each side overstating their advantage. Though the historical reality may be unknowable, we know that Díez believed or wanted to believe that the Castilians had done a great deal of damage. W. Turner, J.P. "The Town Cellar, or the Church of the Monastery of St. Clement's, and Other Buildings Supposed to be Connected Therewith, in the Town of Poole," *Proceedings of the Dorset Natural History and Antiquarian Field Club*, vol. IX (1888), 90–92.

an absence of personal defense of one's peasantry was worth the cost? We cannot be certain about the answers to these questions, but we can be sure that, in nearly all our sources, defense of one's own peasant population was a secondary concern, serving more as a convenient spur to vengeful bloodshed than as a real chivalric imperative.

Nor was Poole an exceptional case for Pero Niño's warriors. Before happening upon Poole the Castilians had been "following the coast, each day burning and robbing many houses ..."[16] Having wrought destruction on the English coast, as the Castilians sailed back to France they met a group of Normans who encouraged them to win great honor in attacking the island of Jersey. The captain and his knights sailed to the island and fought with the English in glorious and honorable battle, Díez crowing that the "fight was very strong" and that "both sides were so good and had such will to fight".[17] Interrogating some English prisoners captured during the battle, Pero Niño was told that "[T]he other people, burgesses and peasants and fishermen had taken to a village, the largest of the island ... in which they had their possessions, and women and children, and the greater part of the people who had escaped the battle had collected there ..."[18] The captain and his knights discussed what to do with these people (whom modern nomenclature would designate refugees) and agreed that the city must be taken and the whole country fired.[19] "[Pero Niño] ordered some reserve men to put fire [to the country]. The land was well populated with many houses and orchards, and many crops, and livestock; and all the land blazed, which was a very piteous thing to see ..."[20] Even as Díez appears to lament the burning of Jersey, he acknowledges that the knights and men-at-arms, led by the heroic knight Pero Niño, were responsible for it. Even so, Díez is silent about the actual effect on the "other people." He seems to lament the destruction of the *things* rather than the effect on the peasants, burgesses, and fishermen. It is almost as if Díez sees the economic infrastructure as more valuable than the human lives of the inhabitants of Jersey.

On this point, we must remember that even when the common folk themselves were not targeted, the activities of knights likely wrought havoc

---

[16] Díez de Games, *El Victorial*, 206. "siguiendo la costa, cada día quemando e robando muchas casas ..."

[17] Ibid., 269. "La pelea hera tan fuerte ... Tan buenos heran de amas partes, e tan a voluntad lo avian ..."

[18] Ibid., 271. "E que la otra gente, burgueses e labradores e pescadores, que tenían vna villa, la mayor de la ysla, çercada de madera e buenas cabas llenas de agua, en que tenían sus algos, e mugeres e hijos, e que allí se abrían recogido la mayor parte de la gente que de la batalla escaparon ..."

[19] Ibid., 270–271.

[20] Ibid., 272. "Mandó el capitán honbres ahorrados que fuesen poniendo fuego. La tierra hera muy poblada de muchas caserías e huertas, e muchos panes, e ganados; e ardía toda la tierra, que hera vna cosa muy piadosa de ber ..."

in their lives anyway. The poor medieval family might not have witnessed the incredible devastation brought by modern warfare, but it did take much less to push them over the edge than it would a modern family. Medieval peasants, living close to subsistence, could find themselves starving to death if their crops were burned, their orchards and vineyards cut down, or their livestock stolen or slaughtered.[21] Such was indeed the case in late medieval warfare. As Pero Niño and his French allies left England to return to France, they slaughtered livestock on the Channel Islands, not only for their own benefit, but to punish the English, though Díez assures his reader that, beyond slaughtering livestock, the Castilian knights "did no other evil, for [the Englishmen] were a poor people."[22] Díez may or may not have seen any evil done to the Channel Islanders, but one wonders if any of them starved to death when their food supply was destroyed. The same evidence of economic disruption and social violence is present in the chronicles. Over and over again, chroniclers speak of knights and men-at-arms burning, cutting, and making damages and robberies. Against the English, the Portuguese, the Navarrese, and even against Castilian rebels, Castilian knights "made damage" throughout the land, effectively inflicting injury on the townsfolk and peasants of late medieval Europe.

The chivalric preference for habitual destruction was so prevalent that chroniclers came to use the simple term *la tala* with regularity. *La tala*, literally "the cutting" or "the chopping" today often refers to the activity of lumberjacks or loggers, but in the late Middle Ages it referred to the regular and expected cutting down of enemy crops by knights and men-at-arms. It often referred specifically to grapevines, but was regularly applied to orchards, wheat, and other agricultural products. Chroniclers rarely needed to explain the term, suggesting that readers would have known precisely the activity that it referred to. So, just as Juan I had cut down vines and orchards in Portugal in 1385, in 1429, King Juan II ordered the men-at-arms of the eastern frontier to invade Navarre and Aragon. The chronicler and knight Fernán Pérez de Guzmán wrote that the king "sent to order to all the villages of the frontier that they should make cruel war in the Kingdoms of Aragon and Navarre, [and his men] made great damages and cuttings [*talas*] and burnings in [those kingdoms]."[23] Later that year, Juan's Constable, Álvaro

---

[21] There were certainly wealthier peasants in medieval Europe, but for the most part the rural workers lived in incredible poverty and destruction of their immediate food supply would have been disastrous. See Hilario Casado Alonso, *Señores, mercaderes y campesinos* (Valladolid: Junta de Castilla y Leon, 1987). For a more general assessment of Castile's peasantry in the late Middle Ages and the early modern period, see Teófilo F. Ruiz, "The Peasantries of Iberia, 1400–1800," in *The Peasantries of Europe*, ed. Tom Scott (London: Longman, 1998).

[22] Díez de Games, *El Victorial*, 214. "e non fiçieron otro mal, por quanto es gente pobre ..."

[23] Fernán Pérez de Guzmán, "La crónica del serenísimo príncipe don Juan, segundo rey

de Luna, "entered six leagues into Aragon with 1500 lances, men-at-arms, and jinetes, cutting [*talando*] and burning all the places and everything he found in the countryside."[24] In this instance, the chronicler also notes that the behavior of Luna and his entourage was so ghastly that it sowed terror among the population. The people of the area were so incredibly afraid of the Castilian chivalry that they surrendered the fortress of Monreal to him without resistance, in an attempt to ensure their security.[25] Luna continued destroying and robbing other places in Aragon and it is unclear whether the protection money paid by the people around Monreal had the desired effect or not.

La tala had a particularly vigorous usage when discussing the war against Islam on the southern frontier. During the regency of Fernando de Antequera and the personal rule of Juan II, the concept of *la tala* was a constantly recurring strategic component of the holy war with Granada. In 1410, as the Infante Fernando undertook the invasion of Granada which would earn him the sobriquet "de Antequera," he and his knights and señores ravaged Granada's territory, "burn[ing] the suburbs and all the bread that they had, and then cut[ting] the orchards and vines" of Cártama, a village to the west of the city of Málaga on the southern coast.[26] As the Castilian army approached Málaga and ran into the olive and almond groves outside the city, the defenders sallied forth to protect the trees, but "the Christians cut [*talaron*] all the orchards and vines ... and they left nothing outside the city that they did not destroy, save a house of the King."[27] Twenty years later, in 1431, the young Juan II called a council to discuss a possible renewal of the holy war against Granada. One significant piece of advice he received was to "enter through all parts into the Kingdom [of Granada], cutting [*talando*] and burning as much as he could."[28] As Juan undertook one of his few successful forays across the southern frontier, he appears to have kept this advice in mind. Juan fought a major battle against his Muslim enemies on the Vega de Granada, the fertile plains to the west of the capital

---

deste nombre en Castilla y en Leon," in *Biblioteca Autores de Españoles*, vol. 68, 462–463. "el Rey embió á mandar á todas las villas de las frontera que hiciesen guerra cruel en los Reynos de Aragon é Navarra ... los quales habian hecho grandes daños y talas y quemas en los Reynos de Aragon é Navarra ..."

[24] Ibid., 464. "Y el Condestable entró seis leguas en el Reyno de Aragon con mil é quiñientas lanzas, hombres darmas é ginetes, talando é quemando lugares é todo lo que en el campo halló ..."

[25] Ibid.

[26] Ibid., 324. "[P]usieron su Real esa noche cerca de la villa de Cártama, é quemáronle el arraval é todo el pan que tenian, é talaron ende las huertas é viñas ..."

[27] Ibid. "los Christianos les talaron todas las huertas é viñas ... é no dexaron cosa fuera de la cibdad que no destruyeron, salvo una casa del Rey ..."

[28] Ibid., 496. "unos decian que el Rey debia entrar por todas partes en el Reyno, talando é quemando quanto pudiese ..."

of the Nasrid Kingdom. Even after defeating the Muslim army, "the King still ordered [his men] to cut the grains and vines and orchards and all that which was found in the countryside, all the towers and houses and buldings which were within three leagues of the city were demolished; [this activity] lasted lasted for six days after the battle was won."[29] The goal was clearly to starve out his enemy, to force the capitulation of the king of Granada, no doubt a time-honored military tactic. We can only imagine how much agricultural produce was destroyed over the course of nearly a week and with what intensity the citizens of Granada and the poor peasants of its countryside suffered.

Evidence of Social Violence: Commoner Voices

Cutting down crops, burning fields, tearing down buildings, setting cities alight, demolishing walls and homes, sowing terror among enemy populations; it comes as no surprise that the means of war that had been practiced for centuries in European warfare should appear in the late Middle Ages. Chivalric violence and destruction were not reserved for violent attacks in another king's territory or in Muslim lands. The lowest members of Castilian society themselves felt the blows of swords and lances, and witnessed the fires of Castilian chivalric violence. Reading between the lines of our sources, we can just barely hear the small voices of the late medieval peasants and urban dwellers. The proceedings of the *cortes*, the medieval consultative institutions comparable to parliaments throughout Europe, record the plaints of the commoners and are one of the few places where the voices of the common folk can be heard.[30] While the representatives of the urban elite no doubt were the most powerful in the *cortes*, we must remember that there were likely other representatives of urban and possibly even rural interests in the *cortes* of the 14th and 15th centuries. After all, the unique history of the Iberian kingdoms as expanding frontier zones suggests

---

[29] Ibid., 499. "El Rey mandaba todavía talar los panes é viñas é huertas é todo lo que en el campo se hallaba, é fueron derribadas todas las torres é casas y edificios que habia en derredor de la cibdad tres leguas en torno, lo qual duró en se hacer seis dias despues de la batalla vencida."

[30] Most historians of the *cortes* agree that by the Trastámara period, the representatives of the third estate present in these assemblies were primarily the urban elite, at times even local aristocracy. The classic work on the *cortes* is Wladimiro Piskorski's *Las cortes de Castilla en el período de tránsito de la Edad Media a la Moderna, 1188–1520* (Barcelona: Ediciones el Albir, S.A., 1977). Other works are useful but also focus on an earlier period, in a search for the origins of Castilian representative government. See, for example, Evelyn S. Procter, *Curia and Cortes in León and Castile, 1072–1295* (Cambridge: Cambridge University Press, 1980) and Joseph F. O'Callaghan, *Alfonso X, the Cortes, and Government in Medieval Spain* (Brookfield, VT: Ashgate Publishing Company, 1998).

that the commoners of Castile were likely not as far removed from the halls of power as they might have been in English parliaments or French *parlements*. Where the records of the *cortes* reflect the sober conveyance of the concerns of commoners, popular ballads and poems offer bitter and satirical objections to knightly and lordly violence. These sources help to flesh out the sparser evidence of chronicles and chivalric biography, confirming that violence was being perpetuated by knights against those below them in the social hierarchy.

From the beginning of the Trastámara period, Castilian kings recognized the reality of violence and received petitions from their subjects asking that they respond to social violence. At his first *cortes* upon securing the throne in 1369, Enrique II promulgated legislation laying out punishments for those who stole or committed evils, whether against churches or anyone else.[31] In the chaos of the civil war, it should come as no surprise that Enrique would attempt to end the problems of that strife. The *cortes* of 1369 suggests not only that violence was being committed but also that Enrique intended, at least at some level, to rein it in. A year later the representatives of the cities, villages, and rural areas of the kingdom requested that the king cleanse the land of those who were committing robberies and doing evil.[32] Who were these robbers and evildoers? We might be tempted to believe that the petitioners were simply referring to the highwaymen and petty thieves with which any society in history might have to deal. In the *cortes* held only a year later in 1371, though, the king's response to a similar petition specified that "if some *powerful knight or squire, with his company* robs or takes something against the will of its owner" he would have to pay thrice the value to its owner.[33] In the same *cortes*, the king responded to a petition in which the Castilian clergy complained of

> powerful men and others who violate the churches and the monasteries and enter into them very irreverently and without the fear of God, and rob them of their ornaments and other things which they find ... [and] they take food and other things in the churches and occupy them with many of their men, eating, and extorting, and destroying the said places against the will of their prelates.[34]

---

[31] *Cortes* held at Toro in 1369. *Cortes de los antiguos reinos de León y de Castilla*, ed. Real Academia de la Historia (Madrid: M. Rivadeneyra, 1861–1866), vol. 2, 165–166.

[32] *Cortes* held at Medina del Campo in 1370. Ibid., vol. 2, 186–187.

[33] *Cortes* held at Toro in 1371. Ibid., 200. Italics are mine. "sy algunt cauallero o escudero poderoso, el con su conpanna rrobare o tomare alguna cosa en qual quier manera quelo tome contra voluntad de cuya fuere ..."

[34] *Cortes* held at Toro in 1371. Ibid., 247. "ommes poderosos e otros que quebrantan las eglesias e monesterios e entran dentro muy sin reuerençia e temor de Dios, e rroban los ornamientos dellas e las otras cosas que y fallan ... e que toman viandas e otras cosas enlos delas eglesias e posan enellas muchas vezes con muchas conpannas comiendo e confechando e destruyendo los dichos lugares contra voluntad delos perlados dellas."

The repeated use of terms such as "knight," "squire," and "powerful men," as well as references to companies of armed men, should alert us to the fact that the people perpetrating these deeds against city dwellers, peasants, churches, and monasteries were not simply local hooligans and minor criminals, but strong, armed men accompanied by similar followers – the chivalric elite.

Enrique, eager to assert his authority after coming to the throne through violent insurrection and aware of the possibility of challenges to his legitimate rule, appears to have responded vigorously in the *cortes* to petitions concerning social violence. The responses of Enrique's government ranged from the specific to the general. In 1371, Enrique specified that any man in his entourage who should stop at an inn and injure or kill the host would have his hand cut off for the former and would be put to death if he should kill. Indeed, Enrique's legislation specifies that anyone of any condition, whether *hidalgo* or not, "murders justice" by killing or injuring while in the king's service, and prescribed the same punishments of death or manual amputation.[35] As we have seen in Chapter 1 the actions which Enrique took against his political opponents, amputation and execution seem well within the realm of reality for the Trastámara dynast. The year before, Enrique had undertaken a more general institutional solution to the problem of violence by allowing communities to institute *hermandades* or local police or militia forces in order to protect themselves from the evils being perpetrated. We will return to the *hermandades* later in this chapter, but at the moment the significance is that Enrique recognized the problems of violence which were being communicated to him by his subjects.

Despite Enrique's efforts, the situation failed to stabilize. The *cortes* proceedings suggest that violence against the lowest members of society remained and may even have been augmented, with more specific complaints brought to the *cortes* during the reign of Enrique's son and successor, Juan I. At a *cortes* in Soria in 1380, the second of Juan's reign, the king received a fairly comprehensive list of grievances from the representatives of the commons and cities, asking that people should "neither cut nor hack nor burn nor knock down nor violate houses nor vineyards nor orchards ... nor rob nor take cattle or beasts, nor violate churches, nor seize anything against the will of their owners, nor seize laborers nor merchants nor men or women."[36] King Juan agreed that these actions were illegal and the perpetrators should be brought to justice. Significantly, the

---

[35] *Cortes* held at Toro in 1371. Ibid., 196.
[36] *Cortes* held at Soria in 1380. Ibid., 306. "que non corten nin tajen nin quemen nin derriben nin quebranten casas nin vinnas nin arboles ... nin robben nin desjarreten ganadaso nin bestias, nin quebranten eglesias nin tomen nin saquen dellas cosa alguna contra voluntad de sus duennos, nin prendan labradores nin mercadores nin algunos varones nin mugeres ..."

king added to the complaints of the petitioners that those lords or knights or squires who harbored the evildoers should pay twice the amount of the damage to those who received it.[37] Clearly, if the perpetrators were not knights themselves they were often part of a knight's retinue – this is what Juan is referring to when he mentions *harboring* evildoers. In 1385, Juan again responded to a petition asking that malefactors be punished. The petitioners insisted that if royal officers would not punish evildoers, then the *hermandades* ought to be allowed to arrest and punish them. Juan agreed.[38] In 1386, in an attempt to bring malefactors and evildoers out of the shadows and allow them to live honestly and peacefully, Juan even offered a general amnesty to those who were responsible for deaths and injuries.[39] The Trastámara kings claimed to have heard the suffering of their subjects and were laboring to right the situation.

And yet, year after year, the violence continued. At a *cortes* held in 1390, Juan I acknowledged and attempted to respond to the violence in his realm.

> Because of the enmity and hatred that occur between the prelates and *ricos hombres* and Military Orders and *hidalgos* and knights and other persons of our kingdoms, it happens many times that they apprehend and kill and wound peasants and vassals of those against whom they have enmities or hatred, and they demolish and burn down their houses, and take their goods, and cause them many other evils and damages and wrongs; therefore we establish and order that for no enmity nor hatred that the aforesaid should have one against the other, should they apprehend or kill or wound the peasants and vassals of their opponents, nor to the foodstuffs of the said vassals and peasants, nor should they take them nor burn nor cause other wrong, neither to their houses nor property, nor goods … nor burn down their houses …[40]

The king specifically ordered that anyone who burned crops or chopped [*talare*] vines ought to be put to death. In 1425 Juan II received a petition asking that knights and other powerful men stop intruding into cities and

---

[37] *Cortes* held at Soria in 1380. Ibid.
[38] *Cortes* held at Valladolid in 1385. Ibid., 323.
[39] *Cortes* held at Segovia in 1386. Ibid., 342–343.
[40] *Cortes* held at Guadalajara in 1390. Ibid., p. 427–428. "Por quanto por las enemistades e mal querençias que acaeçen entre los perlados e rricos omes e Ordenes e fiios dalgo e caualleros e otras personas delos nuestros rregnos, acaesça muchas vezes que prenden e matan e fieren alos labradores e vasallos de aquellos contra quien han las enemistrades e mal querençia, e les derriban e queman sus casas, e les toman sus bienes, e les fazen otros muchos males e dannos e desaguisados; por ende estableçemos e mandamos que por enemistad nin mal querençia quelos sobre dichos e cada vno dellos ayan vnos contra otros, que non prendan nin maten nin ffieran alos labradores e vasallos de sus contrarios, nin alos apaniguados delos dichos sus vasallos e labradores, nin les tomen nin quemen nin ffagan otro desaguisado, nin asus casas e heredades e bienes … o le quemare su casa … o talare vinnas, que mera por ello muerte qual deue morir aquel que matare a otro sin rrazon e sin derecho …"

villages and other places and forcefully taking clothes, crops, wood, and other things, which the common people were suffering. The petition notes "the knights and prelates and lords to be great and powerful people, that [the common people] cannot resist, and they had by force to suffer and endure the said wrongs and evils and damages."[41] In 1440, during the civil wars which erupted around the role of Álvaro de Luna, we find a very long and belabored petition to the king begging him to stop the widespread destruction in his realm. In this last the typically praiseworthy language addressed to the king (e.g. "most high lord, most powerful lord") is powerfully augmented, praising Juan's special relationship with God and with his people, and agreeing that all ought always loyally to serve such a great prince – the urgency in the pleas of Castile's people for an end to the violence is manifest here. Indeed, the complaints to the king in the *cortes* continue throughout the period.[42] As late as 1473, Enrique IV received a petition from the representatives in which they alleged that castellans across the kingdom were using force and imprisoning people and causing many other damages to the people of Castile.[43] If the evidence of petitions and royal responses is valuable at all, then we must accept that the chivalric elite were regularly injuring, abducting, and killing the common people of Castile.

For more than a century between the accession of Enrique II in 1369 and the death of Enrique IV in 1474, the urban dwellers (and perhaps the peasants) of Castile loudly complained to their king that they were being abused by knights and men-at-arms. As the petitions kept coming in at nearly every meeting of the *cortes*, the Trastámara kings promised to resolve the situation, to punish the knights responsible, and to hold the chivalry of Castile to a higher standard. But the problem never seems to have been resolved. That petitions continued to reach the king's court verifies the reality that social violence continued to be a problem and that there was little that the king could do to ameliorate the situation.

Sometimes we hear the voices of peasants and commoners outside of formal petitions as well, often in a biting tone. Angus MacKay has proposed a useful framework for considering the relationship between the ballad and its social setting. MacKay sets out to "relate the vision of the ballads and the ballad audience to a description of aspects of the behavioural system of the

---

[41] *Cortes* held at Palenzuela in 1425. *Cortes de los antiguos*, vol. 3, 63. "que por quanto muchas vezes auia acaesçido e acaesçia que algunos cauallleros e perlados e otras personas poderosas demis rregnos e sennorios, que tienen vezindat en algunas mis çibdades e villas e logares dela mi corona rreal o biuen o comracan çerca dellas ... e que les tomauan por fuerça e contra su voluntad la rropa e paja e lenna e otras cosas muchas ... e que por los tales caualleros e perlados e sennores ser grandes e poderosos, non los podian rresistir, e que auian por fuerça de sofrir e padesçer los dichos agrauios e males e dannos ..."

[42] *Cortes* held at Valladolid in 1440. Ibid., 369–373.

[43] *Cortes* held at Santa María de Nieva in 1473. Ibid., p. 872.

society in its own terms."[44] In other words, ballads likely represent general social complaints rather than the specific episodes of which they sing. A popular ballad of the mid-15th century imagined a meeting between the king of Castile and the duke of Arjona. The duke, a real historical figure, was a distant cousin of King Juan II and was actively involved in the troubles of Juan's reign, taking different sides at different times and leading his troops across the kingdom as he burned, cut, and killed.[45] The ballad had the king summoning the duke, feeding him, and then, strolling in the garden, saying to him, "Of you, Duke of Arjona, great complaints have been given me by the people; / That you force their women, married and betrothed / That you drink their wine, and eat their bread / That you take their barley without being willing to pay for it."[46] The duke denies the charges, the king counters with the petitions of the commoners, and has the duke imprisoned. No doubt such a ballad embodies the bitter anger of the folks singing it as well as their hope that all such perpetrators would meet the duke's fate. The mention of the petitions strongly suggests that the petition evidence needs to be taken seriously, as it seems to have mattered to society outside of the formalities of the *cortes*.

Other times, the common voice is expressed through venomous satire, as is the case with the *Dança General de la Muerte*. The "Dance of Death" was a general European motif in art and literature in the late Middle Ages, a period marked by the Black Death, Mongol and Turkish invasions, and endemic war in western Europe. In its iteration as a Castilian poem, as in other works of poetry, the *Dança* takes the form of a spirited yet dark *memento mori*, with the personification of Death inviting various members of society to join the dance. As each member of society explains to Death that he or she should not have to dance yet, Death calls them out for their sins and errors and explains that they will join the dance, regardless. Each interaction between Death and someone else offers a little window through which we might glean a broad understanding of satirical social criticism.

---

[44] Angus MacKay, "The Ballad and the Frontier in Late Mediaeval Spain," *Bulletin of Hispanic Studies*, 53 (1976): 15–33.

[45] Fadrique, duke of Arjona, lacks a recent biography. For a now dated study of the duke, see Santiago de Morales Talero, "Don Fadrique de Castilla y Castro, Duque de Arjona," *Boletín del Instituto de Estudios Giennenses*, no. 40 (1964): 17–36. We can also imagine the ballad being written of Fadrique of Aragon, who may have also been duke of Arjona and was also involved with the troubles of Enrique's reign. See José Manuel Calderón Ortega, "La donación de Arjona a Fadrique de Aragón," in *Historia medieval: actas del II Congreso de Historia de Andalucía, Córdoba* (Córdoba, Spain: Consejería de Cultura y Medio Ambiente de la Junta de Andalucía, 1994).

[46] *Antología de poetas líricos castellanos*, ed. M. Menéndez Pelayo (Madrid: Librería de Hernando y Compañía, 1945), 140. "De vos, el duque de Arjona, – grandes querellas me dan; / que forzades las mujeres – casadas y por casar; / que les bebiades el vino, – y les comiades el pan; / que les tomais la cebada, - sin se la querer pagar."

When Death calls the king to dance, the king frantically calls on his knights to save him, shouting, "My worthy, worthy knights! / I do not want to go to such a low dance; / come with the archers, / all of you protect me by the strength of your lances." Death replies: "Strong king, tyrant, who always robs / all your kingdom and fills up your treasure chest, / in doing justice you have healed very little, / as is notorious through your country."[47] The problems with kings in late medieval Castilian society were multifold. They failed to do justice to their people and they used the armed knights as bodyguards and bullies in order to rob their subjects. It is difficult not to hear the inefficacy of the Trastámara royal government in response to commoner petitions.

When Death calls on the duke, he is taken by surprise as well:

> Oh, what evil news is this! ... I had thought to do battle: / wait for me a little, Death, I beg you, / for if you do not stop, I fear that soon / you will seize me or kill me; I will have to leave / all my delights, for I cannot be / such that my soul should escape from that lasting fire. [Death says] Powerful duke, cunning and brave, / now is not the time to make delays, / join in the dance with good countenance, / leave to others your horse tack: / never will you be able to prime your falcons, / to join the joust nor participate in tournaments; / now you have to end your desires.[48]

Like the king, the duke is a man whose life is centered on battle and horsemanship. He is not ready for death because he knows that his sinful life will result in damnation. Without much difficulty, we can imagine a peasant enjoying the poem, snickering about Death's sarcastic jibes at the duke's power and bravery, feeling no regret if such a fate were visited on a lord such as the duke of Arjona.[49] When the peasant is called by Death, we

---

[47] "Dança general de la muerte," in *Poesía crítica y satírica del siglo XV*, ed. Julio Rodríguez Puértolas (Madrid: Clásicos Castalia, 1984), 48. "*Dize el Rey:* ¡Valía, valía, los mis caballeros! / Yo non quería ir a tan baxa dança; / llegad vos con los ballesteros, / amparadme todos por fuerça lança ... *Dize la Muerte:* Rey fuerte, tirano, que siempre robastes / todo vuestro reino e fenchistes el arca, / de fazer justiçia muy poco curastes, / según es notorio por vuestra comarca."

[48] Ibid., 49–50. "*Dize el Duque:* ¡Oh, qué malas nuevas son éstas ... Yo tenía pensado de fazer batalla: / espérame un poco, muerte, yo te ruego, / si non te detienes, miedo he que luego / me prendas o me mates; habré de dexar / todos mis deleites, ca non puedo estar / que mi alma escape de aquel duro fuego. *Dize la Muerte:* Duque poderoso, ardid e valiente, / non es ya tiempo de dar dilaçiones / andad en la dança con buen continente / dexad a los otros vuestras guarniçiones: / jamás non podredes çebar los halcones, / ordenar las justas nin fazer torneos; / aquí habrán fin los vuestros deseos."

[49] The Dance of Death has been well studied as a piece of art and literature, but has received somewhat less attention from historians. One of the few studies that does an excellent job of connecting the Castilian "dança" to late medieval society and social criticism is Helena Alonso García de Rivera, "Estructuras sociales en la Baja Edad Media Española según el anónimo 'Dança General de la Muerte,'" *Revista de folklore*, no. 388 (2014): 26–43. Rivera argues that the poem represents typical understandings of each of

see one of the few moments when Death is less sarcastic. The peasant, like everyone else, protests Death's arrival, asking, "How should the villein dance / who never raised his hand from the plowshare?" and asking Death for another labor. Death's reply is almost salvific for the tired peasant, who, like everyone else, cannot avoid joining the dance. Death says, "If your work was always without artifice, / not making furrows in the land of others, / you will have a great part in eternal glory."[50] Though certainly far from the reality of Trastámara Castile, the thought of dukes and kings being punished for their violent depredations while the hard-working peasant shared in the glory of God must have been a pleasant fantasy.

Why did social violence continue unabated in Trastámara Castile? Kings were publicly sympathetic to the plight of commoners and regularly legislated punishments for knights and men-at-arms who perpetrated such violence. As we saw in the last chapter, there was a political component to the inability of kings to control knightly violence. We must recall that a key component of knightly political violence was an ideology that valorized knightly independence from an overbearing king. It was the *right* of knights to act independently of the king. Similarly, social violence continued because the chivalric framework of knightly violence was something larger than any of the early Trastámara kings. They were unable to check knightly impulses which were supported by chivalric ideology. In the absence of any higher earthly power controlling knightly social violence, it was left to the knights themselves to police their behavior. Conversely, even when the Trastámara kings wished to stop noble violence, they had little means to actually do so. The only effective way to stop knights from performing violence was to send other knights to physically prevent violence from being done. In other words, kings could enforce decrees designed to rein in violence only by sending knights to fight knights. In all cases, the chivalric elite of late medieval Castile would oversee any resolution of social violence or lack thereof.

---

the characters called by Death. For example, the knight, whose calling was violence, is portrayed in the poem as a man whose life revolves around violence. Rivera notes that only three figures escape damnation in the poem, each perceived to be purer and more humble members of society: the peasant, the monk, and the hermit. In contrast, she notes, the poem was designed to be a scathing condemnation of the powerful in society, especially powerful lay figures, but also powerful religious figures. For more general studies on the Dance of Death in medieval Europe see Sophie Oosterwijk and Stefanie Knoell, eds., *Mixed Metaphors: The Danse Macabre in Medieval and Early Modern Europe* (Newcastle upon Tyne: Cambridge Scholars Publishing, 2011); and Elina Gertsman, *The Dance of Death in the Middle Ages: Image, Text, Performance* (Turnhout, Belgium: Brepols, 2010).

[50] "Dança general de la muerte," 59. "*Dize el Labrador:* ¿Cómo conviene dançar al villano / que nunca la mano sacó de la reja? ... *Dize la Muerte:* Si vuestro trabajo fue siempre sin arte, / non faziendo surco en la tierra ajena, / en la gloria eternal habredes gran parte ..."

The Ideology of Social Superiority and Social Violence

Because chivalric social violence did not exist in an ideological vacuum it could not easily be reined in. Late medieval knights were not simply beasts who acted on amygdalar impulses. They thought about their place in society and they thought about what that meant concerning the exercise of violence. Chivalry, sitting at the heart of late medieval Castilian social violence, asserted that knights and men-at-arms were fundamentally different from, even intrinsically better than, those below them in the social scale because the chivalric elite alone had a claim to honor, which implied a right to practice violence. The idea that chivalric warfare was a mark of social superiority is not new. Francisco García Fitz has argued convincingly that the martial role of knights helped to create their social identity. Where Fitz emphasized that knights derived their social prestige from *warfare*, I wish to emphasize that it was through violence more broadly defined, including violence at home, in minor wars, or even in tussles with locals or neighbors, that social identity was created.[51] A peasant or merchant could not win honor as knights conceived of it and therefore had no right to commit violence, especially against their social betters. Bound up with the right to honor and the right to violence was a knight's bloodline, or *linaje*. A viable *linaje* guaranteed that a man was of knightly or arms-bearing status.

Legally, the rights of commoners were curtailed, while knights and nobles had a number of unique legal rights and privileges. The basic assumptions of Castilian law were that commoners and knights were inherently different kinds of people. In the *Siete Partidas*, the great law code of the late 13th century which was fêted by the Trastámara nobility, knights enjoyed special privileges and rights by virtue of their possession of honor. Impeachment, for example, was a process wherein a nobleman was accused of wrongdoing or dishonoring someone else of rank; this legal process was reserved for fellow noblemen.[52] The law was very clear that only nobles could bring an impeachment against a fellow nobleman, because it opened an avenue for the accuser to redeem his honor. Several means for responding to an impeachment existed, including, importantly, a trial by battle. An impeached nobleman could respond to the accusation with a martial challenge to his accuser, in which case, the man left standing on the field would be the legal victor.[53] Because commoners could not have their honor impugned

---

[51] Francisco García Fitz, "'Las guerras de cada día en la Castilla del siglo XIV," in *Edad Media. Revista de Historia*, 8 (2007), 145–181.
[52] Samuel Parsons Scott provides the term "impeachment" as a translation of the term "riepto". *Las Siete Partidas*, trans. Samuel Parsons Scott and ed. Robert I. Burns, S.J., vol. 5 (Philadelphia: University of Pennsylvania Press, 2001), 1322.
[53] *Las Siete Partidas del Sabio Rey don Alonso el nono, nueuemente Glosadas por el Licenciado Gregorio Lopez del Consejo Real de Indias de su Magestad* (Salamanca: Boletin

by a knight or nobleman, they could not bring a charge of impeachment. Therefore, violent retribution under the law was not a possibility for a non-noble. The *Partidas* enshrined in law the ideoogical separation between the chivalric and the subchivalric on the basis of a person's honor.

Punishments for crimes were similarly different for knights and for those below the knightly class. For homicide, a knight was to be banished to some remote area, but a person of low degree was to be executed. In both cases, the criminal's property was to be dealt with as though he were dead.[54] From a legal standpoint, a knight's public persona, his public reputation, ability, and existence, indeed all the features of a man's honor, were the equivalent of a commoner's life. Knightly honor was something at least as precious as an ordinary man's existence. Similarly, the *Partidas*, as an expression of royal intent as much as chivalric ethos, even tried to forbid precisely some of the violence we have seen committed, specifically stating that anyone who should use weapons and armed men to set fire to houses and crops ought to be punished. Again, though, the punishment varied based on the social standing of the criminal. Nobles and men of distinction who committed such a crime were to be banished, their honor suffering the punishment. An inferior man was to be punished by being thrown into the fire that he started or, if he should be found after the damage was done, he was to be burned to death.[55] The weight of the Castilian law code may well have been one component of the difficulty that the Trastámara kings encountered as they futilely attempted to proscribe noble violence during the proceedings of the *cortes*.

The legal process as much as legal punishments functioned differently for the knightly class. The *Partidas* decreed that knights were capable of committing two kinds of offenses: those which were unique to knighthood and those which were forbidden to everyone. In the former class were offenses such as selling arms or disobeying military orders. Knights guilty of these offenses could be arrested, tried, or punished only by the king or their military commander. For other offenses, such as murder, robbery, and the use of force, knights could be arrested and taken before local magistrates, who could decide their guilt and prescribe punishment. For any knightly crime which required punishment, though, the magistrate had to send the knight to the king or the knight's military commander, who would then decide whether and how severely the knight ought to be punished.[56] While the law code of medieval Castile was generally quite progressive in its insist-

---

Oficial del Estado, 1555), Part. 7, Tit. 3, Ley 1. While I have cited the 1555 edition of the *Partidas*, readers may find it useful to consult the English language translation by Scott, cited in n. 52.

[54] Ibid., Part. 7, Tit. 8, Ley 15.
[55] Ibid., Part. 7, Tit. 10, Ley 9.
[56] Ibid., Part. 7, Tit. 29, Ley 3.

ence that all free men had recourse to the law, exceptions were carved out and special rights were built in for knights and noblemen. These people had institutional advantages which reflect an ideological framework that held knightly and noble lives to be fundamentally more valuable than the lives of commoners, primarily because of their accumulation of honor and their ability to defend that honor violently.

The legal division of knights and commoners was buttressed with cultural expressions of knightly superiority and special privilege. From the chivalric perspective, peasants and commoners were often valued roughly equivalent with livestock. A fictional raid recorded in the *Mocedades de Rodrigo* describes a count and his company bringing war to his neighbor by attacking his shepherds and stealing his livestock. The neighbor responds by setting fire to homes and fortifications, and taking his neighbor's possessions. "[A]nd [the neighbor] takes [the count's] vassals and all they have in their hands, / and he takes their livestock, all the ones grazing in the fields, / and he takes to their dishonour the washerwomen washing at the water's edge."[57] The two men agree to do battle and, as a sign of good faith, the neighbor gives back some of the count's washerwomen and vassals but keeps the livestock he has plundered. As a result, the battle continues. In short, the knights could have fought over any of the captured chattels, whether they were humans or animals.[58] Indeed, at times, it is easy to believe that knights saw certain animals as more valuable and worthwhile than the peasants working the land. In a later episode in the same poem, a Muslim army has invaded Castile and their army has brought along stolen livestock and Christian captives. Rodrigo smashes the enemy army and recaptures the livestock and the captive Christians. These two kinds of chattel are grouped together in the poem and, in fact, the king of Castile is truly delighted when he sees the recovered livestock grazing in the field.[59] No further mention is made of the human loot.

At times, we might be forgiven for believing that Castilian knights even valued some animals *above* human life precisely because some animal life was considered chivalric itself. The most clearly chivalric animal, naturally enough, was the horse, which carried knights into battle and which exhib-

---

[57] *Las Mocedades de Rodrigo: The Youthful Deeds of Rodrigo, the Cid*, ed. and trans. Matthew Bailey (Toronto: University of Toronto Press, 2007), 74–75. I have used Bailey's translation here instead of supplying my own, which would be inferior to Bailey's. Bailey's edition includes the original language on p. 40: "e trae los vassallos e quanto tienen en las manos, / e trae los ganados, quantos andant por el campo, / e tráele por dessonra las lavanderas, que al agua están lavando." It is noteworthy here that the washerwomen are referred to as having their own honor. As we will see in Chapter 5, the reference here is likely to a woman's sexual honor rather than to anything like the honor we have seen with knights and men-at-arms.

[58] Ibid., 75. Original language on p. 40.

[59] Ibid., 79. Original language on p. 44–45.

ited the characteristics of chivalry. Gutierre Díez de Games, describing Pero Niño in the heat of battle during an encounter with the Granadans, gushes over the chivalric nature of Pero Niño's horse. As the enemy attacked the great knight with stones the horse began to turn back, much to its rider's displeasure. Feeling Pero Niño's will, the horse, which was "good and loyal," turned back around and charged into the enemy.[60] The knight fought on and soon found himself surrounded by the enemy, who were overwhelming him. As he turned his horse to return to his men, he saw that the horse had lost a great deal of blood and was dying. In lamentation, Díez writes, "the horse was of good nature, and although its strength failed it because of the blows and great wounds which had been given it, its heart did not fail it, and it brought its lord out of that place … and shortly thereafter the good horse fell dead on the ground, its stomach and guts hanging out through many places."[61] Roland or Olivier would appreciate such a death for their steeds. *The Book of the Knight Zifar* similarly valorizes horses as chivalric creatures. Indeed, the plot of the first half of the book is driven by the terrible curse suffered by Zifar: any horse he rides will drop dead after ten days. The practical problems associated with this are clear, but Zifar and his wife also express the emotional challenge of doomed horses. The connection between knight and horse is even *explicitly* commented on by Díez, who claims that knights are "robust, and strong, without fear, and brave … there is no animal more concordant to the knight than the good horse."[62] We cannot imagine a knight writing so effusively of a peasant or merchant or laborer.

Other animals, as well, were more valuable than people as a result of their chivalric virtues. In *The Book of the Knight Zifar*, the devil tempts the Emperor Roboán by telling him that his wife has three secret prizes. Unbeknownst to Roboán, if he should ask his wife for each of these three prizes, husband and wife will never see one another again and the empress will be left disconsolate and empty for the rest of her life. The three prizes that are able to tempt this great knight and emperor are a powerful hunting mastiff, unrivalled in its ability to take down stags and boars; a beautiful hawk which could seize any kind of bird, including ostriches; and a horse whiter than snow and swifter than any other steed. The emperor fails this test, gaining each of these animals and leaving the empress forever.[63] Though this is

---

[60] Díez de Games, *El Victorial*, 291.
[61] Ibid., 292. "el cauallo hera de buena natura, e avnque le falleszía le fuerza, de los golpes e grandes feridas que la auían dado, non le fallesçía el caraçón, porque sacó a su señor de tal lugar… e dende a poco cayó el buen cavallo muerto en tierra, colgando las barrigas e las tripas fuera por muchos lugares."
[62] Ibid. "hombres rebustos e fuertes, sin temor, e esforçados; por ende, no es enimalía más concordante al cavallero que es el buen cavallo."
[63] *El Libro del Cauallero Zifar*, ed. Charles Philip Wagner (Norwood, MA: The Plimpton Press, 1929), 461–480.

meant to be a moral lesson, it is difficult to imagine many knights refusing such a powerful temptation. Each of these types of animals, especially the horse, was precious to late medieval knights because they represented their own ideals and pleasures; these were animals used in battle or the hunt. In the grand chivalric worldview, the world was essentially divided into the chivalric and the non-chivalric. Knights, ladies, and men-at-arms, horses, hounds, and hawks were in the former group while peasants, burgesses, and merchants, cattle, sheep, and pigs were in the latter.

The final component of establishing an honor-based social hierarchy lies in the concept of *linaje*. Many knights and chivalric authors could point to the prestigious and ancient *linajes* to which they belonged. Lineage and the honor that was attached to it was crucial enough that it became one of the markers of social identity; it marked someone as worthy of social status, of knighthood, and of the right to commit violence. Similarly, low lineage, or *bajo linaje*, was a damning accusation used to question a man's ability and right to action. Several of our chivalric biographies open with a glorious investigation of the hero's *linaje*. These introductions serve to establish for the reader that the man in question was born with a certain amount of honor simply by virtue of his ancestors. The first chapter of the *Crónica de don Álvaro de Luna*, for example, appropriately titled "Of the diversities of *linajes*, and of the house and *linaje* of don Álvaro de Luna, Master of Santiago and Constable of Castile," begins by explaining that the best men are those who descend from a glorious and pure *linaje* because they receive the virtue and glory of the acts of their predecessors. These men not only receive such glory from their ancestors, but also understand that it is incumbent upon them to work night and day to maintain the nobility and greatness of their *linaje* and to achieve new fame for their family through great deeds. The author then assures his reader that Álvaro de Luna was exactly this kind of man.[64] Although the author assures his reader that he will be brief in recounting the deeds of the Luna *linaje*, he goes on to recount in detail the deeds of Álvaro's ancestors, father, and uncles, men who achieved greatness in serving Enrique de Trastámara during the civil war that brought him to the throne, in fighting for the Trastámara monarchs, and, in one famous case, in being acclaimed as Pope Benedict XIII (r. 1394–1423) by "all the world."[65] Few men could hope to have a more glorious and acclaimed *linaje*.

Gutierre Díez de Games similarly labors to emphasize Pero Niño's ancestry. He acknowledges that Pero Niño was not a man of great estate –

---

[64] *Crónica de don Álvaro de Luna*, ed. Juan de Mata Carriazo (Madrid: Espasa-Calpe, S.A., 1940), 8.

[65] Benedict XIII was pope during the western schism and was thus not recognized by much of the Christian world, let alone all of it. For the author of a Luna biography, of course, this was a point that had to be made as vigorously as possible. *Crónica de don Álvaro de Luna*, 8–13.

that is, he was not wealthy — but one of Díez' first priorities is to outline the great knight's *linaje*. Just as the Lunas had generations of great knights fighting for their kings, the Niños also fought for the Trastámaras, finding success and an increase in their honor and glory on the battlefields of the civil war of the 1360s. In particular, Pero Niño's father, Juan Niño, was a man who had performed great deeds on the battlefield, though he was not always on the winning side of the intrigues of Trastámara politics. Nonetheless, Díez emphasizes that Pero Niño's ability to be a great knight was bound up with his *linaje*. Because the Niños had served the Trastámara kings, because they had been good knights, because they had accumulated honor for themselves, Pero Niño was in a position to build upon the name of his family. In a very practical sense, Pero Niño was raised in the household of the king because his father had been close to the royal family. In a more ideological sense too, his family's honor spurred him both to defend the honor he was born with and to perform great deeds of arms in order that the honor of his family would be increased.

In both of these cases, the concept of *linaje* serves as the starting point for understanding the glorious lives of great knights whose careers, naturally, were characterized by the exercise of violence. *Linaje*, a marker of social superiority, served as a precondition in the minds of these authors for an honorable life of prowess and achievement. Without having the pedigree of great knights, neither Álvaro de Luna nor Pero Niño, in the eyes of their biographers, would have had the hereditary framework to perform great deeds. Their sense of honor extending back through generations of ancestors was central to their understanding of themselves and their public personas in late medieval Castile.

Two collections of short profiles of notable Castilians in the 15th century, Fernán Pérez de Guzmán's *Generaciones y Semblanzas* and Fernando del Pulgar's *Claros Varones de Castilla*, exhibit the same consciousness of *linaje* seen in chivalric biographies. Indeed, in both of these collections, the authors follow a fairly neat formula in describing their subject, the first component of which is describing the subject's *linaje*.[66] Such a formulaic approach itself testifies to the importance of *linaje* in the intellectual environment of Castilian knights. Thirteen of the fifteen knights that Pulgar describes receive some account of their *linaje*. Fernan Álvares de Toledo, the count of Alba, for example, was "the son of Garci Álvares de Toledo and the grandson of Fernando Álvares de Toledo; he was of a noble *linaje* of the ancient knights of that city."[67] Diego Hurtado de Mendoza, the duke of the

---

[66] For an assessment of Guzmán's literary and historical framework, see Robert Folger, *Generaciones y semblanzas: Memory and Genealogy in Medieval Iberian Historiography* (Tübingen, Germany: Gunter Narr Verlag Tübingen, 2003.

[67] Fernando del Pulgar, *Claros varones de Castilla* (Buenos Aires: Espasa-Calpe Argentina, S.A., 1948), 46. "Don Fernan Áluares de Toledo, conde de Alua, fijo de Garci

Infantado, was "the son of the Marqués don Iñigo Lopez de Mendoza, and grandson of the admiral don Diego Furtado … He was of a most ancient noble Castilian *linaje*."[68] In the dozen or so other cases, the language is similar, with Pulgar recounting in the first or second sentence his subject's parentage and *linaje*. Guzmán's approach is similar and perhaps even more explicit. As Guzmán describes each of his subjects, he notes not only the man's immediate parentage, but describes at some length the man's *linaje*. Diego López de Estúñiga, "on the side of his father, … was of [the house of] Estúñiga. The manor of this *linaje* is in Navarre. I heard tell of them that the Estúñigas are descended from the kings of Navarre … On the side of his mother, he came from the Horoscos, a good *linaje* of knights."[69] That both Guzmán and Pulgar place an assessment of a man's *linaje* before any other assessment demonstrates its central importance. A good *linaje* could speak to a man's public persona – to his honor – before his own deeds or reputation could. A man might tarnish, maintain, or augment the honor and reputation left to him by his family, but it was the foundation upon which all else was built. In short, a man's *linaje* was the first means of judging his standing in society.

Only a few individuals in either collection were men of or close to *bajo linaje* and they fall into two categories. In the first are those men who sit right on the edge of having low lineage, often men of *hidalgo* ancestry but not members of one of the great *linajes*. These men parlayed what little lineage they had into something greater through great deeds of arms. Pulgar mentions Juan de Saavedra, "an *hidalgo* knight" for whom the author offers no *linaje*. Saavedra's honor, though, was never in doubt because he spent all his life fighting on the southern frontier against the Muslim enemy.[70] The holy war, as we will see in the next chapter, functioned as the superlative means for a man to accumulate honor beyond that with which he was born. Even a relatively minor *linaje* could be built into something larger. In the second category are men who were clearly of *bajo linaje* and for whom

---

Áluares de Toledo, e nieto de [Fernando Álvarez de Toledo], era de linaje noble de los antiguos caualleros de aquella ciudad."

[68] Ibid., 72. "Don Diego Hurtado de Mendoça, duque del Infantadgo, marqués de Santillana, e conde del Real de Mançanares, fijo del marqués don Iñigo Lopes de Mendoça, e nieto del almirante don Diego Hurtado … Era de linaje noble castellano muy antiguo."

[69] Fernán Pérez de Guzmán, *Generaciones y semblanzas* (Buenos Aires: Espasa-Calpe Argentina, S.A., 1947), 32. "De parte del padre, fue de Astuñiga. El solar de este linaje es en Nauarra. Yo oy dizir a algunos dellos, que los d'Estúñiga vienen de los reyes de Nauarra … De parte de su madre, venia este Diego Lopez de los de Horosco, un buen linaje de caualleros."

[70] Pulgar, *Claros varones*, 94. In a similar case, Pulgar mentioned Rodrigo de Narvaes, "an *hidalgo* knight" whose *linaje* is left unmentioned but who fought against the Muslims throughout his career. 95–98.

this was indicative of greater problems. Fernán Alfonso de Robles, a man of *bajo linaje*, was a clerk who acquired the favor of Queen Catalina of Lancaster and managed to wield some power in her entourage. Guzmán is clear about the effects of this man of low *linaje* wielding any power. Instead of the honor so valued and jealously guarded by knights, this man brought "no small confusion and shame to Castile," because too many of the great knights and señores of the kingdom "to a man of such low condition as this should submit themselves."[71] In other words, a man of low lineage finding power at court was an inversion of the appropriate social order. Instead of honor, knights would experience shame because of such an event; instead of building on the glory of their own *linajes*, they dishonored their ancestors in allowing such a man to wield power. Guzmán even acknowledges that there is no good reason to include a biography of this man, saying:

> I should make such singular mention now of this Ferrand Alonso de Robles, not because his *linaje* nor condition should require that he, amidst such noble and notable men, should be written about, but in order to demonstrate the vices and defects of Castile in the present time.[72]

The very reality that a man of low lineage should wield power represented a serious defect for Castilian society.

As in the case of Fernán Alfonso de Robles, there were moments when men of low *linaje* achieved positions of power. For a clerk in the queen's entourage, there was no redeeming quality. For others, low *linaje* would remain a tool of their political rivals and enemies even as they found success through martial ability and the favor of the king. The great Miguel Lucas de Iranzo himself was a man without a clear *linaje* and his enemies would continue to level this charge against him throughout his career, suggesting that he attained a position of power only through inappropriate, perhaps homosexual, liaisons with the king. Unlike the authors of *El Victorial* or the *Crónica de Don Álvaro*, the author of Iranzo's biography, *Hechos del condestable don Miguel Lucas de Iranzo*, does not begin with an assessment of Iranzo's *linaje*, precisely because Iranzo did not have a great *linaje* to his name. Aware of this shortcoming, Iranzo's biographer instead spends a significant section of the early part of the work ignoring his *linaje* and instead emphasizing his service and devotion to King Enrique IV. With the spectacle of various noblemen shouting "Nobility! Nobility! Nobility!" Miguel Lucas was raised to his position as a baron of the realm and was

---

[71] Pérez de Guzmán, *Generaciones*, 67. "Non pequeña confusion e vergueña para Castilla que los grandes perlados e vaualleros … que a un onbre de tan baxa condiçion como este asi se sometiesen."

[72] Ibid., 69. "Fazese aqui tan singular mençion deste Ferrand Alonso de Robles, non porque su linaje nin condiçion requiriese que el, entre tantos nobles e notables, se escriuiese, mas por mostrar los viçios e defetos de Castilla en el presente tienpo."

invested as a knight.[73] Instead of focusing on Iranzo's *linaje*, the author relies on a created nobility for the Constable. But not everyone was prepared to accept the author's glossing-over of Iranzo's low birth. Diego de Valera, the famous knight, treatise writer, and historian, jealously observed the rise of Iranzo and others during the reign of Enrique IV. Valera wrote of Iranzo that he was a man of little estate and low *linaje* and noted that, despite these flaws, he had been made a baron and Constable of Castile in the space of a day. King Enrique's favor of Iranzo, Valera cries acridly, should be "no small marvel to those who see it, because it did not follow from merits, nor *linaje*, nor virtues" – all components that would have rightly awarded such honors to men of high *linaje*.[74] Chivalry asserted that one's lineage was a social marker that made one's actions and behaviors legitimate by default. The absence of *linaje*, implying a commoner background, meant that a man was not entitled to the same rights, dignities, and honor that a knight would be. Though we have several examples of men who overcame low *linaje*, their lack of acceptable ancestry haunted them in the vicious world of Castilian politics and rivalries.

If we accept that the knightly class of Trastámara Castile had established for itself a uniquely privileged position, based on honor, *linaje*, and violence, we still must ask how this translated into violence committed against commoners. What honor was there to be gained from killing peasants and burning down their fields? After all, in theory, the greatest honor for medieval Castilian knights was ideally found in fighting strong enemies or fighting the infidel. Knights saw their profession, though, as blessed by God and worthy of an increase in honor, no matter whom they fought against. Early in *El Victorial*, Díez includes a chapter titled "How Our Lord Jesus Christ wanted that the victors in battle should be honored." Díez goes through a list of great knights in history, from Joshua to Judas Maccabeus to Charlemagne to the crusaders of the 11th century and notes that all of them fought and won many battles and were honored by God and men for their deeds of arms. It is perhaps noteworthy that a number of these great knights were famous for burning down cities, massacring populations, and wreaking havoc among the enemy. Judas Maccabeus, for example, regularly slaughtered citizens and burned towns to the ground. It is not that Díez is valorizing violence against the poor and downtrodden, but that he simply is not truly concerned about the welfare of those who had die to produce honor for his lord. And, more importantly, Díez firmly believed that a great knight wins honor and plaudits from God in any battle, whether it is single

---

[73] *Hechos del condestable Don Miguel Lucas de Iranzo*, ed. Juan de Mata Carriazo (Madrid: Espasa-Calpe, S.A., 1940), 7–13.
[74] Valera, "Memorial de diversas hazañas", 17. "no poco fueron maravillados todos los que lo vieron, porque no parecia preceder merecimientos, ni linage, ni virtudes...."

combat against another great knight or general hell-raising among a peasant or urban population.

Violence of the type we have seen knights committing – burning down crops, plundering towns, killing peasants – was also a legitimate way for a knight of borderline *linaje* to prove himself to his peers. If his *linaje* and family honor was present but questionable, he might erase the doubts of his fellow knights by performing any sort of violence, confirming that he was a member of the chivalry and knew how and when to perform violence. One of the knights of borderline *linaje* in Pulgar's collection of profiles was a man named Rodrigo de Villandrando. Pulgar describes him as "the son of an *hidalgo* squire, a native of the ville of Valladolid."[75] He was a man of some ancestry, but without a strong claim to a great *linaje* populated with vigorous knights of generations past. Finding himself "young and poor and alone," Villandrando did what a good knight ought to do in his situation: he travelled to France, where the Hundred Years' War was raging, and joined a company of foreign fighters. In that company, Pulgar gushes, "he did those things which a young man ought to do, and he won through his arms estimation as a valiant and vigorous man."[76] By now we might suspect that the "things which a young man ought to do" are not romantically inspired individual combats against a fellow knight. Pulgar confirms this:

> And as the fame of his courage and of the prisoners he had taken were divulged through the land, there came to him some men, and his heart increasing day by day with his deeds, and his deeds with the men, and the men with the interest, there came to him many more men ... until he was captain of ten thousand men, and his power was of the greatest of the captains who served the King of France. And with that, his great power, he robbed, and burned, and destroyed, and demolished, and depopulated villes and places and towns in Burgundy and France ...[77]

On hearing of such worthy behavior, King Juan II of Castile sent a message to Villandrando ordering him to return to Castile to fight against the factions that had formed in Castile. Villandrando's exceptional talents, demonstrated in France and maintained in Castile, won him special recognition from Juan II: he was raised to a count, given the ville of Ribadeo, and

---

[75] Pulgar, *Claros varones*, 58. "Don Rodrigo de Vallandrando, conde de Ribadeo, fué fijo de un escudero fijodalgo natural de la villa de Valladolid ..."
[76] Ibid. "e después en las cosas que omme mancebo deue fazer, que ganó por las armas estimación de omme valiente e esforçado ..."
[77] Ibid., 59–60. "E como la fama de su valentía e de las presas que tomaua se diuulgó por la tierra, llegáronse a él algunos ommes, e creciendo de día en día el coraçon con las fazañas, e las fazañas con la gente, e la gente con el interese, allegáronse a él muchas más gentes, fasta ... ser capitán de dies mil ommes, e su poder fué de os mayores que tenía ninguno de los otros capitanes del rey de Francia a quien seruía. E con aquel su grand poder robó, quemó, destruyó, derribó, despobló villas e logares e pueblos de Borgoña e de Francia ..."

he and his descendants were invited to eat at the king's table. What better way to confirm to skeptical peers that a man was of noble *linaje* than by perpetrating violence against the common folk, a social marker in itself?[78] Vigorous fighting was itself the primary means of achieving honor. Medieval knights and authors developed nuance by adding layers of increasing honor – fighting against great knights, religious enemies, or in the king's service may have been *better* means of winning honor, but fighting against peasants was still a worthwhile endeavor.

Once in a while, imaginative literature offers a neat capsulation of the chivalric framework of social violence. In an early episode from *El Libro del Cauallero Zifar*, the knight Zifar, who has fallen on hard times, is on foot, leading his wife on his horse. Another knight approaches and, believing Zifar and his wife to be commoners, orders them to leave the area. When Zifar refuses, the other knight declares that he will kill Zifar for his insolence and do with the woman what he pleases. Zifar, his honor offended, insists that the other knight cannot do violence to a fellow *hidalgo* without cause, to which the other knight responds "How can you pretend to be a knight, being that you are a servant of this woman!?" The other knight then issues a sardonic challenge to Zifar. "If you are a knight, climb up on this woman's horse and defend her!"[79] For these literary knights, a knight is within his rights to kill commoners if they defy him. If the other knight had known that Zifar was himself a knight, this encounter would have unfolded differently. In the event, the only way in which Zifar can defend himself is by violently proving himself to actually be a knight himself.

Chivalric social identity was founded first of all on the assumption that a social chasm separated knights from commoners – the two were not meant to mix. The chivalric framework of this chasm was rooted in the concept of honor. Knights and men-at-arms were born with the honor bestowed upon them by their ancestors, while commoners and their brood were akin to a litter of pigs.[80] In life, honor was a force that allowed knights to defend themselves violently and to preemptively attack another. Commoners, with no honor to speak of, had no right to commit violence. We might insist from a modern perspective that commoners did indeed have honor and

---

[78] For an explanation of the economic incentives of social violence, see Rosa Maria Montero Tejada, "Violencia y abusos en los señoríos del linaje Manrique a fines de la Edad Media," in *En la España Medieval*, 20 (1997), 355.

[79] *Zifar*, 41–42. "'Commo,' dixo el otro, 'cuydades escapar por cauallero, seyendo rapas desta dueña? Sy cauallero sodes, sobit en ese cauallo de esa dueña e defendetla.'"

[80] In a much broader cultural sense, this comparison is particularly apt. The Latin legal term *sequela* denoted the children of an unfree serf. It carried an implication of the animalistic production of a litter of young, rather than the production of a human child. For a noble or knightly family, the Latin term would have been *familia*. Christopher Corèdon with Ann Williams, *A Dictionary of Medieval Terms and Phrases* (Cambridge: D.S. Brewer, 2004), 254.

rightly speculate that if their father were killed or their sister were raped they too would seek vengeance.[81] But the dominant lay elite of late medieval Castile – the knights and men-at-arms – did not recognize such a reality themselves. From a knightly perspective, the concept of a peasant vindicating honor through violence was laughable at best and frightening at worst. Finally, the framework of knightly thought offered both divine and earthly sanction and reward for violence performed against the common folk. Just as God had smiled on Judas Maccabeus, so he would smile on Castilian knights as they burned crops and fields. Just as the Lord of Heaven had needed good fighters to destroy His enemies, so the lord king needed good fighters to destroy his enemies. In the mode of warfare of late medieval Europe, this meant blessings and rewards from the king for wreaking havoc among the foundation of the economic structure: peasants, fields, urban dwellers, merchants, and infrastructure.

Contesting Chivalric Ideology: The Case of the *Irmandiños*

The nearly unrestrained violence of late medieval knights did not go on indefinitely without some response. The common folk of Castile were not willing to accept their ongoing destruction and persecution. Instead, at several moments in the 15th century, the common people rose up against the chivalric elite and violently demanded a solution to the problem. Of the several popular risings in the Kingdom of Castile in this period, the largest and best attested is the series of revolts in Galicia known as the *Irmandiños* revolts.[82] These revolts were based in the largest *hermandad* in Galicia, the *Santa Hermandad* (Galician *Irmandad*), an institution which, as we saw above, devolved peacekeeping and policing powers to the regional government rather than the central royal government. In 1431 and 1451 the members of the *Santa Hermandad* rose and were put down, barely making a mark in contemporary sources. In 1467, in an event with much wider significance, the *Santa Hermandad* rose again, an event that did draw the notice of chroniclers and historians. The *Irmandiños*, led by a few *hidalgos* (petty

---

[81] For evidence of violent criminal acts by the common folk, see Ricardo Córdoba de la Llave, "Violencia cotidiana en Castilla a fines de la edad media," in *Conflictos sociales, políticos e intelectuales en la España de los siglos XIV y XV*, ed. José Ignacio de la Iglesia Duarte (Logroño, Spain: Instituto de Estudios Riojanos, 2004), 393–443.

[82] There were other risings during the 15th century, some of them small and local, others regional. Rosa María Montero Tejada identifies several risings in the 1480s against the Manrique *linaje*. Like the *Irmandiños*, these risings were directed against the abuses of knights and lords. Montero Tejada, "Violencia y abusos," 366–371. See also Emilio Cabrera, "Conflictos en el mundo rural. Señores y vasallos," in *Conflictos sociales, políticos e intelectuales en la España de los siglos XIV y XV*, ed. José Ignacio de la Iglesia Duarte (Logroño, Spain: Instituto de Estudios Riojanos, 2004), 49–80.

nobility) but consisting primarily of peasants, targeted the castles and strong houses of the knights and lords of Galicia.[83] Like the rebels of the *Jacquerie* in France more than a hundred years earlier or the Catalan *Remençes* only a few years earlier, the *Irmandiños* also violently targeted knights and nobles, with gruesome stories of the attacks of the peasants. When the peasants stormed the castle of Santa Marta, for example, "they killed the Countess of Santa Marta, their *señora*, in a crude manner, cutting her into pieces."[84]

Irmandiño violence, like its chivalric counterpart, was not undirected fury; it rose out of an ideological foundation. Carlos Barros, in his unrivalled work on *Irmandiño* mentality, firmly posits two root causes of commoner dissatisfaction: (1) that the *señores* of Galicia failed to do justice as the king or his agents ought and (2) that commoners were distraught by knights and lords constantly robbing and killing the common folk.[85] Barros has identified something close to an *Irmandiño* ideology which was solidified over the course of the Trastámara period. In other words, all of the social violence that we have seen directly cultivated a popular mentality which led to several popular revolts. Peasants and commoners in the second half of the 15th century saw no other recourse to their complaints than to rise up and attack knights and lords. Even so, the *Irmandiños* does not represent an effort on the part of the peasants to do away with the knights and *señores*, even if they did attack them. Instead, the rebels had their own agenda, a program which they wished to see instituted. Teofilo Ruiz described the commoner rebels as "upholders of royal power and supporters of the very social structure that assigned them ... a subordinate position." For Ruiz and Barros alike, the rebels inserted themselves into and laid claim to what they perceived as a just and harmonious social order.[86] Cecilia Devia takes this logic a step further, arguing not only that the *Irmandiños* were articulating a social and political ideal, but that they were *returning* to a status quo wherein the *bellatores* protected the other two *ordos* of medieval society. In

---

[83] Carlos Barros, "Lo que sabemos de los Irmandiños," in *Clio et Crimen*, no. 3 (2006), 39. Since the 1990s, Barros has been the leading expert on the Irmandiños revolts and their place in Galician history. The short piece cited here is a brief but useful point summary of his years of diligence.

[84] Lope García de Salazar, *Libro de las bienandanzas e fortunas*, transcribed in Harvey L. Sharrer, "The *Irmandiño* Movement and the Revolt of 1467–69 According to Lope García de Salazar's Libro de las bienandanzas e fortunas," in *Estudios Galegos Medievais*, ed. Antonio Cortijo Ocaña, Giorgio Perissinotto, and Harver L. Sharrer (Santa Barbara, CA: Centro de Estudios Galegos, 2001), 151. "E despues que mataron los villanos de Ribadavia a la Condesa de Santa Marta, su señora, de cruda muerte, faziendola pedaços ..."

[85] Carlos Barros, *Mentalidad justiciera de los irmandiños, siglo xv* (Madrid: Siglo XXI de España Editores, S.A., 1990), 83.

[86] Teofilo Ruiz, *Spanish Society, 1400–1600* (Rochester, NY: University of Rochester Press, 2001), 194. See also Barro, *Mentalidad justiciera*.

other words, Devia accepts that before the rise of the Trastámara nobility the three *ordos* functioned as a harmonious symphony, working together to produce an ordered and peaceful society.

Certainly the common folk *wanted* such a society. A society in which the clerics prayed and the knights protected the peasants who diligently worked would have been a relatively pleasant society, especially in comparison with the society that the peasants *actually* inhabited. A few writers do lament the destruction in the realm and, like the *Irmandiños*, long for a past golden age, even if they would not condone the violence of a peasant uprising. Diego de Valera, in two letters to King Juan II in the 1440s, lamented the evils that were visited on the Kingdom of Castile. Employing a blend of theological and humanistic ideas, Valera noted that it was the king's responsibility to seek the "salvation" of his subjects through the establishment of order within the kingdom. Recalling the destruction of Spain in the 8th century, Valera implied that there was an ancient period when society worked for the protection of all its members, and he reminded the monarch that "it is not pleasing to God [that] your royal lordships are plunged into war." Finally, Valera called on Juan to restore *concordia* in his kingdoms, ending the damages and robberies and injuries and destruction that disorder and strife had brought to the kingdom. In all his exhortations to peace, Valera insists, at times explicitly and at times implicitly, that Juan can achieve once again the glories of a previous age if he can restore order to his realm.[87] Valera's call for peace, of course, largely fell on deaf ears, but even if the writer had had more influence over the events of his time, he was emphatically not embracing the violence of peasant revolt. For Valera and his more bellicose fellow knights, the peasant uprising and the ideology that accompanied it were no solution to the problems of the kingdom, but represented further evidence of disorder in society.

Most knights were not only hostile to *Irmandiño* ideology, but dismissed the legitimacy of peasant revolt altogether. Indeed, although the revolt of the *Irmandiños* is one of the best-attested risings of medieval Castilian commoners, most of the late medieval chivalric authors have little to say about it. Again, we get the sense that the activities of the common folk were simply not worth dignifying from the perspective of chivalric chroniclers. Lope García de Salazar, a Vizcayan knight and lord, compiled various documents during his life and offered a brief commentary on the uprising, one of the only chivalric authors to do so. After drily listing the numerous castles and fortifications torn down by the commoners, Salazar comments on the death of the countess of Santa Marta, calling it a "crude death."[88] Finally, he offers his thoughts on the greater historical meaning of the *Irmand-*

---

[87] BNE MSS/9263.
[88] García de Salazar, *Libro de las bienandanzas*, 151.

iños revolt, asserting that the violence was a punishment from God for the sins of the knights of Galicia. Notably, Salazar does *not* suggest that the knights' sins had anything to do with their violence, rather suggesting that they simply needed to have a bit more "discipline". He then goes on to speak briefly of the excessive cruelties and disobedience of the villeins against their natural lords, suggesting that they were only temporarily a tool of the Almighty before being put back in their proper place, rebuilding the fortifications they had torn down.[89] No ideal order based on the harmony of the three *ordos* appears in Salazar's account. Instead, things returned to normalcy when the commoners were defeated. As in European explanations of the incomprehensible Black Death or the inscrutable Mongol invasions of eastern Europe, the knightly author can find no explanation for the rising other than God's vengeance. Fernán Pérez de Guzmán, another knightly chronicler, dismisses the legitimacy of the peasants in fine Foucauldian form. In a chronicle that runs to 418 pages in a modern print edition, Guzmán uses the term *loco* – crazy or mad – only twice; once when the Infante Fernando's confessor attempts to restrict important strategic news from reaching the infante's ear, and once when describing the first rising of the *Irmandiños*. Guzmán notes that the vassals of the Galician nobleman Nuño Frayre de Andrade had risen against him because he was "saying he was a lord most forceful and severe and they could no longer suffer him and three thousand men and more made war on him … and carried a flag of Santiago."[90] According to Guzmán, King Juan II attempted to make peace between the rebels and the Galician nobles but was unable to do so because the commoners "moved so powerfully and were so crazy, that not only did they not want [to make peace] … but they attempted to violently enter into the city of Santiago," where the archbishop of Santiago defeated them in battle.[91] Like Salazar, Guzmán, a good knight, could not comprehend that the commoners had legitimate grievances or an ideological program. They were simply *loco*.

Non-chivalric chroniclers who were more sympathetic to the *Irmandiños* confirm that the reality of the rising was alien to chivalry. The chronicler Alfonso de Palencia, a man whose life was spent at court and in churches describes the behavior of well-respected knights in terms incongruous with the chivalric ethos. Palencia relates that as the peasants and commoners took

---

[89] Ibid., 151.
[90] Pérez de Guzmán, "don Juan, segundo," 493. "[É] sus vasallos de la Puente de Hume é Ferror é Villalva que eran suyas, que se habian todos levantado contra él, diciendo que era señor muy fuerte é duro é que no lo podian comportar, é hacianle guerra tres mil hombres é más … é traian un pendon de Santiago."
[91] Ibid. "los dichos hermanos se vieron tan poderosos y estaban tan locos, que no solamente no quisieron estar por cosa de lo que por los dichos Arzobispo é Obispo les fué mandado de parte del Rey, mas atentaron de entrar en la cibdad de Santiago …"

up arms the renowned knight Pero Niño, "one of the principal personages of Valladolid, and one of the infamous captains of King Enrique, fearing the rigorous punishment of the *Hermandad*, fled to Simancas."[92] Palencia also observes that the troubles in the north "added to the fear which news of various portents in different parts of the kingdom instilled, and induced the great lords of both parties [in the ongoing civil war] to seek the dissolution of the *Hermandades*."[93] Fear (*temor*) was a dangerous subject for late medieval knights. In Castilian knightly chronicles, fear is rarely ever mentioned except in warning knights not to fear death, injury, or their opponents. The only time fear is mentioned as a trait of knights is when they fear God, a noble yet humbling experience. For Palencia to observe not just one knight's fear, but to suggest that the great knights of the realm reacted to the *Irmandiños* with fear, indicates an inversion of chivalry. In a world where peasants were committing violence – an activity typically reserved for knights – against their social betters, knights initially could not react through their honor-based *modus operandi*. They sought the dissolution of the *Hermandades* in order to return the world to the way it ought to be – with commoners in the fields and cities, and not wielding weapons in a fit of topsy-turvy social violence.

No doubt there was a material interest on the part of nobles and knights. In their eyes, the *Irmandiño* rising threatened their privileged economic and political positions as well. We have good reason, though, to emphasize the role of chivalry and honor in the knightly understanding of and response to the rising. Noble political and economic privilege was conceived of in the terms of chivalry and honor. When knights and chivalric authors wrote about the rising, *they* conceived of it in chivalric rather than economic terms.

The rising of the *Irmandiños*, the most significant episode in a series of late medieval commoner revolts, ultimately reveals two realities of social violence and the knightly ideological framework in the late Middle Ages. On one hand, the *Irmandiños* rising confirms that knightly social violence was a serious problem of the period. Castilian commoners could suffer only so long the reality of knights destroying homes, burning crops, pillaging livestock, violating women, and spilling blood, leaving ashes and bones in their wake. By the end of the first century of the Trastámara period, commoners

---

[92] Palencia also refers to Pero Niño as "infamous," an indication of Palencia's antipathy toward leading knights and men-at-arms in Castile. Alfonso de Palencia, "Crónica de Enrique IV," ed. and trans. Antonio Paz y Meliá in *Biblioteca de Autores Españoles* (Madrid: Ediciones Atlas, 1973), vol. 257, 210. "Temiendo el riguroso castigo de la Hermandad huyó a Simancas D. Pedro Niño, personaje principal en Valladolid, y uno de los infames capitanes de D. Enrique …"

[93] Ibid. "Todo esto, unido al temor que infundían los avisos de diversos prodigios en diferentes partes del reino observados, indujo a los Grandes de ambos partidos a procurar la disolución de las Hermandades."

devised a political program for which they were willing to take up arms in a quixotic effort to solve the problem of chivalric social violence. On the other hand, the reaction of knights and knightly writers to the risings of the late 15th century underlines that the program of the *Irmandiños* was precisely a prescriptive program. Knights and chivalric thinkers already operated within an ideological paradigm which suited them. Unchivalric peasants and commoners, those barely human creatures that existed alongside cattle and sheep, had no right to commit violence, especially against their social betters. When precisely that event occurred, the paragons of knightly virtue were initially caught unaware, unsure of how to react. Fleeing from the armed brotherhood, perhaps motivated by the eminently unchivalric impulses of fear and confusion, knights realized that their world was being turned upside down. In the midst of a violent civil war, the chivalry of both sides briefly came together in order to put down this frightening challenge to their world.

Conclusions

Violence in late medieval Castile functioned not simply as an economic impulse nor as a ritualistic resolution of grievances. Knightly identity generally was defined by acts of violence, and knightly *social* identity was inseparable from the knightly performance of violence. Born into families with a "bank account" of honor, knights were raised knowing that they had a right to defend their honor through violence and that to be perceived well by their peers they had to wreak havoc on someone. More often than not, that someone was the commoner in the field or the city. To be sure, some knights surely sought to avoid violence against the impoverished, as Pero Niño hoped, even if the evidence for such behavior is lacking. Undoubtedly, many of the chivalric elite defended the peasants and economic resources of their territories in order to protect their own wealth and status, though this is a far cry from a noble-minded desire to protect the weak. Although knights dreamed about testing their mettle against another great knight, the reality was that honor could be sustained and increased in both this life and the next by breaking peasant bodies and property. Knights were defined socially by their martial calling, whether that meant fighting in formal wars or harassing the peasants of their neighbors.

As people who were little more than animals or chattels, commoners had no fundamental right to honor and therefore no fundamental need to violently defend or augment it. When commoners did respond to the oppression of knightly violence with organized violence of their own, it was an inversion of the knightly world order and had to be stopped at all costs. The *Irmandiños* uprising, and others like it, were moments of terror and confusion for the Castilian chivalry. Perhaps it is unsurprising that as the hierarchical pyramid of society broadened in the later Middle Ages more people sought entry into the ranks of knighthood, establishing a new *linaje* for themselves and appropriating the right to violence against efforts on the part of knights to protect their privileged status. From a social standpoint, knights exercised a near monopoly on the usage of violence. Little wonder that they would endorse and propagate an honor-based ideological framework that continued to guarantee them such a powerful claim over their fellow men.

3

Holy War

Warfare was the *raison d'être* of medieval knights. Whatever debates might have existed about the importance of courtliness, romantic love, or economic stewardship, late medieval chivalry prized warfare as its central component, idealizing prowess in battle as a valorizing achievement for which the warriors of Christian Europe ought continually to strive. Across Europe and throughout the High and Late Middle Ages, knights emulated the heroes of chivalric literature and history: Roland, El Cid, Judas Maccabeus, Godfrey de Bouillon; warfare was truly a knight's calling. Not all fighting was equally valorous, though. In the 14th century, the French knight Geoffroi de Charny outlined a hierarchy of various types of deeds of arms, each being more honorable than the last. Jousting and participating in tournaments (we might call them practice for war) are the first and second steps, certainly honorable pursuits, for they require physical strength, hardship, "crushing and wounding, and sometimes danger of death."[1] Above "practice war," Charny declares that fighting in wars, whether for oneself, for one's family, or for one's lord, accrues great honor to a knight. He initially calls fighting in war the highest honor that a man can find in this world, "for it is from good battles that great honors arise and are increased, for good fighting men prove themselves in good battles."[2] Upon further reflection, Charny recognizes one particular form of warfare which is better than others, asserting that

> the man who makes war against the enemies of religion in order to support and maintain Christianity and the worship of Our Lord is engaged in a war which is righteous, holy, certain, and sure, for his earthly body will be honored in a saintly fashion and his soul will, in a short space of time, be borne in holiness and without pain into paradise ... [O]ne can lose in [religious war] neither one's reputation in this world nor one's soul.[3]

---

[1] Richard W. Kaeuper and Elspeth Kennedy, *The Book of Chivalry of Geoffroi de Charny: Text, Context, and Translation* (Philadelphia: University of Pennsylvania Press, 1996), 85–87.
[2] Ibid., 91.
[3] Ibid., 165.

For Charny, then, all war was positive and rewarding to a knight, but religious warfare was the highest good. We might expect that chivalry on the south side of the Pyrenees would look somewhat different; historians have convincingly argued that societies on the religious frontier in Iberia were often more tolerant of their Muslim neighbors than were their northern European neighbors, at least up until the second half of the 15th century. Despite this tolerance, Castilian chivalry in the late Middle Ages was remarkably similar to that of France or England concerning warfare. The ideas expressed by Charny were applicable south of the Pyrenees as well.

The idea of holy war in the Castilian context has a messy historiography, developed over recent centuries. In the 19th and early 20th centuries, Spanish historians, seeking to locate the unique national history of a united Spain, articulated the concept of the *reconquista* as a united effort on the part of all Spaniards to push back the Muslim conquest and reestablish a united Catholic Spanish kingdom, beginning at the moment of the Islamic invasion in 711 and continuing until its fulfillment in 1492.[4] Historians in the early 20th century also argued that the reality of the 800-year *reconquista* was what gave Spain its unique history among European nations. Claudio Sánchez Albornoz, for example, argued that no other nation experienced such a long and continuous struggle against the Islamic world.[5] With the benefit of hindsight, we can see multiple problems with such an interpretation. The 800 years between the Islamic invasion and the conquest of Granada saw changes in ideological, political, military, and religious situations. There is not a single history of *reconquista*, nor of the Islamic presence in Iberia. We must ascribe the concept of historically driven holy war to a very particular historical context with a very particular historical purpose. In this chapter we will use the term *reconquista* to refer to a specific idea at the heart of the chivalric framework of holy war – the idea that Castilian knights had a historical imperative to reclaim lands taken from them by the Muslims. Holy war itself was larger than *reconquista*, although in late medieval Castile the two concepts become closely linked.

Contemporary historians have considered the ideological development of holy war at some length. Francisco García Fitz, for example, has argued that the key to a medieval understanding of the process of holy war in Iberia was the nuanced and sometimes confused differentiation between holy war

---

[4] Ramón Menéndez Pidal, *Los españoles en la Historia* (Madrid: Espasa-Calpe, S.A., 1947)
[5] Sánchez Albornoz agreed with Américo Castro in positing the question of how different history would have been if the Muslim armies in 711 had landed not at Gibraltar but at Marseilles. The implication, of course, is that the Muslim presence, and the consequent Christian effort to repel that presence, was Spain's own unique struggle. Claudio Sánchez Albornoz, *España, un enigma histórico* (Buenos Aires: Editorial Sudamericana, 1956), vol. 2, 596–597.

and Augustinian just war. Drawing on clerical writers (and a few knightly writers) throughout the Middle Ages, Fitz concludes that late medieval thinkers focused on the injustice of the Islamic conquest and worked to restore justice in the world by reclaiming the territory for Christians.[6] Indeed, the concept of righting a historical wrong was central to the knights and men-at-arms of Trastámara Castile, and the old clerical theology of holy war continued to inform their actions.[7] We must add to Fitz' argument that knightly writers relied on chivalric ideas – the desire for vengeance and the vindication of familial honor – to justify war against Islam. And, importantly, when they drew on existing ideas of just war and holy war, they understood these concepts on their own terms.

Fitz and others who have studied holy war and *reconquista* in medieval Iberia have almost all avoided a particular period in the history of Castile: the Trastámara period. Fitz himself, like most scholars of the Iberian holy war, prefers to focus on the period between about 1050 and about 1350. This was the period of the most significant Christian victories in the peninsula and, as a result, the most fertile ground for clerical, royal, and literary imaginings of the holy war. After the death of Alfonso XI in 1350, the few historians who pick up the thread of the intellectual development of holy war resume in about 1485 as the Catholic Monarchs undertook the final conquest of Granada.[8] In other words, there is no significant study in

---

[6] Francisco García Fitz, "La Reconquista: un estado de la cuestión," in *Clio et Crimen*, no. 6 (2009), 199.

[7] On this concept more broadly defined, Thomas Devaney has demonstrated that late medieval Castilians identified strongly with their Visigothic predecessors. See Thomas Devaney, "Virtue, Virility, and History in the Fifteenth-Century Castile," *Speculum*, vol. 88, no. 3 (2013): 721–749.

[8] Joseph F. O'Callaghan, arguably the leading Anglophone historian of holy war in medieval Spain, examined in detail the period from the mid-11th century to the death of Alfonso XI in his *Reconquest and Crusade in Medieval Spain*. He devotes just about a page to the Trastámara century, arguing fairly that the *reconquista* largely ended during this period. The implication of this short treatment, though, is that because the activity itself ended, an ideology of holy war also was unimportant. This is problematic. Joseph F. O'Callaghan, *Reconquest and Crusade in Medieval Spain* (Philadelphia: University of Pennsylvania Press, 2003). For the section on Trastámara Castile, see pages 212–213. In his book devoted only to what he calls the "Gibraltar Crusade," O'Callaghan similarly passes over most of the Trastámara period in less than a page, again implying that there was not much going on intellectually. Joseph F. O'Callaghan, *The Gibraltar Crusade* (Philadelphia: University of Pennsylvania Press, 2011), 263–264. Hispanophone scholarship, surprisingly, is not much more complete on the ideology of the Trastámara period. José Rodríguez Molina, in his work on the frontier discusses the development of crusading and holy war ideology in the early Middle Ages, follows it through to the Battle of Las Navas de Tolosa in 1212, dwells briefly on the Alfonsine efforts of the early 14th century, and then jumps to the legacy of the holy war in the early modern period, stopping ever so briefly to mention Miguel Lucas de Iranzo at the end of the 15th century. José Rodríguez Molina, *La vida de moros y cristianos en la frontera* (Jaén: Alcalá

English or Spanish on the chivalric framework of holy war itself between 1369 and 1474.

This chapter uses knightly sources – chronicles, chivalric biographies, poetry, and romance – in order to describe the chivalric ideology concerning holy war in the period in Castilian history when the war against Islam was less vigorous than at any other point in the Middle Ages. The chapter will argue that holy war remained theoretically the greatest achievement for late medieval Castilian knights. All wars were considered a valorous opportunity for Castilian knights to demonstrate their prowess and win honor, but the war against the Kingdom of Granada was considered the most important variety of warfare and the war in which knights could *best* win honor. A complex combination of crusading theology, the idiosyncratic Iberian tradition of holy war, the desire to defend Christendom from foreign attack, and the hope of destroying a hostile infidel presence animated ideas about holy war in late medieval Iberia. This theology combined with existing chivalric values in Iberia – the drive for honor and the importance of *linaje* – to create a unique Castilian desire to reclaim lost territory through military power. *Reconquista* was not simply a religious or martial goal but a historical imperative. Castilian history, from a chivalric perspective, had been interrupted by a great tragedy, namely the destruction of Visigothic Spain by the forces of Islam. Late medieval Castilian knights felt themselves pulled to a fulfillment of their historical destiny through the process of *reconquista*. To right the wrongs of the past, Muslim sovereignty had to be driven out of Iberia. The impulse of *reconquista* functioned not only at the level of the Kingdom of Castile and the knights of Castile but at a personal and familial level. Knights looked to the vigorous deeds of their forebears who had fought in the holy war and sought to preserve and expand upon the honor they inherited as a result. All of these ideas complemented the others, leading to a powerful ideological environment that compelled knights to perform great deeds of arms against their Islamic foes.

Grupo Editorial, 2008), 167–175. Jesús Rodríguez Velasco is one of the few who set out to examine ideologies of chivalry and knighthood in the Trastámara period, but he focuses almost exclusively on the work of Diego de Valera. While Valera was a knight, he was only a single knight. Velasco explicitly discounts the use of imaginative literature as a legitimate source for the 15th century because it is only secondary to formal treatises or legalistic works. Jesús Rodríguez Velasco, *El debate sobre la caballería en el siglo XV* (Salamanca, Spain: Europa Artes Gráficas, S.A., 1996). Francisco García Fitz has written an article arguing precisely that the "cooler" frontier during the Trastámara period has less to tell us about the ideology of holy war. Francisco García Fitz, "Una frontera caliente: la guerra en las fronteras castellano-musulamans (siglos XI–XIII)," in *Identidad y representación de la frontera en la España medieval (siglos XI–XIV)*, ed. Carlos de Ayala Martínez, Pascal Buresi, and Phillippe Josserand (Madrid: Casa de Velázquez, 2001), 159–180.

To be sure, not every knight was enamored with holy war and, of those who espoused the commitment to holy war, it is possible that some did so insincerely. However, embrace of holy war was widespread enough that it did not require the *sincere* commitment of *every* knight. As a key component of chivalry, the chivalric elite as a whole operated under the assumptions of the concept of holy war. Even if they were out to secure only their own economic or political advantage, they found that they could do so only in the context of the ideology of holy war. Their peers, most of whom did embrace the idea of holy war, would not have taken their claims seriously without some grounding in it.

Chivalric ideas, powerful as they were, frequently were contested by interested supra-knightly parties. For Trastámara kings, who embodied not only knighthood but statecraft, holy war was certainly a worthy enterprise, but it often had to be passed over in favor of more pressing concerns. Wars with other Christian kingdoms, dynastic intrigues, civil wars, diplomacy, financial concerns, and political expediency all weighed on the minds of the Trastámara kings and influenced their actions. As a result, the Trastámara period is one in which the holy war progressed only in fits and starts. From a Machiavellian perspective, the royal preference for expediency over holy war is eminently sensible; for the chivalric purists of late medieval Castile, this preference showcased weakness and a faltering commitment to their great cause. When kings of Castile understood and embraced the apical position of holy war in the hierarchy of warfare, they tended to earn the support and admiration of powerful knights and nobles.[9] Kings or regents who made the holy war a priority tended to enjoy greater support from the Castilian chivalry and suffered fewer challenges to the stability of their reigns.

Kings and regents might have been less likely to have sincerely embraced the chivalric emphasis on holy war, precisely for the reasons outlined above. As the ruler of a kingdom, they had to consider a greater range of issues, priorities, and commitments than, say, an Andalucian nobleman had to. For kings, there was a calculation about the expenditure of resources, and holy war was not always at the top of the list, for practical reasons. The knights and nobles of the realm, having fewer responsibilities across a narrower world of competing interests, could prioritize the holy war and expected their monarch to do the same. This tension is crucial for understanding the vicissitudes of the Trastámara monarchs. As we will see, it also led to

---

[9] Timothy Guard has examined the relationship between crusading ideas and the late medieval English state. A similar ideological process was at work there, linking king, country, God, and knights together. In Castile, these ideological forces played out in a very real way on the southern border. Timothy Guard, *Chivalry, Kingship and Crusade: The English Experience in the Fourteenth Century* (Woodbridge: Boydell Press, 2013), 186–190.

some incongruities in words and deeds on the part of some monarchs or favorites. Often kings would proclaim their commitment to the holy war in order to try to placate their bellicose subjects but, ultimately, chose not to follow through with it.

In the context of the relative doldrums of holy war in Trastámara Spain, Castilian kings and knights did find honor and glory in fighting their coreligionists, as we will see in Chapter 4. Surely there was even some ambivalence on the part of several kings and, undoubtedly, many knights and men-at-arms. But, as the Trastámara period progressed, ambivalence toward holy war tended to fade more and more. The drumbeat of holy war continued to grow louder through the late 14th and 15th centuries, as knights and nobles insisted that the holy war was the most central part of their identity. Even in the absence – perhaps *because* of the absence – of vigorous prosecution of the holy war, chivalry functioned as a call to arms more than ever.

The Chivalric Framework of Holy War

When Pope Urban II (r. 1088–1099) inaugurated the crusades with a speech at Clermont in 1095, he was innovating more in the tools of papal leadership, public framing, and scale of ambition than in theology. Gregory VII (r. 1073–1085) had articulated many of the same ideas concerning holy war and even considered initiating and personally leading a martial expedition to the East decades before Urban urged Frankish knights to set aside their differences and liberate Christ's homeland.[10] In recent years, historians have noted that a Christian effort to stem and roll back the Islamic advance in Iberia predates the First Crusade by decades, if not centuries.[11] Certainly, in the mid-11th century Alexander II (r. 1061–1073) and Gregory VII encouraged Christian military action against Muslim polities in southern Iberia, using the same sorts of tools that Urban would use to encourage the First Crusade. Alexander granted remission of sins to those Christians who took part in the campaign to take the city of Barbastro from Muslim hands. His justification for such remission lay in his assertion that Muslims had driven the Christians from their own lands and continued to persecute Christians living under Muslim rule.[12] Urban's call at Clermont would echo the language of the Barbastro campaign, with Muslims accused of conquering and defiling Christian territory while visiting terrible suffering on innocent Christians.[13]

---

[10] John France, *The Crusades and the Expansion of Catholic Christendom, 1000–1714* (London: Routledge, 2005), 10.
[11] O'Callaghan, *Reconquest and Crusade*, 5–10.
[12] Ibid., 24–27.
[13] Paul Halsall has collected several versions of Urban's speech at Clermont in English

The clerical innovations of the 11th century helped to give birth to the chivalry that would persist in various forms for the next 500 years. The idea that knights were not only *permitted* by God to fight and kill but that they could actually win forgiveness of their sins would embed itself in chivalric *mentalité* and transform the knightly relationship with the divine. Medieval knights would so firmly seize the idea of meritorious suffering won on the battlefield that they would embrace the idea above and beyond the theaters of war that Alexander, Gregory, and Urban had ever thought possible. Indeed, in much of western Christendom throughout most of the High and Late Middle Ages, the idea of divine sanction for knightly bloodshed formed one of the most powerful threads of chivalric ideology.[14]

The institution of crusading theology laid the foundation for a broader Christian approach to holy war through the High and Late Middle Ages. Three large concepts would dominate this approach. First, knights understood that in attacking the enemies of Christendom they would receive remission of their sins. Fighting was itself a holy and salvific activity, something that numerous popes, monks, and preachers had promised them. Second, because Muslims were held to be perpetrating atrocities on Christians, it was incumbent on Christian knights to push back Muslims, liberating and protecting fellow Christians. Third, Christians were justified in attacking Muslims because Muslims had taken Christian land. In seizing the Holy Land, especially Jerusalem, Muslims had assaulted the honor of Jesus Christ himself. It was incumbent upon Christian pilgrims (read: crusading knights) to restore the honor of their Lord by revenging themselves on the Muslim enemy. These three ideas held true as much in Castile as in the rest of Christendom, though local conditions would develop Castilian idiosyncrasies as well.

The first of these three ideas, salvation through warfare, and especially war against non-Christians, had become a key component of chivalry across much of Europe. In France, England, the Empire, and other areas, the salvific nature of crusade had transferred so easily into chivalry at large because the potential of regular holy war against non-Christians was a relatively remote possibility.[15] Knights and knightly thinkers north of the Pyrenees continued to value war against Islam as the highest good, but it required more resources, time, and effort for warriors to actually travel to a place

---

translation at the website of Fordham University's Internet Medieval Sourcebook. http://legacy.fordham.edu/halsall/source/urban2-5vers.html.

[14] The unrivalled work on this topic is Richard Kaeuper, *Holy Warriors: The Religious Ideology of Chivalry* (Philadelphia: University of Pennsylvania Press, 2009).

[15] The ideal of holy war remained important and a number of knights and kings actively sought it out. Timothy Guard's work on this subject in the English context is illuminating. Guard, *Chivalry, Kingship and Crusade*. See especially his chapter dealing with Spain, pp. 51–57.

where they could fight against Muslims or pagans. It was therefore easy for Englishmen, Scots, or Frenchmen to transfer the glory of crusade to quotidian warfare. In Castile too, the saving grace of holy war had been transferred to all warfare. But in Castile holy war still remained a practical and easy alternative to war against fellow Christians. As a result, Castilian knights explicitly emphasized that war against Islam guaranteed them reward in the next world.

Jorge Manrique, a knight and poet of the late 15th century, inverted the satirical message of the *Dança General de la Muerte*, which we saw in the last chapter. Where the *Dança* imagined a personified death carrying away knights and dukes and suggesting their violent lives would lead to damnation, Manrique imagines Death as more sympathetic to the highest knightly calling of holy war.[16] In his long poem *Coplas por la Muerte de su Padre*, a lament on the death of his father, Manrique imagines Death coming to his father's door. Instead of laughing at his victim, Death is sympathetic and reassuring. True, Death says, life is fleeting and all people die at some time. But there are degrees of a valuable life. A "lasting life" – that is, eternal life after death – is not won with money and wealth and fineries, "but the good religious men earn it with prayers and with chants; the famous knights, with labors and tribulations against Moors."[17] The classic language of knights "laboring" on the battlefield in the same way that monks and priests labor in monasteries and churches ensures that they are saved.[18] In the Castilian knightly mind, fighting against Islam was a holy calling, a sort of suffering that they undertook in order to win them life after death. Neither was this an empty or hollow promise; Death speaks directly to the actions of Manrique's father, saying, "And because you, eminent baron, / spilled so much blood / of the pagans, / await the reward / which in this world you won / by your hands; / and with this confidence / and with the complete faith / which you have, / depart with good hope / that you win eternal life."[19] Too often knightly attitudes toward the salvific nature of their

---

[16] For a full account of Manrique's life and a detailed analysis of the *Coplas* see Frank Domínguez, *Love and Remembrance: The Poetry of Jorge Manrique* (Lexington, KY: University Press of Kentucky, 1988).

[17] Jorge Manrique, *Obra Completa*, ed. Augusto Cortina (Buenos Aires: Espasa-Calpe Argentina, S.A., 1966), 133. "mas los buenos religiosos / gánanlo con oraciones / y con lloros; / los caballeros famosos, / con trabajos y afliccones / contra moros."

[18] Kaeuper, *Holy Warriors*, 137–144.

[19] Ibid., 133–134. "Y pues vos, claro varón, / tanta sangre derramasteis / de paganos, / esperad el galardón / que en este mundo ganasteis / por las manos; / y con esta confianza, / y con la fe tan entera / que tenéis, / partid con buena esperanza, / que esta otra vida tercera / ganaréis." When Manrique uses the term "pagans" (*paganos*) here, he is referring to Muslims, not to any pagan. This was commonplace in medieval literature, both in Iberia and in other parts of Europe. See See Debra Higgs Strickland, *Saracens, Demons and Jews: Making Monsters in Medieval Art* (Princeton, NJ: Princeton Univer-

bloody profession are subtle and reside behind the text. For the Castilian knight Manrique, in the context of holy war, it was central enough to his understanding of chivalry that he stated it explicitly. Perhaps Manrique also wanted to assert an idea similar to that articulated in this book: knights themselves lived a life thinking about their actions. Manrique allows his father to speak at the end of the poem, responding to Death's praise in order to claim that "We have so little time / in this miserable life, / by such way / that my will is / consistent with the divine in / all things."[20] Manrique himself was sure that the knightly shedding of Muslim blood was divinely sanctioned and he naturally imagined that his father, at death, could rest assured that this was true.

As a corollary to the idea that fighting the holy war won a knight salvation, failing to press the holy war implied that knights had fallen into sin and drifted from the path of God. Pedro López de Ayala, whom we have met as a chronicler, also wrote poetry critiquing the society in which he lived. His *Libro de Rimado de Palacio*, written sometime in the late 14th century, laments the religious errors that the knights of Castile have fallen into because of their failure to fight against Islam. "[Knights] have forgotten the Moors, those on whom they make war, / who in their own lands can eat ... The Christians had wars, the Moors are rested, / in their kingdoms, already [Christian] kings have been injured; / and all this comes through our evil sins, / for we are against God in all erroneous things."[21] For Ayala, Christian infighting, the recuperation of Muslim Spain, and the decline of the Spanish kingdoms are connected to a failure to press the holy war, a terrible sin in God's eyes. To remedy the sin, logically, the holy war needed to be renewed. It is telling that Ayala wrote these words in the last quarter of the 14th century, when the holy war was at one of its lowest ebbs. The world looked sinful and broken from a chivalric perspective because Christian knights were not more vigorously attacking their religious enemies.

The second of the three ideas pertaining to holy war, the old crusader goal of protecting Christians from the persecuting hand of Muslims, similarly occupied the minds of knights. In the Castilian context, this was most often expressed through a concern over Christians who had been captured

---

sity Press, 2003), 157. The term Manrique uses which I have translated as "eternal life" is "esta otra vida tercera," literally "this third afterlife". This is a strange term, but one which likely refers to eternal life.

[20] Manrique, *Obra Completa*, 134. "No tengamos tiempo ya / en esta vida mezquina / por tal modo, / que mi voluntad está / conforme con la divina / para todo ..."

[21] Pedro López de Ayala, *Libro Rimado de Palacio*, ed. Kenneth Adams (Madrid: Ediciones Cátedra, S.A., 1993), 196. "Olvidado han a los moros e las sus guerras fazer, / que en otras tierras llanas asaz fallan que comer ... Los cristianos han las guerras, los moros están folgados, / en todos los demás regnos ya tienen reyes doblados; / e todo aquesto viene por malos nuestros pecados, / ca nos somos contra Dios en todas cosas errados."

by Muslims during raids across the border. The question was important enough politically that in 1429 King Juan II required King Muhammad VIII of Granada (r. 1417–1419, 1427–1429) to repatriate Christian captives in order to obtain a six-month or year-long extension of the truce between the two kingdoms. Incidentally, Juan had no intention of maintaining a truce at this point, seeking only to move forward with one of the goals of the holy war. Ayala asserts that making a demand for the freeing of Christian captives was tantamount to denying Muhammad's request for a truce and that Juan immediately began marshalling knights and men-at-arms for an invasion of Granada.[22] If Ayala is correct, King Juan's political and propagandistic calculus must have been a clever one. Not only could Juan play the part of the concerned Christian king, seeking to have his subjects returned to him, but he could be sure that Muhammad would reject the offer. With a guaranteed renewal of the holy war, Juan could then use the question of Christian captives as the *causus belli* of the war, making himself a great Christian holy warrior. Only a year later Ayala confirmed such an approach in more explicit language. King Muhammad IX (r. 1419–1427, 1430–1431, 1432–1445, 1448–1453) asked Juan for a new truce and even offered to send soldiers to aid the Castilian king in an ongoing war with the kingdoms of Navarre and Aragon. Juan proudly made the same demand that he had in 1429, offering to renew the truce for a year or more if Muhammad would pay a great tribute and release all Christian captives in Granada. Ayala claims that Juan did this "knowing that [Muhammad] would not grant it, and that [Juan] would have cause to make war."[23] In the games that kings played, the question of Christian captives was a useful bargaining chip, allowing Castilian kings to express their pastoral concern for their Christian subjects and offering a perpetual cause for war.

These great political calculations worked because there existed in the world of ideas a general concern for Christian captives. In 1471 the Constable Miguel Lucas de Iranzo wrote a letter to Pope Sixtus IV (r. 1471–1484) lamenting the state of affairs in Andalucía. After recounting the terrible deeds of Muslim raiders in a general sense, Iranzo begs the pontiff to think about the Christians who suffer under Muslim rule: "Look, your most clement Holiness! Look how fiercely and savagely the blood of your innocent lambs is shed! Look how without hope of remedy some are bound up forever to be captives! Look how grievous and terrible is the yoke of servitude in which those unhappy ones are!"[24] This propagandistic argu-

---

[22] Fernán Pérez de Guzmán, "La crónica del serenísimo príncipe Don Juan, segundo Rey deste nombre en Castilla y en Leon," in *Biblioteca de Autores Españoles*, vol. 68, 451.
[23] Ibid., 484. "Esto hacia el Rey conosciendo que se le no otorgaria, porque él hubiese cause para hacer la guerra."
[24] *Hechos del condestable Don Miguel Lucas de Iranzo*, ed. Juan de Mata Carriazo (Madrid: Espasa-Calpe, S.A., 1940), 473. "Míre Vuestra clementísima Santidad. Mire

ment that a holy war was needed precisely to protect and recover Christian captives taken by the Muslims of Granada was followed with a rhetorical question to the pope, asking who would save the captives. The answer, of course, was Iranzo himself, but before coming to that conclusion Iranzo entertains the heroes of the past as possible saviors of Iberian Christendom. "Charlemagne, who regularly [fought the Muslims], Godfrey de Bouillon, who dared [to fight them], our most holy kings [of Castile] who won this land"; each of these heroes would have been a welcome leader of the holy war, but alas, they were all "taken by death, and they do not come."[25] It would remain for Iranzo and other 15th-century Castilians to move forward with the holy war and rescue their captive coreligionists.

Fortunately for Castilian knights, the heroic past provided exemplars of men fighting Muslims to rescue Christian captives. Drawing on the Matter of France, Castilian poets of the late Middle Ages had created a figure unique to Iberian chivalry who taught an important lesson to the knights of Castile, calling on knights to press the holy war and rescue Christian captives from the grip of the Muslim enemy. So Gaiferos was born. According to a number of long ballads (or very short epic poems), Gaiferos was a vassal of Charlemagne, and the husband of one of the emperor's many daughters, a woman named Melisenda. This Frankish princess, it would seem, had been carried away by the Muslims of al-Andalus, where she was held as a captive. Gaiferos had idled for seven years without going to her rescue – he blamed his poverty, having neither horse nor arms. Charlemagne finally shames Gaiferos into action, bringing the knight's personal honor into question should he fail to return to France with his wife. In a fury, Gaiferos leaves the emperor's palace and borrows his Uncle Roland's horse and arms and rides to al-Andalus. He fights with the Muslims of the city of Sansueña, before rescuing his beloved and returning triumphantly to France, his honor vindicated.[26] The story's message speaks for itself: sitting idly in the peace and comfort of Christendom while fellow Christians are captive in the south is not only intolerable but shameful. The great knights of the past urged Gaiferos to action against Islam, and knights of the present needed to emulate him.. Protecting Christians from Muslim persecution, whether real or imagined, was an imperative of the chivalric approach to

---

quán fiera y saluajemente se derrama la sangre de vuestros ynoçentes corderos. Mire quán sin esperança de remedio alguno los lieuan para sienpre catiuos. Mire quán pesado y terrible sea el yugo de seruidunbre en que ya los tristes están."

[25] Ibid., 474. "¿A quién yremos … Ya Carlos el Grande, que solía, Godofré de Bullón, que osaua, nuestros muy santos reyes que ganaron esta tierra, ocupados por la muerte, no vienen."

[26] Baltasar Fra-Molinero suggests that by the 16th century Sansueña was understood to be Zaragoza. See Baltasar Fra-Molinero, "Don Quijote Attacks his Muslim Other: The Maese Pedro Episode of *Don Quijote*," in *Contextualizing the Muslim Other in Medieval Christian Discourse*, ed. Jerold C. Frakes (New York: Palgrave Macmillan, 2011), 130.

holy war, and served as a personal as well as a political call to action. The lesson of Gaiferos, a hero from the past, embodied this imperative.[27]

A link to the past in the form of a single literary figure was only one component of the historical character of Trastámara holy war, just as the protection of Christian captives was only one component. Castilian knights and knightly writers also thought about the third idea concerning holy war – reclaiming the very land of Iberia – and they conceived of it as a historical imperative for Castilian knights as a group. Like the ideas of early crusaders, 15th-century Castilian holy warriors were driven by the desire to reconquer land that belonged to Christendom by ancient right. In the context of this chapter we cannot resolve this larger question of when precisely the concept of *reconquista* came into being but we *can* say that in the late 14th century, and especially in the 15th century, the idea of *reconquista* became a central component of Castilian chivalry. Knights felt a divine historical calling to restore Christian authority across the Iberian Peninsula, and perhaps beyond.

The Matter of Spain

The clearest topic recommending warfare against Granada is what might be called the Matter of Spain, the imaginative literature that dealt with the *destruición*, or the loss of Visigothic Spain to Islam, as well as the literature concerning the *reconquista*.[28] The two closely related topics together were unique to Iberia and formed a corpus of literature that reflected the issues at stake in the perpetuation of the war against Islam. Where the Matter of France and Rome are often best expressed in epic poetry and the Matter of Britain in romance or pseudo-chronicle, the Matter of Spain consists of a

---

[27] Four *romances* exist that deal primarily with the question of Gaiferos and his captured wife and follow the theme as outlined in the body of this chapter. Additionally, Gaiferos appears as the nephew of Roland in several other *romances*. All of these *romances* can be found in *Antología de poetas líricos castellanos*, vol. IX: Romances caballerescos del ciclo Carlovingio, ed. Fernando José Wolf and Conrado Hofmann (Madrid: Librería de Hernando y Compañía, 1899). For the Gaiferos *romances* see 57–72.

[28] Several scholars have recently used the term "Matter of Spain" to complement the traditional triad of the Matter of Britain (Arthur), the Matter of France (Charlemagne), and the Matter of Rome (classical antiquity). Sylvia Federico used it to describe the active efforts by Alfonso XI to marry Castile to the heroic traditions of the Matters of Britain and Rome. Similarly, R.F. Yeager has similarly identified a "Matter of Spain" but recognizes it only in relation to Chaucer and English literature. We must be somewhat careful with this term – the traditional triad was used by medieval authors to refer to the various genres of literature, while the term "Matter of Spain" was not. See Sylvia Federico, "Chaucer and the Matter of Spain," *The Chaucer Review*, vol. 45, no. 3 (2011): 299–320 and R.F. Yeager, "Chaucer Translates the Matter of Spain," in *England and Iberia in the Middle Ages, 12th–15th Century: Cultural, Literary, and Political Exchanges*, ed. María Bullón-Fernández (New York: Palgrave Macmillan, 2007), 189–202.

variety of works across literary genres. We have already seen the ballads of Gaiferos, and we will see that the idea of *reconquista* was similarly dealt with through other ballads and poetry. In addition to poetic works, the desire for holy war was expressed in what we might call imagined history, appropriate to a subject that consists of an idealized past. Principal among the works concerning the Matter of Spain is Pedro de Corral's *Crónica del Rey Don Rodrigo*, which deals with the loss of Spain to the Muslims under the ultimate Visigothic king, Rodrigo (r. 710–712). *Rodrigo*, produced around 1430, is ostensibly a historical chronicle of the 8th century, but in fact is Corral's own creation, based on previous Iberian legend, history, and myth.[29] James Donald Fogelquist has noted that Corral reworked the legend of Rodrigo as a critique of his own society during the tumultuous reign of Juan II.[30]

The lengthy *Rodrigo* opens with the efforts of the titular King Rodrigo to unify Spain under his rule, particularly focusing on the subjugation of the city of Córdoba in the years before the Islamic invasion of the peninsula. With the submission of Córdoba, Rodrigo successfully unifies not only all of Iberia, but significant parts of northwestern Africa as well. All is right with the Spanish world, united under a Christian king, but a storm is brewing in Africa as the Arabs explode onto the scene and begin attacking Rodrigo's vassal, the Count Julián, on the southern shores of the Mediterranean. Fortunately, Rodrigo, a good and strong Christian king, initially decides to assist Julián in defending against the onslaught of Islam; the invasion is temporarily repulsed as Rodrigo's vassals defeat the enemy in battle, and a truce is agreed between Muslims and Visigoths.[31] The first section of the chronicle shows a society functioning well: Christian kings and knights recognize their duty to God to preserve Christendom and prevent an Islamic expansion.

In stark contrast, the second section presents an image of Visigothic Spain wracked by internal problems. Rodrigo's vassals, the great lords and knights of Spain, make war on one another and largely ignore the menace of the Islamic presence on their borders. Even as these significant military encounters progress, King Rodrigo becomes enamored of the beauty of a woman named La Cava, the daughter of Count Julián. When La Cava denies Rodrigo's advances, he simply takes what he wants and rapes La

---

[29] Pedro de Corral, *Crónica del Rey don Rodrigo (Crónica sarracina)*, ed. James Donald Fogelquist (Madrid: Editorial Castalia, S.A., 2001), vol. I, 8–12 and Rafael Ramos, "A vueltas con la *Crónica del rey don Rodrigo*," *Tirant*, vol. 16 (2013): 353–368.

[30] Fogelquist has pointed out that the "true" history of the 8th-century Islamic conquest of Spain was lost almost immediately after it happened and that long before Corral produced *Rodrigo*, around 1430, any reliable information concerning the last Visigoths was "obscured by dense layers of legendary accretion." James Donald Fogelquist "Pedro de Corral's Reconfiguration of La Cava in the *Crónica del Rey don Rodrigo*," *eHumanista*: Monographs in Humanities, 3.

[31] Corral, *Rodrigo*, vol. I, 182–183.

Cava, an episode that will be discussed more fully in Chapter 5. Corral leaves unanswered the question of whether La Cava was an innocent victim, a seductress, or a pawn in the intrigues between Julián and Rodrigo.[32] Whatever the case, Count Julián responds by offering legendarily awful advice to Rodrigo. Julián advises the king that he ought to dismiss the great many knights he has in his pay, disarm them, have them return to work their lands, and abandon the castles in the south of his land; the king agrees to all this, because he has no better counselor than Julián in all the land.[33] Count Julián then travels to the south, aggregating knights about him, and writes a letter to the Muslims, inviting them to invade a Spain which no longer had men prepared to defend it, and promising to aid them in conquering the territory from King Rodrigo.[34] This is the turning point of the chronicle and, for Corral, the turning point of Spanish history. What will come after Julián's treason is the destruction (*destruición*) of Spain.

Late medieval Castilians were left with something of a mystery concerning the destruction of Spain. Who was at fault? Was it the Muslims, frightening pagans from across the sea? Was it Count Julián, an ambitious and disloyal man whose treasonous acts invited the enemy into Spain? Perhaps it was King Rodrigo himself, a king who thought so highly of himself and his royal office that nothing, not even his vassal's daughter, was beyond his reach. Did Rodrigo's pride and lust provoke Julián's treason? Or maybe La Cava herself was to blame, for allowing her feminine sexuality to entice Rodrigo's attack on her. Other writers of the 15th century were fairly certain that Julián bore the brunt of the responsibility. Gutierre Díez de Games and Pedro López de Ayala, for example, were both sure that it was the treason of Julián that led to the *destruición*. Corral himself acknowledged that the actions of Julián were the immediate cause of the *destruición*, but he was much more willing to entertain the idea that King Rodrigo, La Cava, and the nobles of Spain also bore some responsibility for the loss. Whoever was at fault, most authors agreed that the *destruición* was made possible only because

---

[32] Ibid., 449–455. On this question, historians themselves have proposed different interpretations, not just in Corral's work, but in the longer legacy of La Cava. Indeed, as Patricia Grieve has noted, La Cava today is seen as a sort of Helen of Troy, responsible for the terrible destruction of Spain. This interpretation probably dates most clearly from 16th-century interpretations of the legend of La Cava. Patricia E. Grieve, *The Eve of Spain: Myths of Origins in the History of Christian, Muslim, and Jewish Conflict* (Baltimore: The Johns Hopkins University Press, 2009). See also Marjorie Ratcliffe, "Florinda la Cava: víctima historíca, víctima literaria: la Crónica sarracina en el Siglo de Oro," in *Memoria de la palabra: Actas del VI Congreso de la Asociación Internacional Siglo de Oro, Burgos-La Rioja 15–19 de julio 2002*, vol. 2, ed. Francisco Domínguez Matito and María Luisa Lobato López (Frankfurt: Iberoamericana Vervuert Verlagsgesellschaft, 2004), 1485–1494.

[33] Corral, *Rodrigo*, vol. I, 464–466.

[34] Ibid., 476–480.

the knights, nobles, and king of Visigothic Spain were too distracted by their own failures (internal warfare, royal pride, lust, treason) to fight the religious enemy. The results of the blame game tell us less than we would like to know about holy war in late medieval Castile, but the fact that it was an issue up for debate is significant. Each of these writers – Corral, Ayala, Díez, and others – was invested in discussing the topic. *They* thought it was a matter of some importance to determine why Spain had come to ruin in the 8th century, suggesting that the nuances of holy war and its justification were an important issue for late medieval Castilian knights. Writers were willing to spill ink on this question because getting holy war right mattered to them.

Blame for the *destruición* was an important issue precisely because the *destruición* was such an important event in the Castilian mind; it was a moment when evil triumphed over good and the proper course of history was upset.[35] Much of the rest of *Rodrigo* details the loss of Spain to Islam, the final defeat of Rodrigo and the Visigoths, and the ensuing flight of the Visigoths to the northern mountains. In all of these events, the Muslims are equated with the forces of evil. Even as Rodrigo and Julián and others were sinners and flawed men who brought the *destruición* upon themselves, still the enemy was terrifying and demonic. In an inversion of the biblical story of God stopping the sun in the sky so that Joshua could finish killing the enemies of Israel, Corral claims that one of the days of the *destruición* was two hours shorter than it should have been. For when "the devils saw that the Moors had the worse [of the fighting] and were beaten, they all came together to change the day into night and empower blackness and darkness."[36] The greatest tragedy, the greatest historical transgression, comes when the Muslims take the city of Toledo, the capital of Visigothic Spain and the center of Christian religion and culture in the peninsula. The city is taken only when treasonous Jews in the city collaborate with the Muslim enemy, opening a postern gate to let the Muslim army in. Once the army is inside the city, they and their disloyal Christian allies perpetrate a great slaughter on the Christian inhabitants. "They began to kill whoever they encountered … And as they arrived they met with voices so loud and such terrible shouts wanting heaven to take them away; and they killed the men

---

[35] Indeed, as Patricia Grieve has noted, writers much more often used the term *destruición* than a term connoting loss, such as *perdido*. Where the latter would call to mind Adam and Eve's fall from grace and the loss of paradise, *destruición* implies an active error on the part of Spaniards and active violence on the part of those who caused the destruction. See Grieve, *The Eve of Spain*, 130–133.

[36] Corral, *Rodrigo*, vol. I, 495. "que como los diablos vieron que los moros avían lo peor e eran vencidos, que todos fueron juntos a tornar el día noche a poder de nublos e de escuridat."

and the women, and the children ..."³⁷ Corral laments the loss of Toledo as a key moment in the destruction of Visigothic Spain. As with the entire story, the loss of the city is ultimately a result of the sins of the Christians of Spain, but it is effected through historical wrongs – the betrayal of Julián and his Christian allies, the nefariousness of the Toledan Jews, etc. The *destruición* was a great tragedy, not only because it represented a failure on the part of Spanish knights, but also because the course of history was changed for the worse.

Not all was bleak for Visigothic Spain, though. Corral offered hope to his readers in the form of exemplary Spanish knights, who vigorously and devotedly fought against the Muslims. Overflowing with examples of laudable fighting against Muslims, *Rodrigo* leaves no doubt that warfare against Islam is an honorable endeavor. One particularly good example among these is the great effort exerted by the Infante Sancho. In battle against the religious enemy, he is regularly set upon by dozens of the enemy; always he strikes great blows and kills many of them, such that the Muslims themselves recognize that this is "the best knight in the world."³⁸ Sancho is then targeted by the Muslim leader and killed, his head cut off and paraded around the battlefield on the end of a lance. Truly, from Corral's perspective, this enemy is a particularly brutal and heartless one. When King Rodrigo hears of Sancho's death, he cries out to God, asking why the "mirror of chivalry of all the world" has been taken.³⁹ The language employed in King Rodrigo's memorial of Sancho suggests that Sancho's death in fighting against a religious enemy carries special weight. King Rodrigo, in his cry to God, acknowledges that Sancho has been martyred for Rodrigo's sins. In the traditional understanding of the *destruición*, the Muslims are often seen as being sent to Spain for the punishment of Visigothic sins.⁴⁰ That Corral connects Sancho's death with God's retribution against the Goths suggests that his martyrdom is directly related to fighting the forces of Islam, not simply to dying in battle.

The general direction and lesson of the chronicle, too, offers hope for correcting the historical error that was the *destruición*. Early in the work, King Rodrigo and his men witness a strange event: a tornado sweeps through the camp and plucks up the bishops of Jaén and Liberia, carrying them up into the sky.⁴¹ For half an hour, the bishops are held aloft, while Rodrigo

---

³⁷ Corral, *Rodrigo*, vol. 2, 76. "E los otros començaron de matar los que fallavan ... E como llegaron fallaron las bozes tan grandes e los gritos tan terribles que al cielo querían llegar; e matavan los ombres e las mugeres, e a los niños ..."
³⁸ Corral, *Rodrigo*, vol. 1, 513. "el mejor cavallero del mundo"
³⁹ Ibid., 519. "¿cómo ... que te plaze que yo vea morir el espejo de cavallería de todo el mundo?"
⁴⁰ Fogelquist, "Reconfiguration of La Cava," 55.
⁴¹ I have been unable to determine what see the bishop of Liberia is meant to corre-

and his knights look on, terrified. After the half hour is over, the king asks the bishops what happened and the Bishop of Jaén gives an explanation. God, he says, allowed the devil to have power over him for the space of half an hour because of the bishop's sins, but did not allow the devil to kill him. Once the bishop realized his sins, God allowed him to return to earth, to walk again in the land where he belonged.[42] What a delightful metaphor for Corral's understanding of Castilian history! The bishop of Jaén, a city which in the 15th century was important on the southern frontier, promised that the rule of the devil was only temporary and that such vexations would be righted after a short period of terror and tragedy. Perhaps, for Corral, the historical "half hour" was the period from *destruición* in the early 8th century to the glorious *reconquista*.

Corral did not even need to wait for the 15th century to arrive before "the devil" could be turned back and Christians could start walking their land again. Toward the end of the chronicle, Corral foreshadows the hope and promise of the next 700 years of Castilian history through the figure of King Pelayo (r. 718–737). Relegated to the mountains of northern Spain, Pelayo, who is a virtuous man in contrast to Rodrigo's sinfulness, begins the long process of the *reconquista*, marshalling Castilian knights to take back the lands of Iberia.[43] The superlative example of a holy warrior in Corral's chronicle, Pelayo is encountered by the reader only as a fighter of the Muslims; indeed his election as king is made after fighting the enemy and then retreating to the mountains with the remaining Christians.[44] After becoming king, Pelayo starts to become a holy hero. On one of Pelayo's first campaigns against the Muslims as king, God performs a miracle for him, causing all the arms of the enemy to be cast from their hands, such that Pelayo's army would be able to kill them all. Immediately a mysterious man gives Pelayo a shield with a white cross on a red field and the name of Christ written on it in Chaldean letters. The man, whom Pelayo recognizes as a messenger of God, tells the king to strive and go forth in the name of Jesus Christ to conquer the enemy. "And so Our Lord fought for the King Pelayo who killed there Alcamar [a Muslim leader]."[45] Corral could hardly be more clear in his message: Fighting against religious enemies earns

---

spond to. It is possible that Corral is referring to the Basilica of Santa Maria Maggiore, one of the sees of Rome. If this is the case, it would represent a grander project on the part of Corral, suggesting that the events of the 8th century had greater import for Christendom than the loss of Spanish bishoprics alone.

[42] Corral, *Rodrigo*, vol. 1, 610–616.

[43] Certainly this is a much simplified account of Corral's work, but it suffices for the purpose of examining the greater arc of the story and analyzing Corral's thoughts on chivalry and warfare on the southern frontier.

[44] Corral, *Rodrigo*, vol. 2, 328–329.

[45] Ibid., 345. "E ansí peleó Nuestro Señor por el Rey Pelayo que mató allí a Alcamar."

knights not only the honor which they always win while fighting, but merits special recognition from God, whether that entails His hand in their victory, or their assured martyrdom on the holy battlefield.

In a more precise sense, and in language that was clearly designed as a critique of Corral's contemporary Castile, the narrator laments infighting within the kingdom, precisely because it leaves the frontier open to Muslim assault. Although Count Julián is the villain of the story, having betrayed the king and invited the Muslims in, words of legitimate complaint about the king's behavior are put into his mouth before his daughter is raped by the king. Julián's lands are the first to be assaulted by the advancing Islamic armies and Rodrigo acts after receiving a letter from the count begging for aid:

> "[A]s you, lord, have many men with you, and are well garrisoned, it is not necessary to wait for counsel; I see a great evil, and the great loss cannot be recovered if you do not send many men. I have great grief over such evil, and it will be in my heart until your great power with the sword of justice comes in my aid and defense."[46]

Not only does Corral want to make clear that fighting against Islam is a knightly virtue, but he wants to emphasize that the king has a responsibility to aid those living on the frontier and to defend the land of Spain from the Muslim onslaught. In the same vein, *Rodrigo* presents the argument that King Rodrigo's preoccupation with internal wars and intrigue decreases the great chivalry of the kingdom, thereby weakening Christendom against the Islamic advance. Early in the story, during King Rodrigo's reduction of Córdoba, there is a general sense that all the good knights of Spain are killing one another, which the narrator refers to as "la *primera* destruición de España," implying that the bricks in the road to the later and more horrific *destruición* were laid by King Rodrigo and those who fought him in ignoring the greater calling.[47] At one point during the siege of Córdoba, the narrator gives voice to a passionate lament articulating precisely this point:

> Oh! Sad Spain, now this day you are put in a position to be destroyed (*destruida*) forevermore! Born in such a strong place in the noble lineage (*linaje*) of the Goths who have been killing one another, and so coming to the great destruction (*destruición*) of all Spain, that the ancient sages said ... that with strength the most noble men would destroy (*destruirían*) each other, and

---

[46] Corral, *Rodrigo*, vol. I, 235–236. "[C]omo, tú, señor, ayas contigo muchas gentes, e bien guarnidas, no es menester esperar luego consejo; ca el grand mal a ojos es, e el grand perdimiento non puede ser recobrado si muchas gentes no enbías. Grand duelo he tenido por tanto mal, e todavía será en mi coraçón fasta que el tu grand poder con espada de justicia venga en mi ayuda e defendimiento."
[47] Corral, *Rodrigo*, vol. I, 153; italics are mine.

that with them killed and destroyed (*destruidos*), strange men would capture the lordships of Spain for a long time.[48]

The knights of the 15th-century frontier, as we will see, might easily have made the same sorts of claims against Juan II or Enrique IV. In the minds of many late medieval Castilian knights, the war against Islam was the highest possible good. A society properly organized was a society where a good monarch boldly led the knights of his kingdom into the battlefields of the *reconquista*. A bad king, on the other hand, would ignore the war and allow Islam to recover the lands reclaimed by the Christians over the centuries. The move from internal warfare to the loss of Spain further suggests that Corral was dissatisfied with the efforts of knights of his time to press the war against Islam.

Implicit in Corral's account of the *destruición* is that the *reconquista* constituted an act of vengeance on the part of Castilians.[49] Through the loss of the territory of Spain, the honor of the Castilian kingdom and its knights had been impugned and it was incumbent on them to vindicate the honor of the kingdom in taking vengeance on the religious enemy. In *Rodrigo*, as the forces of Islam advance through Africa, Rodrigo calls his council together and explains his decision to send knights to defend against them. His first and presumably most important reason for defending North Africa is so that "we will not lose that which our predecessors won with sword in hand."[50] Rodrigo and all his knights agree that preventing the loss of their

---

[48] Ibid., 139. "¡O España triste, cómo oy este día eres puesta en condición de ser destruida para siempre jamás! En fuerte punto nasció tanto orgullo en el noble linaje de los godos que unos a otros así se han de matar, e ya se viene llegando la gran destruición de toda España, que los sabios antiguos dixeron … que con orgullo se destruirían la más noble gente unos a los otros, y éstos muertos y destruidos que gentes estrañas cobrarían los señoríos de España por luengos tiempos …"

[49] Susanna Throop has emphasized the larger theological understanding of crusade as an act of vengeance. Susanna A. Throop, *Crusading as an Act of Vengeance, 1095–1216* (Burlington VT: Ashgate Publishing, 2011). For this point see pages 1–4, but the entire book makes essential contributions to our understanding of crusading ideology. Throop's other work has further expanded our knowledge of ideologies of holy war in the eastern Mediterranean. See Susanna A. Throop, "Zeal, Anger and Vengeance: The Emotional Rhetoric of Crusading," in *Vengeance in the Middle Ages: Emotion, Religion and Feud*, ed. Susanna A. Throop and Paul R. Hyams (Burlington, VT: Ashgate Publishing, 2011); and Susann A. Throop, "Acts of Vengeance, Acts of Love: Crusading Violence in the Twelfth Century," in *War and Literature*, ed. Laura Ashe and Ian Patterson (Cambridge: D.S. Brewer, 2014). Throop's work is in dialogue with Jonathan Riley-Smith's own assertion that crusaders themselves thought of crusading as an act of feudal obligation to God and that, in doing so, crusading was a loving act rather than simply a violent act. See Jonathan Riley-Smith, "Crusading as an Act of Love," *History*, vol. 65, no. 214 (Jun. 1980): 177–192.

[50] Corral, *Rodrigo*, vol. I, 183. "non perderemos lo que nuestros antecesores ganaron con el espada en la mano."

predecessors' gains would be the honorable thing to do. The interesting aspect of placing these words in a Visigoth's mouth is that the Visigoths had no legacy of the *reconquista* – Corral deploys it as a message to his contemporaries. Undoubtedly, this sentiment would have resounded in the mind of a Castilian knight of the 15th century as a reference to the *reconquista*. A similarly implicit sentiment is also expressed in the great Iberian Arthurian romance *Amadís de Gaula*. After Amadís has defeated King Abies, he leaves the field of battle "with that glory which victors in such deeds often accumulate, not only of honor, but of restitution of a kingdom to he who lost it."[51] The idea of the *reconquista* is present in a story not set in *reconquista* Castile – the ideal of holy war was absorbed by this Castilian imagining of the Matter of Britain. A powerful idea was not contained only within the imagination of Iberian history.

If the idea of *reconquista* as an act of shame and honor vindicated through vengeance against Islam is implicit in Corral's work, it becomes explicit in the sources which make up much of the rest of the Matter of Spain: short poems and folk ballads, which are typically referred to as *romances*, not to be confused with the episodic romances of Arthurian literature. Representing a blending of folk tradition and chivalry, the *romances* deal at length with the real and imagined history of the *reconquista*, confirming for us that this drive for holy war as an act of vengeance writ large was central to Castilian knights in the late Middle Ages. The frontier ballad *Romance de la vengaza de Fernandarias* speaks of a desire to fight with the Muslims, the singer proclaiming "before twenty days have passed I will be dead or revenged / on the Moors of Ronda." The singer's inspiration in this case came from an earlier campaign to conquer the fortress of Cañete in which the knight Fernando de Sayavedra was "very well revenged, / for the Moors were broken; few escaped. / With honor and a great mounted raid Cañete was returned."[52] The honor gained through seeking vengeance on the Muslims of Ronda is more than the typical honor won in battle. As part of a specific act of vengeance continuing the long history of *reconquista*, fighting against Islam in the 15th century was part of a divine historical and chivalric imperative.

In Castile, then, as in much of Europe, there was a superlative position in chivalry which marked war against a religious enemy as the highest calling.

---

[51] *Amadís de Gaula*, ed. Edwin B. Place (Madrid: Consejo Superior de Investigaciones Cientificas, 1959), vol. 1, 80. "con aquella gloria que los vencedores en tales autos leuar suelen, no solamente de honrra mas de restitución de vn reino a quien perdid lo tenía."
[52] *Antología de poetas líricos castellanos*, ed, Fernando José Wolf and Conrado Hofmann (Madrid: M. Rivadeneyra, 1876), vol. 8, 144–145. "antes de veinte dias yo seré muerto ó vengado / entre esos moros de Ronda" "Sayavedra de ellos fué muy bien vengado, / que rotos fueron los moros; pocos se han escapado. / Con honra y gran cabalgada á Cañete se ha tornado."

Unlike in the rest of Europe, though, Castile's geopolitical situation made such a calling a realistic undertaking and one that the knights of southern Castile readily embraced. Also unlike the rest of Europe, Castile's particular history infused holy war with a particular kind of justification beyond doing God's work by slaying His enemies. In the Castilian context, there was a clear historical imperative that formed part of the very identity of Castilian knights. As subjects of the kingdom of Castile, they had a special historical relationship with holy war and the honor it provided. Knights could participate in what they saw as a centuries-long effort unique to their corner of Christendom, the opportunity to exact vengeance on Muslims for the shame of the *destruición*.

The idea of the *reconquista* was a call for vigorous war against Granada, not only as a kingdom-level impulse to complete the destruction of Islamic polities in the peninsula, but also as an emotional and passionate desire to maintain the honor and glory of one's ancestors. In other words, the same concepts of shame, honor, and vengeance which were present for Castilians knights as Castilians reverberated equally strongly at a personal and familial level. Many of the noble families of Trastámara Castile understood their families' honor as residing largely in those families' historical accomplishments in the long *reconquista*. Pressing the *reconquista* not only honored a knight in God's eyes and placed him in a grand historical narrative, but also allowed him to maintain and vindicate the achievements of his *linaje*. Similarly, a knight's failure to continue the *reconquista* implied that a knight did not value the honor his family had won in fighting against Islam. Failure would result in the Muslims reclaiming the *linaje*'s accomplishments, heaping shame on the idle knight and his family.

Jorge Manrique's late 15th-century poem *Coplas por la Muerte de su Padre*, which we encountered earlier, embodies precisely the ambitions and emotions of the *reconquista*, localized to the author's own life and ancestry. Often read today for its beautiful language and poetic turns of phrase, the poem evokes Manrique's passionate and emotional desire to honor his father, and particularly his father's conquests against the Muslims.[53] The author acknowledges that his father did not bequeath any great economic fortune, but left his son something greater: the honor and legacy of *reconquista*. Manrique eulogizes his father, proudly saying "you did not leave great treasures, / nor accumulate much riches / nor finery; / but you made war against the Moors, / winning their fortifications / and their villages; / and in battles you conquered them."[54] It was in the war against Islam that Manrique's father "achieved the dignity / of the great Chivalry / of

---

[53] For the historical context of the poem see Nancy Marino, *Jorge Manrique's* Coplas por la muerte de su padre: *A History of the Poem and Its Reception* (Woodbridge, England: Tamesis, 2011), 22–33.

[54] Manrique, *Obra Completa*, 129. "No dejó grandes tesoros, / ni alcanzó muchas

the Sword."⁵⁵ Manrique's pride in his father's achievements is based in the concept that Castilians had a historical obligation to pursue holy war against Islam. Indeed, before introducing his father's great accomplishments, Manrique rhetorically asks what great labors King Juan II or the infantes of Aragon had achieved. They spent their lives worried about heraldry and tournament and fine clothes – useless pursuits in Manrique's mind.⁵⁶ The lament ends with the heartfelt observation "that although you lost life, / your memory / left full consolation."⁵⁷ The connection between his father's vigorous deeds on the field against Islam and the memory he leaves behind must be understood not simply as a universal expression of human loss, but as a particular recognition of the cultural values endorsed by the Manrique family. Jorge himself was an active knight, and his pride in his father's participation in the holy war lends insight into how he understood his own purpose, heritage, and context.

As we saw in the last chapter, knights were proud of the glorious deeds of their families, no matter whether those deeds were done against the Muslims of Granada or against someone else. So what are we to make of knights like Manrique who so vigorously trumpeted the superlative nature of their *linajes*' accomplishments in the holy war? For one thing, we might accept precisely that such a superlative nature circulated among the chivalric elite. There is never any debate over whether or not the holy war was the *highest* calling for Castilian knights. More importantly, that some knights emphasized holy war in their family history more than others suggests to us that actually committing to holy war was a prescriptive move as well on the part of knightly authors.⁵⁸ As a public pronouncement, a text written in the Castilian language would have served as an inducement to Castilians to commit to the highest calling. If it was a reality for Manrique's *linaje*, for the *linajes* of the Guzmanes and the Ponce de Leones, it was realistic for Castilian knights at large to participate in the holy war. More than almost any other single component of chivalry, the idea of holy war and of *reconquista* served as a call to action for Castilian knights. On the southern frontier, they would continue to find honor, reward, and redemption. If they would simply take up the historical imperative that God had granted them – an imperative that was not granted to the knights of France or England or Florence – they could win a glory unlike any other imaginable.

---

riquezas / ni vajillas; / maz hizo guerra a los moros, / ganando sus fortalezas / y sus villas; / y en las lides que venció."
⁵⁵ Ibid., 130–131. "alcanzó la dignidad / de la gran Caballería / de la Espada."
⁵⁶ Ibid., 122–123.
⁵⁷ Ibid., 135. "que aunque la vida perdió, / dejónos harto consuelo / su memoria."
⁵⁸ For a comparison with northern Europe on this point see Nicholas Paul, *To Follow in Their Footsteps: The Crusades and Family Memory in the High Middle Ages* (Ithaca, NY: Cornell University Press, 2012).

For these knights, the Kingdom of Castile was specially blessed by God with such an opportunity.

Holy War, Political Stability, and the Trastámara Kings

Holy war constituted such an important intellectual component of chivalric ideology in late medieval Iberia that it contributed directly to the stability and instability of the Trastámara kings and their grip on the throne. Precisely because of the call to action presented by knights and knightly authors, the ideal of holy war as a unique and special opportunity granted by God to Castile was projected as an undeniable responsibility of the Trastámara kings. Those monarchs who understood the importance of the holy war tended to enjoy a smoother relationship with the knights of the realm. Those who did not embrace the holy mandate to reconquer all of Iberia saw more disobedience from their vassals and challenges to their rule. In short, the power of knightly ideas was strong enough to affect the fortunes of kings on the throne.[59] At the dawn of the Trastámara age in 1369, the ideal of holy war was not particularly powerful, but as the Trastámara nobility became more entrenched, kings of Castile found that the chivalric drive for holy war impinged more often upon their royal prerogative. From a modern perspective, we might be able to identify a number of reasons for this phenomenon, principal among them that engaging in the holy war kept armed and violent knights busy on the southern frontier, physically far from the centers of royal power, and too busy to contemplate challenging the king. As accurate as this may be, the chroniclers and knightly writers of the Trastámara period did not conceive of holy war with such a realpolitik approach. In their words and often in their deeds, they saw the success of kings as fundamentally wrapped up in their prosecution of the holy war simply because it was the honorable and chivalric thing to do. Under the early Trastámaras, knights and nobles who were recently established as victors in the civil war consolidated their gains and slowly began to call for holy war. As their calls were rebuffed in the late 14th century, they became louder and insisted that their monarch embrace their chivalric ideas. Far from being a story of monarchs manipulating knights, in late medieval Castile knights and nobles influenced the monarch's actions as well.

The first hints of a renewed chivalric emphasis on holy war came in the late 14th century, at just about the time that the nobility that came to power with the ascension of the Trastámara dynasty was moving into its second generation. The uncertainty over the Trastámara accomplishment had begun to fade and it became clear that Enrique II's order would be long lasting.

---

[59] For a comparison on this point with England and France, see Richard W. Kaeuper, *War, Justice, and Public Order* (Oxford: Oxford University Press, 1988).

Towards the end of Juan I's reign, in 1390, he had proposed placing himself on the Portuguese throne and renouncing the Castilian throne in favor of his son, the Infante Enrique. A major part of the objection to this scheme was that leaving the eleven-year-old Enrique in charge of Castile would expose the southern frontier to risk of invasion by the Muslims, which would lead to a great loss for Christendom. A strong king was needed to lead the fight against the Muslims.[60]

The reign of Enrique III has often been lauded as one in which Castile's fortunes improved and the relationship between Crown and knights improved.[61] Yet, even then, tensions concerning the southern frontier ran high. Despite a truce with Castile, the Muslims of Granada raided into Murcia in 1392, testing Enrique, who the new king of Granada perceived to be weak and ineffective, and no doubt worrying the inhabitants of the frontier. A particular event suggests this worry and hints at a debate among the leading men of Castile concerning the war against Granada. Two years after the Granadan raids into Murcia, in an episode resembling a romance, Martín Yañez de Barbudo, the Master of Alcantara, sent a message to the king of Granada, insisting that he acknowledge the truth and goodness of the faith of Christ while renouncing Islam and declaring it to be false and deceitful. The Master went on to challenge the king to formal combat, offering him a two-to-one advantage in manpower. Apparently finding the request ridiculous, the king of Granada had the Master's messengers arrested, causing him much dishonor, whereupon he sought to vindicate his honor in the default method of chivalry, by attacking Granada.[62] King Enrique, on hearing this news, was upset; he sent messengers to Barbudo, insisting that it was not only wrong to break the king's truce with Granada, but that he was also embarking on a suicide mission, with too few men to effectively fight the Muslims. The Master rebuffed the messengers, insisting that the cross that led his army would not turn back.[63] Clearly, the Master and the king did not see eye to eye.

The debate about the Master's commitment came when two nobles, the lord of Aguilar and the marshal of Castile, came to him to try to dissuade

---

[60] López de Ayala, "Don Juan el Primero," in *Biblioteca Autores de Españoles*, vol. 66, 128.
[61] Joseph O'Callaghan describes Enrique III as "an effective ruler who closely guarded his authority and succeeded in containing the ambitions" of men who would disrupt the status quo. Joseph F. O'Callaghan, *A History of Medieval Spain* (Ithaca, NY: Cornell University Press, 1975) 537–538. Emilio Mitre Fernandez' landmark work has demonstrated that in granting magistracies to the leading nobles of his realm, Enrique III incorporated them further into the governance of the realm, what Fernandez refers to as a "tight oligarchy," suggesting that Enrique did so as part of a program seeking to centralize power. Emilio Mitre Fernandez, *La extension del regimen de corregidores en el reinado de Enrique III de castilla*, 44–50.
[62] López de Ayala, "Don Enrique Tercero," in *Biblioteca Autores de Españoles*, vol. 66, 221.
[63] Ibid., 221–222.

him from his holy mission. In a long argument, these two men suggested that the Master was wrong for going against his lord king's wishes, but they highlighted two significant reasons why he ought to stand down. Firstly, Andalucía was not prepared for war, and provoking the king of Granada into attacking would result in great loss to the Castilian frontier. Secondly, Barbudo did not have enough men to do real damage to the Muslims; the two nobles reminded him that the many victorious leaders of the *reconquista* always had large armies to fight their enemies. As part of the remembrance of the *reconquista*, the lord and the marshal noted that kings leading their people into war with a great host was the most effective way to defeat the enemy. The war against Granada was certainly a laudable endeavor, but one in which the king needed to lead and which needed to be better planned. Some of the knights in the Master's force were convinced, and abandoned the mission, but Barbudo refused to turn back, trusting in a miracle from God. He was killed in the ensuing battle.[64] When King Enrique heard of his death, he sent a message to the king of Granada, explaining that the Master had acted without his license and declaring that "if evil had befallen him there, he deserved it."[65] The tension between Enrique and some of his knights over his Granadan policy was on full display.

Still one more dimension of the episode suggests not only tension between Enrique and some of his knights, but the way in which it might be leveraged by a clever man. The Master of Santiago, hearing of the Master of Alcantara's debacle, went to the king and advised him on his next course of action. Knowing that there were still several lords in Andalucía who had not reconciled themselves to Enrique's rule, the Master advised Enrique to raise an army in Andalucía and make as if he were planning to invade Granada. As Enrique followed this advice, he summoned the malcontent lords to join his army and prepare to attack the Muslims, ostensibly because the king of Granada had opened a war on Castile. The malcontents came and made their peace with Enrique, who received them well. He did not follow through on his reported desire to go to war against his southern neighbor; the suggestion of holy war itself was enough to bring Castilian knights to his side. Perhaps this option was enough to maintain stability through the rest of Enrique's reign. One wonders if the promise of war without war itself would have been enough thereafter.

We need not speculate about whether Enrique's successor could have gotten away with empty promises of warfare, for on Enrique's death, one of the two people named regent for his infant son, Juan II, was the child-king's uncle, the Infante Fernando. The 15th century brought much more dynamism to the fortunes of the Castilian crown vis-à-vis the nobility

---

[64] Ibid., 222–223.
[65] Ibid., 223. "si mal se avia fallado della, él se lo merescia."

as the martial efforts of the Trastámara monarchs developed. The period between the minority of Juan II and the reign of Isabel and Fernando shows a clear decline of central authority. Juan II's reign (1406–1454) can be logically divided into two markedly different periods – the first being his minority, dominated by his uncle and regent Fernando de Antequera, and the second being his personal rule, from 1419 on. Perhaps unexpectedly, the long minority was "a time of comparative tranquility,"[66] which is to say that during the thirteen-year period when others ruled in Juan's name, there were few internal problems. It appeared as if the regency of Fernando and Juan's mother, Catalina, helped to stabilize Castilian government. During Juan's minority, the nearly constant war with Granada was the only major external conflict, though the Hundred Years' War did flare up again, with England proclaiming war against Castile in 1418.

Known to Castilian history as Fernando de Antequera in recognition of his conquest of that town from the Kingdom of Granada, the regent Fernando devoted much of his attention to the *reconquista*. Fernán Pérez de Guzmán, in his chronicle of the reign of Juan II, wastes little time before training his focus on the frontier, observing that Muhammad VII had broken the truce and invaded Castile, that he had been defeated by the marshal of Castille, and that Fernando and his co-regent, the Queen Mother Catalina of Lancaster, "knowing this, were greatly pleased."[67] Upon receiving news that Muhammad had renewed the war, Fernando proposed to lead the war effort himself. One by one, and at great length, Guzmán reads out the praises sung by all present at court on Fernando's announcement. The queen praises the infante's love of the kingdom and his willingness to place himself in travails and danger to preserve the estate of her son and subjugate the infidels. Sancho de Roxas, the bishop of Palencia, extols Fernando's virtue and goodness, calling him a "true Christian zealous in the service of God." Responding for all the counts and *ricos hombres* and knights and squires, Admiral Alfonso Enriquez pledges their support and all that is necessary to serve God and the king. Even the representatives of the towns and rural places take the opportunity to declare their support for Fernando's "most noble proposition."[68] Quite possibly Fernán Pérez de Guzmán invented some of the particular words he placed in the mouths of those at court; the enthusiastic response is probably less contrived. The armies raised for the ensuing war against Granada were well populated with the leading knights of the realm, and Guzmán himself operated among the elites of Castilian society – he likely shared many of the views of those elites.

---

[66] O'Callaghan, *Medieval Spain*, 541.
[67] Pérez de Guzmán, "don Juan, segundo," 280.
[68] Ibid., 280–282.

The intention declared, Fernando, unlike his brother, Enrique III, moved to make the Granadan campaign a reality. At nearly every step our sources paint a picture of Fernando aggressively working in concert with his knights to defeat the Muslim enemy and, significantly, fully embracing the chivalric ethos as he goes. Early in the campaign, in 1407, the infante sent Martín Alonso de Montemayor to reconnoiter the Granadan castle of Audita. The knights were attacked by the Muslims and Martín, filled with righteous anger, took the castle by force and burned and pillaged the village below the castle, killing and imprisoning dozens of men and women. The infante was greatly pleased with Martín's initiative.[69] At other times, Fernando proved himself to demonstrate chivalric virtue even more strongly than his knights. Late in 1407, he ordered Juan de Velasco to lead a raiding party past a certain point in enemy territory. Juan's knights were encouraged by the infante's aggressive stance, but Juan himself refused to continue, insisting that he and his men needed to rest. As a result, the Muslims outmaneuvered Juan and denied his ability to raid effectively. The chronicler assures us that the infante was most angry with Juan's reluctance to fight.[70] Shortly after this incident, the infante was laying siege to Setenil, an effort which was going poorly for the Castilians. In response to some of his knights, who suggested that they ought to abandon the siege, Fernando castigated them, saying

> I would have great shame to depart from here without doing more … I came here with so many and such noble knights as you … and it has been nineteen days that we are here without accomplishing more … and to have to depart now seems most shameful to me; and think well on this, and see if it seems good to you that we should fight a day or two [longer].[71]

The infante artfully deployed the chivalric fear of shame in order to maintain the chivalric virtue of prowess. Importantly, the siege of Setenil not only displayed the infante's understanding of chivalry in its most basic form, but also enshrined his emphasis on holy war against Islam, for after the siege ended successfully for the Castilians, he went to Sevilla, kissing a cross on the way to the church, and gave thanks to God for his victory over the enemies of the Holy Faith.[72]

---

[69] Ibid., 294.
[70] Ibid., 297.
[71] Ibid., 299. "[Y]o he gran vergüenza de partir de aqui sin mas hacer, porque desde que aquí estamos nunca probamos hacer cosa de lo que se debia; que razon fuera, pues yo aquí vine con tantos y tan nobles caballeros como vosotros … é ha diez y nueve dias que estamos aquí sin hacer mas de lo que vedes; é haber de partir así, á mí parece muy vergonzoso; é pensad bien en ello, é ved si os parecerá bien que la combatamos un dia ó dos …"
[72] Ibid., 301. Devaney and Ruiz have provided deeper analyses of Fernando's entry into Sevilla. Thomas Devaney, *Enemies in the Plaza* (Philadelphia: University of Pennsylvania

Several years before his campaign against Granada, on the Feast of the Assumption of the Blessed Virgin in 1403, Fernando had founded a new chivalric order, which he named the Order of the Jar and the Griffin. Dedicated to the Blessed Virgin, Fernando's order was designed with one goal in mind: the destruction of Muslims and the protection of Christendom. As Amy Remensnyder has observed, Fernando's contemporaries gushed about his dedication to the Blessed Virgin and his prosecution of the holy war, with one poet noting that because he was "devoted to the Blessed Virgin … he vanquishes and conquers the great land of the Moors."[73] Fernando's military action certainly represented his commitment to holy war; that he also labored to show his dedication to holy war in cultural and political acts speaks to his intellectual dedication to that chivalric priority.

Throughout early 1408, the infante, preoccupied with administrative business, was absent from the frontier, leaving its defense to the frontier lords – a tactical mistake – as the king of Granada raided through Andalucía. The knights of the frontier sent word to the queen and the infante, requesting that they send more troops to the south, and both regents quickly agreed to do so, realizing that they had been greatly shamed in allowing the war effort to falter. Though it may seem counter-intuitive, later in 1408, the regents continued to prioritize the holy war by arranging a truce with Granada. Far from attempting to avoid a war, the queen and infante set about raising funds from the kingdom in order to enable them to continue the war at a later date.[74] Even in peace, Fernando (and Catalina) kept the effort against Granada at the forefront of their policies. We might begin to suspect that the regents were falling into the pattern of Enrique III, promising action without undertaking it, but the evidence we have suggests that they were sincere in their intentions, moving to raise funds for a resumption of the war.[75] In addition, the newly enthroned king of Granada, Yusuf

---

Press, 2015), 1–4. Teofilo Ruiz, *A King Travels: Festive Traditions in Late Medieval and Early Modern Spain* (Princeton, NJ: Princeton University Press, 2012), 79–84. Certainly, a vigorous knight might give thanks to the Lord for a victory over any enemy, even if he was Christian. It is significant, though, that the language here explicitly emphasizes the war against unbelievers.

[73] The poet was Alfonso Alvarez Villasandino, quoted in Amy Remensnyder's *La Conquistadora*. Remensnyder offers a full account of Fernando's Marian devotion and links it to his commitment to holy war. Amy Remensnyder, *La Conquistadora, The Virgin Mary at War and Peace in the Old and New Worlds* (Oxford: Oxford University Press, 2014), 70–71. See also Angus MacKay, "Don Fernando de Antequera y la Virgen Santa María," in *Homenaje al profesor Juan Torres Fontes*, vol. 2 (Murcia: Universidad de Murcia, 1987), 949–958.

[74] Pérez de Guzmán, "don Juan, segundo," 306.

[75] Indeed, the records of the *cortes* held at Valladolid in 1411, after the conquest of Antequera had been completed, indicates that the people of Castile continued to support these efforts, agreeing to additional taxes, so long as it was guaranteed that such taxes

III (r. 1408–1417) saw fit to break the truce with an attack on Priego, likely expecting that the Christian resumption of war was not far off.

With Yusuf's attack on Priego, Fernando returned to the frontier to prosecute the war which would define his legacy in Castile. Arriving outside the town of Antequera in 1410, the infante and the bishop of Palencia engaged the Muslims in tough fighting, with a Cistercian brother carrying the crucifix at the center of the army. With the strength of the Christian armies and their leaders, the Muslims outside Antequera were defeated and the Castilians sacked the enemy camp, full of many valuable goods. Fernando himself took nothing from the camp, as he "wanted nothing, save the honor of the victory."[76] As the siege of Antequera continued, the infante, channeling his noble anger into the war effort, thrust forward, embracing chivalry. As he had done at the siege of Setenil, Fernando angrily raised the specter of shame to drive his knights forward, at one point shouting out to the knights and men-at-arms who were performing less admirably than he liked, "Have shame, and do that which I ask!" The knights did indeed do that which he asked, redoubling their efforts.[77] Before assaulting Antequera, Fernando sent for the banner of Santo Isidro de León, which he desired to carry into battle. The significance, as Guzmán eagerly notes, is that the banner had since ancient times been carried into battle by the kings of Castile whenever they fought the Muslims in person.[78] That particular Castilian component of chivalry, an emotional connection to the glorious *reconquistadores* of the past, is writ large in Fernando's desire to carry the banner with him. He actively and publicly linked himself with the long history of the *reconquista*. Time and time again the infante behaved in this manner and the knights of Castile cleaved to him as a result. Fernando fully understood the powerful ideology of chivalry. He used the language of honor and shame to encourage the men in the army, and appears himself to have lived the chivalric ideal.

Whether or not the historian can judge if Fernando was indeed such a model of knightly behavior, his contemporaries appear to have endorsed the idea wholeheartedly. Fernando had news that Yusuf was on his way to relieve Antequera with a large army, and the infante sent letters to the cities of Córdoba, Sevilla, Xerez, and Carmona, ordering them without delay to send as many men as they could. The cities respond enthusiastically, not, we are told, because they recognized Fernando as their rightful lord who was entitled to call up levies, but because he was much loved. Fernando's marshalling of more troops effectively dissuaded Yusuf from attacking, but

---

would be used to continue prosecuting the war against Granada. *Cortes* held at Valladolid in 1411. *Cortes de los antiguos*, vol. 3, 5–7.

[76] Pérez de Guzmán, "don Juan, segundo," 319–320. "el Infante ninguna cosa quiso, salvo la honra de la victoria."

[77] Ibid., 321. "*Habed vergüenza, é haced lo que yo hago.*"

[78] Ibid., 328.

Fernando, wanting to ensure that his campaign was a success, sent letters to Córdoba and Sevilla, requesting that they send money and goods to pay the troops. Again his request was granted, because "the Infante was much loved by all."[79] When Antequera finally fell to the Castilians, there was a debate over which knights entered the tower of the village first; Fernando intervened to ensure that all the men who claimed to have been first into the tower were greatly honored, as well as a dozens more men who were known to be at the fore of the fighting.[80] Over and over, Fernando's efforts were supported by the fighting men of Castile because of his embrace of the chivalric impulse for war against Granada and their desire for honor and glory in that martial effort; the holy war functioned to unite the warriors of Castile around their ruler. With the conquest of Antequera complete, Fernando, known thereafter as Fernando de Antequera, made a victory march back to Sevilla, where he was received in the fashion usually reserved for a king.[81]

For most of Fernando's regency, it is telling that he faced little possibility of revolt or open civil war. Early in the minority government, there were some tensions between Queen Catalina and the infante about the proper ordering of the regency, but these were resolved without conflict by dividing the geographical areas over which each regent ruled. Moreover, Catalina fully supported Fernando's presence on the front and gloried in his victories as much as did other lords. We do not have explicit evidence that the knights and lords of Castile avoided internal conflict and the ensuing destabilization of Castile *because* of Fernando's embrace of chivalric virtues, but the implicit evidence infuses most accounts which we have of Fernando's career. Guzmán's chronicle continuously and effusively praises Fernando in exactly these terms and leaves little doubt that the respect and love he commanded arose from his vigorous prosecution of the war. As with any of the rulers of Castile in this period, there is the possibility that the stability of Fernando's regency was due to non-ideological factors. True, Fernando denied the knights of the realm the *opportunity* to rebel against him, because they were busy on the frontier. True, there were economic incentives for them to remain complacent while they served with him in the south; booty gained from the war would have kept them happy. But it is telling that our sources are silent on these issues. Chroniclers and knightly writers argued either that Fernando was a good leader or that he was a good knight. The preeminence of chivalry and its emphasis on holy war trumped discussions of economics or realpolitik during Fernando's regency. In short, Fernando de Antequera was a consummate politician and a man who understood the nature of his time. A central component of his understanding of his time

---

[79] Ibid., 327. "el Infante fuese de todos mucho amado."
[80] Ibid., 330.
[81] Ibid., 332–333.

and his ability to manipulate public perceptions of him was grounded in his understanding of chivalry. He was able to influence knightly perceptions *because* he knew what the knights of the realm expected from a king. He cleverly used the ideological tools available to him in order to provide himself with a strong foundation of support and to avoid challenges to his rule as regent.

Perhaps the best evidence for Fernando's comprehension of chivalry and his embrace of it in prosecuting the holy war presents itself in contrast to the personal rule of Juan II. At age thirteen, Juan took the reins of the government of Castile on the death of his mother. Fernando had himself died in 1416, after reigning as Fernando I of Aragon for four years. Juan's personal rule would be marked by precisely the kind of internal disruptions that were absent throughout Fernando's regency government, and these disruptions began almost immediately after the regency ended; in 1419 armed men of the kingdom entered the king's chambers in order to imprison his favorite, Juan Furtado de Mendoza.[82] The best way to characterize Juan's approach to the war against Granada is one of indecision and hesitancy; Juan sometimes acted as if he would go to war and sometimes even opened hostilities with his Muslim neighbor, but the effort was always half-hearted and subject to revision. The troubles of Juan's reign are complex and have much to do with the personal ambitions of powerful men in Castile. Ideas were nevertheless still important, and criticism and praise of Juan during his personal reign was often couched in the language of holy war and chivalry. Indeed, Juan's problems with his favorites and his ambitious cousins, the infantes of Aragon, contributed to his confused policy concerning Granada, which in turn helped to open a gap between Juan and the Castilian knights in chivalric terms, which led to further instability. This vicious cycle is at the heart of the troubles of Juan's reign, and his failure to embrace chivalry in the way that his uncle had needs to be seen as one piece of this puzzle.

Almost from the beginning of his personal rule, the Castilian government was plagued both by Juan's willingness to allow his favorites to effectively rule in his name and by the efforts of the infantes of Aragon to secure land and power throughout Castile.[83] Before her death, Juan's mother had negotiated a truce with Granada, partly because of further challenges for Castile, namely the renewal of the Hundred Years' War and Henry V of England's proclamation of war against Castile as part of that renewal. By 1421, these various challenges were clearly dominating Juan's policies concerning Granada. In that year, ambassadors from the king of Granada arrived at Juan's court, requesting that the truce be renewed for three more years and that the tribute Granada was paying to Castile be lessened. The ambassa-

---

[82] Ibid., 381.

[83] For a full biography of Luna see Nicholas Round, *The Greatest Man Uncrowned, A Study of the Fall of Don Alvaro de Luna* (London: Tamesis Books Limited, 1986).

dors, well aware of Juan's challenges, openly noted that such an action was Juan's wisest choice, given his internal troubles; the king agreed with the ambassadors and renewed the truce with Granada.[84] Clearly, at this point, and through most of his reign, Juan's choices were limited concerning his foreign policy; the king was forced to react to situations as they developed rather than causing situations to develop as he pleased.

Throughout the 1420s, the situation remained difficult. Castile was frequently either at war with some combination of Aragon, Navarre, and England, or effectively so, due to the support of the infantes of Aragon, particularly of their brother, King Alfonso V of Aragon (r. 1415–1468). As this intra-Christian warfare continued, we have evidence that Juan was not particularly disliked or resented for this violence. As we will see in the next chapter, all fighting, even against other Christians, was still a valorous endeavor. In 1429 Juan sent to order all the men of the frontiers in the northeast that they should "make cruel war" in the kingdoms of Navarre and Aragon, an order to which the knights of the frontier happily responded.[85] The bishop of Calahorra found himself besieged by the king of Navarre in 1430 and begged King Juan to come personally to relieve him; the king sent men to relieve the bishop, but failed to come himself. The evidence of the northern wars suggests that the chivalric elite were willing to support Juan, given the difficult realities, even though the holy war had been delayed.

Even as he dealt with his Christian neighbors and unwelcome cousins, Juan was thinking about his southern frontier. Shortly before Aragon and Navarre had renewed their war with Castile in 1429, Granadan ambassadors had arrived at Juan's court requesting an extension of the truce for another four or five years. Juan, with the agreement of the *cortes*, granted Granada an extension of just six months, and then only if the king of Granada turned over more Christian captives. After the ambassadors departed, we are told, Juan began preparing to raise funds and armies for a war against Granada at the expiration of the six months. A year later, Muhammad IX, a man who would be king of Granada four times over thirty-five years, given Granada's own internal vexations, sent an embassy to Juan not only requesting a renewal of the truce, in recognition of Juan's northern wars, but even offering to send troops to aid Juan in his struggle. The Castilian king responded by rejecting Muhammad's alliance, but offering to renew the truce for another year and a half if Muhammad would send a great tribute and release all Christian captives in his kingdom. Guzmán informs his reader that Juan "did this knowing that he would not grant it, for he had cause to make war [on Muhammad]."[86]

---

[84] Pérez de Guzmán, "don Juan, segundo," 405.
[85] Ibid., 462–463.
[86] Ibid., 483–484. "Esto hacia el Rey conosciendo que se le no otorgaria, porque él hubiese cause para hacer la guerra."

That war would be slow in coming, but would indeed arrive in grand fashion. In August of 1430, some months after receiving Muhammad's embassy, the kingdoms of Aragon, Navarre, and Castile finally agreed on a truce and Juan moved his focus south. However, August was a less than optimal time to open a campaign, with the heat making for a most unpleasant experience for men and horses. Nonetheless, Juan ordered that supplies be prepared on the frontier and that levies be raised, and he went himself to Burgos to make a great display of power, wherein he declared his intention to march against Granada in March of the following year. As the year wore on, Juan's ambassadors convinced the king of Tunis to cut off support for Muhammad, while the bishop of Jaén along with the *adelantado mayor* of Andalucía raided into Granada, skirmishing with their Muslim enemies. During the first months of 1431, Juan held "many counsels" about the coming campaign, during which various strategies were debated. Some knights advised Juan to enter through all parts of the kingdom, cutting and burning as much as he could. Others, perhaps remembering Fernando de Antequera's glorious victory, recommended that the king attempt to take a major city or fortification, such as Málaga. Ultimately, Juan took the advice of a Muslim convert to Christianity that he ought to head straight for the Vega de Granada (around the city of Granada itself), at which point a prince of the Nasrid royal family named Yusuf would come to him and work to overthrow Muhammad.[87] When Juan finally arrived outside of the city of Granada, a large army of Muslims sallied from the city and attacked the Christian army, putting the Master of Calatrava, the Constable of Castile and several counts in dire straits. As the Christian army looked to be heading for defeat, Juan broke his camp and joined the battle, turning the tide and producing a glorious Christian victory. Guzmán sings Juan's praises, declaring that the Christians won through their bravery and strength "and the grace of Our Lord, and the good venture of the King."[88] He goes on to list the numerous knights who took part in the battle, noting the great glory that accrued to them all. For the next six days, Juan and his army cut down all the grain and vines and orchards in the area around Granada, and demolished all the buildings and towers and houses within three leagues of the city. In the space of a year, Juan took advantage of the internal dissension in Granada to place his own man, Yusuf IV, on the throne. Yusuf offered his kingdom as a tributary state and a vassal of the great king of Castile. For a brief, shining moment, Juan II appeared to be living up to the legacy of his great forebears, whether they be Fernando de Antequera or the great *reconquistadores* of the past.

---

[87] Ibid., 496.
[88] Ibid., 498. "que por la gracia de Nuestro Señor é buena ventura del Rey …"

The moment was fleeting. Having defeated the Muslims, Juan held a council to determine his next move. Most of the knights and the grandees of the realm recognized that the Muslims were now fearful of Juan's potency on the field of battle, as well as the fact that the Muslims had reduced numbers after the battle outside Granada, and they advised the king that he should lay siege to the city and expect to be there for several months, until the king of Granada should surrender. A small minority, led by Álvaro de Luna, suggested that Juan's victory was sufficient and that the Muslim king would no longer be a threat to Castile, fearful as he was of the Castilian king's might. This smaller faction argued that Juan ought to return to his own land, and perhaps prepare for a future campaign against Málaga or another city.[89] The king took the advice of the Constable and the rest of the knights present were apparently flabbergasted. How on earth could Juan, on the brink of fulfilling the promise of the *reconquista*, walk away from such glory? Guzmán, expressing the perplexity of the larger faction, identifies this as a key moment in divine history by observing that both before and after the council, great earthquakes struck various cities in Castile.[90] Apparently, the Almighty Himself frowned on Juan's poor decision. In words which perhaps understate the shock at the king's decision, Guzmán speaks for the assembled knights and men-at-arms, saying, "It was a thing of wonder that with all the evils which the Moors received in this war, never was the party of the king moved."[91] Guzmán's only explanation for the king's decision is either that the existing discord between the grandees and the Constable led Luna to advocate for a contrary position, or, just as likely, that the Constable had been bribed by the infidels. Whatever the case, Luna's position (and therefore the king's position) made no sense in a chivalric framework.

As the truce between Castile and Granada expired in 1433, Juan ordered men to the frontier but refrained from making a return trip himself. Throughout the mid-1430s, Juan was distracted, choosing not to prosecute the war with Granada himself and working to conclude a lasting peace with Aragon and Navarre, the treaty being approved in 1436. By 1437, the dam had broken. The magnates of the realm who were not tied to Luna by marriage or patronage formed a league against him and civil war broke out. It is worth noting that the troubles at the beginning of Juan's personal rule centered on his cousins, the infantes of Aragon. While the magnates certainly took sides in the early troubles, their initiative in opposing the king truly came to fruition with the rising against Luna. Given what we know about chivalric ideology, though, and our chronicler's description of the events after Juan's successful campaign, we ought to seriously consider

---

[89] Ibid., 499–500.
[90] Ibid.
[91] Ibid. "Fue cosa de maravillar que con todos quantos ales los Moros en esta guerra rescibieron, jamas se movió partido al Rey."

the possibility that Juan's (or rather, Luna's) decision to curtail the holy war was a significant factor in the decision of the chivalric elite to rise against Luna's position of privilege.

In the ensuing civil war, the league of nobles, together with Juan's son and heir apparent, Enrique, defeated the king's forces, and in negotiations in 1439 they had Luna expelled from the court. The civil war continued, though, as Luna's supporters retained their positions of authority. After the decisive Battle of Medina del Campo in 1441, Juan was again defeated and captured by his enemies. This time, Luna was exiled from Castile for six years, a new counsel favoring the magnates was installed and royal powers were curtailed to such an extent that Juan was effectively a puppet ruler for a regency government dominated by the leading nobles of Castile as well as the infantes of Aragon. By 1444, the prince Enrique switched sides, joining Luna in a new coalition against the power of the infantes. In May of 1445, Enrique defeated the infantes at the Battle of Olmedo and restored his father and the Constable to power, at the same time carving out a position of privilege for himself. Ultimately, though, Luna thought himself more secure than he was, ordering a number of arbitrary arrests in 1448 which precipitated noble insurrections across the kingdom. Throughout these troubles, the king of Granada took advantage of the wild disorder in Castile, and, in what must have been a living nightmare for the knightly ideal of the *reconquista*, the Muslims retook several castles and towns of the frontier. As the troubles in Castile continued, the Muslims raided as far as Jaén and Utrera, burning, pillaging, and killing. The knightly fear of the undoing of the *reconquista* was given voice by Guzmán:

> The Moors, knowing the tumults which were occurring in these kingdoms, entered through various parts, and made many great damages, not only carrying off steeds and cattle and men and women, but taking by force some villages and fortifications which the Christians had taken with great expenses and travails and deaths and the shedding of much blood.[92]

All the great work of the past heroes of the *reconquista* might be undone because Juan had lost control of the kingdom. While stability seemed to be a thing of the past, the troubles would eventually die down, with Luna being executed in 1453, a year before Juan himself passed away. For centuries, Juan's reign was remembered as a period of weakness and uncertainty.

Juan's successor, Enrique IV, was likely a masterful military strategist. His military policy concerning Granada was essentially to slowly bleed and

---

[92] Ibid., 654. "Los Moros conosciendo las turbaciones que en estos Reynos habia, entraron por diversas partes, é hicieron muy grandes dañoa, no solamente llevando grandes cavalgadas de ganados é hombres y mugeres, mas tomando por fuerza algunas villas é fortalezas que los Christianos habian ganado con grandes gastos y trabajos, é muertes y derramiento de mucha sangre."

starve the Muslim kingdom to death. There would be few great battles or major campaigns, but, from a 21st-century military historian's perspective, his strategy was not bad. For all his experience and sound martial policy, though, Enrique IV failed to embrace chivalry in the way that Fernando de Antequera had so masterfully done and that Juan II had nearly achieved midway through his reign. The dissonance between objectively good military strategy and powerful cultural ideals is nothing short of breathtaking and speaks precisely to the incredible power of ideas. By the late 15th century, the knights of Castile did not want to be slowly fed the Kingdom of Granada; they wanted to hunt and kill it. In disregarding this impulse, Enrique opened himself to criticism of his policy on the southern frontier, even if it was a sound policy.

Shortly after Enrique succeeded his father in 1454, he made clear his intention to roll back the gains which the Muslims had made during the last decades of Juan's reign. It was a promising start to his time on the throne. In 1455, Enrique assembled the noblemen of Castile in a council, in part to prepare for a resumption of the holy war. Historians have been blessed to have several different chronicles of Enrique's reign, some friendly to the king, and some decidedly less so. In both friendly and unfriendly chronicles, Enrique's motives at his council are lauded. Both Diego de Valera, no friend of the king, and Diego Enriquez del Castillo, the king's chaplain, record his desire to reopen the holy war in chivalric terms, emphasizing the completion of the *reconquista*. Valera, recording the opinions of the gathered knights, notes that

> since it was pleasing to Our Lord to give to the king so many and so great means to recover the land which the Moors in Spain had usurped, in injury to the Kings past and of [Enrique himself], and with such noble chivalry such as he had in his kingdoms, his proposition in wanting to make war was holy and good, and it should be done.[93]

Castillo, giving voice to the king himself, records a similar sentiment:

> [I]t is a just and most necessary thing that we the Catholic and true Christians want to undertake [war against Granada], for by discarding vices and taking on virtues, we destroy the enemies who persecute our faith; we fight against the Moors who usurped our land ... we have clear justice ... our purpose is holy and the zeal of God guides us, whose cause is that which we do ... Whereby we hope in the infinite goodness of our Redeemer that He

---

[93] Diego de Valera, "Memorial de diversas hazañas," in *Biblioteca de Autores Españoles*, vol. 70, 4. "pues á nuestro Señor habia placido dar al Rey tantos é tan grandes aparejos para recobrar la tierra que los moros en España usurpada, en injuria de los Reyes antepasados é dél, é de tan noble caballería cuanta en sus Reynos habia, el propósito suyo en les querer facer guerra era sancto é bueno, é que lo debia luégo poner en obra ..."

will give us victory over them, and in such a manner, that we will return with honor, and recover that which our ancestors lost.[94]

No doubt the king's move for war against Granada was perceived by the leading men of the realm as a strong endorsement of the chivalric program of holy war. Enrique prepared even further to ensure the success of the war, both in a theological sense and in a practical sense, by sending messengers to Pope Nicholas V (r. 1447–1455), requesting that he grant a plenary indulgence for the war against Islam. This request would eventually be granted by Nicholas' successor, Callixtus III (r. 1455–1458).[95]

With the chivalry of Castile supporting him, a papal grant of indulgence forthcoming, and a powerful army raised, Enrique stood ready in March of 1455 to destroy the Kingdom of Granada, winning glory and honor for himself for decades to come as he set out for the city of Granada itself, his army burning and pillaging as it went. Then, with little fanfare, Enrique dismissed the greater part of his army and departed himself for Écija, in his own kingdom, while the remaining knights were left to raid as they pleased. According to Valera, "many of the knights were very much awed for having seen such great preparations made and not making more of that which was done."[96] As the small groups of knights raided and skirmished with the enemy, Enrique ended up setting up his camp near Málaga for a time while his men completed *la tala*, the cutting down of wheat in the Granadan countryside. While Valera suggests that the king had no desire to fully undertake the holy war and even suggests that he was in league with infidels, Castillo defends the king's strategy as thoughtful and cautious, designed to starve and weaken the Muslims before going on to besiege their cities and castles. Whatever their opinions about the king's strategy, both chroniclers agree that Enrique did not want to engage the Muslims in pitched battle; the opportunity for knights to win honor through prowess under Enrique's strategy was diminished. Without taking sides in a debate more than half a millennium old, it is clear that Valera represents the dominant opinion of the chivalric elite. A knight himself, Valera carefully notes multiple examples

---

[94] Diego Enríquez del Castillo, "La historia del rey Don Enrique el Cuarto," in *Biblioteca de Autores Españoles*, vol. 70, 104–105. "[J]usta cosa é muy necesaria es que nosotros los católicos como verdaderos christianos la queramos emprender, porque con ella desechando los vicios omando las virtudes, destruyamos los enemigos que persiguen nuestra fe; peleemos contra los morors que usurpan nuestra tierra ... tenemos clara justicia ... nuestro propósito es sancto, y el celo de Dios nos guia, cuya causa es la que se hace ... Por donde espero en la infinita bondad de nuestro Redentor que nos dará vencimiento de ellos tal, é de tal manera, que tornaremos con honra, é recobraremos lo que nuestros antepasados perdieron."
[95] Valera, "Memorial de diversas hazañas," 4.
[96] Ibid., 5

of knights seeking engagements with their enemies against the king's will, desiring to win honor through vigorous deeds of arms.

A third chronicler, Alfonso de Palencia, also showered Enrique with vitriol. Although Palencia was not a knight himself, he used the language of chivalry to attack the king, partially titling a chapter dealing with the campaign "The shameful conduct of Don Enrique, and wickedness in which was revealed his secret intentions."[97] The chronicler notes that the king had assembled a mighty force of knights and infantry, perhaps some 3,000 horse and 10,000 foot, and great knights such as Juan Ponce de León, the count of Arcos. He goes on to claim that such a force was fully capable of destroying the Muslims at Málaga. Yet "all this host was powerless to execute some memorable deed, for it encountered an obstacle in the perverse will of the king," who apparently ordered his men only to "impose themselves on the fruitpickers" and "cut off the ears of some peasants."[98] Palencia was certain that the city of Málaga was ready to fall if only the king had pressed the attack. Indeed, echoing the ideals of the corporate interest of all Castilians in completing the *reconquista*, Palencia described the failure at Málaga as a missed opportunity to increase the "honor and glory of the nation."[99] Searching for an answer to Enrique's inexplicable waffling on the holy war, Palencia concludes that the monarch must have been in league with the Muslims, even asserting that the king had secretly converted to Islam. Enrique would face constant troubles over the next twenty years. We can only wonder if his fortunes might have been different if he had embraced the holy war at this key moment outside Málaga.

Where in the case of Juan II we are unsure how clearly the king's Granadan policy affected the risings against him, in the case of Enrique IV we have some clearer evidence. In addition to the fact that Valera was angry at the king's policy on the southern frontier, we have Castillo identifying a connection between noble grumblings and the war effort. Immediately after explaining and defending Enrique's strategy, Castillo angrily notes that the knights were discontent over the policy and that *as a result of this discontent*, many of them set up secret confederations planning to arrest the king.[100]

---

[97] Alfonso de Palencia, "Crónica de Enrique IV," ed. and trans. Antonio Paz y Meliá in *Biblioteca de Autores Españoles* (Madrid: Ediciones Atlas, 1973), vol. 257, 70. "Capitulo VIII *Relajada disciplina del ejército. – Conducta vergonzosa de D. Enrique, y maldades en que se iban revelando sus secretas intenciones.*"
[98] Ibid., 73. "Toda esta muchedumbre fue impotente para ejecutar alguna hazaña memorable, por hallar un obstáculo en la perversa voluntad del Rey … que llagaba hasta imponer a los que arrancaban los frutales, castigos vergonzosos, como el de mandar cortar las orejas a algunos peones."
[99] Ibid. "era el honor y la gloria de la nación."
[100] Enríquez del Castillo, "Don Enrique el Cuarto," 105–106.

Though the king departed for Córdoba before the knights were able to act, Castillo attacks them in a fine prose:

> Oh! False disloyalty of vassals! Ugly thoughts of natural subjects! Dishonest enterprise of subject knights! Cruel presumption of knights! That such boldness you dare to make ... for to besmirch the nobility of your blood! Tell me now, then, indiscrete barons, who would defend your purity, when you destroy it without fear of having infamy? Who would sustain your honor when you revile it, without worrying about shame?[101]

Certainly Castillo was using the language of chivalry in the broadest sense, appealing to the knights' sense of honor and loyalty to their rightful lord. He took a very particular position about the right behavior of knights, but ultimately he, like his king, failed to understand the centrality of active prowess exercised against Muslims. Enrique's behavior, contrary to the ideal understood by the chivalric elite, resulted immediately in a plot to seize him and indirectly in general hostility towards and distrust of the king, as we will see.

Often the most cutting criticism of a man comes from his most devout supporters; without meaning to do so, they allow a glimpse of his true faults and errors. Such is the case with Enrique's Constable, Miguel Lucas de Iranzo. A man of relatively humble origins, he rose first through service to the marques of Villena and then in Enrique's retinue before his accession to the throne, being named Constable of Castile in 1458. Although he might have remained in the king's court and been active in politics at the center of the kingdom, Iranzo ended up spending most of his career on the southern frontier, either because he was devoted to the holy war (as he insists) or because he had powerful enemies at court (as historians have observed).[102] In any case, Iranzo both defended the frontier towns against Muslim incursions and brought the war across the border. His biography claims that he was always occupied in "prosecuting and continuing the war against the infidel enemies of our holy faith."[103] The praise of the Constable as a holy warrior extends to suggesting that everyone ought to be so great, claiming that "if more of those in the kingdom around the king had been filled with the same desire which the Constable had," not only Granada but all of the pagan kingdoms beyond would be vassals and tributaries

---

[101] Ibid., 106. "¡O falsa deslealtad de vasallos, feo pensamiento de súbditos naturales, deshonesta empresa de caballeros súbditos, cruel atrevimiento de caballeros, que tal osadia atrevíades, é presumíades emprender, para desdorar la nobleza de vuestra sangre! Decidme pues agora, indiscretos varones, ¿quién defendiera vuestra limpieza, quando vosotros la destruiais sin temor de haber infamia? ¿quién sostuviera vuestra honra, quando vosotros la denostábades, sin recelar vituperio?"

[102] See Carriazo's introduction to *Hechos del Condestable*, xxxvii–xliii.

[103] *Hechos del Condestable*, 85.

of Castile.[104] Although Iranzo's biography never directly criticizes Enrique, his message is clear: the king ought to be fighting against the Muslims. The biography, ostensibly praising the king for his grand military strategy, suggests the problem of Enrique's priorities, for when the Constable asked the king to continue the war against Islam, Enrique responded that it would be a glorious and magnificent thing if he made war against Aragon and Sicily and Navarre while his men did the same against the infidels.[105] The Constable went back to the frontier to continue the holy effort, leaving the king to do whatever it was he was engaged with in the north. The preoccupation of the southern lords and the prosecution of the *reconquista* was less important to the king.

In stark contrast to Fernando de Antequera's understanding of the chivalric ethos, and his willingness to lead personally at the front, awarding honor and glory to his knights and resolving disputes, Enrique IV's absence from the front allowed knightly rivalries born in the holy war to fester and erupt into local "private" wars. In 1462, long after Enrique had effectively left the prosecution of the holy war to the frontier lords, a number of lords and their retinues converged on the city of Gibraltar, aiming to take it from the Muslims. In a campaign that we will examine more fully in Chapter 4, two Andalucian families, the Guzmanes and the Ponce de Leones, both of whom claimed the city of Gibraltar as their familial right in the history of the *reconquista*, disputed who ought to take control of the city.

The contest between the Guzmanes and the Ponce de Leones at Gibraltar would quickly develop into a fully fledged feud. The two families, who between them controlled most of the land in Andalucía, expressed their disagreement over the rights to Gibraltar by turning Andalucía into a war zone, burning churches and monasteries, slaughtering one another's peasants and vassals, and generally wreaking havoc on the stability of the kingdom. One could imagine that, had Enrique been present at the siege of Gibraltar or willing to arbitrate effectively between the two families at the time, he might have avoided such tensions. In a more direct sense, Enrique's inability to consider the question of Gibraltar from a perspective that took into consideration the claims to the city on both sides also directly led to the Guzmán family rising in revolt against the king. In 1462, the Guzmanes had petitioned the king to resolve the issue, pressing their claim to the city of Gibraltar against the insidious craftiness of the Ponce de Leones. Enrique, disregarding the bases of the Guzmanes' claim, simply seized the city for himself and appointed his own governor. As a faction of nobles rose in revolt against Enrique in 1465, proposing to place his half-brother Alfonso on the throne, Juan de Guzmán, extracting a promise from Alfonso to grant

---

[104] Ibid.
[105] Ibid., 95–96.

the city to him, joined the rebels and fought against the king for the next three years, in one of the most tumultuous periods in the history of Trastámara Castile.[106] Enrique, like Juan before him, faced complex challenges during his time on the throne; his failure to readily embrace several key elements of chivalry compounded these challenges, leading to dissent and even rebellion among the chivalric elite.

Conclusions

The chivalric elite of late medieval Castile, like their counterparts north of the Pyrenees, held holy war to be the greatest and most worthy activity in which they could participate. Unlike their northern cousins, Castilians shared a frontier with the world of Islam and could relatively easily go to that frontier and fight against their religious enemies, if they so desired. Leading voices among Castilian chivalry called for the prosecution of the holy war, sometimes in order to redirect the destructive energies of knightly violence, other times to advance personal or familial agendas. Whatever the specific goal of holy war from the perspective of *realpolitik*, the ideology looked similar. Drawing on a centuries-old theology of crusade, Castilian knights maintained a vigorous desire for holy war even, or especially, during a period when the holy war had largely ground to a halt.

Blending a Church-approved theological valorization of slaughtering the infidel with concepts of honor, shame, and vengeance, medieval Castilians constructed a chivalric concept of *reconquista* in the 15th century. Postulating a historical narrative animated by sin, loss, and destruction, the idea of *reconquista* was more than simply holy war – it was holy war with a vengeance. In reclaiming the territories which had been lost to Islam some 700 years earlier, Castilian knights sought to vindicate the honor of their kingdom, of their faith, and of their families. The Trastámara kings, often slow to recognize the power of chivalry, suffered an ideological disconnect from many of the knights of their realm, regularly contributing to civil strife and political intrigues. The idea of holy war was able to trump sound military policy, political obedience on the part of royal vassals, and *convivencia* on the frontier itself. This powerful idea, which had fermented in the minds of knights as much as in those of clerics, would eventually be embraced by the Catholic Monarchs and would remake Spanish foreign policy at the dawn of the modern world.

---

[106] Phillips, *Enrique IV*, 57–58.

4

War Against Christians

Castile was at war again in 1396. In the last entry of his partial chronicle of the reign of Enrique III, Pedro López de Ayala writes simply: "And in this year the King [João I] of Portugal took to Badajoz, the King Don Enrique [III of Castile] being in Sevilla."[1] Ayala's terse statement is perhaps unremarkable; from 1396 we can look backwards and observe near constant war for the last thirty years: the Castilian civil war from 1366–1371, a territorial dispute with Portugal in 1372–1373, a similar dispute with Navarre in 1378–79, and an attempt on the part of Juan I to claim the Portuguese throne, a debacle that lasted from 1384 to 1389. Going forward, too, Castile and its knights would constantly be at war with their neighbors in the 15th century. Throughout much of this period, the Hundred Years' War raged between France and England, with Castilian knights often participating through piracy and naval raids on English and Portuguese territory, if not through engagements on land.[2] For Ayala, who had lived through and participated in many of these campaigns, even being captured by the enemy twice, a new war with Portugal, which ultimately proved to be a small and insignificant campaign, would have been business as usual. Not only from the royal chronicler's perspective, but from the perspective of knights and men-at-arms, a new war would not have been a shocking development. To be sure, another theater of war opening on the western frontier meant further opportunity for the chivalric elite to exercise their sword arms and win precious honor for themselves.

What may strike the modern reader as somewhat more remarkable is that nearly all of Castile's wars in the late 14th century, and many throughout the 15th century, were fought against fellow Christians: England, Portugal,

---

[1] Pedro López de Ayala, "Don Enrique Tercero," in *Biblioteca Autores Españoles*, ed. M. Rivadeneyra (Madrid: Impresores de Camara de S.M., 1876), vol. 66, 246. "E en este Año tomó el Rey de Portogal á Badajoz, estando el Rey Don Enrique en Sevilla."
[2] For examinations of Castilian kings and knights in various components of the Hundred Years War see *History of Warfare: The Hundred Years War (part II): Different Vistas*, ed. L.J.A. Villalon and D.J. Kagay (Boston: Brill, 2008); and Teofilo F. Ruiz, *Spain's Centuries of Crisis: 1300–1474* (Malden, MA: Blackwell, Publishing Ltd., 2011), especially pages 38–44.

Navarre, and occasionally Aragon and other Castilians. In the same thirty-year period that closed the 14th century, Castile fought non-Christian enemies only in small campaigns, often no more than raiding Granada, defending against raids from Granada, or fighting Muslim pirates in the Mediterranean. Given the paramount position of holy war in chivalric ideology discussed in the last chapter, why did the chivalry of late medieval Castile so consistently make war against their coreligionists? And what did they think of this? For the martial nobility that was brought to power with the Trastámaras, was there any sense of hesitation in raising one's sword against a brother in Christ?

Knights in Castile turned their swords and lances on their fellow Christians without too much difficulty. More importantly, they built an ideology specific to that task which saw religious and chivalric valorization of their inter-Christian violence. Although violence perpetrated against fellow Christians may not represent the romantic modern ideal of the medieval knight, it was very much a reality in the late Middle Ages.[3]

This chapter will argue that inter-Christian violence was a normal part of life in late medieval Castile. Indeed, the chivalric ideology of the Trastámara nobility placed such a high premium on honor achieved through violence that a Christian neighbor was a viable target against whom violence could be perpetrated and honor vindicated or won. Warfare in late medieval Castile was not some pure crusading virtue, it was not directed by popes or bishops, and it could rarely even be controlled by the Castilian Crown. Even as clerics and some knightly authors called for reforms in the violence of knights directed against fellow Christians, Castilian warriors kept shedding Christian blood for their own honor and advantage and even articulated an ideology that continued to valorize warfare against Christians. At the same time, warfare against fellow Christians often drew on the theology of the holy war – the two were not easily separable. Knights and lords whose personal and family history were washed in the blood of the infidel drew on precisely that tradition in order to justify and allow their violence against Christian neighbors. When the glory of their successes in the holy war was threatened, knights jealously defended them against usurpers or challengers.

---

[3] David Nirenberg's well-received study has dealt primarily with the Crown of Aragon and southern France and focuses on the persecution of religious minorities, especially Jews and Muslims. David Nirenberg, *Communities of Violence: Persecution of Minorities in the Middle Ages* (Princeton, NJ: Princeton University Press, 1996). Similarly, R.I. Moore has suggested that the development of a fundamentally Christian society which excluded religious minorities, sometimes violently, had begun by the 11th century. R.I. Moore, *The Formation of a Persecuting Society: Power and Deviance in Western Europe, 950–1250* (Oxford: Basil Blackwell, 1987). Teofilo Ruiz also discussed holy war and its effects, arguing that "the Reconquest also had a pernicious impact on Castilian society." Teofilo F. Ruiz, *Crisis and Community: Land and Town in Late Medieval Castile* (Philadelphia: University of Pennsylvania Press, 1994), 7.

Evidence of Inter-Christian Violence

Chronicles present the clearest evidence that late medieval Castilian Christians regularly participated in warfare against their coreligionists. From the beginning of the Trastámara period, chronicles discuss the chivalry of Castile at war. When, in 1369, the newly enthroned Enrique II saw Galicia invaded by King Fernando of Portugal (r. 1367–1383), he moved against the Portuguese with "all the great lords and knights of his realm."[4] The Castilian knights caused a great deal of damage in Portugal, while Portuguese knights did the same in Castile. A decade later, in 1378, Enrique II found himself at war again, this time with the king of Navarre. Ayala points out that in addition to Castilian and Navarrese knights, there was an English knight named Sir Thomas Trivet, who came with a company of armed men to fight for Navarre, and a knight of Caen named Per Ducas de Lebret, who similarly came to Navarre seeking plunder in a war against Castile. "And these men began to enter into Castile, and to make robberies and wars, and those men of Castile in Navarre did the same, and the war was opened."[5] In each of these cases, Enrique de Trastámara led his men into war and a great number of them willingly participated in fighting against fellow Christians. This phenomenon is not unique to Enrique II's reign, but spans the Trastámara period. In 1384, with the Portuguese succession in question, Juan I besieged Lisbon even as he had trouble engaging the Portuguese king, who had no stomach for a direct engagement with the Castilians. During this war, Juan called all his knights and vassals to him and said that they should enter Portugal and "cut down the crops and the vines and make all the damage that they could"[6] – language reminiscent of the complaints about knights made during meetings of the *cortes*.

The way Ayala writes about these events tells us a great deal about the regularity and ubiquity of inter-Christian warfare in late medieval Castile. Keeping in mind that Ayala was an eyewitness to and often a participant in these wars, it is perhaps unsurprising how casually he mentions the outbreak of war between Christian kingdoms. To be sure, the warfare and its activities were worth recording in a chronicle, but Ayala's language accepts these wars as normal. Rare is the lament from the chronicler bewailing the sad state of affairs in which Christians are killing one another. More often, he uses short,

---

[4] López de Ayala, "Don Enrique tercero," 3. "otrosi todos los grandes Señores é Caballeros del su Regno."
[5] Ibid., 33–34. "E estas gentes comenzaron á entrar en Castilla, é á facer robos é guerras, é mesmo facian los de Castilla in Navarra, é la guerra era abierta."
[6] López de Ayala, "Don Juan Primero," in *Biblioteca Autores Españoles*, vol. 66, 98. "é que dende entrasen en Portogal á facer talar los panes é viñas, é facer todo el daño que pudiesen ... é ellos ficieronlo asi."

direct, and sterile statements; "the war was opened" is a typical description.[7] For Ayala and his fellow men-at-arms, there was nothing shocking about fighting fellow Christians. Indeed, it was a familiar part of their lives, close to their hearts, and a key part of their lives as vigorous warriors.

Such fighting was not simply blind obedience to their king's foreign policy. Ducal and comital actions demonstrate that even when Castilian knights were not traveling to Portugal or Navarre to make war, they still found ample reason to fight their fellow Christians within Castile. One particular case study provides a clearer image of inter-Christian warfare within Castile: the war between the Guzmanes and Ponce de Leones in Andalucía in the second half of the 15th century. These two powerful *linajes* held a number of titles, notably the duchy of Medina Sidonia and the county of Arcos de la Frontera, respectively. Through the late 14th and early 15th centuries, the families had been on friendly terms, regularly intermarrying and working together to further their goals in Andalucía and Granada. Yet several factors helped to cultivate an atmosphere of mutual suspicion and hostility between the two families: Juan Ponce de León, a patriarch of the *linaje*, married a Guzmán and treated her disrespectfully, taking multiple mistresses, staining his wife's honor, insulting the Guzmanes, and eventually living separately from her; during the political troubles of the 1440s and 1460s, both clans sought political and local advantage by supporting the factions of Álvaro de Luna, the Infante Alfonso, or others as appropriate, and often took opposite sides; by the early 1470s, the Ponce de Leones concluded a marriage with the powerful Pacheco family, perhaps driving a wedge between the two families.[8]

---

[7] For an excellent biography of Ayala and a discussion of his craft, see Michel Garcia, *Obra y personalidad del Canciller Ayala* (Madrid: Editorial Alhambra, 1983). For a narrower study of Ayala and his relationship to the nobility, see Helen Nader, *The Mendoza Family in the Spanish Renaissance, 1350–1550* (New Brunswick, NJ: Rutgers University Press, 1979), 56–75.

[8] A significant body of scholarship exists on the Andalucian nobility in the late Middle Ages. In particular, the work of Juan Luis Carriazo Rubio is essential in understanding the nuances and subtleties of marriage, power, and politics in the region. See especially *La memoria del linaje. Los Ponce de Leon y sus antepasados a fines de la Edad Media* (Sevilla, Spain: Universidad de Sevilla, 2002) and *La Casa de Arcos entre Sevilla y la frontera Granada (1374–1474)* (Sevilla, Spain: Fundación Focus-Abengoa, 2003). Rafael Sanchez Saus provided a wide-ranging analysis of the major families of late medieval Andalucía and discussed the importance of the concept of *linaje* in the region, arguing that *linaje* was "much more than a link of blood between generations. It is a community of affections and interests, a receptacle of a familiar past without which the medieval man would not be able to conceive of himself, and a projector made into the future of his set of values and his aspirations." Rafael Sanchez Saus, *Caballería y linaje en la Sevilla medieval: estudio genealogico y social* (Cádiz, Spain: Universidad de Cádiz, 1989), 39. Saus' protégé, Miguel Ángel Ladero Quesada, expanded on his efforts to document the nobility of the region in his *Los señores de Andalucía: Investigaciones sobre nobles y señoríos*

With all of these factors in the background, war broke out in 1471 and the region experienced what Juan Luis Carriazo Rubio has called "a terrible explosion of violence."[9] The chronicler and knight Diego de Valera, using the same language that we have seen before, noted that the duke and the count "made cruel war" between one another and damaged one another as often as they were able.[10] The violence perpetrated during this war was indeed great and is essentially indistinguishable from warfare against other kingdoms. The city of Sevilla, the jewel of Castilian Andalucía, was besieged by the count of Arcos, Rodrigo Ponce de León in 1473. Valera had no doubt that Rodrigo wreaked havoc in the region to such a degree that to the citizens of Sevilla "it appeared a grave thing to endure such great injury which [Rodrigo] with so few men would make to the city of Sevilla."[11] The armies marching through Andalucía in this war of neighbors were significant in size. If we trust our chroniclers' numeracy, the duke of Medina Sidonia at one point marched with an army of 20,000 infantry and 1,800 horsemen.[12] And when these armies met on the field of battle, the blood flowed copiously. Outside Alcalá de Guadayra in 1473, the two Castilian armies met

---

en los siglos XIII a XV (Cádiz, Spain: Universidad de Cádiz, 1998). In particular, see the chapter by Ladero Quesada and his description of the foundations of the late medieval nobility, "La consolidación de la nobleza en la Baja Edad Media," and María Concepción Quintanilla Raso's examination of the Fernández family, "Los grandes linajes. Una investigación histórica sobre el linaje de Fernández de Córdoba". See also *Nobleza y sociedad en la España moderna*, ed. María del Carmen Iglesias (Madrid: Fundación Central Hispano, 1996), and Marie-Claude Gerbet, *Las noblezas españolas en la Edad Media: siglos XI–XV*, trans. María José García Vera (Madrid: Alianza Editorial, S.A., 1997), 176.

[9] *Historia de los hechos del marqués de Cádiz*, ed. Juan Luis Carriazo Rubio (Granada: Editorial Universidad de Granada, 2003), 25.

[10] Diego de Valera, "Memorial de diversas hazañas," in *Biblioteca de Autores Españoles*, vol. 70, 75. In some sources, the counts of Arcos are referred to as "Marqués" in reference to another of their titles, Marquis of Cádiz.

[11] Ibid., 74. "como les pareciese grave cosa de comportar quel Marqués con tan poca gente tan grande injuria pudiera hacer á la cuidad de Sevilla …"

[12] Ibid., 75. If these numbers are accurate, this would have been a sizeable force, especially for a private war against one's neighbor. Philippe Contamine notes that in 1335 Edward III of England marshalled some 15,000 men for a campaign against the Scots. He estimates that "a large army" in France near the end of the 15th century "could total 20,000 or more" infantry. Though Contamine treats Castile only briefly, he lists the size of the armies that campaigned against Granada in the 1480s. These large armies, designed to fully conquer Granada, each had slightly more than 10,000 horse and roughly 40,000 foot, roughly double the size of the Duke's army during the Andalucian war. It is possible, therefore, that the Duke's side mustered half as much as a monarch-led national campaign. This is to say nothing of how much the count of Arcos might have mustered. See Philippe Contamine, *War in the Middle Ages*, translated by Michael Jones (New York: Basil Blackwell Inc., 1984), 132–134.

in a battle where many men on both sides ended their lives, including the two brothers of the duke of Medina Sidonia, Pedro and Alfonso Guzmán.[13]

One tragedy for the lords of Andalucía followed another, due to the ongoing war. Following the battle at Alcalá de Guadayra, King Abu al-Hasan 'Ali of Granada (r. 1464–1482, 1483–1485) invaded Castile. Hoping to take advantage of the conflict between the Guzmanes and Ponce de Leones, the Muslim monarch attacked the city of Cardela. The count of Arcos went to succor the city, but the duke of Medina Sidonia, seeing his own opportunity, set out to attack the count's possessions in his absence. As a result, the count withdrew to parry the duke's maneuvers; the result was a Muslim conquest of the city of Cardela. One of the last martial successes of Iberian Islam came because the lords of Andalucía were engaged in an inter-Christian feud. In response to the loss of Cardela, the count of Arcos set out to have his vengeance – not on the king of Granada, but on the duke of Medina Sidonia. Valera writes that Rodrigo, "being very hurt from the loss of Cardela, each day went searching for how he could injure the Duke in a way which would cause him much pain."[14] Rodrigo's solution was to strike at the center of the duke's holdings in Andalucía: the city of Medina Sidonia itself. After a siege of some time, the count's men scaled the city walls and killed the mayor of the city in battle, a lance being thrust through his mouth and out the back of his neck. Valera relates that the villagers and townsmen of the area welcomed the count as their natural lord, because the mayor had allowed his men to injure them and rape their women.[15] Violence followed upon violence as the families pursued their feud.

The Andalucian war was certainly remarkable to contemporaries. But it was the *scale* of the fighting rather than its Christian-on-Christian nature that was noteworthy to most chroniclers and authors. Valera and the royal chronicler Diego Enríquez del Castillo both reported the events of the war, but they rarely passed judgement on either the lords or the knights and squires who took part in it for killing their Christian brethren. Indeed, they rarely even commented on the fact that it was a war between Christians. Instead, they concerned themselves much more often with how knights behaved in battle or in life. The mayor of Medina Sidonia, mentioned above, was condemned by Valera for his decadent lifestyle and unwillingness to engage his enemy with a full company, not for spilling Christian blood.[16] Just as fighting under one's king against Christians in other kingdoms was considered acceptable, so fighting against one's neighbor in a dispute over land or honor was acceptable to many chivalric authors.

---

[13] Valera, "Memorial de diversas hazañas," 75.
[14] Ibid. "Estando el Marqués muy lastimado por la pérdida de Cardela, cada dia andaba buscando como pudiese dañar al Duque en cosa que mucho le doliese ..."
[15] Ibid., 77.
[16] Ibid.

Leaving the chronicles behind, our final component in confirming that warfare against fellow Christians was accepted as a normal state of affairs comes not from chronicles but from imaginative literature, though we have to look a bit closer in order to see it at work.[17]

The battlefield enemies of the great literary knight Amadís and his fellow "good knights" are nearly all Christians. In an early episode in the great Spanish romance, Amadís has a grand final duel with Abies, the Christian king of Ireland. At the beginning of the duel, the author emphasizes that Abies was commended to God by his people before battle and that, when he lies dying at Amadís' hand, his final request is to have confession, as a good Christian ought. His dying wish is granted to him "[a]nd receiving all the sacraments of the holy Church, King Abies' soul left his body."[18] In slaying Abies, Amadís goes on to receive great glory and honor from his own king for defeating Abies. A duel to the death with a fellow Christian is a perfectly legitimate way for an exemplary knight to win honor. For Abies' part, he dies a properly Christian death, with no indication that his soul was punished for fighting against Christians. Indeed, the language for suggesting just such an eternal punishment would not have been difficult to find. Knightly chroniclers of the late Castilian Middle Ages frequently explain that men's souls are in perdition for errors and sins in this life.[19] The absence of such language, and the very willingness to confirm that Abies received the body of Christ at the end of his life, suggests that the author and his readers would have found nothing inherently sinful in fighting against fellow Christians.

In a later episode Abies' brother, King Cildadan, seeks revenge on Amadís and engages him in battle. Cildadan is nearly killed but Amadís and his friends remind their king that he is a good king and a man who kept his word. Cildadan lives, joins Amadís' company, and goes on to fight alongside Amadís' friends, proving himself to be indistinguishable from the other great knights of the realm, fighting with them on God's side.[20] Amadís and his growing company choose to serve the king of Bohemia,

---

[17] Bautista Martínez Iniesta, "Los romances fronterizos: Crónica poética de la Reconquista Granadina y Antología del Romancero fronterizo," in *Lemir*, 7 (2003). http://parnaseo.uv.es/Lemir/Revista/Revista7/Romances.htm. The regular battles among Christian kings and knights that fill the pages of romance and epic poetry offer what we might call an intellectual backscatter. They reflect the assumptions and unspoken expectations of the chivalric elite. Inter-Christian battles in imaginative literature do not generally warrant comment from their authors; they were simply accepted as a normal state of affairs.

[18] *Amadís de Gaula*, ed. Edwin B. Place (Madrid: Consejo Superior de Investigaciones Cientificas, 1959), vol. 1, 79. "y ruégote que me fagas hauer confession … y recevidos todos los sacramentos de la santa Yglesia el rey Abies salióle el alma."

[19] Valera, "Memorial de diversas hazañas," 77.

[20] *Amadís de Gaula*, vol. 2, 491–504.

who is at war with "the most powerful man of the Christians, who is Patín, emperor of Rome."[21] The story peters out without a clear resolution, but the battle scenes are typically chivalric, with Amadís and others striking signal blows and then being honored highly for their deeds. Great honor is won by fighting and killing great Christians. Each of these examples has eminently chivalric justifications behind it – defending against an aggressive invader, participating in a feud, or upholding the honor of maidens – but the result in each case is the same: good knights win honor fighting against Christian enemies.

Castilian epics confirm that intra-Christian fighting is acceptable, with *Mocedades de Rodrigo* suggesting in one case that the might of Castile is so great that fighting against the other Christians of continental Europe is a logical step, indeed that the king of Castile rightly ought to be emperor. Rodrigo (El Cid) declares that he desires war with France and Germany to acquire the imperial throne for his king, disdains the offered negotiation of the pope, and shouts "¡Dévos Dios malas graçias, ay, papa romano!", apparently cowing the pontiff.[22] In the *Crónica del Rey don Rodrigo*, the normative behavior of inter-Christian violence is augmented even further. Indeed, we see the eminently chivalric assertion that the Christian God approves of knightly violence, even when perpetrated against other Christians. During a war against fellow Christians in southern Spain, a knight takes a blow from a lance (wielded by a fellow Christian) through his arm and towards his body, "but God willed that the lance did not enter into the body."[23] Violence against Christians in this case is not only acceptable, but even overseen by the Lord of Hosts.[24] Where the historical record of chroniclers and biographers demonstrates clearly that violence against Christians was constantly being committed by the knights and men-at-arms of Castile, the imaginative literature offers an ideological backscatter confirming that such

---

[21] *Amadís de Gaula*, vol. 3, 759. "yo he Guerra … con el más poderoso hombre de los christianos, que es el Patín, emperador de Roma."

[22] *Las Mocedades de Rodrigo: The Youthful Deeds of Rodrigo, the Cid*, ed. and trans. Matthew Bailey (Toronto: University of Toronto Press, 2007), 61. Bailey translates this as "Cursed be your offer, oh Roman Pope!" A less poetic, though perhaps more literal, translation might be "You give poor regards to God, oh Roman Pope!" Rodrigo is clearly suggesting that the pope is on the wrong side of the battle and disrespects the divine in doing so. Divine sanction, in *Mocedades*, does not necessarily flow from the institutional church, but instead through right exercised through prowess on the battlefield.

[23] Pedro de Corral, *Crónica del Rey don Rodrigo (Crónica sarracina)*, ed. James Donald Fogelquist (Madrid: Editorial Castalia, S.A., 2001), vol. I, 112. "pero quiso Dios que no le entró la lança por el cuerpo."

[24] Kaeuper has reminded us that God was indeed the bellicose Lord of Hosts, the ideal form of God for a knightly class. He argues that knights saw God as "the giver of their great prowess and ordainer of all victories." Richard W. Kaeuper, *Holy Warriors* (Philadelphia: University of Pennsylvania, 2009), 56–57.

violence was accepted, normalized, and sometimes even divinely sanctioned. There can be no doubt that such violence was occurring and that it was not a delicate, ritualized affair. Inter-Christian violence was real, blood flowed, and people died.

The Ideology of Inter-Christian Violence

If inter-Christian violence was being performed so vigorously and regularly, what animated it? Why were Christian knights, despite their immersion in the language of holy war and the regular reminders from priests of the identity of the true enemy, so willing to maim and kill their fellow Christians? On a macrohistorical level, we could attribute this violence to the traditional and universal motives of human violence, such as economic incentives or the acquisition of political power.[25] Indeed, part of the settlement of the Andalucian war was a guarantee that the count of Arcos had perpetual liberty to fish tuna off the coast of Cádiz.[26] But while these grand motives may supply part of the explanation, examining the ideology of inter-Christian violence will help us to define the cultural and intellectual milieux in which the knights and men-at-arms of late medieval Castile operated. It may well be that tuna fishing was the material issue central to the Andalucian war; but how did the Castilian knightly class think about and justify perpetuating violence against one another, even if only for the acquisition of delicious tuna meat?

At the heart of the ideology of inter-Christian violence was the sacrosanct chivalric concept of honor won through martial ability and sustained through the preservation of the accomplishments of one's *linaje*. Indeed, the abstract concept of honor functioned as a very real and very pragmatic phenomenon. It provided the means for great lords and knights to interact with one another, to attack one another, and to preserve their economic interests. The tuna itself was not crucial – it was secondary to the question of honor, which served as the matrix for knightly identity and chivalric interaction with the wider world. In order to address the question of economic interests or claims to territory or title, knights and lords relied

---

[25] José Rodríguez Molina perhaps overplayed his hand when he argued that knights preferred material reward and payment to honor and praise. Molina, *La vida de moros y cristianos en la frontera* (Jaen, Spain: Alcalá la Real, 2007), 59. Ladero Quesada rightly notes the ever-important roles of *botín* (booty), *dineros* (money), and *una carrera política* (a political career) in late medieval Castilian warfare. Miguel Ángel Ladero Quesada, "Una biografía caballeresca del siglo XV: 'La Coronica del yllustre y muy magnifico cauallero don Alonso Perez de Guzmán el Bueno'," in *En la España Media*, 22 (1999), 258–260.

[26] Valera, "Memorial de diversas hazañas," 85.

on the concept of honor. In short, inter-Christian violence was not only acceptable but valuable, because it was a sure and reliable way to maintain and augment a man's honor – his reputation among his peers.

As we saw in Chapter 3, the idea of historical achievement was crucial to a knight's sense of honor. Any assault on the glory of one's family and forebears had to be defended vigorously.[27] This concept – rather than economic need or the acquisition of power – was the proximate cause of the Andalucian war and continued to be central throughout the war's progress. The beauty of the Andalucian war, for the historian, is that we have documents written from various perspectives offering differing points of view of what exactly happened and what was important in this conflict. Two chronicles record the events of the war itself: Diego de Valera's *Memorial de Diversas Hazañas*, and Diego Enríquez del Castillo's *La Historia del Rey Don Enrique el Cuarto*. Valera sometimes sides with the Guzmanes even as he thinks of Rodrigo Ponce de León as a "new Cid,"[28] while Castillo offers a thinner but more neutral account. Additionally, we have three chivalric biographies, all written by anonymous authors: the *Hechos del Condestable don Miguel Lucas de Iranzo*, the *Historia de los Hechos del Marqués de Cádiz*, and *La Coronica del yllustre y muy magnifico cauallero don Alonso Pérez de Guzmán el Bueno*. The first focuses on the deeds of the titular Constable and is markedly generous to the Guzmanes while hostile to the Ponce de Leones. The second, written toward the end of the 15th century, makes a hero of Rodrigo Ponce de León, one of the two antagonists in the Andalucian war. The third lionizes Alonso el Bueno, the founder of the Guzmán *linaje*. Ostensibly a historical work dealing with the late 13th century, it was written in the mid-15th century, shortly before the conflict in Andalucía began, and offers us a view of the Guzmán position.

The origins of the Andalucian war (an inter-Christian conflict) lie in the Castilian conquest of Gibraltar from the Nasrids of Granada (an instance of Christian holy war). Castillo's sterile account offers a starting place, as he simply notes that in 1462 news came to King Enrique IV that "Don Juan de Guzmán, Duke of Medina Sidonia … with his men and those from the city of Xerez … had taken the city of Gibraltar from the power of the Moors."[29] This much is agreed on by the several accounts. The story,

---

[27] Sanchez Saus, *Caballeria y linaje*, 39.
[28] *Historia de los hechos del marqués de Cádiz*, 28. Indeed, MacKay has marshalled evidence showing that multiple nobles of the period ostensibly bought into Rodrigo's projected identity not only as the new Cid but also as the new Fernán González, a hero of the *reconquista*. See Angus MacKay, "Un Cid Ruy Díaz en el siglo XV: Rodrigo Ponce de León, Marques de Cádiz," in *El Cid en el valle del Jalón: Simposio Internacional* (Calatayud, Spain: Centro de Estudios Bilbilitanos, 1991), 192–202.
[29] Diego Enríquez del Castillo, "La historia del rey Don Enrique el Cuarto," in *Biblioteca de Autores Españoles*, vol. 70, 124. "Llególe nueva como Don Juan de Guzmán,

of course, is not so simple. The question of honor and *linaje* was deeply embedded in the conquest of Gibraltar. The Guzmanes claimed Gibraltar as a special part of their *linaje*, a key component of their identity as holy warriors of the frontier. Alonso el Bueno's short epitaph in his chivalric biography, summing up his most glorious and important deeds, notes that he was "first in service of God and of the kings" and "was with the most noble king don [Fernando IV] … and went on to win Gibraltar [from the Muslims]."[30] One of the greatest legacies of the founder of the Guzmán *linaje* was the extravagant accumulation of honor gained through the taking of Gibraltar in the holy war. Because the city had been retaken by Muslim forces in the intervening years, the prospect of the reconquest of Gibraltar in 1462 would have been an emotional and powerful moment for Alonso el Bueno's descendants. Indeed, for Duke Juan de Guzmán, the man who was present at the reconquest of Gibraltar in 1462, the impact would have been significantly augmented, as his own father, Enrique de Guzmán, had died in 1436 during a Castilian assault on the city.[31] Taking Gibraltar was the violent vindication not just of Juan's honor but of his entire *linaje*'s honor.

For the Guzmanes, their personal and familial honor had become intimately connected to a particular place. The abstract concept of the honor of the Guzmán *linaje* became manifest in the physical space of Gibraltar. While the city had been held by the Muslim enemy, it served as a burning ember of Guzmán desire, a perpetual goal for the Guzmanes to target as part of the holy war. There was perhaps no place where members of this great family could better win honor than in the reconquest of the city. When that moment finally came to fruition in 1462, it was a great vindication of the entire *linaje*'s honor. The acquisition of the city would deposit an immense quantity of honor in the family's collective repository and after seizing it, Gibraltar would serve as a physical rallying point for Guzmán knights, a material space where knights could demonstrate their commitment to their *linaje*'s ancient history, preserve its honor from those who would besmirch it, and set out for greater conquests against the enemy. Gibraltar would function as a nerve center for the augmentation of Guzmán honor in a multitude of forms.

But if the Guzmanes were not the Christians to take the city, it could never produce so much honor. The potential loss of this physical honor base is what was so upsetting to the Guzmanes as the conquest of Gibraltar nearly slipped out of their grasp. Valera provides an account of events as

---

Duque de Medina-Sidonia, Conde de Niebla, con su gente é la de Xerez é de aquellas comarcas al derrador avian tomado la cibdad de Gibraltar de poder de los Moros …"

[30] Ladero Quesada, "biografía caballeresca," 283. "que fue el primero en seruiçio de Dios e de los reyes, que fue con el muy noble rey don Alonso (*sic por Fernando*) en la çerca de sobre Algezira y estando el rey en este çerco fue en ganar a Gibraltar …"

[31] Ibid., 247.

follows. Rodrigo Ponce de León had overseen the siege of Gibraltar, a siege that led the Muslim inhabitants to tender their surrender to Rodrigo. He was pleased with this offer but he knew that his ailing father, Count Juan of Arcos, was on his way to Gibraltar, and Rodrigo decided to wait to accept the surrender because he wanted his father to be able to take the city with him. His personal honor was on the line, but so was the larger honor of his *linaje* and a joint acquisition of Gibraltar would benefit them both. At the same time, Duke Juan de Guzmán was on his way to the siege as well. On learning that the city would fall to Rodrigo, the duke secretly sent a messenger to the inhabitants of the city, asking them to refuse to surrender to Rodrigo and hold out until he arrived at Gibraltar so they could surrender to him instead; in exchange the duke guaranteed the inhabitants the security of their lives and goods. When the men of Xerez, fighting for the Guzmanes, arrived at Gibraltar, the inhabitants opened the gates to surrender to them. Rodrigo, unwilling to see the city given to someone else, quickly mounted his horse and led his men into the city to seize it before the men of Xerez could. Rodrigo's men seized the towers of the city and unfurled Rodrigo's banner, killing and robbing inhabitants in the process. According to Valera, it appeared at this point that the Ponce de Leones had won the day, snatching the victory and honor from the Guzmanes.

However, the castle of Gibraltar was still in Muslim hands and this small piece of Castilian history becomes almost farcical. On his arrival the duke, through some intrigue, arranged for the castle to surrender to him rather than to Rodrigo. When the defenders opened the gates of the castle, both Rodrigo and the duke's standard bearer entered. A Muslim man asked for the banner of the duke in order to fly it in the castle and Rodrigo "had such great anger that he put his hand to his sword and gave a blow to the standard bearer of the duke in the arm, which made him drop the banner on the ground, for which the duke had great anger."[32] Although Rodrigo's father and the duke would make temporary amends, the enmity between Rodrigo and the Guzmanes had been sown, all over the question of who would win more honor through prowess done on a battlefield of the holy war. It is perhaps noteworthy that Rodrigo's father died in the years after the conquest of Gibraltar, and so it was Rodrigo, the son, who would be left to vindicate his *linaje*'s honor; Rodrigo could claim not only that he had been slighted but that his father – his ancestor – had been slighted.[33] Whatever the case, both Rodrigo and the duke of Medina Sidonia now

---

[32] Valera, "Memorial de diversas hazañas," 27–28. "Don Rodrigo ovo tan grande enojo que puso mano á la espada y dió un golpe al Alférez del Duque en el brazo, que le fizo derribar la bandera en el suelo, de lo qual el Duque ovo grande enojo."

[33] For a thorough account of the Ponce de Leones and their conceptual relationship to their history, see Carriazo Rubio, *memoria del linaje*.

seethed with the fury that came from their honor and the honor of their *linajes* being tarnished.

Valera's account explicitly offers one explanation for the hatred between these two men. He paints Rodrigo as an ambitious and proud young man, whose hunger for glory and honor ran up against the intrigues of Juan de Guzmán, an older man obsessed with his family's history and legend. In Valera's assessment, then, it was the desire of both men to do good deeds, preserve or augment their honor, and protect their family's achievements that led to such hatred. These eminently chivalric virtues were at the heart of the enmity that would lead to a serious and destructive war between fellow Christians. The anonymous chivalric biography of Rodrigo comes to similar conclusions, though a few key details change. The biography leaves most of the narrative in place – the Muslim desire to surrender, the duke's "deceptions" to acquire the victory and glory for himself, and the eventual surrender of the castle.[34] Rodrigo's encomiastic chronicler offers slightly different details concerning what happened in the castle of Gibraltar that led to such hostility and violence between the two families. When the Muslims opened the doors to the castle, there was confusion among them about whom they were surrendering to and, in order to protect themselves from Christian violence, they agreed to raise both men's banners above the fortification. Given the chivalric emphasis on holy war, such a calculation seems apt. The chronicler, noting that "envy is the root of all evils," writes that through some deception the duke had the Guzmán banner raised very high and that of the Ponce de Leones very low.[35] According to the Ponce de León chronicler's account, the slight of honor was not done to the Guzmanes, but to the Ponce de Leones, when the duke of Medina Sidonia intentionally insulted them and sapped the glory of Rodrigo's military victory. When Rodrigo's father arrived in Gibraltar, "some anger and points of honor passed between these two knights" and it was only through the intervention of prelates and good knights that the feud did not erupt immediately.[36] Even with such pacific intervention, there were skirmishes. At one point Juan Ponce de León raised a thousand men and fought with Juan Guzmán's men, fighting so well "that Roland in his time could not have done more."[37] Faced with a fellow Christian knight challenging his honor, the Count of Arcos channeled one of the greatest heroes of chivalric epic in exacting violent vengeance on his enemy. The ideals of imaginative

---

[34] *Historia de los hechos del marqués de Cádiz*, 172–174. The author uses the term "enganno" several times to describe Juan's actions.

[35] Ibid., 172–173. "la ynbidia es rays de todos los males."

[36] Ibid., 174. "algunos enojos e pundonores pasados entre estos dos caualleros …"

[37] Ibid., 175. "Y todos los suyos lo fizieron tanto bien, que Roldán en su tiempo non pudo más fazer."

literature, fantastic and exaggerated though they could be, manifested as aspirations for the historical figure of Juan Ponce de León.

The image that the Ponce de Leones created of the duke as an envious man who wanted to publicly broadcast his family's superiority over the count's may not be far off the mark. Indeed, the Guzmán family's chivalric biography suggests exactly that image. In several places in the chronicle, the Ponce de Leones make an appearance, each time as a junior partner to the Guzmanes. In the first, the chronicler emphasizes that while both families descend from a daughter of the king of León, the Guzmán line can be traced from fathers to sons, while the Ponce de León *linaje* is traced through a female line.[38] The implication is that the Guzmanes are senior, masculine, and strong while the Ponce de Leones are junior, feminine, and weak.[39] The second appearance of the Ponce de Leones in the biography has their progenitor, Fernando Pérez, begging the Guzmanes to allow him to become their vassal, so that he can attain wealth and glory. The generous and noble Alonso el Bueno grants Fernando's wish, bestowing upon him riches and estates and goods. Leaving no doubt about the message, the chronicler writes: "and so in this manner the house of Niebla [the Guzmanes] made the house of [Ponce de] León."[40] The Guzmanes, long the dominant *linaje* in Andalucía, wished to guarantee that they would remain so. By emphasizing their superiority over the rising Ponce de Leones, both in their ideological tracts and in their behavior at Gibraltar, they were preserving their *linaje*'s honor and legacy.

Certainly all sides believed that the hostility that erupted in the 1470s was a result of one or the other *linaje*'s slighted honor at the holy war battlefield of Gibraltar, the only vindication for which was violent retribution. In a broad sense, the war itself was built around honor and *linaje*, but even individual instances of violence during the course of the war centered on these concepts. Indeed, each city and fortification of the coast of Andalucía played a role in the institutional memory of one or the other families. The Andalucian cities and castles mentioned in the chronicle of Alonso el Bueno were the same places now threatened by the Ponce de Leones. Neither was it simply a greedy possession of territory that mattered to the Guzmanes, as there was a real emotional connection between the places and the Guzmán

---

[38] Ladero Quesada, "biografía caballeresca," 269–270.
[39] Louise Mirrer has argued that Christian men feminized Muslim enemies as well as Jews in order to demonstrate their supremacy over these other groups. This approach makes sense in the context of family rivalries as well. Louis Mirrer, *Women, Jews, and Muslims in the Texts of Reconquest Castile* (Ann Arbor, MI: University of Michigan Press, 1996). This argument is writ large throughout the book but is particularly well articulated in her section on Christian descriptions of Muslim men, especially on pages 47–55.
[40] Ladero Quesada, "biografía caballeresca," 282. "y ansí de esta manera la casa de Niebla hizo la casa de León."

linaje. In the chronicle's portrayal of the Battle of Río Salado (1340) at the city of Tarifa, Alonso el Bueno literally mixes the blood of his *linaje* with the soil of Tarifa itself. According to the chronicle, Alonso, besieged inside Tarifa by the Muslim king of Morocco, learned that his enemy had custody of Alonso's two young sons. The king demanded that Alonso turn over the city of Tarifa if he wanted his sons to live, swearing by Allah that he would behead the boys then and there. Alonso shouted down to his enemy, "If such is your will, take this, my knife, with which you can make the sacrifice." The chronicler notes: "In this way Tarifa was defended, leaving the innocent sons of Alonso Pérez de Guzmán dead and beheaded."[41] Once the Muslims were defeated, the king of Castile granted most of Andalucía to Alonso, specifying the territory all the way from Gibraltar, north past Cádiz. Importantly, this territory contained the major cities that would one day be claimed by the Ponce de Leones, including Gibraltar, Tarifa, Vejer de Frontera, and Cádiz, as well as the Guzmanes' base of Medina Sidonia. The chronicler explains that the grant of these lands was not only because Alonso was a good, brave, and loyal knight, but "for the knife which Alonso gave with which his sons were beheaded."[42] An act of violence performed against the Guzmán *linaje* during the holy wars created an honor-based emotional and chivalric connection to the territory which would allow them to commit their own acts of violence against the Ponce de Leones.

How disheartening it must have been, then, when Rodrigo Ponce de León made such great destruction in the lands of Enrique de Guzmán, who had succeeded his father in 1468, just before the Andalucian war broke out.[43] What anger and desire for vengeance must have coursed through Enrique when Rodrigo's men, led by Hernando de Rivadeneyra, a "brave knight desirous of winning honor," brought down the walls of Alanís and seized that fortification.[44] Indeed, placing the whole war in the context of slighted honor and commitment to *linaje* offers an approach that makes sense of otherwise apparently petty actions. The siege of Medina Sidonia by Rodrigo was not simply a tactical maneuver, but one that was designed to strike at the heart of the Guzmán *linaje*, as the Ponce de Leones well knew

---

[41] It is interesting, although perhaps less central in the context of the argument here, that the King of Morocco has just executed his own grandsons – Alonso had married the King's daughter. Ladero Quesada, "biografía caballeresca," 279. "y dixo al rey: 'Pues tal es vuestra coluntad toma este mi cuchillo con que agades el sacrificio'. Por esta vía se defendió Tarida, quedando muertos y degollados los ynoçentes hijos de don Alonso Pérez de Guzmán."

[42] Ibid., 280. "por el cuchillo que dio con que sus hijos fueron degollados."

[43] For the family tree of this branch of the Guzmán family, see Sanchez Saus, *Caballería y linaje*, 209–220.

[44] Valera, "Memorial de diversas hazañas," 74. "Hernando de Rivadeneyra, como fuese caballero esforzado é deseoso de ganar honra …"

that the city was "all the honor of the duke."[45] It makes sense that Enrique would have attacked Rodrigo's holdings when the king of Granada invaded. Seizing the opportunity to vindicate his wounded honor was far and away more important than worrying about a small Muslim raid across the border; that so much of this Christian honor was rooted in the holy war remains a delicious irony. When the dust finally settled in 1474, it is no wonder that Rodrigo's partisans felt that he could return home "with much honor," having brought such destruction and violence to Andalucía. His honor, and that of his family, had been vindicated in war against the Guzmanes, his Christian Castilian neighbors.

The Andalucian war pitted two great Christian families against one another in a destructive and devastating encounter. The cause for this war, according to the chivalric writers who recorded it, was the contest for knightly honor between them. The ability to claim to be better knights and warriors was so crucial for the identities of the two families that they would willingly set aside the holy war and even allow their religious enemies to reassert themselves in order to have their vengeance and vindicate their tarnished sense of pride and honor. Yet the particular points of honor at stake in the prelude to the Andalucian war were rooted in the long history of the holy war against Islam. This seemingly contradictory state of affairs reveals the powerful impulse to violence rooted in late medieval chivalry. Violence on one battlefield yielded honor that could subsequently be challenged by fellow Christian knights. Once challenged, that honor must be defended against a knight's coreligionists.

The Guzmanes and the Ponce de Leones clearly put on a showy display of honor, *linaje*, and violence, but they were not the only Castilian noblemen operating under these assumptions. Indeed, such chivalric assumptions extended across Castile and throughout the Trastámara period, with almost every instance we have detailing inter-Christian violence relying on these concepts. In 1385, some ninety years before the Andalucian war began, the desire for winning honor against the Portuguese drove several knights into a suicidal battle. The knights saw their Portuguese enemies nearby and discussed whether or not they ought to fight a battle which they expected to lose. After a debate among the knights, they agreed that "there would be great shame on them to see the enemies with their eyes and not go to fight with them, and that those who should hear of it in Castile would think poorly of it."[46] Sure enough, the Castilian knights were defeated, and two of their captains were killed. Pedro López de Ayala does not report on how

---

[45] *Historia de los hechos del marqués de Cádiz*, 177. "Medina Sidonia, que era toda la honrra del duque."

[46] López de Ayala, "Don Juan primero," 98–99. "les era gran vergüenza ver los enemigos á ojo é non ir pelear con ellos; é que los que lo oyesen en Castilla, que se lo razonarian mal."

highly everyone in Castile thought of this decision. Although we do not know how their actions were received, we know that they were operating under the assumptions of chivalry. They were concerned about the vindication of their honor and how the rest of elite society would view their actions. Always worried about public perceptions – the foundation of the concept of honor – knights chose to fight fellow Christians in order that their peers would think highly of them.

Other knights also relied on the projection of the ideals of honor, *linaje*, and violence – even when they had comparatively weak claims to a great family lineage. During the Andalucian war, one potent participant was Miguel Lucas de Iranzo, the Constable of Castile and self-described devout holy warrior who had written to the pope about the blood of his innocent Christian lambs being shed by Muslims. He fought on the side of Enrique de Guzmán not only because the Constable was a vigorous knight who desired battle, but "for the great debt of love which his father had had with the Duke Don Juan [de Guzmán]."[47] The Constable himself relied on the deeds and feelings of his father – the honor of his *linaje* – for his *casus belli* against the Christian count of Arcos. Iranzo himself was made a noble only in 1454, less than twenty years before the Andalucian war began. Nonetheless, Iranzo used the same language of paternal devotion and commitment to his ancestors' loyalties as he chose to fight on the side of the Guzmanes. He offers us no economic incentive, no political stratagem, no tactical logic for joining one side or the other. The only express justification is the vindication of his father's honor. Iranzo understood the social and ideological norms of the society in which he operated and worked to participate within those norms, despite the absence of any real basis to do so. In other words, the Constable entered into the behaviors of elite society by speaking their language and behaving as if he actually had a great ancestry. He may have been posturing, but in his posturing he put on a fine chivalric display, leading his men onto the battlefield to shed the blood of those innocent Christian lambs.

In addition to the concepts of honor and *linaje*, the ideology of interChristian violence incorporated divine and royal blessings. As we saw in the previous chapter, the holy war was the highest calling of Castilian knights. Warfare against Christians, though, was also a good and divinely appointed mission in the minds of many of the chivalric elite. Indeed, Castilian knights and men-at-arms could expect that fighting in a war against Christians would yield blessings and rewards, both in this world and the next. Chivalric ideology borrowed language and concepts from holy war in valorizing warfare against fellow Christians. The power of late medieval Castilian

---

[47] *Hechos del condestable Don Miguel Lucas de Iranzo*, ed. Juan de Mata Carriazo (Madrid: Espasa-Calpe, S.A., 1940), 477. "por el grand debdo de amor que con el duque don Juan su padre avía tenido ..."

chivalry rested in its ability to constantly reassure knights and men-at-arms that their activities were justified and valid.

The king of Castile himself and the knights surrounding him expressed this idea incontrovertibly in official documentation. In December of 1445, Juan II issued a confirmation of the grant of the city of Trujillo to his Constable and favorite, Don Álvaro de Luna. This document carries a lengthy explanation of Juan's reasons for confirming the grant to Don Álvaro. The confirmation opens with a detailed recollection of the Battle of Olmedo, a battle amongst Christians which pitted Juan's forces, led in part by Don Álvaro, against the forces of the infantes of Aragon, led by Juan, king of Navarre (*jure uxoris*). The Castilian side won the battle and Don Álvaro's leading role was ostensibly the reason for Juan confirming the Constable's holdings.[48] The language of divine favor is heavy in the description of the battle. The document begins by noting that the king of Navarre and his supporters "*with the aid of God* would know and come to realize through experience in what manner [Don Álvaro] served [the King of Castile]."[49] The king goes on to remember that Don Álvaro fought most bravely and, *with the aid of God*, vanquished and scattered the enemy, and finally speaks of the battle and the victory *which God gave to [Juan II] and [Don Álvaro]*.[50] At nearly every juncture, Juan reminds his subjects that the Christian God favored the Castilians over the king of Navarre and the infantes of Aragon – all of whom were Christians. As importantly, he is emphasizing that Don Álvaro, in leading this fight against a Christian enemy, fought in the name of God and achieved victory over his enemies because of a divine blessing upon his mission. For Juan and Luna, God liked some Christians better than others.

Certainly King Juan's larger cause was favored by God, and the confirmation suggests that Don Álvaro, as a vigorous knight, was specifically favored by God. Addressing Álvaro directly, the king says:

> "You, my constable, took a wound from an encounter with a lance through the right thigh and other wounds, through which you persisted and suffered in very great danger. And through the grace of God you fought most forcefully and virtuously and with great spirit and loyalty as a virtuous and strenuous knight and for this you deserve and merit many great plaudits and rich rewards and remunerations ... and gifts beyond the blessed and most

---

[48] The best account of the career of Álvaro de Luna and a summary of his relations with the *Infantes* remains Nicholas Round's *The Greatest Man Uncrowned* (London: Tamesis Books Limited, 1986). The most detailed reconstruction of the Battle of Olmedo is Fernando Castillo Cáceres, "¿Guerra o torneo?: la Batalla de Olmedo, modelo de enfrentamiento caballeresco," *En la España medieval*, no. 32 (2009): 139–166. Cáceres' assessment of the battle as markedly chivalric is correct, though he may be too willing to believe that that meant that it was a gentlemanly encounter.

[49] Biblioteca Nacional de España MSS/18697/73

[50] Ibid., "vencerastes & desbarastes los enemigos." Italics in text are author's emphasis.

laudable and glorious memory and fame which, in that [battle] and through that [victory] you won."[51]

Aside from the fact that once again Don Álvaro is acting with the grace of God, we must note the combination of the Constable's wounds, his chivalric virtues, and God's divine sanction. Richard Kaeuper has described chivalry as a religious ideology and has suggested that there was a theological aspect to the knight's calling which revolved around the fact that knights *suffered* on the battlefield.[52] This suffering, akin to the suffering of a penitent, of a devout monk, or to the suffering of Christ himself, won knights divine merit in the eyes of God. How very significant that the king specifically mentions the Constable's wounds and describes the Constable as "suffering" them. In fighting against his Christian enemies, the Constable was winning divine merit for the next life. On this same point, the king describes Álvaro's chivalric virtues piece by piece – he is forceful, virtuous, has great spirit (courage or bravery) and great loyalty. From a chivalric point of view, the Constable is being held up, just as Tristan might have been, as a great Christian knight, and a key implication of that is devotion to and favor from God. Finally, this passage in praise of the Constable serves as the pivot for the whole document. Having described the Battle of Olmedo and praised Don Álvaro for his leadership, King Juan moves on to observe that the Constable has already won "the blessed and most laudable and glorious memory and fame" and declares that in addition to these social or spiritual rewards, the Constable's leadership in the recent inter-Christian war also merits material recognition from his sovereign – the confirmation of the city of Trujillo. For King Juan, for Don Álvaro, and presumably for the chivalric class of late medieval Castile, valorous fighting won spiritual and material rewards, even when that fighting was against fellow Christians.

The confirmation is already a fascinating document for its description of the Battle of Olmedo and the clear valorization of inter-Christian warfare.

---

[51] Ibid. "Vos el dicho my condestable fuestes ferido de un encuentro de lanca por el muslo derecho & de otras feridas en lo qual vos persisteis … & sufreisteis en ello muy grand peligro & por la gratia de dios vos oviesteis en todo ello muy esforzada & virtuosamente & como grand animosidat & lealtad como virtuoso & estrenuo cavallero & por ello vos digno & merecent' de muy grandes senalados & ricos gualardones & remuneraciones & guas' merads' & donaciones allende de la bienaventurada & muy loable & gloriosa memoria & fama quel en ello & por ello ganasteis." I have translated *oviesteis* here as "you fought," despite its literal translation as "you did". The term "to do" is ubiquitous in chivalric literature and language as standing in for doing deeds of prowess in a fight or battle.

[52] For an incisive assessment of the role of suffering in chivalric religious ideology see Kaeuper, *Holy Warriors*, 94–104. Kaeuper has made a convincing argument that knights saw their profession as one of suffering on the battlefield and that such suffering won them merit for eternal life. The language of suffering here must be understood in that context.

But before actually confirming his grant of the city of Trujillo, Juan mentions one more piece of the Constable's career. Having justified the renewal of the grant by noting the Constable's service at Olmedo, Juan then recalls an episode fourteen years earlier, in which the Constable led the king's troops on a different battlefield. In remembering this battle, Juan uses much of the same language as he did about the Battle of Olmedo. The Constable entered powerfully into the land of the king's enemies and fought with them, and through the grace of God he vanquished them and scattered them. Juan emphasizes that this victory, in which the Constable faced travails and dangers, was done with the aid of God.[53] Just as in the Battle of Olmedo, this earlier battle results in divine sanction and favor and contributes to the king rewarding Don Álvaro materially as well. This earlier battle, though, was the Battle of Higueruela, in which Don Álvaro led the king's troops in victory against the Muslim Kingdom of Granada. The only significant difference in the description of these two battles is that the Muslim enemies are described as "enemies of the faith," whereas the Christian enemies are simply described as "enemies." Otherwise, the language of valorization, reward, and divine sanction is nearly identical. Juan's choice to record the Battle of Olmedo alongside the Battle of Higueruela strongly suggests that he perceived (and that he existed in a chivalric context which allowed him to perceive) that a knight performing valiantly in battle against Christians deserved nearly the same material and spiritual rewards as a knight fighting against the enemies of the faith. The valorization of chivalric activity in a battle against Christians used nearly identical language to the battle against an infidel.

With this diverse and ubiquitous evidence, we can begin to reconstruct a chivalric ideology of inter-Christian violence in late medieval Castile. The first component, sitting at the center of chivalry, is the concept of personal honor. Just as we have seen in all chivalric violence, the drive to win personal honor was a mighty motivation for knights and men-at-arms. The unique component of honor-based violence pertaining to inter-Christian warfare lies in the fact that, when it came to personal combat or individual glory, a knight won more honor by fighting with or defeating someone with greater honor and prowess than himself. Despite its pervasiveness and its importance in creating and reinforcing social hierarchy, there was much less honor to be gained in destroying peasant levies than there was in engaging with a fellow warrior of equal or greater martial ability. The pages of romance are rife with examples of knights eagerly riding into combat upon seeing the great prowess of a potential rival. Christian knights were almost always regarded as the best warriors, the best knights, and the most honorable men. In the Castilian redaction of the story of Tristan, for example, both Tristan

---

[53] BNE MSS/18697/73.

and Galeote were delighted after they essentially fought one another to a draw, believing that they had distinguished themselves and won great honor in such a contest.[54] In tournaments, which both imitated and informed knightly literature, we see the same mechanics at work. Jousting knights were proud to win honor by "practicing" against their fellow Christian warriors. The chronicler of the *passo honroso* of Suero de Quiñones diligently recorded which knights jousted against which, the precise location of each blow delivered to each knight, and which knight was the winner of each encounter, when such could be determined.[55] The knights of Quiñones' tournament were interested in every detail of the tournament because those details showed who the best and most honorable knights were. Indeed, knights came not only from Castile but from across Europe to test their mettle against their fellow Christians, seeking out the best and most skilled to fight against.[56] The jousting wherein they won honor was different only in degree from the real battle they might see against the very coreligionists with whom they jousted.[57] The records of jousting and of battles in imaginative literature leave no doubt that knights saw fighting against the most honorable and powerful Christians as a sure way to win honor.

The honor to be gained in fighting the greatest and most respected Christian knights helps us to understand an ostensibly confusing component of chivalric descriptions of non-Christians. We might expect all medieval Christians to simply abhor the Muslim or pagan enemy. Yet we often find a certain amount of respect for formidable non-Christian warriors, even an attempt to paint them with Christian and chivalric attributes. With the understanding that the greatest possible warrior was a powerful *Christian* knight and that knights gained the most honor from fighting against the greatest possible enemy, we can begin to comprehend this approach to non-Christian enemies. Giving a Muslim enemy the attributes of a Christian knight increased his reputation among Christian knights, making him a

---

[54] *El Cuento de Tristan de Leonis*, ed. George Tyler Northup (Chicago: University of Chicago Press, 1928), 119. Outside the Castilian context, see Malory's *Morte d'Arthur* as one excellent example of great Christian knights eager to fight great Christian knights. Over and over, Lancelot rides into battle seeking combat with the greatest knight around.

[55] Most of the chapters in the chronicle operate in this way. For a particularly good example, see the chapter on Pedro de los Ríos. Pedro Rodríguez de Lena, *El passo honroso de Suero de Quiñones*, ed. Amancio Labandeira Fernández (Madrid: Fundación Universitaria Española, 1977), 204–205. "Noel Fallows has provided an English translation of selections of the *passo honroso*. Noel Fallows, *Jousting in Medieval and Renaissance Iberia* (Woodbridge: Boydell Press, 2010).

[56] For example, Antón de Funes was one of several knights who travelled from Aragon to try his hand at the lists, while a knight named Arnaut travelled from the court of the duke of Brittany in order to participate. Rodríguez Lena, *passo honroso*, 173 and 422.

[57] David Crouch, *Tournament* (London: Hambledon and London, 2005), 4–5.

more worthy enemy. Chivalric authors wanted to Christianize great Muslim enemies as much as possible so that the heroes of Christendom, when fighting them, could win the greatest possible honor. Fernán Pérez de Guzmán, in his *Mar de las estorias*, describes Saladin as so many medieval Christians did: in essentially chivalric terms. Although there is a page missing from the manuscript, which interrupts the passage, we know that Guzmán called Saladin "a magnificent and marvelous prince ... a baron most practiced and notable in arms, [and] most frank ..."[58] In Christianizing and chivalrizing Saladin, Guzmán simultaneously praises him and allows that the Christians fighting him could win that much more honor. Together with the immense honor that could be won from the grander ideal of fighting against the religious enemy, making individual Muslim enemies paragons of chivalry allowed their honor to be augmented. The concept of fighting fellow Christians was powerful enough that its intellectual and prescriptive components could, counter-intuitively, be applied to non-Christians with a bit of authorial propagandistic finesse.

The second component, arising from the first, is that same particularly Castilian ideal that we saw in connection with holy war in the previous chapter: the honor and memory of a knight's *linaje*. Remembering one's father, or grandfather, or distant ancestors and their deeds was crucial to the Trastámara nobility. In an ironic twist, the essential relationship between *linaje* and holy war actually helped to lead to and inform an ideology of inter-Christian warfare. Because the holy war of the misty past of the 11th, 12th, and 13th centuries functioned as the superlative avenue for winning honor in Trastámara Spain, competition among the *linajes* to claim that legacy became fierce. The Guzmanes' asserting their claims to Andalucía so strongly is excellent evidence of this. Even before being challenged by the Ponce de Leones, the Guzmanes were aware of how important it was to articulate a claim to this history. Moreover, the elevation of holy war and its past to a paramount position in chivalric thought led to severe competition among *linajes* to assert themselves in the holy war of the 15th century. The impulse to claim Gibraltar was one of the highest possible honors for *both* the Guzmanes and the Ponce de Leones; with so few opportunities to assert themselves in the holy war, both *linajes* seized every initiative. This competition, inspired by the holy war, could essentially set the knightly elites of late medieval Castile on a violent, honor-based collision course.

Finally, the third component was a blending of lay warrior culture with theology. In its broadest form, this was neither particularly Castilian nor new in the late Middle Ages. Nevertheless, it was a crucial component of the chivalric approach to inter-Christian violence in late medieval Castile. There is little doubt that Christian knights would have performed violence

---

[58] BNE, MSS/7575, 80.

against one another without any religious justification. A chivalric warrior culture already existed that allowed for violence between Christian knights. Knights and chivalric authors successfully applied the Christian theology of violence to that culture. Drawing on the same language that might be applied to the holy war, authors, knights, and kings credited their victories over Christian enemies to a Christian God who loved knights and their profession. God turned aside enemy lances and guided friendly swords into enemy skulls while knights and men-at-arms suffered in *imitatio Christi* on the battlefield. For many warriors of late medieval Castile, there was little doubt that God appreciated their breaking of Christian bodies and spilling of Christian blood.

Complications

Even as these ideas dominated the literature and written works of knights and men-at-arms, there were problems and contradictions built into them. At times, knights, courtiers, or prelates recognized, lamented, and even attempted to reform the problems of chivalry that allowed for and praised inter-Christian violence. Other times, the problems simply appeared without a clear solution presenting itself. Indeed, as with any ideology, it did not function perfectly in the real world.

One problem of inter-Christian violence, naturally, was that its excesses were destructive to the Christian religion in Castile. During the Andalucian war, for example, the church of Sant Marcos in Sevilla was burned. This was a point of contention among the various sides and reflects a concern over the excess of inter-Christian violence. The chronicle of Miguel Lucas de Iranzo mentions that during the fighting, "some of the men of [Rodrigo] burned a church which they call Sant Marcos, which had some of the men of the duke in it," because Rodrigo's men knew that the duke was so powerful and that his *linaje* was older and more honorable than Rodrigo's.[59] The competition between *linajes* and the drive for honor, according to Iranzo's chronicle, led to a reprehensible act of destruction. Diego de Valera acknowledges that Rodrigo's men burned the church, but was sure that it was a terrible regret. Indeed, he notes that Rodrigo was much aggrieved at the burning of the church and that after he died his wife helped to have the church rebuilt.[60] Perhaps the best evidence that there was a broad recognition that excessive inter-Christian violence was destructive to the religion lies in the fact that the chronicle of Rodrigo Ponce de León acknowledges the excess and

---

[59] *Hechos del condestable*, 476–477. "Y los de la parte del dicho marqués quemaron vna yglesia que dicen Sant Marcos, que tenía onbres del duque."
[60] Valera, "Memorial de diversas hazañas," 63.

the rumors of Rodrigo's involvement, and steadfastly refutes that he had anything to do with it:

> And some say that [Rodrigo] had ordered [his men] to burn Sant Marcos, and certainly in this they do not speak the truth, for he was most Christian and he knew of no such thing; he grieved much for this act, and if time would allow, he would have made a great punishment for it. But as for his men who made great damage to that church, there were some of them who wanted to put fire to the doors in order to enter them, not thinking that the whole would be burned, and nothing remained save the chapel of the high altar and sanctuary, which God wished to preserve.[61]

By all accounts, Rodrigo was as upset as anyone at the burning of Sant Marcos, but he was certainly not willing to take responsibility for it, nor even to allow his men to be accused of deliberately burning a church. There is a quiet recognition here that chivalric violence could go too far and that fighting against fellow Christians could be too destructive, and even a small voice that nobody wanted to hear too clearly, calling for limits to such violence.

Given the pervasiveness of inter-Christian violence in the Trastámara period and the destruction that it wrought on Castilian Christendom, it comes as little surprise that there were those who called for a change in this late medieval practice of violence against fellow Christians. The reform effort is perhaps best represented in the person of Alfonso de Cartagena, bishop of Burgos. As a leading intellectual of his day, Cartagena was prepared to offer a new way forward for the chivalric elite. Indeed, Cartagena was well aware of the knightly lifestyle and chivalric ideals and he attempted to prescribe for knights realistic and achievable changes in their behavior.[62] Cartagena's program was articulated through two works: his speech to the Council of Basel in 1434 and a treatise on chivalry called the *Doctrinal de los caualleros*.

---

[61] *Historia de los hechos del marqués de Cádiz*, 176. "E algunos dixeron que el marqués avía mandado quemar a Sant Marcos, y por çierto en esto non dixeron verdad, ca él era chistianísimo y la tal cosa non supo; antes le pesó mucho dello, y si el tinpo lo padeçiera, él diera sobre ello grand castigo. Mas commo de aquella yglesia fazían grand danno a los suyos, ovo algunos dellos que quisieron poner fuego a las puertas por les entrar, non pensando que así avía de ser de se quemar toda, que no quedó saluo la capilla del altar mayor e sagrario, que Dios quiso guardar."

[62] Noel Fallows, "Chivalric Manuals in Medieval Spain: The *Doctrinal de los cavalleros* (c. 1444) of Alfonso de Cartagena," *Journal of Medieval and Renaissance Studies*, vol. 24, no.1 (1994): 53–87; Noel Fallows, "Just Say No? Alfonso de Cartagena, the *Doctrinal de los caballeros*, and Spain's Most Noble Pastime," in *Studies on Medieval Spanish Literature in Honor of Charles F. Fraker*, ed. Mercedes Vaquero and Alan Deyermond (Madison, WI: Hispanic Seminary of Medieval Studies, 1995); and Noel Fallows, *The Chivalric Vision of Alfonso de Cartagena: Study and Edition of the* Doctrinal de los caualleros (Newark, DE: Linguatext, Ltd., 1995).

In his speech at Basel, Cartagena was arguing for the superiority of the king of Castile over the king of England. In addition to arguments about the ancient past and the lineage of both houses, Cartagena suggested that in deciding between two otherwise equal kings, their acts in war could decide which carried precedence. In the case of England and Castile, Cartagena was certain that "the war which is made against the infidels is said to be the war of God."[63] Because the king of Castile (at the time Juan II) "continually makes war against the pagans and the infidels," he clearly held precedence over the king of England.[64] It seems that Cartagena's speech at Basel was more than simply a description of the greatness of Castile; rather, it ought to be read as a call to his countrymen to reach their greatest potential. The surest sign that this was a reform speech rather than simply a description of reality is that King Juan was, in fact, *not* continually making war against the pagans and infidels. By emphasizing that kings of Castile were great *because* they made war against the infidel, Cartagena implicitly called out Juan's inaction and encouraged Castilians to prove that they were better than Englishmen. At Basel, Cartagena never said that warfare against fellow Christians was categorically wrong – that was for God to decide. But he did say that war against pagans and infidels was *always* good. If Noel Fallows is correct in suggesting that Cartagena had a practical approach to chivalry, perhaps we see it on display in this speech. The bishop was not willing to wholly condemn inter-Christian warfare because he knew that eradicating the practice was simply unrealistic. But it would have been possible to redirect knightly energy to the southern frontier. In emphasizing that the way to fight God's war with certainty was in fighting against Muslims, Cartagena made a realistic effort to redirect the energies of Christian Europe against Islam, and specifically of Castile against Granada.

Cartagena's *Doctrinal de los caualleros* compiles the ancient and recent laws of Spain in an effort to demonstrate what knights ought to do and how they ought to behave. Cartagena was articulating a political theory in this work, one in which knights would loyally serve their king and arrange themselves in an ideal hierarchy.[65] This political theory was paired with a reduction in inter-Christian warfare and a focus on the holy war. At times, the bishop made this call explicitly. He lamented, for example, that the men of Granada enjoyed peace while Castilian knights exercised their arms "against relatives and against those who ought to be friends, or in jousts or

---

[63] "Discurso pronunciado por D. Alfonso de Cartagena en el Concilio de Basilea acerca del derecho de precedencia del Rey de Castilla sobre el Rey de Inglaterra," in *La Ciudad de Dios*, 35 (1894): 352. "la guerra que sse fase contra los ynfieles sse dise guerra de dios …"

[64] Ibid., 353. "pues manifiesta cosa es que mi sseñor el rey de castilla continuamente fase guerra contra los paganos e ynfieles."

[65] *Chivalric Vision of Alfonso de Cartagena*, 70–71.

in tournaments, of which the one is abhorrent and abominable and a thing which carries dishonor and destruction, and the other a game or rehearsal, but not a principal act of chivalry."[66] Indeed, Cartagena insists quite clearly that knights should stop menacing their friends and ignoring the legacy of their ancestors in order to go and fight for the holy faith.

Even implicitly, Cartagena's *Doctrinal* is an attempt to reform chivalry. Cartagena famously called on the knights of Castile to read not the popular romances of Tristan and Amadís, but to read of the historical deeds of the great heroes of Spain. For Cartagena, the historical figures were better exemplars of good chivalry than the literary figures were. Throughout the text, Cartagena mentions a few of these Spanish knights by name. There is King Ramiro (r. 842–850), who defeated the Muslims at Calahorra in 844, a battle during which Santiago (St James) appeared in the sky to aid the Christian fighters. There is Diego Pérez de Vargas, who helped to reconquer the city of Jerez de la Frontera in 1231; incidentally, Santiago was visually present at this battle as well. In contradistinction, Cartagena also offers the example of Diego de Haro, who, during the Battle of Alarcos in 1195, abandoned a castle, an action that contributed to the Muslim victory.[67] Part of the reason why Cartagena was so insistent that knights read chronicles and history rather than romance was that the chronicles of Spanish history often took the holy war as their subject. The bishop recognized that knights were influenced by what they read and, as a result, wanted them to read works which would whet their appetite for holy war and drive them away from killing their fellow Christians.

The same reform effort appears in the chronicle of Miguel Lucas de Iranzo, the Constable of Castile toward the end of the 15th century. As we have seen, the *Hechos del Condestable Don Miguel Lucas de Iranzo* reads as a manifesto of holy war.[68] The Constable is almost always cast as the superlative crusading warrior, ever mindful of the struggle for the faith against the Muslim enemy. Indeed, like Cartagena, Iranzo actively notes at times that the holy war was a solution to an existing *problem* of violence against fellow Christians. In his letter to Pope Sixtus VI, which we encountered in Chapter 3, Iranzo laments the terrible destruction brought by inter-Christian warfare. We can almost hear him weeping as he recounts the violence done against

---

[66] Ibid., 255. "contra los parientes e contra los que duian ser amigos, o en justas o en torneos, de lo qual lo vno es aborescible e abominable e cosa que trae desonrra e destruyçion, lo otro vn juego o ensaye mas non prinçipal acto de la caualleria."
[67] Ibid. For King Rodrigo see pp. 178–179; for Vargas and Haro see pp. 224–225.
[68] Iranzo, in one sense, represents the meeting point between frontier culture, which could accommodate cultural exchange and accommodation, and Trastámara nobility. See Rodríguez Molina, *La vida de moros y cristianos*, 418–419 and Thomas Devaney, *Enemies in the Plaza: Urban Spectacle and the End of Spanish Frontier Culture, 1460–1492* (Philadelphia: University of Pennsylvania Press, 2015).

himself and the Christians of central Andalucía by the vicious and deceitful Master of Calatrava. He goes on to decry the actions of the count of Cabra, whom he accuses of allying with the Muslims, leading them to attack Christian enemies near Córdova and allowing them to commit a litany of atrocities: butchering men and boys, raping women and girls, burning Christians in their beds, washing themselves in Christian blood, blaspheming the name of Christ, burning the figure of the Blessed Virgin, desecrating churches, and so on in that manner. For Iranzo, there was compelling and regular evidence that inter-Christian violence had led directly to Muslim assaults and the loss of the Christian frontier.[69] Iranzo had a solution. More holy knights like himself were needed, and the pope could encourage knights to leave behind their petty and destructive inter-Christian squabbles, to fight the enemies of the faith by offering plenary indulgences to any knights who would defend the frontier or any Christians who would send money for that purpose.[70]

Devout Christians such as Alfonso de Cartagena and Miguel Lucas de Iranzo had identified the same ideas of inter-Christian warfare which we have outlined in this chapter, they recognized them as problematic, and they offered a solution. Their efforts, though, did not have the effect they might have hoped for. Noel Fallows has claimed that Cartagena's prescriptions would lay the foundation for the Catholic Monarchs' consolidation of Spanish Christian society and their successful establishment of a state centered on a powerful monarch.[71] He may well be correct in this assessment, but Cartagena's call for an end to inter-Christian violence in favor of the holy war must be judged a failure. The bishop of Burgos died in 1456, and perhaps he died happy, knowing that the new King Enrique IV was renewing the war against Granada, even if that war was not as vigorous as some might have hoped.[72] We have seen, of course, that some of the most intense inter-Christian warfare was yet to come, both in Andalucía and across Castile, as factions rose and fell against Enrique. As for Iranzo, we must be somewhat skeptical of his own dedication to the holy war.[73] He certainly wanted to be known as a holy warrior and he surely did raid the Granadan frontier and wreak havoc among the Muslims from time to time.

---

[69] *Hechos del condestable*, 470–475.

[70] Ibid., 475.

[71] *Chivalric Vision of Alfonso de Cartagena*, 70–71.

[72] Valera, "Memorial de diversas hazañas," 14–18. Where Valera is often mild in his criticism of Enrique, Alfonso de Palencia is unforgiving. His entire chronicle is hostile to the king. Alfonso de Palencia, "Crónica de Enrique IV," ed. and trans. Antonio Paz y Meliá, in *Biblioteca de Autores Españoles* (Madrid: Ediciones Atlas, 1973), vol. 257.

[73] For more sympathetic understandings of Iranzo see O'Callaghan, *The Last Crusade in the West: Castile and the Conquest of Granada* (Philadelphia: University of Pennsylvania Press, 2014), 118–119, and Juan Torres Fontes, "Las treguas con Granada de 1469 y 1472" *Hispania: Revista española de historia*, no. 90 (1963): 163–199.

It is no coincidence, though, that in the months immediately following his heartfelt letter to Sixtus, Iranzo was at war again, indulging his honor and his father's legacy by joining in the Andalucian war. For Iranzo, of course, it was his Christian enemies who were defying God's will while he and his allies fought in the name of God. Iranzo's last military action before his death was to aid the duke of Medina Sidonia against the count of Arcos. Chivalric ideas were just as powerful to Iranzo, a relative newcomer to the chivalric elite, as they were to old *linajes*. Ideas mattered at least as much as, if not more than, economic interests or military strategy. Indeed, Iranzo's chronicler never even mentions the important issue of who controlled the tuna fisheries.

Conclusions

The late 14th and 15th centuries were marked by fighting among Christians across Europe, with Castile being no exception. As pious Castilian knights struck one another down, they were not operating purely under unchained and incomprehensible barbaric impulses. The chivalry of Trastámara Castile committed inter-Christian violence in the context of an ideological framework. At the heart of this violence, as at the heart of so much medieval violence, was the high premium placed on winning, and defending one's honor. The honor of the individual in late medieval Castile was deeply connected to the honor of one's *linaje*. Great deeds of one's ancestors weighed heavily on the hearts and minds of knights who wished to preserve the honor of generations past and meet or exceed the expectations placed on them by their forebears. Honor both individual and familial was given the sanction of God Almighty, in whose service all knights believed they were always fighting. Guzmán, Ponce de León, Iranzo, Luna, Trastámara – all were God's holy warriors in their own eyes, even when their Christian enemies believed exactly the same thing. It is perhaps no surprise that calls for reform, whether sincere or propagandistic, did not fundamentally change chivalric behavior for decades. Knights certainly recognized that the holy war was more valorous and that more honor could be won there, but commitment to their own and their family's honor often dictated that they fight a war at home, a war which, if not holy, was often divinely sanctioned. These impulses were a component of chivalry for nearly all Castilian knights. Although Miguel Lucas de Iranzo vigorously projected his identity as a holy warrior, he regularly fought against Christians. Although Rodrigo Ponce de León fought an extensive war against his Christian neighbors in Andalucía, he also understood his family's honor to be connected to the war against Islam and he saw himself as a holy warrior. These two components were not mutually exclusive. Quite the contrary; war against the infidel and war against fellow Christians were both valorous exercises that knights participated in, depending on the opportunities available, the exigencies of the moment, or the particular challenge to their individual or familial honor.

That late medieval Christians were actively and enthusiastically killing and wounding one another and that they intellectually conceptualized such violence is a reminder that religious violence is more complex than might first appear. Our dominant narrative of late medieval Spanish history rightly highlights religious violence against minority populations, particularly Muslims and Jews. But we must remember that religious violence was not targeted *only* at religious Others. The ideology of violence of the Trastámara nobility was comprehensive, offering a means for justifying, valorizing, and encouraging the killing of fellow Christians.

5

Chivalry, Men, and Women

Enrique IV's masculinity was faltering. After his dethronement in effigy at the Farce of Ávila in the summer of 1465, Juan Pacheco and his allies had called into question not only the king's right to rule, but also his Christianity, heterosexuality, and even his masculinity. As they fought against Enrique in a civil war, they championed the royal claim of Alfonso, the king's eleven-year-old half-brother, who was apparently sufficiently masculine. A few years into the civil war, though, the rebels lost their champion when the fourteen-year-old Alfonso died in 1468. With no viable male candidates remaining for the throne, the rebels rallied behind Enrique's half-sister, Isabel. By the end of the summer, the two sides had negotiated the Treaty of the Bulls of Guisando, whereby Enrique would remain on the throne but would accept Isabel as his heir. Enrique's daughter, Juana la Beltraneja, was cut out of the succession and Enrique ended his marriage with Juana's mother. These stipulations all confirmed Enrique's impotence, both as a ruler and as a man, both of which had been components in resistance to his rule in the first place.

The one other stipulation of the treaty was that Isabel would have to obtain Enrique's permission before she married anyone. She herself was placed in submission to the men around her, first by the noble supporters who hoped to control her and then by her half-brother, weak though he might be. Almost immediately, though, Isabel took her fate into her own hands by secretly agreeing to a marriage with her second cousin, the future Fernando II of Aragon. When the marriage was actually concluded in October of 1469, Enrique abandoned the terms of the treaty, insisting that his daughter would be his heir once again. When Enrique died in 1474, both Isabel and Juana were proclaimed queen of Castile.[1] Two women would fight for the throne in the War of the Castilian Succession, a remarkably rare occurrence in medieval history. Isabel and her supporters would eventually prevail, but the reality of having a choice between two female claimants reflected a chal-

---

[1] Biographies of Isabel have flourished since the late 20th century. Among the best is Peggy K. Liss, *Isabel the Queen* (Oxford: Oxford University Press, 1992). For an analytical approach to Isabel's reign as queen see Barbara F. Weissberger, *Isabel Rules: Constructing Queenship, Wielding Power* (Minneapolis: University of Minnesota Press, 2003).

lenge to comfortable norms of gender in late medieval Castile.[2] How could a woman effectively lead in war? With no male option, how should a queen's legitimacy be constructed? How should her identity be constructed? These questions were difficult precisely because of the gendered nature not only of kingship, but of chivalry. Warfare, violence, and prickly honor seemed easier to understand from a male perspective.

Studies of the female role in medieval chivalry have traditionally focused on women as the inspiration for male behavior. The love of a woman was expected to make a knight fight more vigorously on the field of battle or at the tournament. Women were often depicted as bystanders or spectators at chivalric events. Noble ladies appear throughout chivalric literature, endangered and in need of protection by none other than a strong and virtuous knight.[3] More recent scholarship has sought to foreground the female role in chivalry a bit more clearly. David Crouch, while acknowledging that women were typically spectators at chivalric events, emphasized that as spectators they still could influence the course of events and knightly behavior.[4] Both Amy Vines and Louise Wilkinson have emphasized an even more active role for women in the chivalric world, especially from a cultural perspective, the former arguing that female figures in romances helped to reinforce and reproduce historical norms of female authority, while the latter has made the case that women embraced chivalric virtues such as lineage and courtesy even as their own virtuousness inspired knights to be gentlemanly.[5] Both traditional scholarship and newer research have helped to illuminate women's role in chivalry, particularly as it applies to courtliness, romance, and male behavior and not to the female relationship with chivalric violence directly.

This chapter will explore the relationship between gender and violence in late medieval Castilian chivalric ideology, with an emphasis on three main points. First, chivalric violence was theoretically understood to be a fundamentally masculine quality. Men were expected to perform violent acts, while their failure to do so eroded their masculine reputation. Second,

---

[2] On Isabel and questions of her right to rule, see Ana Isabel Carrasco Manchado, *Isabel I de Castilla y la sombra de la ilegitimidad: Propaganda y representación en el conflicto successorio (1474–1482)* (Madrid: Sílex Ediciones, S.L., 2006).

[3] A few works that present a more traditional understanding of the female role in chivalry include Richard W. Kaeuper, *Medieval Chivalry* (Cambridge: Cambridge University Press, 2016), 321–329 and Georges Duby, "Women and Power," in *Cultures of Power: Lordship, Status and Process in Twelfth-Century Europe*, ed. Thomas. N. Bisson (Philadelphia: University of Pennsylvania Press, 1995), 73–75.

[4] David Crouch, *The Birth of Nobility: Constructing Aristocracy in England and France, 900–1300* (Harlow, England: Pearson Longman, 2005), 318–319.

[5] Amy N. Vines, *Women's Power in Late Medieval Romance* (Cambridge: D.S. Brewer, 2011). Louise J. Wilkinson, "Gendered Chivalry," in *A Companion to Chivalry*, ed. Robert W. Jones and Peter Coss (Woodbridge: Boydell Press, 2019), 228–239.

chivalric ideology opened no space for valorized violence against women. Rape and attacks on ladies were constantly castigated in Castilian chivalric literature. The very frequency with which sexual violence is reviled, though, suggests to us that rape and male violence against women was all too common among knights and the chivalric elite. Third, women had a role to play in committing violence. Women were seen as the inspiration for male violence, as objects of romantic affection who loved nothing more than a powerful and violent knight.[6] Furthermore, women had a space to shame men into committing violence in order to uphold family and individual honor. Perhaps most importantly, women in late medieval Castile pushed the boundaries of chivalric gender roles as they related to violence. Although women rarely took up arms, they eagerly incited or directed chivalric violence when it suited them.[7] At times, late medieval Castilian women transformed gender roles to allow for their leadership of violent men.

Masculine and Feminine Honor

Generically speaking, honor societies typically operate differently for men and women. Masculine honor arises out of physical strength, audacity, the ability to make good on one's promises, and an aggressive and jealous sexuality.[8] Each of these characteristics represents a man's ability to dominate rather than to be dominated. On the battlefield, in society, and in the bedroom, honor societies present an expectation and a reward for a raw and agonistic masculine power. In ancient and medieval European cultures, both in the Mediterranean and in northern Europe, such masculinity is writ large in literary, religious, and historical texts. Men are good men when they fight well, but also when they lead well in warfare – another indication of dominance. Beyond the plaudits offered to men for dominance, one need only think of the way in which men are mocked for submissive behavior or shamed into more dominant behavior. Numerous examples come to mind: the sign of the horns in Mediterranean traditions given to a cuckold, a man who has been sexually humiliated by a more dominant rival;[9] the bitter

---

[6] Richard W. Kaeuper and Elspeth Kennedy, *The Book of Chivalry of Geoffroi de Charny: Text, Context, and Translation* (Philadelphia: University of Pennsylvania Press, 1996), 66–68.

[7] For an assessment of medieval women who *did* take up arms in some capacity, see Megan McLaughlin, "The Woman Warrior: Gender, Warfare, and Society in Medieval Europe," *Women's Studies*, vol. 17, no. 3–4 (1990): 193–209.

[8] Julian Pitt-Rivers, "Honour and Social Status," in *Honour and Shame: The Values of Mediterranean Society*, ed. Jean G. Peristiany (London: Weidenfeld and Nicolson, 1965), 21–23; Frank Henderson Stewart, *Honor* (Chicago: University of Chicago Press, 1994), 108.

[9] Pitt-Rivers, "Honour and Social Status," 46–51.

charge of cowardice for a soldier on the battlefield;[10] even the language used to demean and belittle a man and provoke him into more aggressive and dominant behavior in the medieval or even the modern world, whether we mean Enrique IV being called a *puto* or modern adolescent taunts about a man's perceived homosexuality or weakness.[11] In each of these cases, the desired outcome is to publicly humiliate and shame a man by emasculating him in front of his peers. The typical solution for a shamed man in an honor society is to dominate someone else – through a fistfight, through renewed vigor on the battlefield, or the sexual conquest of a woman. Domination of other people, often violently, rests at the heart of masculine honor in an honor society.

Honor and violence in medieval chivalry, so deeply tied to one another, represent precisely these theoretical gender constructions. Chivalric men are typically only men once they have dominated someone else. The young Cid in *Mocedades de Rodrigo* goes into his first battle at age twelve – an appropriate age of adolescence – and one of his very first acts is to go into battle where he slays his enemy, Count Don Gómez.[12] The great knight Pero Niño was educated in chivalry at age ten. His tutor told him that he should not spend time in the school of letters at his age because he needed to focus on his martial training. He went into battle against his enemies at age fifteen, striking signal blows, spilling blood, wounding, and ultimately defeating them. In doing so, "he began well and showed that he would reach great honor through the art of arms and office of chivalry."[13] Edward III of England's assertion as he watched his sixteen-year-old son struggle in the press at the Battle of Crécy, that his boy should win his spurs, echos loudly.[14] Indeed, it is nearly a trope in chivalric literature and history that great heroes begin their adult lives only once they have fought (and preferably won) in battle. Boys became men through violent domination.[15] Once

---

[10] Richard W. Kaeuper, *Chivalry and Violence in Medieval Europe* (Oxford: Oxford University Press, 1999), 274.

[11] Pitt-Rivers, "Honour and Social Status," 46.

[12] *Las Mocedades de Rodrigo, The Youthful Deeds of Rodrigo, the Cid*, trans. Matthew Bailey (Toronto: University of Toronto Press, Inc., 2007), 40.

[13] Gutierre Díez de Games, *El Victorial*, ed. Juan de Mata Carriazo (Madrid: Espasa-Calpe, S.A., 1940), 334. "él començava bien e mostrava que grand honra avía de alcançar por arte de armas e ofiçio de cavallería."

[14] Inversely, when a knight loses the honor of knighthood, his spurs are removed from him, symbolically emasculating him. Stephanie Trigg, *Shame and Honor: A Vulgar History of the Order of the Garter* (Philadelphia: University of Pennsylvania Press, 2012), 136–137. Also, see Maurice Keen, *Chivalry* (New Haven, CT: Yale University Press, 1984), 175.

[15] William Ian Miller, *Humiliation, and Other Essays on Honor, Social Discomfort, and Violence* (Ithaca, NY: Cornell University Press, 1993), 55–60.

they had become men, they were expected to maintain themselves through the violent domination of others on the battlefield.

If male honor is about domination, female honor emphatically is not. Yet this is not to say that female honor is *only* about submission. In honor societies, submissiveness to one's father, husband, brothers, or sons is indeed a key part of a woman's good behavior, partly because it allows her male relatives to exhibit their dominance over her. Her submissive behavior towards her relatives augments her family's masculine honor, demonstrating the dominant and powerful men who head the family and represent them publicly.[16] Submission itself, though, does not yield honor. Instead, feminine honor is rooted in sexual purity and the production of healthy and legitimate heirs, especially sons.[17] As such, on the one hand, a woman's amorous and sexual love of a man under the circumstances of marriage and loyalty can bestow honor on and even ennoble a man.[18] On the other hand, a woman who becomes sexually promiscuous or bears children outside of approved marriage risks permanently damaging her family's honor. This is partly because she has allowed an outside man to dominate her without the approval of the men in her family. As such, they themselves are shamed by her sexual behavior.[19] Additionally, a pregnancy outside of marriage usurps the certainty of her family's line. In the case of a married woman, her husband can no longer be certain about the paternity of his wife's children; in the case of an unmarried woman, her family is placed in the unwelcome situation of submissively taking care of a more dominant man's brood.[20] If masculine honor is predicated on dominance and prowess, feminine honor is predicated on sexual purity and prudence.

Elite women in the Middle Ages found agency to some extent through the appropriation of chivalric gender roles. Barbara Weissberger has argued that feminine gender and sexuality served to threaten masculinity and to cultivate an "anxious masculinity," particularly after Isabel secured the throne for herself.[21] To be sure, Isabel's femininity and appropriation of masculinity in her self-fashioning was transgressive. But Isabel also fashioned her femininity cleverly, blending traditional chivalric femininity with elements of

---

[16] Pitt-Rivers, "Honour and Social Status," 45–46.

[17] Nancy Huston, "The Matrix of War: Mothers and Heroes," in *The Female Body in Western Culture, Contemporary Perspectives*, ed. Susan Rubin Suleiman (Cambridge, MA: Harvard University Press, 1985), 123–135.

[18] C. Stephen Jaeger, *Ennobling Love: In Search of a Lost Sensibility* (Philadelphia: University of Pennsylvania Press, 1999), 94–101.

[19] Halvor Oxnes, "Honor and Shame," *Biblical Theology Bulletin: A Journal of Bible and Theology*, vol. 23, no. 4 (Nov. 1993):167–176.

[20] Pitt-Rivers, "Honour and Social Status," 46.

[21] Weissberger, *Isabel Rules*, 1–2, 71.

chivalric masculinity.[22] She was simultaneously a traditional queen even as she grasped chivalric ideology and violence more fully than many of the men around her. Even as she caused anxiety to masculine thinkers, she was capable of lifting up the knights and chivalric men of Castile by providing an avenue for their chivalric impulses.

Rape and Sexual Violence

As we have seen over and over, violence was ubiquitous in late medieval Castile and was particularly prominent among the chivalric elite. Knights defined themselves through their capacity for violence and their affection for it. Far too often, violence was directed by knights and men-at-arms against women. This included not simply physical abuse but also rape. Our chronicle, literary, and legal evidence suggests that while violence against women was a familiar problem to the elite of late medieval Castile, chivalric ideology did not allow for it. We have seen a place for violence against Muslims, fellow Christians, kings, fellow nobles, and peasants expressed in late medieval Castilian chivalry. Violence against women was emphatically *not* a component of this ideology. Indeed, most ideological evidence rails against knightly violence against women, emphasizing the regularity and gravity of the problem all while attempting to reform knightly behavior. Quite the contrary, women were to be protected and violence against them demanded reciprocal violence.

The legal evidence of the Trastámara period offers only a few rare glimpses of knightly men attacking women physically and sexually. In 1380, Juan I received a petition at the *cortes* held in Soria in which the petitioners complained that some men were "taking married or betrothed women or other women by force" before retreating to their castles or strong houses or the fortifications of ecclesiastical and secular lords in order to avoid being punished for such violence.[23] The king responded with strong words, observing that the desire for justice was "reason and right," and ordering that "whoever or whatever *señor* or castellan of the castles or *alcazares* or strong houses, that they defend the said women."[24] And, Juan continued, if some *señor* or castellan should refuse to turn over the kidnappers and

---

[22] This is not to say that Isabel was queer; she had several models of gender identity open to her and she used them appropriately. She did not break out of clearly normative roles. For an approach to queer gender roles see *Queer Iberia: Sexualities, Cultures, and Crossings from the Middle Ages to the Renaissance*, ed. Josiah Blackmore and Gregory Hutcheson (Durham, NC: Duke University Press, 1999).

[23] *Cortes* held at Soria in 1380. *Cortes de los antiguos reinos de León y de Castilla*, ed. Real Academia de la Historia (Madrid: M. Rivadeneyra, 1861–1866), vol. 2, 306.

[24] Ibid.

rapists, the king's officer "should go to the said fortification and take it and tear it down, so that it is an example and a lesson for others not to dare to do the same."[25] Coming just a decade into the Trastámara period, this petition confirms that the powerful men of Castile did abduct and rape women. But, unlike our earlier evidence of social violence, the question of gendered violence is rarely raised again in the records of the *cortes*. Was Juan I successful in ending male violence targeting women?

The sources suggest not. Instead, it would appear that gendered violence as a unique category was simply subsumed in the legal records under more general complaints of violence. As Castile was riven by civil war and dynastic intrigue throughout much of the 15th century, petitions in the *cortes* focus on the general disorder of the realm and the miscarriage of justice. In 1432, for example, in the middle of ten continuous years of petitions to the king about knightly violence, we find a brief reference to rape. At the *cortes* held in Zamora that year, King Juan II acknowledged to petitioners that "it is notorious in my kingdoms and lordships, that ... highway robbers and rapists of married women and virgins and widows and murderers"[26] could all find safe haven in the cities and towns and rural places. The petition was not focused on these specific crimes, heinous though they may have been. Instead the petitioners complained that the robbers and rapists and murderers could live comfortably because they claimed to be the king's own justices and had letters of privilege issued by the king. Justice and public order were falling apart and sexual violence was one component of this larger problem. We ought to recall the ballad of the duke of Arjona which we saw in Chapter 2 and remember that one of the charges against the duke was that he "forced women, married and betrothed."[27] The language in the ballad closely mirrors the language concerning violence against women in the records of the *cortes* and the language of the chronicles. Clearly there was a concern about the behavior of the chivalric elite towards Castilian women.

Even as we see evidence of violence against women, we can detect hints that chivalric writers scorned knights and men-at-arms who raped, abducted, or otherwise attacked women. In his chronicle, *Memorial de Diversas Hazañas*, Diego de Valera described a key moment in the Andalucian War, when Rodrigo Ponce de León, the marques of Cádiz, besieged and captured a fortification and village outside the city of Medina Sidonia, killing the *alcaide*. Valera commented on the reaction of the citizens of the city when Rodrigo came to occupy the city, observing that they

---

[25] Ibid.
[26] *Cortes* held at Zamora, 1432. Ibid., vol. 3, 151. "era notorio enlos mis rregnos e sennorios ... se acojen muchos rrobadores delos caminos, e forçadores delas mugeres casadas e virgenes e viudas, e matadors."
[27] *Antología de poetas líricos castellanos*, ed. M. Menéndez Pelayo (Madrid: Librería de Hernando y Compañía, 1945), 140. "que forzades las mujeres – casadas y por casar."

went out of the city and received [Rodrigo] and kissed his hand as if he was their natural lord; this was because of the enmity which most of the citizens had with the *alcaide*, for the men of the *alcaide* had wronged them and taken the women away by force, and even though sometimes they complained about [the *alcaide*] to the Duke [of Medina Sidonia], he was never punished.[28]

Valera uses this instance as a moral example, emphasizing that the *alcaide* lost his life and honor and that he deserved to die. Rodrigo, on the other hand, is held up as a chivalric hero who entered the city and restored justice to the citizens, especially because he prevented the ongoing attacks against women that had been perpetrated by the *alcaide*'s men. For Valera, himself a practicing knight and participant in the wars of 15th-century Castile, male attacks on women were fundamentally dishonorable and even evil.

Indeed, medieval Castilian literature highlighted the theme of the knightly treatment of women and regularly excoriated gendered violence and rape. The *Cantar de Mio Cid*, frequently lauded as the national epic of Spain and arguably the foundational poem of Castilian chivalric literature, deals directly with violence against women. One of the key arcs of the original poem concerns the marriage of El Cid's two daughters, Elvira and Sol, to two nobles – the brothers Carrión.[29] Newly attached to the great warrior's family, the brothers achieve great wealth as a result of the battlefield prowess of El Cid and his men. But the Carrións are no honorable warriors; they are exposed as cowards and ridiculed by the other Castilian knights for their fear and dishonor.[30] The Carrión brothers, in short, are some of the first examples of bad knights in Castilian literary history and their villainy presents itself most clearly in the treatment of their wives.

After receiving incredible wealth from their father-in-law, the brothers conclude that, because of their new wealth and the prestige of the Carrión lineage, they are capable of achieving much more advantageous marriages. They aspire to marry the daughters of a king or even an emperor. Standing in their way are the daughters of El Cid, their current wives. The brothers decide to abandon and kill the women, constantly using the verb *escarnir* to describe their intentions.[31] The verb suggests moral or social harm as much as physical harm, connoting mockery, ridicule, and, in the context of an honor society, shame. The intent of the Carrións to shame the daughters of

---

[28] Diego de Valera, "Memorial de diversas hazañas," in *Biblioteca de Autores Españoles*, ed. M. Rivadeneyra (Madrid: Impresores de Camara de S.M., 1876), vol. 70, 77. "los vecinos della le salieron á rescibir é le besaron la mano como si fuera su señor natural, de lo qual fué causa la enemistad que los mas de los vecinos tenian con el Alcayde, é les injuriaban é les quitaban las mujeres por fuerza, aunque algunas veces se quejaban al Duque dél, y ningun castigo en ello puso."

[29] *The Song of the Cid*, trans. Burton Raffel (New York: Penguin Group, 2009), 142–152.

[30] Ibid., 158–174.

[31] Ibid., 176. For example, "escarniremos las fijas del Canpeador"; "Assí las escarinn."

El Cid confirms some of our theoretical approaches. What could be worse for a woman than abusing her reputation, her sexual and marital purity, and denying her a good marriage with the opportunity to produce children? Ultimately, it was not just shame or mockery that the Carrións inflicted on El Cid's daughters. They took the girls into the wilderness and

> with leather straps beat them senseless,
> with sharp spurs attacked them
> and tore both their clothes and flesh,
> and clean blood flowed onto their tunics …
> the brothers tired themselves in wounding the women,
> competing with one another to give greater blows
> until Doña Elvira and Doña Sol could no longer speak;
> they left them for dead in the forest of Corpes.[32]

In the following pages, there is a tone of deep regret and sorrow for the heinous behavior of the Carrións. El Cid himself exhibits sorrow and laments the shame and dishonor done to his daughters once he learns of their suffering.[33] Members of El Cid's court, in high chivalric fashion, vow vengeance on the Carrións for their crime against Elvira and Sol.[34] Indeed, El Cid argues to King Alfonso that the disrespect and violence done to his daughters is a dishonor to the king and kingdom itself. In this case, chivalric literature served as a call for reform. In emphasizing that violence against women dishonored the victim herself as well as her male relatives and the king, who could not prevent it from happening, the great Castilian epic poem sought to condemn violence against women and valorize chivalric defense of women.

El Cid's vengeance for the dishonor he and his daughters suffered at the hands of the Carrións comes first through legal appeal – an eminently unchivalric avenue. At King Alfonso's court, El Cid brings a suit against the brothers and their worldly possessions are all confiscated. Again, there is an emphasis that violence against women is wrong on multiple levels – not only personally, but legally as well. But even after being reimbursed by the Carrións, El Cid and his supporters demand a more chivalric kind of justice: martial vengeance. El Cid insists that he will not allow anything less than physical combat in order to avenge the damage done to his daughters. El Cid's nephew, Pedro Bermúdez – an otherwise mute man – finds his voice and lambasts the Carrións with some of the most cutting words of this

---

[32] Ibid., 186. "con las cinchas corredizas májanlas tan sin sabor, / con las espuelas agudas dón ellas an mal sabor / rronpién las camisas e las carnes a ellas amas a dos, / linpia salié la sangre sobre los ciclatones … Cansados son de ferir ellos amos a dos, / ensayandos' amos quál dará mejores colpes. / Ya non pueden fablar don Elvira e doña Sol; / por muertas las dexaron en el rrobredo de Corpes."

[33] Ibid., 192.

[34] Ibid., 194.

section of the poem, saying to one of the Carrión brothers, "I challenge you, you evil traitor. / I will fight you here before the king Don Alfonso / in the name of the daughters of El Cid, Doña Elvira and Doña Sol, / for what you did to them saps your honor; / they are women and you should be men! / In all ways they have more honor than you."[35] El Cid's champions defeat the Carrións in judicial battle, leaving the brothers alive but dishonored and disgraced, with the narrator moralizing: "Great is the infamy of the infantes of Carrión: / Whoever shames a good woman and thereafter abandons her / may such disgrace or worse come."[36] The abuse of El Cid's daughters is one of the key story arcs of the *Cantar de Mio Cid* and the message is perfectly clear: knightly violence against women is not only unacceptable, but a fundamentally dishonorable act. This centuries-old chivalric epic prescribed the honorable and tender treatment of women.

If the *Cantar de Mio Cid* laid a foundation for thinking about violence against women in Trastámara Castile, there were more immediate literary examples that dealt with the question of gendered violence, and particularly with rape. The rape of La Cava in the legend of King Rodrigo, which we mentioned briefly in Chapter 3, was a well-known and contemporary literary treatment of chivalric rape and responses to it. As James Donald Fogelquist has pointed out, the story of La Cava in Pedro de Corral's *Crónica del Rey Don Rodrigo* is complex and multilayered and could be interpreted in multiple different ways.[37] Yet it can hardly be unclear that King Rodrigo rapes La Cava, the daughter of Count Julián. Methodically, King Rodrigo sends for La Cava and asks if she will sleep with him. When she refuses, he hints that she *must* sleep with him because he is the king. She refuses again and leaves his chamber. Some time later, Rodrigo sends for La Cava when there is only a single attendant in his chamber. "[S]he came at his order, and because, at this hour [the siesta] there was nobody else in his chamber but the three of them, he did with her all that he wanted to."[38]

In case we suppose that this was consensual on La Cava's part, the next chapter discusses how La Cava felt "dishonored" (*escarnida*) by the king, and how she grieved terribly after the incident. Indeed, her physical beauty

---

[35] Ibid., 222. "Rriébtot' el cuerpo por malo e por traidor, éstot' lidiaré aquí ant' el rrey don Alfonso / por fijas del Cid, don Elvira e doña Sol, / por quanto las dexastes menos valeded vós; / ellas son mugieres e vós sodes varones, / en todas guisas más valen que vós."

[36] Ibid., 244. "Grant es la biltança de ifantes de Carrión: / qui buena dueña escarnece e la dexa después / atal le contesca o siquier peor."

[37] James Donald Fogelquist, *Pedro de Corral's Reconfiguration of La Cava in the "Crónica del Rey don Rodrigo," eHumanista*: Monographs in Humanities, no. 3 (207): 37–53.

[38] Pedro de Corral, *Crónica del Rey don Rodrigo (Crónica sarracina)*, ed. James Donald Fogelquist (Madrid: Editorial Castalia, S.A., 2001), vol. I, 455. "e ella vino a su mandando, e como esa ora no avía en toda su cámara otro ninguno sino ellos todos tres, él conplió con ella todo lo que quiso."

soon departed and it became outwardly clear that her sexual honor and her feminine purity had been taken from her. La Cava finds comfort with one of her friends, a woman named Alquifa, when she explains that the king has raped her. She goes on to write a letter to her father, Count Julián, in which she refers to herself as "the dishonored La Cava, your daughter," and begs him to come and take her away from the court, so that her dishonor is not made public.[39] La Cava's words, invented by a male chivalric author, offer crucial insights to the male perspective on rape in late medieval Castile. In Corral's mind, the problem for a woman who is raped is the danger that she will suffer public shame and a loss of her sexual honor. La Cava does not call for violent retribution on the part of her father or others, nor does she seek legal justice for the crime committed against her. Instead, she simply wants to occlude public knowledge of her dishonor. From a male chivalric perspective, it is honor – feminine sexual honor – that is endangered by rape. For if a woman's honor is lost, then her family's honor is also tarnished. Thus knights and powerful men must reject rape in order to preserve an honorable society for both men and women.

But Corral, as a chivalric man, was concerned about rape for a larger reason as well – it was an act that was simultaneously dishonorable, socially destructive, and even treasonous. As Fogelquist has noted, the rape of La Cava is only one among several transgressive actions taken by King Rodrigo that led to the destruction of Visigothic Spain.[40] Still, Rodrigo's rape of La Cava is the final straw leading to the destruction of Spain. Despite the fact that La Cava does not want vengeance taken against King Rodrigo, her parents angrily and violently seek to have vengeance on Rodrigo. As we saw in Chapter 3, Count Julián, one of the key military leaders of the southern frontier, rose up against Rodrigo and invited the Muslims of north Africa to invade the Iberian Peninsula. This was the beginning of the *destruición* and its cause was Julián's anger and desire for vengeance against his daughter's rapist, the king of Spain. Rodrigo's act was triply treasonous. Not only did it lead to the destruction of his kingdom and people, but he betrayed the loyalty of his noble subjects, namely Count Julián and La Cava; he betrayed his fidelity to his wife, the queen; and he betrayed his Christian faith and behavior. This last is a theme which runs throughout the story, with Rodrigo constantly transgressing sacred spaces and concepts. The rape of La Cava is one more example of his betrayal of the tenets of Christianity and of his god. For Corral, rape is intolerable because of the destruction it causes throughout society, politics, and the sacred universe.

This ideological rejection of rape continued in other works as well. As Patricia Grieve has argued, the character of La Cava would be transformed

---

[39] Ibid., 458. "la Caba, desonrada, vuestra fija."
[40] Fogelquist, *Reconfiguration of La Cava*, 36–37.

in the late Middle Ages and the Spanish Golden Age. Instead of being a victim of rape by a lustful Visigothic king, she became "the Eve of Spain," a seductive harlot who willfully fornicated with King Rodrigo and helped to usher in the *destruición*.[41] But, even as this transition of La Cava was under way, other literature continued to rail against the rape of women and to insist that good knights ought to avoid rape and prevent women from being raped by other men. The great Spanish chivalric romance, *Amadís de Gaula*, deals with rape in several instances, every time condemning it with strong words and moral invective. The earliest extant version of the work was written by Garci Rodríguez de Montalvo in the first years of the 16th century, though the general outline of the story dates from much earlier, likely the 14th century at least.[42] Very early in the work Amadís encounters a damsel weeping and tearing her hair, who explains her grief: "'Señor,' she said, 'I come by the order of my lady to one of the good young knights who now are known and four footsoldiers took me and, carrying me to the castle, I was shamed and abused (*escarnecida*) by a traitor ...'"[43] Amadís is outraged by the rape of the damsel and swears vengeance on whoever perpetrated the deed. He ends up killing two of the offending footsoldiers, two knights who defended the castle, and another footsoldier in the castle in his rage. Finally, he encounters the knight who raped the damsel, unarmed and on foot. Amadís exclaims to the knight "Ay! arrogant knight, full of villainy, now you purchase the evil which you have done! Arm yourself now; if not I will kill you as you are, disarmed, for with evildoers such as you one should not display temperance!"[44] In this instance, all potential chivalric restraints are set aside and Amadís allows his knightly anger to carry the moment. Anyone who assisted in the damsel's rape must die, anyone who helps to defend the rapist must die, and any concept of "courtesy" toward his enemy is set aside in order to attain vengeance for a wronged woman.

Amadís also gives the reader the courtesy of a very explicit reason for defending women against violence and rape: it makes a man stronger to demonstrate his ability to physically protect women. Later in the work the

---

[41] Patricia E. Grieve, *The Eve of Spain: Myths of Origins in the history of Christian, Muslim, and Jewish Conflict* (Baltimore, MD: The Johns Hopkins University Press, 2009), 180–185.

[42] *Amadis of Gaul, Books I and II: A Novel of Chivalry of the 14th Century Presumably First Written in Spanish*, trans. Edwin B. Place and Herbert C. Behm (Lexington, KY: University of Kentucky Press, 2003), 9–11.

[43] Garci Rodríguez de Montalvo, *Amadís de Gaula* (Lexington, KY: Plaza Editorial, Inc., 2012), 54. "– Señor –dijo ella–, yo vengo con mandado de mi señora a un caballero mancebo de los buenos que ahora se saben y tomáronme allí cuatro peones y llevándome al castillo fui escarnecida de un traidor ..."

[44] Ibid., 56. "¡Ay, caballero soberbio, lleno de villanía, ahora compraréis la maldad que hicisteis! Armaos luego, si no mataros he así desarmado, que con los malos como vos no se debía tener templanza."

eponymous heroic knight attends a feast of his friends and allies. Amadís is distraught at the thought that his lover, Oriana, is being sent away to marry the emperor of Rome, against her will. He takes the opportunity to speak generally to the assembled audience of knights and lords, proclaiming:

> Since you last saw me, my good *señores*, I have traveled through many strange lands and many misadventures have come to pass for me which would take a long time to recount. But those which most concern me and brought me the greatest danger were those in which I aided ladies and maidens from many wrongs and injuries which were done to them; for just as women are born to obey with weak spirit, and their strongest weapons are tears and sighs, so those with extremely strong hearts, among other things, should take up their own weapons and protect and defend them from those who with little virtue mistreat them and dishonor them, just as the Greeks and the Romans did in ancient times, passing through the seas, destroying lands, winning battle, killing kings or casting them out of their kingdoms, solely to make satisfaction for the rapes and injuries done to women.[45]

To be sure, there is still the major concern with female honor, notably the sexual honor that is considered especially feminine. But for Montalvo (or the other author(s) of *Amadís*) there are other issues at play as well. Amadís is deeply concerned, even chiefly concerned, about the maltreatment, rape, and dishonor of women because of his understanding of man's relationship to woman. Relying on clerical assessments of gender, Amadís argues that women are more delicate, less capable, and that they lack the emotional, spiritual, or moral constitution that men possess. As a result, it is the obligation of men to protect women from abuse at the hands of other men. To be sure, this is a fundamentally patriarchal position and it fits very well with the chivalric virtues of prowess and vengeance. Amadís mentions the ancient world as a sort of moral exemplum for his late medieval audience. Significantly, chivalric men found an avenue for violence that implicitly and explicitly othered women, to borrow a concept from feminist theory. Woman became the passive, incapable, and weak counterpart to the active, able, and strong Man.[46]

---

[45] Ibid., Book 3, 236. "Después que no me visteis, mis buenos señores, muchas tierras extrañas he andado y gran desventuras han pasado por mí, que larga sería de contar, pero las que más me ocuparon y mayores peligros me trajeron fue socorrer dueñas y doncellas en muchos tuertos y agravios que les hacían, porque así como éstas nacieron para obedecer con flacos ánimos, y las más fuertes armas suyan sean lágrimas y suspiros, así los de fuertes corazones extremadamente entre las otras cosas las suyas deben tomar, amparándolas, defendiéndolas de aquéllos que con poca virtud las maltratan y deshonran, como los griegos y los romanos en los tiempos antiguos lo hicieron, pasando los mares, destruyendo las tierras, venciendo batallas, matando reyes y de sus reinos los echando, solamente por satisfacer las fuerzas e injurias a ellas hechas ..."

[46] Although it is an old idea, it is still a useful idea. Simone de Beauvoir, *The Second Sex* (New York: Alfred A. Knopf, 1964), xvi–xvii.

Violent Women

The idealized image of a demure, pious, and passive noblewoman with few other notable qualities appears not only in Amadís, but throughout medieval literature. Fainting women in Arthurian legend, weeping women in *chansons de geste*, and the good nuns of exempla provide just such a picture. As always, we do ourselves a disservice to interpret literary evidence with all its prescriptions as a wholly accurate reflection of medieval reality. Medieval noblewomen were raised and lived in the context of the violent and hypermasculine chivalric culture described above. When the need arose, they embraced that culture themselves. Although it was rare for a woman to take up a weapon herself, she had ample means of inciting men around her to violent acts and to effecting violence for her own ends.

The most typical situation in which a lady might push for violent action arose when she was a lord in her own right – when she held a landed title or the rights to a particular holding or privilege. On its face female lordship led to a problem for women. How could a woman defend herself, her rights, and her honor (both personal and corporate) at the same time that she fulfilled her military obligations to society and the Crown if she was expected to eschew violent action herself? The last component here is the easiest to resolve. Female lords in late medieval Spain still levied troops and sent them into battle in the armies of their lords when called upon to do so, just as female (and clerical) lords had been doing across Europe for centuries.[47] Typically, a female lord might appoint a trusted male advisor, perhaps a son or a brother, to lead her troops on the field and it is unlikely that such women sent their levies off to war and then sobbed and wrung their hands while their menfolk were away.

One example is the powerful Leonor de la Vega, head of the Vega *linaje*, who advanced her family's agenda though diverse means.[48] Leonor vigorously manipulated the legal system in order to advance her family's interests and one component of this was cozying up to the Crown in order to receive favorable legal judgments.[49] In short, Leonor constantly chose to assert herself in a male-dominated world without ever clearly breaking out of a traditional female gender role. In 1407 Leonor chose to send an unknown number of soldiers led by her son to fight alongside the Infante Fernando in the holy war. In exchange, Leonor was paid 3,456 *maravedís*

---

[47] McLaughlin, "The Woman Warrior."
[48] For a sense of Leonor in the Mendoza family, into which she married, see Helen Nader, "Introduction: The World of the Mendozas," in *Power and Gender in Renaissance Spain: Eight Women of the Mendoza Family, 1450–1650*, ed. Helen Nader (Chicago: University of Illinois Press, 2004), 16–17.
[49] Grace E. Coolidge, *Guardianship, Gender, and the Nobility in Early Modern Spain* (New York: Routledge, 2016), 126–127.

for the salary of these men. More importantly, she would have cultivated goodwill with the infante for embracing his eminently chivalric cause of holy war. An interesting footnote to this situation is that Leonor was also paid 7 *maravedís* for her son's soldiers who participated in the campaign. Her son, the famous humanist poet Iñigo López de Mendoza, must have contributed a small number of soldiers to the campaign. However, Iñigo was only eight years old at the time and his participation in the campaign would have been most precocious.[50] Instead, his mother leveraged her son's meager military resources in order to continue improving the position of herself and her family. Leonor de la Vega used the military resources available to her in order to advance her personal and familial agendas. In doing so, she participated in the violent impulse of chivalry, contributing to the holy war and sending men into battle.

Leonor was a remarkable and unique woman but her willingness to send men into battle to accomplish her goals was typical in Trastámara Castile. In a complicated case of the 1470s, two noblewomen were major players in a violent contest over a material possession. It would appear that Juan Manrique, the count of Castañeda, forcefully seized a tower house in the community of Piña.[51] Manrique's audacity certainly rankled a noblewoman named Constanza de Herrera, who claimed the fortification as her own. In response to Manrique's audacity, Constanza sent her son, Álvaro de Herrera, to seize the tower house by force in his mother's name. The manuscript record is unclear as to whether Álvaro was successful in his efforts or not; if he was, his possession of the stronghold was temporary. Over the course of several years, as Álvaro lost control of the tower house (or simply failed to dislodge Manrique), Álvaro petitioned the Crown to rectify the situation and force Manrique to return the property to his mother.[52] Given the weakness of the royal government, which we saw on display in Chapter 1, we should not be surprised that King Enrique IV was unsuccessful in doing so. Despite Enrique IV's inaction, though, Constanza chose to act and, like El Cid, she did so both through a legal petition and through violent action.

As the Herraras and Manrique fought over the Piña tower house, another noblewoman contributed to the violence. Juana Sanchez wrote to the king and informed him that the fortification in question ought to be possessed neither by Manrique nor by Constanza, but belonged by right to her brother, Ruiz Sanchez. As such, Juana directed her brother to occupy the tower house by force and eject Manrique, which he had accomplished by the time Juana wrote to the king. Indeed, Juana wrote that "it will please you [King Enrique] to know that Ruiz Sanchez, my brother, has now taken

---

[50] BNE RES/266/6.
[51] BNE RES/226/12.
[52] BNE RES/226/12 and 14.

and possessed justly and peacefully a tower house of Piña."⁵³ Just as a male lord might, Juana recognized that the Crown would not maintain the rights of her family and she sought out violent self-help in the form of her brother to achieve what she wanted. She defaulted to the sword in order to defend her family's honor; this was eminently chivalric.

The manuscript in question conveys a sense, too, that *Juana* was the individual pushing for military action to claim the tower house, not her brother, the man who actually held a right to the fortification and who led the said military action. Although Juana was incapable, as a woman, of taking up arms herself, she was at the center of her family's material interests and the violent vindication of those interests. The tower house of Piña was most actively contested by one man (Juan Manrique) and two women (Constanza de Herrara and Juana Sanchez). Although this gender balance contradicts a Victorian understanding of medieval womanhood, it was not unusual in the late Middle Ages. Women were not often active warriors, but they could and did direct violence to be undertaken by their male relatives.

Sometimes women were more attuned to the importance of chivalric honor than their male relatives were and they pushed men to be more masculine and more violent in order to defend and augment their personal and familial honor. During the Andalucian war between the Guzmanes and Ponce de Leones, a knight named Pedro de Basurto was the *alcaide* of a fortification near the city of Medina Sidonia. Diego de Valera described Pedro as a knight who, "though he was married, gave himself to many women, such that he rarely slept in the fortification, and in order to avoid spending money, he kept no men with him, and all his money was spent on his horse and on fineries ... and he kept no more than two old men in the fortification."⁵⁴ Instead, the *alcaide* simply kept a great host of dogs to guard the fortification and apparently doted on the animals. Pedro's lax behavior is precisely the kind that chivalric writers such as Geoffroi de Charny railed against, insisting that a knight who focused on luxuries instead of hard fighting was not living up to the knightly calling.⁵⁵ We can imagine that a number of chivalric men might similarly reject Pedro's indulgences; Fernando de Antequera likely would have raged against such silly excesses. More interesting is the story that Valera tells about Pedro. It is not a chivalric man, but a chivalric woman – Pedro's own mother – who cajoles her son into more honorable, vigorous, and chivalric behavior, and she does so in a markedly violent manner. Pedro's mother "had great anger

---

⁵³ BNE RES 226/13.
⁵⁴ Valera, "Memorial de diversas hazañas," 76. "el qual como quiera que era casado, dábase tanto á mugeres, que pocas veces durmia en la fortaleza, é á fin de no gastar no tenia gente, é todo su gasto era en caballo y en jaeces, de que mucho se preciaba, é no tenia mas en la fortaleza de dos viejos."
⁵⁵ Kaeuper and Kennedy, *Book of Chivalry*, 188–191.

at his bad life, and saw the fortification so poorly manned," and had grown tired of arguing with her son over the proper way for an honorable knight to behave. Instead, she ordered all of her son's dogs to be killed, in order to force him to employ the men necessary for the defense of the fortification.[56] Pedro's mother took the burden of her family's honor, won in martial activity, upon herself when her son failed.

Using violent action to force her son to be a better knight was the appropriate response in a chivalric context. Unfortunately for Pedro, her actions came too late. After his dogs were killed, Pedro was indeed forced to leave the fortification and gather men-at-arms to properly defend it. When he returned, he found that the enemy had besieged the palace where his mother, wife, sisters, and children had sought refuge. Pedro and his small force engaged the enemy, but Pedro took a lance through the mouth and out the back of his neck. He did not survive. Valera notes that Pedro "lost jointly his life and honor and goods and soul and passed into such great danger" in the next life, just as he had lived in this life.[57]

What of the poor mother? How great was her grief at the death of her son? After all, she had removed the dogs, which were the only defense at the fortification, and sent her son out into what became a suicide mission. What were her thoughts on the chivalric ideology that had helped to break her family? If we take the chronicler at his word, we find that Pedro's mother did not regret her actions at all. Quite the contrary, she stood by the chivalric principles that had informed her decisions to begin with. After her son was killed, the enemy commander informed the besieged noncombatants that Pedro was dead. "The mother responded, neither raising her voice nor expressing any sentiment, that whoever killed him should be put in charge [of the fortification]."[58] To be sure, Valera intends this situation as an example of bad knightly behavior and its results. Most likely the mother's role in this was exaggerated if not invented. But there is a certain plausibility to the role of Pedro's mother in Valera's story. Never does the chronicler remark that her behavior was absurd or castigate her actions. Indeed, the role of the mother is incidental to the story of Pedro. If Pedro's mother did not actually behave in this manner, if she did not actually embrace the martial ethos of chivalry as fully as Valera suggests, it was certainly a realistic situation.

Noblewomen were active participants in chivalric behavior even though they rarely took up arms themselves. Chivalric violence was a profoundly masculine activity, but powerful women embraced the ideal just as much

---

[56] Valera, "Memorial de diversas hazañas," 76–77.
[57] Ibid., 77. "é así juntamente perdió la vida é honra é bienes y el ánima é fué en tan gran peligro queanto paresce que debe ir, segun se dice de su vida."
[58] Ibid., 77. "Respondió la madre que el que lo mató que lo pusiese en cobro, sin tomar voz ninguna ni hacer ningun sentimiento."

as powerful men did. They pushed their sons, brothers, and husbands into violent action in order to vindicate familial or personal honor, to protect material interests, and even to participate in the holy war. These were chivalric goals and women readily prioritized them.

Queen Isabel: A Model Chivalric Woman

A few months before King Enrique IV died in 1474, the Infanta and heir apparent – Enrique's half-sister, Isabel – wrote a letter to her father-in-law, King Joan II of Aragon (r. 1458–1479). The letter was fairly standard and unremarkable; in it Isabel played the role of intercessor, a role that was typical for medieval European royal women. Isabel was approached by one Joan Ferrandez, who wanted his brother, Goncalo, to be named bishop of Sogorbe.[59] In much the way that a Christian supplicant might pray to the Blessed Virgin to intercede with the Father or the Son, supplicants often approached a wife, mother, sister, or other female relative of the king to intervene on their behalf.[60] There is almost a sense that just as God Himself was too powerful and terrible to approach directly, so kings were too dangerous to approach directly. Instead, a closely connected woman could be humble enough, even in regal glory, for a sinner (or petitioner) to approach. Thus the Infanta played a very traditional female role when she wrote to her father-in-law on behalf of one of his subjects. Indeed, she modestly and humbly approached her superior male relative.

Yet Isabel, like the women we have just examined, was no shrinking violet when it came to chivalric violence – she did not fit *only* into the role of humble intercessor. Two years before writing her intercessory letter to King Joan, she had written a letter to him with a markedly different tenor. Joan had had troubles with his Catalonian subjects for years, even fighting a civil war with them between 1462 and 1472. It was only toward the end of their rebellion that Joan was able to besiege their stronghold of the city of Barcelona, in late 1471 and 1472. Isabel's letter was written in November of 1472, about a month after the fall of Barcelona. Isabel wrote:

Very Excellent Señor,

I received a letter that Your Lordship sent me and through it I came to know the good news of the taking and the reduction of the city of Barcelona to the

---

[59] BNE MSS/20212/30/4.
[60] For the role of queens as intercessors, see John Carmi Parsons, "The Queen's Intercession in Thirteenth-Century England," in *Power of the Weak: Studies on Medieval Women. A selection of papers presented at the annual conference of the Centre for Medieval Studies, University of Toronto, Feb. 1990*, ed. Jennifer Carpenter and Sally-Beth MacLean (Chicago: University of Illinois Press, 1995), 151–152.

service and obedience of Your Excellency, which I take as a singular grace for Your Lordship. For as a thing of this world, I could not have greater pleasure nor joy, as much for the great honor and service which [the taking of Barcelona] has entailed for Your Grace as for the vengeance which you can have for this on all those who do not want nor desire the good prosperity and improvement of Your Excellency ...[61]

Isabel maintains a submissive and humble tone, but the content and language of her letter are fundamentally chivalric. She glories in the honor which will accrue to Joan for his military victory, just as a knight might celebrate augmented honor from martial success. And, importantly, she revels in the vengeance which Joan can take against his enemies – those who dishonored him through their disloyalty – just as a knight might relish the taking of vengeance against a rival who besmirched his name. The Infanta writes as a woman who understands and embraces the violent components of chivalry.

Had the Castilian princess comprehended something that eluded her father and, especially, her brother? As we saw in Chapter 1, Isabel's brother, Enrique IV, had been ritualistically deposed in effigy by his political enemies, who questioned his Christian virtues, his strength, and, significantly, his masculinity, with the charge of homosexuality being levelled against him by political enemies in writing and in speech.[62] And, as we saw in Chapter 3, Enrique and his father, Juan II, were also slow and cautious in pressing the holy war and seeking vengeance on the Muslims of Granada. Even before she ascended the throne in 1474, Isabel was hinting at a different path for herself; she was embracing violence, vengeance, and honor, and committing herself as a good Christian woman in the image of the Blessed Virgin Mary. We have to wonder if Isabel saw an opportunity to move past the disorder and challenges of her brother's reign by becoming his opposite.[63] Where he

---

[61] BNE MSS/20212/30/1. "Señor muy excelente, Recebi una letra que vuestra señoria me envio y por ella me figo saber la buena nueva del tomando y reduccion dela cibdat de barcelona al servicio & obediencia de vuestra excelencia lo qual es singular merced tengo a vuestra señoria por que como cosa deste mundo plaser mayor ni alegria non pudiera aver asy por el grand honor y servicio que dello a vuestra merced se ha seguido comom por la venganca que puede por esta tan la aver de todos aquellos que non quieren ni desean el prospero bien y agracentamiento de vuestra excelencia ..."

[62] For a discussion of accusations of homosexuality in the mid-15th century see Gregory S. Hutcheson, "Desperately Seeking Sodom: Queerness in the Chronicles of Alvaro de Luna," in *Queer Iberia: Sexualities, Cultures, and Crossings from the Middle Ages to the Renaissance*, ed. Josiah Blackmore and Gregory S. Hutcheson (Durham, NC: Duke University Press, 1999), 222–249.

[63] Louise Mirrer has argued that Christian hostility towards Jews and Muslims in the late Middle Ages was deeply connected to ideas about gender and power. Mirrer claims that powerful Christian males not only dominated Christian women, but applied the undesirable traits of women (submission, weakness, maternity rather than paternity) to religious "others." Mirrer has also emphasized that relations between Christian men and Muslims, Jews, and Christian women were in a constant state of struggle, with minori-

was accused of a secret commitment to Islam, she highlighted her Christian devotion; where he was accused of being too feminine, she was willing to embrace masculine chivalric violence. Isabel was capable of playing with the gender roles of late medieval Castile, emphasizing her humble, pious, Christian femininity even as she embraced the chivalric male penchant for violence, honor, and vengeance.

Knights, nobles, and poets who surrounded the queen in the decades after her accession vacillated between imagining her as the perfect model of a humble and pious queen and glorying in her martial and chivalric leadership. The former was perhaps more familiar and more comfortable to many male writers. The Andalucian knight and poet Juan Barba wrote a laudatory poetic history of the reign of Isabel and Fernando sometime between 1485 and 1487, during their war against Granada. The work, dedicated to Isabel, was titled *Consolatoria de Castilla*, or the Consolation of Castile, implying that the queen had rescued Castile from the path of destruction that it had been on for decades. The fact that most of the work deals with the final holy war against the Kingdom of Granada hints that perhaps Isabel was the correction to the great historical error of the *destruición*. Indeed, Barba does think of the queen as a divinely blessed figure who solved Castile's problems, noting at length that she was born in the same year that the problematic *privado* Álvaro de Luna was condemned to death. All of the chaos, disorder, crime, and wickedness that flourished in Luna's day would be brought to an end by the rise of Isabel to the throne.[64] Barba imagined Isabel as a gift from Heaven, calling her the "solace of all evils" and noting that God "had protected this consolation, / for Castile, to whom she was given, / from the High Divine for her respect / because He knew the diligent life / that this lady had to live … His hand conserved her well."[65] Isabel was a unique and beloved figure in Barba's poem.

He conceived of the queen's role, though, in terms that exude a demure femininity. Two of her key roles as savior of Spain, for example, were those of wife and mother. Barba dwells on Isabel's marriage to Fernando, writing, "of the superior gifts / which God placed in this princess / was the marriage, for which she chose / a king of this world better than the best … High and powerful God joined them together … because they had to be two crowns

---

ties, especially women, pushing the boundaries set for them by Christian men. Louise Mirrer, *Women, Jews, and Muslims in the Texts of Reconquest Castile* (Ann Arbor, MI: University of Michigan Press, 1996).

[64] Pedro M. Cátedra, *La historiografía en verso en la época de los Reyes Católicos: Juan Barba y su "Consolatoria de Castilla"* (Salamanca: Ediciones Universidad de Salamanca, 1989) , 171–173.

[65] Ibid., 189–190. "por consolatoria estovo guardada, / para Castilla a quien fue dotada / del Alto divino por su respecto, / porque sabía la vida esmerada / qu'esta señora aví de hazer … su mano la tiene asý conservada."

/ for the comfort of our repose."⁶⁶ Marriage politics brought together two powerful kingdoms, which would allow both for the establishment of better justice and for the prosecution of the holy war against Islam. Indeed, Barba hints at the history of the *destruición* by noting that God had brought the two together partly because they both brought with them the bloodline of the Visigoths.⁶⁷ Isabel's marriage served not only to unite the kingdoms of Castile and Aragon, thereby hinting at the unification of the Spanish kingdoms, but also brought Fernando into Castilian political and military affairs; for Juan Barba, this was an unparalleled accomplishment. Isabel's strength and power as a woman was in finding a powerful man who would help to improve her kingdom. Barba embodies an approach that simultaneously valorizes women while confirming the superiority of masculinity.⁶⁸ Once Isabel had fulfilled her womanly duty to marry, her husband could carry out the historical Christian imperative to restore Christian control of Iberia.

After marriage, the honorable calling for Isabel was to bear children and provide an heir to the throne. The poem's narrative, focused to a great deal on the martial glories of Fernando, is punctuated from time to time with news of the birth of a prince or princess. The birth of the couple's first child, Juan, excellently represents the idea of a woman as the producer of strong men. Barba describes the relevant section as that which "denotes in what time was the glorious birth," emphasizing the honor that was produced by the birth of a son to the monarchs.⁶⁹ He goes on to describe the event by saying that "our queen gave birth to the excellent son, / don Juan, the first of our joy,"⁷⁰ and proclaiming the joy and significance of Juan's birth:

> Proclaim fame, truth, and reason
> through all Spain and foreign kingdoms;
> the infidels should fear the damages
> and loyal men should rejoice for such a blessing;
> with the powerful high lords
> King don Fernando and Queen Isabel,
> Castile and they rejoice with [Juan]
> with all victory of greater kingdoms.
> The just desire long awaited
> of their highnesses and of our lives,
> though other graces she had had,

---

⁶⁶ Ibid., 190–191. "Y sobre los dones superiores / qu'en esta prinçesa Dios influyó / fue'l casamiento, que l'escojó / un rey deste mundo mejor de mejores … Juntólos el alto Dios poderoso, / quier que pesase [a] algunas presonas, / porque tenían de ser dos coronas / para consuelo de nuestro reposo."

⁶⁷ Ibid., 191.

⁶⁸ María Eugenia Lacarra, "Notes on Feminist Analysis of Medieval Spanish Literature and History," *La corónica*, vol. 17, no. 1 (Fall 1988): 14–22.

⁶⁹ Catédra, *Consolatoria*, 216. "Denota en qué tiempo fue el glorioso naçimiento."

⁷⁰ Ibid. "parió nuestra reyna el hijo eçelente, / don Juan el prymero de nuestra alegría."

that of a son had been delayed; / but it pleased eternal God, adored, / to give to the monarchs a male heir ..."[71]

Aside from the joy felt by the parents, the kingdom, and Christendom, Barba declares that the baby Juan will surely be a powerful warrior, for Isabel brought him into the world under the planet Mars.[72] Joyous verses were strung together for the queen's daughters as well, but the birth of Juan was truly special. The queen had performed her life's duty: the production of a strong male heir for her husband and for her kingdom.

With Isabel an honorable woman, having borne a son, Barba turns his attention for most of the rest of the text to the martial glories of King Fernando during the holy war against Granada. By and large, Isabel's role is passive and feminine. Her very presence in Sevilla is a moment of adoration of the queen's womanly virtues. Barba notes that "a most high reception / was made to her highness by all the people: / Since they looked to her fulgent grace, / all her people were very content."[73] We can almost imagine a celebrity walking among the people and waving as they cheer for her, her passive presence alone bringing smiles to faces. The only active role for Isabel was as a supplicant before God. While her strong husband fought actively against the Muslim enemy, Isabel raised her hands to God and prayed to Him for victory.[74] Juan Barba glorified Isabel for her passive, submissive, spiritual and reproductive role as a female ruler. Nor was Barba alone in this assessment of the queen and of this important moment in Castilian history. The royal chronicler Andrés Bernáldez almost has difficulty imagining Isabel as a comprehensive ruler of a major European kingdom. She appears much less frequently in his chronicle than King Fernando does, most often praying or parading about with her daughter. At best, she appears a pious and demure figure.[75]

Others perceived the queen differently. Circulating among the intelligentsia of Castile in the last several decades of the 15th century were works

---

[71] Ibid., 217. "Divulgue la fama verdad y razón / por toda España y reinos estraños / y los infieles teman sus daños / y gozen leales de tal benediçión; / con los poderosos altos señores / rey don Hernando y reyna Ysabel, / goze Castilla y ellos con él / con toda vitoria de reinos mayores. / El justo deseo muy esperado / de sus altezas y de nuestras vidas, / aunque las otras graçias avidas, / ésta de hijo s'avý detardado; / mas plugo al eterno Dios adorado / de dar a sus reyes varón heredero ..."

[72] Ibid., 216–217.

[73] Ibid., 215. "muy alto el reçebimiento / se faze a su alteza por toda la genta: / desque miraron su graçia fulgente, / todo su pueblo fue mucho contento."

[74] Ibid., 259–260.

[75] See, for example, Andrés Bernáldez, "Historia de los Reyes Católicos Don Fernando y Doña Isabel," *Biblioteca de Autores Españoles*, vol. 70, 605–608, when the queen barely appears at all during the crucial moments when the holy war was seriously renewed. All of the initiative is attributed to King Fernando.

which lauded the queen's active commitment to the holy war or encouraged her to lead Castile against her enemies. Such pieces of literature attributed masculine qualities to her even as they embraced her as a female ruler, blurring the lines between male and female chivalric leadership. *La Poncella de Francia*, written sometime between the time Isabel secured her throne in 1474 and the last year of the campaign against Granada in 1491, recounts the history of Joan of Arc in her divinely inspired mission to save France from the English during the Hundred Years' War. Or, more accurately, it rewrites the history of Joan as a sort of chivalric epic. Like Pedro de Corral's *Rodrigo*, *La Poncella* is a work of imaginative history designed to convince its audience of the historical significance of a given individual and advocate for the prosecution of chivalric warfare; Queen Isabel was that audience. In the *prohemio* of the document, the author addresses himself directly to the queen, claiming that he has searched long and hard to find a great lady who can compare to her.[76] The search yielded Joan of Arc, whom the author later implores Isabel to emulate, saying, "your greatness ... should take example from such a little woman, and how she was estimated and valued through exerting herself."[77] Joan's actions, both historical and imagined, would provide both a model for and a celebration of Isabel's female leadership.

In *La Poncella*, Joan's martial leadership is key in building honor for the king and knights of France, in what becomes a self-feeding cycle of success for the French. When Joan hears of the troubles facing France, she resolves to go and fight against the enemy. She runs into battle, initially armed only with a fruit basket, and fights valiantly against the English, beating them back and displaying her chivalric valor. She defeats the enemy and then appears before the king, who feels a new sense of pleasure because he has won such honor through Joan's violent activity. Joan herself is not described as winning honor, but the king has honor accrue to him as a result of her violence.[78] Female prowess in this case accrues masculine honor, but it is transferred to a man who can serve as an appropriate receptacle for it. Female martial leadership cannot function on its own; it requires a male presence. But it is a powerful spur to violence for the knights of France. After news spreads through France of Joan's martial prowess, the knights of France are electrified with the desire to serve their king and to win honor fighting against the English. "[E]very day relatives, and friends, and vassals came to the king's aid, and he found himself with 40,000 combatants in the field."[79] With this powerful army and Joan's battlefield leadership, the

---

[76] *La Poncella de Francia: La historia castellana de Juana de Arco*, ed. Victoria Campo and Victor Infantes, 2nd edition (Madrid: Iberoamericana, 2006), 90.

[77] Ibid., 214. "vuestra grandeza ... tome enxemplo de una tan pequeña muger, y cómo se estimó y valió esforçándose."

[78] Ibid., 107.

[79] Ibid., 120. "cada día de parientes y amigos y vassallos socorrido, fallóse en el campo

English were defeated several times in the field and more French knights joined the army, seeking honor and glory. As more knights joined up, "many knights of France, some who were clearly with the enemy, came asking pardon to serve their king, and others who were biding their time, who for fear of the English gave aid to neither side, as they saw [Joan] prosper, they called their houses together; and so with the fame of the Poncella, an infinite multitude was joined with the party of the king."[80] Joan's effect on the chivalry of France is not only to win honor for them, but to encourage them to fight in a great war in which they can serve the king and win honor themselves. Multiple components of chivalric identity come together as the famous young woman stands up to lead an army in this bit of imaginative literature.

Such was also the case for Queen Isabel. By the winter of 1481/1482, Isabel and her husband had resolved to undertake a total war against the Kingdom of Granada. The chronicler Fernando del Pulgar claims that both Isabel and her husband "always had in the soul the great thought to conquer the Kingdom of Granada, and the throwing out of all of the Spains the lordship of the Moors and the name of Muhammad."[81] So, when the Granadans captured the Castilian village of Zahara in 1481, the monarchs welcomed the arrival of the glorious holy war with open arms. King Fernando travelled almost immediately to the southern frontier and aided the Andalucian knights who had captured the Granadan city of Alhama, while Isabel remained behind in the city of Medina del Campo. But this was not because she had no appetite for war. Instead, she stayed back only temporarily in order to set the affairs of the kingdom in order. First, she wrote to various knights of the kingdom, explaining that the king was in Granada, pursuing the holy war, and

> she sent to order them that they should depart then, because they would be able to enter with him into the Kingdom of Granada ... She similarly sent her summonses to all the knights and squires who held lands and benefits

---

con .xl. mil combatientes."

[80] Ibid., 126. "muchos cavalleros de Francia, unos que eran a lo claro contrarios venían demandando perdón a servir a su Rey, y otros que estavan quedos, que por miedo de los ingleses no ayudavan a ninguna parte, como le vieron prosperar llamaron sus casas; y con la fama de la Poncella infinitos se juntan en el partido del Rey." The word used here is *fama*, which carries a deeper meaning than simply "fame." The word connotes reputation and honor as well as being well-known. See Thomas Kuehn, "Fama as legal status in Renaissance Florence," in *Fama: The Politics of Talk and Reputation in Medieval Europe*, ed. Thelma Fenster and Daniel Lord Smail (Ithaca, NY: Cornell University Press, 2003): 27–46.

[81] Fernando del Pulgar, "Crónica de los señores Reyes Católicos Don Fernando y Doña Isabel de Castilla y de Aragon," in *Biblioteca de Autores Españoles*, vol. 70, 365. "siempre tovieron en el ánimo pensamiento grande de conquistar el Reyno de Granada, é lanzar de todas las Españas el señorío de los moros y el nombre de Mahoma."

from her, ordering them that they should be ready with their arms and horses for when she should send to call them to the war which she intended to make against the King and Kingdom of Granada.[82]

As the war against Granada continued, Pulgar regularly explains how Fernando performed the traditional martial role of a king while Isabel summoned more and more knights to come to the frontier to fight in the holy war.[83] As far as we can tell, Isabel both ordered and encouraged the knights of her realm to engage in the war against Granada and they responded, swelling the ranks of the Christian army, just as Joan's leadership swelled the ranks of the French army. Isabel provided a space for the knights of her kingdom to win honor, just as Joan did. As a queen regnant, she could go further, ordering her vassals to the front.

And, just like Joan, Isabel sought out a place near the front itself. Given that Fernando would be at the head of the army in battle, Isabel could have stayed behind in Medina del Campo, hundreds of miles north of the action. Instead, after summoning knights to head to the south, Isabel, "because she similarly intended to go in person to Andalucía, in order to oversee the things which would be necessary," summoned the Constable of Castile, Pedro Fernández de Velasco, and ordered him to serve as regent during her absence. Given the chivalric focus on prowess in battle and, specifically, in the holy war that we have observed, we might wonder why the queen should go to the frontier while Velasco, the proud warrior, should stay behind, missing an opportunity to win honor. Indeed, Velasco wondered this as well, asking the queen, "Is it a reasonable thing that, the King going to war, I should stay in peaceful lands, since I, as your Constable, have the principal charge of your hosts?"[84] Isabel, recognizing his desire to serve his monarchs loyally and to win honor in the holy war, relented, giving the Constable license to travel with her to Andalucía. The queen's eagerness for the holy war manifested through her summoning of warriors, her own presence at the front, and a recognition of the chivalric desire to win honor among her loyal vassals. She recognized and confirmed the martial desires of the chivalric elite.

As martial figures, both Joan and Isabel were, first and foremost, siege strategists. In *La Poncella*, Joan leads her armies against city after city,

---

[82] Ibid., 369–370. "y embióles mandar que luego partiesen, porque pudiesen entrar con él en el Reyno de Granada. Embió ansimesmo sus cartas de apercebimiento á todos los caballeros y escuderos que tenian tierra é acostamientos della, mandándoles que estoviesen prestos con sus armas é caballos para quando los embiase á llamar para la guerra que entendia facer contra el Rey é Reyno de Granada."

[83] Ibid., 371–372.

[84] Ibid., 370. "¿es cosa razonable que yendo el Rey á la guerra, quede yo en la tierra pacífica, teniendo como vuestro Condestable el cargo principal de vuestras huestes?"

investing Tours, Poitiers, and Paris, among others.[85] Naturally, she is almost always successful in executing the siege and the author mentions multiple times that her success comes partly from knowing when to use force to win the day and when to use stratagem. This typical late medieval or Renaissance military advice is unremarkable on its own. That it was given to a reigning queen is somewhat more interesting; it would seem that the author thought of Isabel as a capable military leader who warranted the same advice as her male counterparts. Yet this advice was never given to her in order to explicitly make her more male, nor was it given with a caveat that her femininity was diminished through battlefield leadership and grand strategy.

As a diligent taker of cities, the Joan of *La Poncella* would have served as an excellent reflection of Isabel. A decade after securing the throne against Juana, Isabel reopened the holy war against Granada. Together with her husband, Fernando, Isabel undertook a strategy of besieging the cities of Granada one by one, slowly picking off the strong fortifications of her Muslim enemy. Indeed, the royal chroniclers give a clear sense that while Fernando led the Castilian hosts in sieges, it was Isabel who often insisted on sieges, picked target cities and fortifications, and helped to arrange the logistics for sieges. As the war against Granada proceeded in the spring of 1484, Isabel coordinated the martial effort, sending knights, animals, and artillery to the front from her base in Córdoba. Indeed, she even agreed to move from Córdoba to the frontier cities of Antequera and Alcalá la Real to better oversee preparations for the war, because "the presence of the Queen … caused her ministers and servants to throw themselves into their work with diligence."[86]

Far from playing a passive role, as she did in *Consolatoria*, Isabel appears in the chronicles (together with Joan in *La Poncella*) as the driving force behind a righteous and vengeful war, and as a monarch who understood better than almost all of her predecessors the significance of the holy war; only Fernando de Antequera grasped this chivalric concept with anywhere near the depth of Isabel. The beginning of the war against Granada looked similar to earlier wars against Iberian Islam. After King Fernando had brought aid to the Andalucian knights who had won the city of Alhama, he took the knights who were with him and began making *la tala* (the cutting) in the Vega of Granada. Meanwhile, the queen, from Córdoba, ordered knights to come from throughout her kingdoms – not just Andalucía, but Extremadura, Toledo, and even Valladolid in northern Castile – to join her and to go into Granada to a camp outside the Granadan city of Loja to besiege it. She also ordered artillery to the camp, a clear indication that she intended to lay siege to the city. Within a few months, Fernando returned

---

[85] For example, *La Poncella*, 121.
[86] Pulgar, "Don Fernando y Doña Isabel," 401.

from *la tala* to Córdoba, presumably to coordinate his strategy with Isabel's, and then moved to the camp at Loja and invested the city. Unfortunately for the Christians, the Muslims sent a large force to relieve Loja and, after a vicious fight, Fernando was forced to withdraw from the city and return to Córdoba. When the queen heard the news, she was grieved over the loss, but she redoubled her efforts. Indeed, Pulgar says that "none could understand the great feeling which she had in her words or her deeds; and she proposed to remedy the situation, outfitting the necessary things so that the king should return and enter powerfully into the land of the Moors."[87] Isabel seems to have been the soul behind the vigorous persecution of the holy war, constantly encouraging her husband to take a role of martial leadership. Fernando did enter again into Granada and made *la tala* before leaving his captains in charge and departing to take care of affairs elsewhere in Spain. Only when the knights of Andalucía were defeated again by the Granadans did Fernando return to make *la tala* once more and, finally, to take the village of Tajara. Having done so, he wrote to Isabel, informing her that the king of Granada had asked for a truce and that he was inclined to grant it. The queen wrote back that it seemed to her that the truce was a poor choice; it had never worked in the favor of Castile and she would prefer to bring war throughout the Kingdom of Granada. Fernando acceded to her request and the truce was denied.[88]

A pattern was developing. Fernando would lead the Christian armies into Granada, burn and chop down crops, and return home, sometimes seeking an end to the war. It would seem that the prosecution of the holy war was not a high priority for the king of Aragon. In this he was similar to many of his Trastámara relatives, who had been content to attack Granada briefly and then let the war come to an unremarkable close. Isabel, in contrast, remained committed to the war. Channeling the chivalric passions of the knights and writers of 15th-century Castile that we examined in Chapter 3, she was constant in her desire for a signal victory over the religious enemy.[89] In April of 1484, Fernando and Isabel had departed from the frontier and traveled to Aragon as their captains cut and burned through the countryside of Granada. In the city of Tarazona, after a session of the Aragonese *cortes*, the monarchs had to assess their priorities. Fernando was eager to go to war with France in order to recover some of his northern provinces. Isabel, on the other hand, knowing that the late spring and summer were excellent

---

[87] Ibid., 373. "ninguno pudo conocer en sus palabras ni autos el gran sentimiento que tenia; é propuso de lo repara, aderesando las cosas necesarias para que el Rey tornase é entrar luego poderosamente en tierra de moros …"
[88] Ibid., 375–389.
[89] For an analysis of the union of the holy war, the Catholic Monarchs, and the Blessed Virgin Mary, see Amy Remensnyder, *La Conquistadora: The Virgin Mary at War and Peace in the Old and New Worlds* (Oxford: Oxford University Press, 2014), 81–91.

times to attack Granada, insisted that the holy war should be their first priority. The queen "had deep in her soul that war against the Moors."[90] The monarchs decided to part ways, with Fernando going north into his kingdom while Isabel returned to the south to carry on the holy war in person. She made it back to Córdoba before her husband decided that perhaps his wife's priorities were greater; within a few months, Fernando arrived at the southern front and joined the army, leading it into the Vega of Granada. Following Isabel to the frontier, Fernando and the army began cutting down the orchards and food supplies of the Granadans, performing *la tala*, the old preference of the Trastámara monarchs. Seeing that his destruction was going well, Fernando ordered his captains to continue and announced that he would head back to the north. But it was not to be.

> The Queen … hearing how the King deliberated so soon to leave the war and depart with all his host from the land of the Moors, sent to say to the King, that if it should please him he should make *la tala* in the *vega*, or lay siege to some other ville, for there was still time in the summer in which he would be able to do so. The King knew the will of the Queen, yet the men had already begun to return; but the great lords, as well as the captains, and all the other knights and men of the host, seeing how the counsel of the Queen was reasonable, returned to enter into the *vega* of Granada with the King.[91]

The queen's counsel, informed by the passionate ideal of Castilian chivalry, won out. Her will and her desire to achieve victory over the old enemy appealed to the knights of the host; the old strategy of the Trastámaras was being overridden in favor of a more vigorous and chivalric impulse. From this point forward, it would seem, Fernando began more and more to embrace Isabel's position. Was it possible that Fernando was concerned about shame, given his wife's more chivalric push for holy war? What we can say is that in the ensuing campaign he captured the city of Álora and then he returned to Córdoba. In consultation with her, they decided to target the city of Setenil rather than simply perform *la tala*. The chronicles begin recording one city after another being targeted and taken by the king, typically with the advice or direction of the queen. It may be that Fernando was the active military leader, but it was Isabel who insisted on the war and who insisted on a different kind of warfare.

---

[90] Pulgar, "Don Fernando y Doña Isabel," 400. "la Reyna, que tenia mucho en el ánimo aquella guerra de los moros."

[91] Ibid., 403. "La Reyna … oido como el Rey deliberaba tan presto dexar la guerra é salir con toda su gueste de tierra de moros, embió decir al Rey, que si le ploguiese debia facer la tala en la vega, ó poner sitio sobre alguna otra villa, pues habia aun asaz tiempo del verano en que se podia facer. El Rey sabida la voluntad de la Reyna, como quier que ya la gente comenzada á se volver; pero ansí los grandes señores, como los capitanes, é todos los otros caballeros é gentes de la gueste, visto como el consejo de la Reyna era razonable; tornaron á entrar en la vega de Granada con el Rey."

As a woman hungry for violence and tuned in to chivalric ideas, Isabel was lauded by her chivalric supporters. In a remarkable incident, Pulgar remarks on the queen's behavior and infuses her words with chivalric fervor. In 1486, the city of Loja was finally taken by the Christians. The queen came to the city in victory and visited the knights and men-at-arms who had been wounded in the battle. She told them "that they should be joyous, for as knights they had offered themselves to danger in order to extol the faith and enlarge the land of the kingdom, and that if she was thankful and would remunerate them in this life, God – whose cause it was – would not forget to remunerate them in the next."[92] She also displayed her largesse by sending them to the treasurer for pay for what they had done. The author of *La Poncella* praised her by comparison with Joan, similarly giving her chivalric speech, and echoing the attitude of Isabel. When Joan first comes to the king of France, she tells him, "I dreamt that I, such a small woman, would remedy the lost Kingdom of France, and your royal person, with great vengeance upon your enemies … With this I felt my strength increase to an extreme degree and I lost the fear which is natural for women to have."[93] The idea of a woman remedying a kingdom and taking vengeance on one's enemies fit so well with the idea of Castilian vengeance against Islam and the restoration of the Visigothic Kingdom that it could not possibly have been misunderstood by Isabel, the intended audience. Joan sloughing off her womanly fear and becoming stronger hints at a different conception of femininity: a chivalric conception of female martial leadership that fit Queen Isabel perfectly. Describing Joan's battle against the English at Poitiers, the author draws an even closer parallel to Isabel's war, lauding the French warriors who "were mixed with such furious engagement and with such great cruelty as if they were conquering the enemies of the faith."[94] Chivalric historians loved Isabel's commitment to the holy war and encouraged her to continue her divine mission.

Historians often do a better job when they make up pieces of their history. *La Poncella*, a work dedicated to the queen by one of her courtiers, is remarkable precisely because of the way in which it blends accurate history with imagination. In the imaginative version of Joan of Arc, she

---

[92] Ibid., 439. "que debian ser alegres, porwue como caballeros se ofrescieron á los peligros por ensalzar la fé y ansanchar la tierra, é que si ella gelo agradecia para gelo remunerar en esta vida, Dios cuya era la causa, no se olvidaria de gelo remunerar en la otra."

[93] *La Poncella*, 108. "soñé como por mí, una tan pequeña muger, se remediava el reino perdido de Francia, e vuestra real persona, con gran vengança de vuestros enemigos … Con esto la fuerça sentí crecer en extremo grado y perder el natural temor de las mugeres …"

[94] Ibid., 124. "puestas las batallas en order de una parte y otra, se mezclan con tan furioso acometimiento y con tan gran crueldad como si con enemigos de la fe conquistaran."

leads her armies to liberate the city of Paris from the English and the king holds a council on the question of whether or not they ought to pursue the enemy back into Flanders and perhaps beyond. All of the knights and nobles of France advise the king to stop the war, since he has won France for himself. But Joan speaks up in fine chivalric fashion, beginning a long speech by claiming that "lust to win honor is the enemy of peace."[95] Far from being a shrinking pacifist, Joan says this as a call to continue the war, emphasizing that peace is a poor choice when honor is at stake. The rest of Joan's speech insists that the king ought to follow the English all the way to England in order to win honor and glory, drawing deeply on classical and medieval historical examples upon which Queen Isabel could model herself. The speech ends with a direct appeal to the king which could just as easily be read as a direct appeal to Isabel:

> If Scipio was content with the defeat of Spain, he would not have undertaken the war with Carthage, nor would he have been willing to eject Hannibal from the lordships of Italy, more so in his same land defeat and conquer him. If the Duke Godfrey de Bouillon was content with the lordships of Lower Germany, he would not have won the victories in Outremer. If Alexander and Julius Caesar with the vanquishing of their enemies were content, they would not have had the glory of the lordship of the world ... Hannibal, if after the great victory and battle of Cannae had gone to Rome, he would have vanquished all those who afterward vanquished him ... Thus it is better to follow and destroy the enemy in his land, than to wait for him to waste and burn ours ... Conquering [your enemies] is greater glory and vengeance than reigning. And these people, as they have learned to suffer, it is good that they should learn to injure; in alien lands fame is won, while in their own nothing can amount to much. Follow, then, Your Highness, the high emprises, for to the great, great things and not low things belong.[96]

---

[95] Ibid., 184. "codicia de ganar honra era enemiga de paz."
[96] Ibid., 184–188. "Si Cipión se contentara con los vencimientos de España, no emprendiera la guerra de Cartago, ni fuera contento de lançar a Aníbal de los señoríos de Italia, mas en su misma tierra lo desbarató y venció. Si el Duque Gudufre de Bullón se contentara con los señoríos de Baxa Alemaña, no ganara las vitorias de ultramar. Si Alexandre y Julio César con el vencimiento de sus enemigos se conterntaran, no tuvieran oy la gloria de la señoría del mundo ... Aníbal, si después de la gran vitoria y batalla de Canas fuera a Roma venciera del todo a quien después le venció ... Pues mejor es seguir y destruir al enemigo en su tierra, que esperarle gastando y destruyendo la nuestra ... [V]encerlos es mayor gloria y vengança que reinar. Y estos pueblos como han aprendido a sofrir, bien es que aprendan a ofender; en las tierras ajenas se gana la fama, que en las suyas ninguno pudo mucho crecer. Siga, pues, Vuestra Alteza las empresas altas, que a los grandes cosas grandes y no baxas pertenecen." The classical references and the nature of the work as a sort of mirror of princes places this work in the early stages of the Spanish Renaissance. Yet, the allusions to Alexander, Caesar, and Godfrey de Bullion echo the old chivalric familiarity with the Nine Worthies. See Richard W. Kaeuper, *Holy Warriors* (Philadelphia: University of Pennsylvania Press, 2009), 156.

A powerful and chivalric speech calling for greater war was put into the mouth of Joan of Arc at a fictional moment, when France began to invade England after Joan's conquest of Paris. The fundamental ahistoricism of the passage must be read as a direct appeal to Queen Isabel in her own historical context, which fits the situation much better. Isabel, not Joan, was the woman who stood poised to lead an army against an old enemy that had invaded and taken away her kingdom. If she had the choice to be satisfied with defending the land she currently held or go forth and win honor and fame in an alien land (Granada), the latter was by far the more honorable choice. Isabel made that choice, embracing the chivalric female leadership of the holy war against Granada.

Queen Isabel's fondness for martial virtue was put on fine display between 1487 and 1489 in the spiritual heart of the Kingdom of Castile. As the Catholic Monarchs sought to broadcast the historical significance of the prosecution of the holy war, they worked to associate holy places and relics with that divine mission, and part of this effort included renovations to Toledo cathedral, the metropolitan seat of Castile. Improvements to the cathedral were overseen by Cardinal Pedro González de Mendoza, the archbishop of Toledo. Cardinal Mendoza, a close advisor to Queen Isabel, was an excellent choice for combining chivalric martial virtue and divine sanction. He hailed from the powerful and glorious Mendoza *linaje*, which had provided men to fight in most of the major battles of the Trastámara period. Indeed, more than a decade after he was appointed bishop of Calahorra by Juan II, Mendoza led troops himself at the second Battle of Olmedo in 1467.[97] Created cardinal in 1473 and raised to the see of Toledo in 1482, Cardinal Mendoza spent much of the reign of Isabel leading troops in the holy war, offering the physical representation of the institutional Church on the battlefield. In the coat of arms of this warrior-priest the words of the Mendoza *linaje* dominated: Ave Maria, Gratia Plena. If the Virgin herself did not appear over Mendoza's army, her presence was still surely felt. As the cardinal violated the Church's strictures on clerical celibacy, too, chivalric ideology was present; the eldest of Mendoza's several children was named Rodrigo Díaz de Vivar y Mendoza, bearing the name of that greatest of Iberian knights, El Cid. The person of Cardinal Mendoza was a living expression of the joining of chivalry, violence, and religious sanction.

Mendoza's influence can still be seen today in Toledo cathedral. Under his direction, the master carpenter Rodrigo Alemán carved the choir stalls of the cathedral.[98] The stalls each depict a scene from the Iberian holy war against Islam, culminating in the victory of the Catholic Monarchs at

---

[97] For the life of Mendoza, see Helen Nader, *The Mendoza Family in the Spanish Renaissance, 1350–1550* (New Brunswick, NJ: Rutgers University Press, 1979).

[98] Héctor L. Arena, "Die Chorgestühle des Meisters Rodrigo Alemán" (PhD diss., Ruprecht-Karl-Universität zu Heidelberg, 1965).

Granada in 1492. Violence and the divine Christian mission come together, trumpeting the glory of martial Christian virtue in a way that surely would have satisfied both the queen and the king. Yet we may detect a bit of Isabel's martial leadership here.[99] In most of the stalls, the battles are typical medieval set pieces, with assembled knights outside a city or fortification, but several also clearly depict Isabel as a presence during the campaign. In one stall, Castilian troops are amassed outside the fortified city of Moclín. The most famous encounter at Moclín was surely that of 1280, sometimes known as the Disaster of Moclín because a successful Muslim ambush left thousands of Christian knights dead. The choir stall, naturally, celebrates a much more favorable event, from the Christian perspective, which took place in 1486. Rodrigo Alemán carved the walls of Moclín surrounded by Castilian knights and soldiers. An artilleryman operates his weapon and flames burst from the crumbling walls of Moclín as the Muslim inhabitants issue forth to surrender the city. In the foreground we see not only King Fernando mounted on his steed, but two royal women: Queen Isabel and the Infanta Isabel. Both women were in fact present for the siege of Moclín; the chronicler Andrés Bernáldez discusses their presence at great length, noting their pious commitment to the holy war, the reverence in which they were held by the knights and soldiers in the army, the fine clothes in which they were dressed, and even the animals upon which they rode; Queen Isabel and her daughter were both mounted on chestnut mules.[100]

By the time the woodcut was produced, the queen had upgraded her steed; she appears mounted not on a mule but on a horse. As we saw in Chapter 2, horses were seen as a particularly knightly animal, bearing the same martial and valiant qualities as their chivalric riders. In the woodcut of the siege of Moclín, a royal woman also rides that noblest of creatures in the chivalric worldview. As Isabel's association with a chivalric animal hints at her feminine embrace of a highly masculine chivalric tradition, the choice of Moclín as a scene in which she is depicted as part of the *reconquista* is telling. The conquest of Moclín was a moment where Isabel was transfigured beyond doubt into a different kind of woman. Even Juan Barba, who in his *Consolatoria* imagined Isabel as a very passive and demure figure, recognized the magnitude of the moment, stringing verses of praise together like pearls in fawning adoration of his queen's martial presence at Moclín:

O clear soul, brilliant memory
of the queen who God wanted to give
in faith, the most singular strength
that reigns in the world shown in its history!

---

[99] The choir stalls are one facet of Isabel's chivalric self-fashioning. For a useful exploration of noble women in northern Europe using seals for a similar purpose, see Wilkinson, "Gendered Chivalry," 230–232.
[100] Bernáldez, "Don Fernando y Doña Isabel," 623.

> This coming denotes the glory
> which she receives with the holy war
> and with which she wanted to trample the land
> of the enemies and see victory ...
> She brought [to Moclín] her prayers
> she brought money for the men
> she brought joyous comfort, clearly,
> which caused the weak to regain their lives;
> she brought that high magnificence
> with obedience to wondrous God
> that the queen should enter from our Castile
> into the land of the Moors for excellence.[101]

The Disaster of Moclín of 1280, a calamity overseen by Isabel's male ancestors was, in 1486, revenged by their female descendant. As we have seen, the whole process of Castilian holy war and *reconquista* was envisioned as an effort to right a historical wrong. The choir stall itself suggests that Isabel was aware of the import of the moment. Juan Barba offers a bit of detail confirming her commitment to correcting a historical error, noting that after the victory

> in that ville of Moclín, which was won ...
> another royal deed so singular
> of great merit, she ordered to be done,
> to take up [and rebury] all the bones
> of the many Christians who had died long ago.[102]

Indeed, a second stall which prominently features the queen depicts the surrender of the city of Almería in December of 1489. The Muslim king, Muhammad XII (r. 1482–1483, 1487–1492), kneels before King Fernando to kiss the Catholic Monarch's foot, and just behind the king is Isabel, with a broad smile on her face. Surely Isabel would have been delighted, at the close of 1489, as the noose continued to tighten around the rapidly shrinking Kingdom of Granada. Just two years later, Granada itself would fall and the *reconquista* would be complete. But if we continue to think of each moment

---

[101] Catédra, *Consolatoria*, 285. "¡O, ánimo claro, fulgente memoria / de reyna que Dios quiso dotar / de fe, fortaleza la más syngular / que reyna del mundo muestra su estoria! / Esta venida denota la glorya / que ella reçibe con la santa guerra / y quiso con esto hollarles la tierra / a los enemigos y ver la vitoria. / Y truxo con esto las sus rogativas, / truxo dinero para la gente, / truxo consuelo alegre, patente, / que haze a los flacos que cobren las vidas; / truxo aquell'alta manifiçençia / con obediençia de Dios maravilla / qu'entrase la reyna de nuestra Castilla / en tierra de moros por eçelençia." The use of the word "reyna" is likely a play on words here, given its meaning both of "queen" and of "to reign." The most singular strength to reign in the world was the queen.
[102] Ibid., 287. "en aquella villa Moclín ya ganada ... y otro hecho real tan estraño / de mérito granda manda hazer, / que todos los huesos hizo cojer / de quantos cristianos murieron antaño."

of the holy war as having historical significance, the taking of Almería was another moment that was correcting a historical error. In 1147, during the second crusade, Isabel's ancestor, Alfonso VII, had taken Almería, giving Castile its first port on the Mediterranean in one of the greater victories of that crusade.[103] But, in less than a decade, it was reclaimed by Islamic forces, reinvigorated by the puritanical Almoravids. Just as Isabel had been present at the retaking of Moclín, so she was present at the retaking of Almería. The fact that Isabel – a royal *woman* – was leading the Castilian effort to fix history speaks volumes about the way in which Isabel and other powerful Castilian women saw their relationship with chivalry and violence.

Isabel's role was eminently chivalric. Yet it was not wholly masculine. Isabel, as far as we know, never wielded a sword, nor rode a charger into battle. But, as a woman, she embraced the core concepts of chivalry that male knights and men-at-arms held dear: honor, holy war, and violent vengeance against one's enemies. In this she was not alone. Other elite women in late medieval Castile similarly moved past the stereotypical role of a woman as being simply a pious and pretty object for male affection, domination, and reproduction. Space existed in chivalric ideology for a different model of femininity. A woman could encourage male violence either through shame or encouragement, could pursue war – especially holy war – in a more serious way than her male counterparts, and could defend the honor of herself and her family, just as a man should. A chivalric man's masculinity had violence at its core; without it he was not a man. A chivalric woman might embrace the Isabelline model of femininity. For men and women, violence was deeply entwined with their gender identity.

---

[103] Joseph F. O'Callaghan, *Reconquest and Crusade in Medieval Spain* (Philadelphia: University of Pennsylvania Press, 2003), 44–46.

Conclusions

The Trastámara period saw the articulation of a powerful and often destructive ideology of chivalry. From a political perspective, knights sought to guard their political prerogatives and wield political power in the kingdom. Always claiming to be loyal servants of the king, they were nonetheless prepared at a moment's notice to go to war with the king or the king's supporters to protect their political privileges. From a social perspective, knights defined themselves through their honor and their *linaje*. Peasants and commoners, who did not have honor or lineage to the same degree that knights claimed, had no right to violence, as far as knights were concerned. As the exclusive owners of violent action, knights felt free to exercise their violence on those below them in the social hierarchy. In war, the Trastámara nobility often clamored for the prosecution of the holy war, insisting that a king ought to prioritize the war against Islam. These men saw their personal, familial, and kingdom-wide honor as bound up in the past successes of the holy war, and continual advancement of the *reconquista* was necessary to preserve that honor. Yet knights had no objection to fighting their Christian neighbors, both in Castile and abroad. They believed that God was pleased with their martial activity even when the blood on their swords was loosed from Christian veins. And though most knights were men, women played a key role in chivalric violence, through the production of male heirs, through marriage alliances, and through active violence itself, directing male relatives and vassals into war for their personal and familial benefit. All of these components were central to the larger ideology of chivalry in late medieval Castile.

Most of these components were characteristic of chivalry as it existed across late medieval Europe. The knightly love of independence from higher government oversight is showcased excellently in the struggles between the popular and elite factions in Florence.[1] The disdain and even dehumanization of the lower orders that was articulated so well by the popular ballads of the frontier appeared throughout western and central Europe. Just as it led to the rise of the Irmandiños in the Kingdom of Castile, so it led to the Jacquerie in France and the Great Rising in England. Castile was clearly a part of the larger cultural world of late medieval Europe and the ideology of chivalry reflects this. Yet medieval chivalry, even if it contained a core set

---

[1] For a brief but insightful assessment of chivalric violence in Florence see Peter Sposato and Samuel Claussen, "Chivalric Violence," in *A Companion to Chivalry*, ed. Robert W. Jones and Peter Coss (Woodbridge: Boydell Press, 2019), 105–111.

of values and ideas that reverberated across medieval time and space, did change a bit in particular locations. Iberia was unique in western Europe in the late Middle Ages because of the real Muslim presence in the peninsula. While France, England, the Empire, and the Italian cities were familiar with Islam and ideals of holy war, the chivalry of these states could not march as readily against their religious enemies as the knights of Castile, Portugal, and Aragon could. True, northern Europeans could and did join crusades to the Holy Land and, occasionally, crusades in northeastern Europe. But the powerful religious element of chivalry came to its fullest fruition in the Kingdom of Castile, where knights had generations of ancestors who had fought and died in the holy war. Their ancestral lands were often won sword in hand from Muslim enemies. The angry grace of a vengeful Christian God was felt nowhere as profoundly and successfully as in Castile.

Chivalry was not simply a veneer lightly placed over medieval life. Chivalric impulses were real and helped to steer the course of Castilian history. Indeed, understanding chivalry in late medieval Castile offers a new explanatory perspective on the trials and tribulations of that kingdom in the late 14th and 15th centuries. This ideology, even as it changed in the 16th century and beyond, continued to play a significant role in the course of Spanish history. Economic, political, and military history can tell us a great deal about the development of the Spanish empire. But a history of ideas is also necessary. We might keep in mind the complexity of ideas in the late medieval world not only in assessing the rise of the Spanish empire, though surely no further reason is needed. But the larger thematic lessons of ideology in Trastámara Castile can offer us reminders about ideology and violence in our own world. If we take the late medieval situation as a case study of the broader subject of an ideology of violence, we might remember precisely this comprehensiveness, complexity, and the difficulties of reforming such violence. Indeed, our own violent modern world might take note of the challenges of checking or directing a virulent ideology of violence.

As the new year dawned in 1492, the Iberian world was different. Muhammad XII of Granada had vacated the Alhambra and turned it over to the Catholic Monarchs. With the conquest of Granada, Castile suddenly saw a boost to the treasury, having captured the wealth of the last Muslim kingdom in western Europe. Several days after the conquest was complete, some of this wealth was earmarked for Christopher Columbus' voyage to the west, where Columbus and other elite men eventually sought to win honor and glory, often through warfare against the native peoples of the Caribbean, Mexico, and Peru. The conquest of Granada had been completed as the monarchs themselves made their headquarters in Andalucía and led a national army of knights and men-at-arms in a holy war against the old Muslim enemy, fulfilling the chivalric ideal of holy war. Within decades, the Catholic Monarchs were sending conquistadors – vigorous fighting men who acted much like medieval knights, indeed conceived of themselves as new crusaders – to the New World to establish an empire among the pagans there.[2] In the New World, old social and political patterns were replicated, conquistadors effectively ruling as viceroys in the name of the king, crushing political resistance among the native peoples, and establishing a social hierarchy with the peninsular military elite at the top.[3] In the 16th century, as other European nations began to establish their own empires, the Catholic Monarchs and their Habsburg successors would enthusiastically fight fellow Christians, both Catholic and Protestant, assured that God was on their side.[4]

Chivalry, in other words, did not suddenly disappear in 1474 or 1492 or 1519. It remained a central part of the Spanish world. What changed was that the Catholic Monarchs and their successors appeared to have learned how to embrace knightly ideology, work with it, and redirect its more destructive components outwards, against fellow Christian states and non-Christians across the world. Fernando de Antequera's adept understanding and manipulation of knightly ideology were simply a prelude to the skillful efforts of Queen Isabel to embrace and even dominate the chivalric world. Isabel's mastery of the chivalric worldview was largely what enabled her to secure order in Castile after decades of chaos. She provided ample avenues for Castilian knights to simultaneously serve their monarch on the battlefield and pursue the divinely sanctioned war against Islam, thus honoring their elite families and ancestors. Yet she never shied away from a just war against her Christian neighbors or countrymen when necessary. While the queen would brook no opposition from her chivalric vassals, she found plenty of wars in Europe and, eventually, in the Americas, where the knights of Castile could pursue their martial calling without heavy oversight or control from the royal government. As a reigning queen, she modeled chivalric leadership as her male predecessors were never able to do, shaming men around her into action and serving as an intercessor with higher powers on behalf of her loyal knights. The Spanish Golden Age would be possible only through the establishment of a stable and centralized state in Castile. And while Isabel's brother and father had laid much of the groundwork for the early modern Spanish state, their achievement could not flourish in the disarray that marked Castile in the late 14th and, especially, the 15th centuries. The most profound accomplishment of Isabel and her husband was not their marriage, the growth of government institutions, or the acquisition of New

---

[2] Jennifer R. Goodman, *Chivalry and Exploration, 1298–1630* (Woodbridge: Boydell Press, 1998), 149–167.

[3] Laura A. Lewis, "Between 'Casta' and 'Raza': The Example of Colonial Mexico," in *Race and Blood in the Iberian World*, ed. Max S. Hering Torres, et. al. (Zürich: Lit Verlag GmbH & Co., 2012), 99–123.

[4] Peter H. Wilson, *The Thirty Years War: Europe's Tragedy* (Cambridge, MA: Harvard University Press, 2009), 314–319.

World territories; it was the transformation of their relationship with the most powerful individuals in their kingdom. Chivalry and its practitioners had to be reckoned with or, more accurately, appropriately accommodated and redirected before the Golden Age was possible.

Timeline of Major Events

1337 – Hundred Years' War begins

1347 – Black Death arrives in Europe

1350 – Death of Alfonso XI; accession of Pedro

1351 – Castilian civil war begins

1358 – Jacquerie Rising in France

1360 – Hundred Years' War pauses

1366 – Enrique de Trastámara claims throne

1369 – Death of Pedro; Castilian civil war ends; Hundred Years' War resumes

1378 – Western schism of the Church begins; Ciompi Revolt in Florence

1379 – Death of Enrique II; accession of Juan I

1381 – Great Rising in England

1385 – Battle of Aljubarrota: Portugal secures independence from Castile

1389 – Hundred Years' War pauses

1390 – Death of Juan I; accession of Enrique III

1406 – Death of Enrique III; accession of Juan II

1410 – Conquest of Antequera from Granada

1412 – Trastámara dynasty established in Aragon

1415 – Hundred Years' War resumes; Battle of Agincourt

1417 – Western schism ends

1418 – Regency for Juan II ends

1429 – Joan of Arc defeats English at siege of Orleans

1431 – Battle of Higueruela: minor Castilian victory over Granada; first Irmandiños rising

1441 – Battle of Medina del Campo: Álvaro de Luna removed from power

1442 – Aragonese conquest of Naples

1445 – First Battle of Olmedo: Álvaro de Luna returns to power

1451 – Second Irmandiños rising

1453 – Álvaro de Luna executed; Hundred Years' War ends; Ottoman conquest of Constantinople

1454 – Death of Juan II; accession of Enrique IV

1455 – Wars of the Roses begin in England

1462 – Castilian conquest of Gibraltar from Granada

1465 – Farce of Ávila: Alfonso proclaimed king, war between Enrique and nobles begins

1467 – Third Irmandiños rising

1468 – Treaty of the Bulls of Guisando; Castilian civil war ends

1469 – Marriage of Isabel and Fernando

1471 – Andalucian war begins

1474 – Death of Enrique IV; Isabel and Juana la Beltraneja both proclaimed queen; Andalucian war ends

1475 – War of the Castilian succession begins

1476 – Isabel and Fernando victorious

1479 – Treaty of Alcáçovas: War of the Castilian Succession ends

1482 – Granada War begins

1485 – Wars of the Roses end in England: Tudor dynasty established

1486 – Castilian conquest of Moclín from Granada

1489 – Castilian conquest of Almería from Granada

1492 – Granada war ends: Castilian conquest of Kingdom of Granada

Bibliography

Manuscript Sources

Biblioteca Nacional de España (BNE) MSS/6526 – Enrique de Aragon, Marques de Villena, *Doce trabaxos de Ercules* and *Libro de guerra*
BNE MSS/7575 – Fernán Pérez de Guzmán, *Mar de las estorias*
BNE MSS/9263 – Diego de Valera, *Correspondence*
BNE MSS/18697/73 – Juan II, *Confirmacion en favor de Álvaro de Luna*
BNE MSS/20212/30/1 & 4 – Isabel I, *Letters*
BNE MSS.MICRO/2063 – Enrique II, *Correspondence*
BNE RES/266/6 & 12–14 – *Miscellaneous Documents*

Published Sources

Amadís de Gaula. Edited by Edwin B. Place. Madrid: Consejo Superior de Investigaciones Cientificas, 1959.
Antología de poetas líricos castellanos, vol. 8–10. Edited by Fernando José Wolf and Conrado Hofmann. Madrid: Librería de Hernando y Compañía, 1899–1900.
Barba, Juan. "Consolatoria de Castilla". Edited by Pedro M. Cátedra. *La Historiografía en verso en la época de los Reyes Católicos: Juan Barba y su* Consolatoria de Castilla. Salamanca: Ediciones Universidad de Salamanca, 1989.
Bernáldez, Andrés. "Historia de los Reyes Católicos." *Biblioteca de Autores Españoles (BAE)*, vol. 70. Edited by M. Rivadeneyra. Madrid: Impresores de Camara de S.M., 1876.
Cantar de Mio Cid: Texto, gramática y vocabulario. Edited by R. Menéndez Pidal. Madrid: Espasa-Calpe, S.A., 1956.
Cartagena, Alfonso de. "Discurso pronunciado por D. Alfonso de Cartagena en el Concilio de Basilea acerca del derecho de precedencia del Rey de Castilla sobre el Rey de Inglaterra." *La Ciudad de Dios*, 35 (1894): 211–217.
——. "Doctrinal de los caualleros." Edited by Noel Fallows. *The Chivalric Vision of Alfonso de Cartagena: Study and Edition of the* Doctrinal de los caualleros. Newark, DE: Linguatext, Ltd., 1995.
Charny, Geoffroi de. "Book of Chivalry." Edited by Richard Kaeuper and translated by Elspeth Kennedy. *The Book of Chivalry of Geoffroi de Charny: Text, Context, and Translation*. Philadelphia: University of Pennsylvania Press, 1996.
"La Coronica del yllustre y muy magnifico cauallero don Alonso Pérez de Guzmán el Bueno." Edited by Miguel Ángel Ladero Quesada. "Una biografía caballeresca del siglo XV: 'La Coronica del yllustre y muy magnifico cauallero don Alonso Pérez de Guzmán el Bueno'." *En la España Media*, 22 (1999): 247–283.

Corral, Pedro de. *Crónica del Rey don Rodrigo (Crónica sarracina)*. Edited by James Donald Fogelquist. Madrid: Editorial Castalia, S.A., 2001.
Cortes de los antiguos reinos de León y de Castilla. Madrid: M. Rivadeneyra, 1861.
Crónica de Don Álvaro de Luna, Condestable de Castilla, Maestre de Santiago. Edited by Juan de Mata Carriazo. Madrid: Espasa-Calpe, S.A., 1940.
El Cuento de Tristan de Leonis. Edited by George Tyler Northup. Chicago: University of Chicago Press, 1928.
Díez de Games, Gutierre. *El Victorial: Crónica de Don Pero Niño, Conde de Buelna*. Edited by Juan de Mata Carriazo. Madrid: Espasa-Calpe, S.A., 1940.
———. *The Unconquered Knight: A Chronicle of the Deeds of Don Pero Niño, Count of Buelna*. Translated by Joan Evans. London: George Routledge & Sons, Ltd., 1928.
Enríquez del Castillo, Diego. "Crónica del rey don Enrique el cuarto de este nombre." *BAE*, vol. 70. Edited by M. Rivadeneyra. Madrid: Impresores de Camara de S.M., 1876.
García de Salazar, Lope. *Libro de las bienandanzas e fortunas*. Edited by Sharrer, Harvey L. "The Irmandiño Movement and the Revolt of 1467–69 according to Lope García de Salazar's *Libro de las bienandanzas e fortunas*." *Estudios Galegos Medievais*, ed. Antonio Cortijo Ocaña, Giorgio Perissinotto, and Harvey L. Sharrer. Santa Barbara, CA: Centro de Estudios Galegos, 2001.
Hechos del condestable Don Miguel Lucas de Iranzo. Edited by Juan de Mata Carriazo. Madrid: Espasa-Calpe, S.A., 1940.
Historia de los hechos del marqués de Cádiz. Edited by Juan Luis Carriazo Rubio. Granada, Spain: Editorial Universidad de Granada, 2003.
Huete, Pedro Carrillo de. *Crónica del Halconero de Juan II*. Edited by Juan de Mata Carriazo. Madrid: Espasa-Calpe, S.A., 1946.
Joinville, Jean de. *Histoire de Saint Louis*. Edited by Natalis de Wailly. Paris: Libraire Hachette, 1890.
El Libro del Cauallero Zifar. Edited by Charles Philip Wagner. Norwood, MA: The Plimpton Press, 1929.
López de Ayala, Pedro. "Crónica del rey don Pedro." *BAE*, vol. 66. Edited by M. Rivadeneyra. Madrid: Impresores de Camara de S.M., 1876.
———. "Crónica del rey don Enrique, segundo de Castilla." *BAE*, vol. 66. Edited by M. Rivadeneyra. Madrid: Impresores de Camara de S.M., 1876.
———. "Crónica del rey don Juan, primero de Castilla é de Leon." *BAE*, vol. 66. Edited by M. Rivadeneyra. Madrid: Impresores de Camara de S.M., 1876.
———. "Crónica del rey don Enrique, tercero de Castilla é de Leon." *BAE*, vol. 66. Edited by M. Rivadeneyra. Madrid: Impresores de Camara de S.M., 1876.
———. *Libro Rimada de Palacio*. Edited by Kenneth Adams. Madrid: Ediciones Cátedra, S.A., 1993.
Manrique, Jorge. *Obra Completa*. Edited by Augusto Cortina. Buenos Aires: Espasa-Calpe Argentina, S.A., 1966.
Mocedades de Rodrigo. Edited by Leonardo Funes and Felipe Tenenbaum. Woodbridge: Tamesis, 2004.
Las Mocedades de Rodrigo: The Youthful Deeds of Rodrigo, the Cid. Edited and translated by Matthew Bailey. Toronto: University of Toronto Press, 2007.

"Morgan Picture Bible." The Morgan Library and Museum Online Exhibits. http://www.themorgan.org/exhibitions/exhibOnlineThumbs.asp?id=OnlineKings
Palencia, Alfonso de. "Cronica de Enrique IV." Edited and translated by Antonio Paz y Meliá. *BAE*, vol. 257. Madrid: Ediciones Atlas, 1973.
Pérez de Guzmán, Fernán. "La Crónica del serenísimo príncipe don Juan, segundo rey deste nombre en Castilla y en Leon." *BAE*, vol. 68. Edited by M. Rivadeneyra. Madrid: Impresores de Camara de S.M., 1876.
———. *Generaciones y semblanzas*. Buenos Aires: Espasa-Calpe Argentina, S.A., 1947.
Poesía crítica y satírica del siglo XV. Edited by Julio Rodríguez Puértolas. Madrid: Editorial Castalia, 1984.
La Poncella de Francia: La historia castellana de Juana de Arco. Edited by Victoria Campo and Victor Infantes. 2nd edition. Madrid: Iberoamericana, 2006.
Pulgar, Fernando del. *Claros Varones de Castilla*. Buenos Aires: Espasa-Calpe Argentina, S.A., 1948.
———. "Crónica de los señores Reyes Católicos Don Fernando y Doña Isabel de Castilla y de Aragon." *BAE*, vol. 70. Edited by M. Rivadeneyra. Madrid: Impresores de Camara de S.M., 1876.
Rodríguez de Lena, Pedro. *El passo honroso de Suero de Quiñones*. Edited by Amancio Labandeira Fernández. Madrid: Fundación Universitaria Española, 1977.
Rodríguez de Montalvo, Garci. *Amadís de Gaula*. Lexington, KY: Plaza Editorial, 2012.
Las Siete Partidas. Glossed by Gregorio Lopez. Salamanca, Spain: Andrea de Portonaris, 1555.
Las Siete Partidas. Translated by Samuel Parsons Scott. Edited by Robert I. Burns, S.J. Philadelphia: University of Pennsylvania Press, 2001.
The Song of the Cid. Translated by Burton Raffel. New York: Penguin Group, 2009.
Valera, Diego de. "Memorial de diversas hazañas." *BAE*, vol. 70. Edited by M. Rivadeneyra. Madrid: Impresores de Camara de S.M., 1876.

Secondary Sources

Arraco, José Manuel Pérez-Prendes y Muñoz de. "Consideraciones sobre el derecho señorial." *Ariadne*, no. 18 (2006): 119–132.
Arena, Héctor L. "Die Chorgestühle des Meisters Rodrigo Alemán." PhD diss., Ruprecht-Karl- Universität zu Heidelberg, 1965.
Bachrach, David S. *Religion and the Conduct of War c. 300–1215*. Woodbridge: Boydell Press, 2003.
Barros, Carlos. "Lo que sabemos de los Irmandiños." *Clio et Crimen*, no. 3 (2006): 36–48.
———. *Mentalidad justiciera de los irmandiños, siglos XV*. Madrid: Siglo Veintiuno Editores, 1990.
Belinchón, José Serrano. *El condestable: de la vida, prisión y muerte de don Álvaro de Luna*. Guadalajara, Spain: AACHE Ediciones, 2000.
Bennett, Matthew. "The Development of Battle Tactics in the Hundred Years' War." In *Arms, Armies and Fortifications in the* Hundred Years' War, ed. Anne Curry and Michael Hughes, 1–20. Woodbridge: Boydell Press, 1994.

Beresford, Andrew et al., eds. *Medieval Hispanic Studies in Memory of Alan Deyermond*. Woodbridge: Tamesis, 2013.
Blackmore, Josiah and Hutcheson, Gregory S., eds. *Queer Iberia: Sexualities, Cultures, and Crossings from the Middle Ages to the Renaissance*. Durham, NC: Duke University Press, 1999.
Boulton, D'Arcy Jonathan Dacre. *The Knights of the Crown: The Monarchical Orders of Knighthood in Later Medieval Europe 1325–1520*. New York: St. Martin's Press, 1987.
Bull, Marcus and Housley, Norman, eds. *The Experience of Crusading*, vol. 1: *Western Approaches*. Cambridge: Cambridge University Press, 2003.
Cabrer, Martín Alvira. "La muerte del enemigo en el pleno medievo: cifras e ideología (el modelo de Las Navas de Tolosa)." *Hispania: Revista española de historia*, vol. 55, no. 190 (1995): 403–424.
Cabrera, Emilio. "Conflictos en el mundo rural. Señores y vasallos." In *Conflictos sociales, políticos e intelectuales en la España de los siglos XIV y XV*, ed. José Ignacio de la Iglesia Duarte, 49–80. Logroño, Spain: Instituto de Estudios Riojanos, 2004.
Calderón Ortega, José Manuel. "La donación de Arjona a Fadrique de Aragón." *Historia medieval: actas del II Congreso de Historia de Andalucía, Córdoba*. Córdoba, Spain: Consejería de Cultura y Medio Ambiente de la Junta de Andalucía, 1994.
Camillo, Ottavio di. "Interpretations of Humanism in Recent Spanish Renaissance Studies." *Renaissance Quarterly*, vol. 50, no. 4 (1997): 1190–1201.
Carbajal, Eva Belén Carro et al., eds. *Libros de caballerías (de 'Amadís' al 'Quijote'): poética, lectura, representación e identidad*. Salamanca, Spain: Seminario de Estudios Medievales y Renacentistas, 2002.
Carceller Ceviño, María del Pilar. "Alvaro de Luna, Juan Pacheco y Beltrán de la Cueva: un estudio comparativo del privado regio a fines de la Edad Media." *En la España Medieval*, no. 32 (2009): 85–112.
Carrasco Manchado, Ana Isabel. *Isabel I de Castilla y la sombra de la ilegitimidad: Propaganda y representación en el conflicto successorio (1474–1482)*. Madrid: Sílex Ediciones, S.L., 2006.
Carriazo Rubio, Juan Luis. *La Casa de Arcos entre Sevilla y la frontera Granda (1374–1474)*. Sevilla, Spain: Fundación Focus-Abengoad, 2003.
———. *La memoria del linaje. Los Ponce de Leon y sus antepasados a fines de la Edad Media*. Sevilla, Spain: Universidad de Sevilla, 2002.
Casado Alonso, Hilario. *Señores, mercaderes y campesinos*. Valladolid: Junta de Castilla y Leon, 1987.
Castillo Cáceres, Fernando. "¿Guerra o torneo?: la Batalla de Olmedo, modelo de enfrentamiento caballeresco." *En la España medieval*, no. 32 (2009): 139–166.
Castro, Américo. *España en su historia*. Buenos Aires: Editorial Losada, 1948.
Ceballos, Francisco Toro and Molina, José Rodríguez, eds. *IV Estudios de Frontera. Historia, tradiciones y leyendas en la frontera*. Jaén, Spain: Soproargra, S.A., 2002.
Cervigón, José Ignacio Ortega. "La nobleza peninsular en época trastámara. Principales líneas de investigación (1997–2006)." *eHumanista*, vol. 10 (2008): 104–132.
Classen, Albrecht, ed. *Violence in Medieval Courtly Literature: A Casebook*. London: Routledge, 2004.

Contamine, Philippe. *War in the Middle Ages*. Translated by Michael Jones. New York: Basil Blackwell, 1984.

Coolidge, Grace E. *Guardianship, Gender, and the Nobility in Early Modern Spain*. New York: Routledge, 2016.

Córdoba de la Llave, Ricardo. "Violencia cotidiana en Castilla a fines de la edad media." In *Conflictos sociales, políticos e intelectuales en la España de los siglos XIV y XV*, ed. José Ignacio de la Iglesia Duarte, 393–443. Logroño, Spain: Instituto de Estudios Riojanos, 2004.

Corédon, Christopher with Williams, Ann. *A Dictionary of Medieval Terms and Phrases*. Cambridge: D.S. Brewer, 2004.

Corral, José Luis. *La torre y caballero: El ocaso de los feudales*. Barcelona: Edhasa, 2002.

Corfis, Ivy A. and Harris-Northall, Ray, eds. *Medieval Iberia: In Contact and Transition*. Woodbridge: Tamesis, 2007.

Cowell, Andrew. *Medieval Warrior Aristocracy: Gifts, Violence, Performance, and the Sacred*. Cambridge: D.S. Brewer, 2007.

Cristianos y musulmanes en la Península Ibérica: la guerra, la frontera y la convivencia. Avila, Spain: Fundación Sánchez Albornoz, 2009.

Crouch, David. *Birth of Nobility: Constructing Aristocracy in England and France, 900–1300*. Harlow, England: Pearson Longman, 2005.

———. *The English Aristocracy, 1070–1272: A Social Transformation*. New Haven, CT: Yale University Press, 2011.

———. *Tournament*. London: Hambledon and London, 2005.

Delgado, Juan Álvarez. "Alonso de Palencia (1423–1492) y la Historia de Canarias." *Anuario de Estudios Atlanticos*, vol. 1, no. 9 (1963): 51–79.

Devaney, Thomas. *Enemies in the Plaza: Urban Spectacle and the End of Spanish Frontier Culture, 1460–1492*. Philadelphia: University of Pennsylvania Press, 2015.

———. "Virtue, Virility, and History in Fifteenth-Century Castile." *Speculum*, vol. 88, no. 3 (2013): 721–749.

Devia, Cecilia. "Pedro I y Enrique II de Castilla: la construcción de un rey monstruoso y la legitimación de un usurpador en la Crónica del canciller Ayala." *Mirabilia*, 13 (Jun.–Dec. 2011): 60–78.

———. *La violencia en la Edad Media: la rebelión irmandiña*. Vigo, Spain: Editorial Academia del Hispanism, 2009.

———. "Violencia y dominacion en la Baja Edad Media castellana." PhD diss., Universidad de Buenos Aires, 2013.

DeVries, Kelly, ed. *Medieval Warfare 1300–1450*. Burlington, VT: Ashgate Publishing Company, 2010.

Deyermond, Alan. *El "Cantar de Mio Cid" y la épica medieval española*. Barcelona: Sirmio, 1987.

———. *Epic Poetry and the Clergy: Studies on the "Mocedades de Rodrigo."* London: Tamesis Books Limited, 1968.

———. *A Literary History of Spain: The Middle Ages*. London: Ernest Benn Ltd., 1971.

Deyermond, Alan and Lawrance, Jeremy. *Letters and Society in Fifteenth-Century Spain: Studies presented to P.E. Russell on his eightieth birthday*. Llangrannog, Wales: Dolphin Book, Co., 1993.

Domínguez, Frank. *Love and Remembrance: The Poetry of Jorge Manrique*. Lexington, KY: University Press of Kentucky, 1988.
Doubleday, Simon R. *The Lara Family: Crown and Nobility in Medieval Spain*. Cambridge, MA: Harvard University Press, 2001.
Duby, Georges. "Women and Power." In *Cultures of Power: Lordship, Status and Process in Twelfth-Century Europe*, ed. Thomas N. Bisson. Philadelphia: University of Pennsylvania Press, 1995.
Edwards, John. *Christian Córdoba: The city and its region in the late Middle Ages*. Cambridge: Cambridge University Press, 1982.
———. *Ferdinand and Isabella*. Harlow, England: Pearson Longman, 2005.
———. *The Spain of the Catholic Monarchs, 1474–1520*. Oxford: Blackwell Publishers Ltd., 2000.
Entwistle, William J. *The Arthurian Legend in the Literatures of the Spanish Peninsula*. New York: Phaeton Press, 1975.
Erdmann, Carl. *The Origin of the Idea of Crusade*. Translated by Marshall W. Baldwin and Walter Goffart. Princeton, NJ: Princeton University Press, 1977.
Estepa Díez, Carlos. "Rebelión y rey legítimo en las luchas entre Pedro I y Enrique II." In *Lucha política: condena y legitimación en la España medieval*, ed. Alfonso, Isabel, 173–185. Lyon: ENS Éditions, 2004.
Estow, Clara. *Pedro the Cruel of Castile, 1350–1369*. Leiden, Netherlands: Brill, 1995.
Fallows, Noel. "Chivalric manuals in medieval Spain: The *Doctrinal de los cavalleros* (c. 1444) of Alfonso de Cartagena." *Journal of Medieval and Renaissance Studies*, vol. 24, no.1 (1994): 53–87.
———. *Jousting in Medieval and Renaissance Iberia*. Woodbridge: Boydell Press, 2010.
———. "Just Say No? Alfonso de Cartagena, the Doctrinal de los caballeros, and Spain's Most Noble Pastime." In *Studies on Medieval Spanish Literature in Honor of Charles F. Fraker*, ed. Mercedes Vaquero and Alan Deyermond. Madison, WI: Hispanic Seminary of Medieval Studies, 1995.
Federico, Sylvia. "Chaucer and the Matter of Spain." *The Chaucer Review*, vol. 45, no. 3 (2011): 299–320.
Fernández Flórez, Darío. *Dos claves históricas: Mío Cid y Roldán*. Madrid: Signo, 1939.
Fernández, Manuel García. "Sobre la alteridad en la frontera de Granada: (una aproximación al análisis de la guerra y la paz, siglos XIII–XV)." *Revista da Faculdade de Letras. Historia*, no. 6 (2005): 213–235.
Fogelquist, James Donald. *Pedro de Corral's Reconfiguration of La Cava in the "Crónica del Rey don Rodrigo.*" eHumanista: Monographs in Humanities, 3, University of California–Santa Barbara, 2007.
Folger, Robert. *Generaciones y semblanzas: Memory and Genealogy in Medieval Iberian Historiography*. Tübingen, Germany: Gunter Narr Verlag Tübingen, 2003.
Fra-Molinero, Baltasar. "Don Quijote Attacks his Muslim Other: The Maese Pedro Episode of Don Quijote." In *Contextualizing the Muslim Other in Medieval Christian Discourse*, ed. Jerold C Frakes. New York: Palgrave Macmillan, 2011.
France, John. *The Crusades and the Expansion of Catholic Christendom, 1000–1714*. London: Routledge, 2005.
Galván, Luis. "'A todos alcança ondra': consideraciones sobre el honor y la relación del Cid y el rey en el 'Cantar de mio Cid'." In *"Sonando van sus nuevas allent*

parte del mar". El Cantar de mio Cid y el mundo de la épica, ed. Alberto Montaner Frutos. Toulouse: Presses université de Toulouse, 2013.

García Fitz, Francisco. "Una frontera caliente: la guerra en las fronteras castellano-musulamans (siglos XI–XIII)." In *Identidad y representación de la frontera en la España medieval (siglos XI–XIV)*, ed. Martínez, Carlos de Ayala et al., 159–180. Madrid: Casa de Velázques, 2001.

——. "'Las guerras de cada día' en la Castilla del siglo XIV." *Edad Media. Revista de Historia*, 8 (2007): 145–181.

——. "La Reconquista: un estado de la cuestión." *Clio et Crimen*, no. 6 (2009): 142–215.

García, Michel. *Obra y personalidad del Canciller Ayala*. Madrid: Editorial Alhambra, 1983.

García de Rivera, Helena Alonso. "Estructuras sociales en la Baja Edad Media Española según el anónimo 'Dança General de la Muerte'." *Revista de folklore*, no. 388 (2014): 26–43.

Gerbet, Marie-Claude. *Las noblezas españolas en la Edad Media: siglos XI–XV*. Translated by María José García Vera. Madrid: Alianza Editorial, S.A., 1997.

Gertsman, Elina. *The Dance of Death in the Middle Ages: Image, Text, Performance*. Turnhout, Belgium: Brepols, 2010.

Gilmore, David D. *Aggression and Community: Paradoxes of Andalusian Culture*. New Haven, CT: Yale University Press, 1987.

——. "Honor, Honesty, Shame: Male Status in Contemporary Andalusia." In *Honor and Shame and the Unity of the Mediterranean*, ed. David D. Gilmore, 90–103. Arlington, VA: American Anthropological Association, 1987.

González, María Asenjo. "Acerca de los linajes urbanos y su conflictividad en las ciudades castellanas a fines de la Edad Media." *Clio et Crimen*, no. 6 (2009): 52–84

Goodman, Jennifer R. *Chivalry and Exploration, 1298–1630*. Woodbridge: Boydell Press, 1998.

Grieve, Patricia E. *The Eve of Spain: Myths of Origins in the history of Christian, Muslim, and Jewish Conflict*. Baltimore, MD: The Johns Hopkins University Press, 2009.

Guard, Timothy. *Chivalry, Kingship and Crusade: The English Experience in the Fourteenth Century*. Woodbridge: Boydell Press, 2013.

Harper-Bill, Christopher, and Harvey, Ruth, eds. *The Ideals and Practice of Medieval Knighthood: Papers from the first and second Strawberry Hill conferences*. Woodbridge: Boydell Press, 1986.

Hatton, Vikki and MacKay, Angus. "Anti-Semitism in the *Cantigas de Santa Maria*." *Bulletin of Hispanic Studies*, vol. LX, no. 3 (Jul. 1983): 189–199.

Herrer, Hipólito Rafael Oliva. "El mundo rural en la corona de Castilla en la baja edad media: dinamicas socioeconomicas y nuevas perspectivas de analisis." *Edad Media. Reivsta de Historia*, vol. 8 (2007): 295–328.

Heusch, Carlos. "La pluma al servicio del linaje: El desarrollo de los nobiliarios en la Castilla trastámara." *e-Spania: Revue interdisciplinaire d'études hispaniques médiévales et modernes*, no. 11 (Jun. 2011). http://e-spania.revues.org/20313.

Horden, Peregrine and Purcell, Nicholas. *The Corrupting Sea: A Study of Mediterranean History*. Oxford: Blackwell Publishing, 2000.

Howard, Michael. *War in European History*. Oxford: Oxford University Press, 2009.
Huizinga, Johan, *The Autumn of the Middle Ages*. Translated by Rodney J. Payton and Ulrich Mammitzsch. Chicago: University of Chicago Press, 1996.
Huston, Nancy. "The Matrix of War: Mothers and Heroes." In *The Female Body in Western Culture, contemporary perspectives*, ed. Susan Rubin Suleiman, 123–135. Cambridge, MA: Harvard University Press, 1985.
Hutcheson, Gregory S. "Desperately Seeking Sodom: Queerness in the Chronicles of Alvaro de Luna." In *Queer Iberia: Sexualities, Cultures, and Crossings from the Middle Ages to the Renaissance*, ed. Josiah Blackmore and Gregory S. Hutcheson, 222–249. Durham, NC: Duke University Press, 1999.
Iglesias, María del Carmen, ed. *Nobleza y sociedad en la España moderna*. Madrid: Fundación Central Hispano, 1996.
Jaeger, C. Stephen. *Ennobling Love: In Search of a Lost Sensibility*. Philadelphia, University of Pennsylvania Press, 1999.
Jones, Robert W. and Coss, Peter, eds. *A Companion to Chivalry*. Woodbridge: Boydell Press, 2019.
Kaeuper, Richard W. *Chivalry and Violence in Medieval Europe*. Oxford: Oxford University Press, 1999.
———. *Holy Warriors: The Religious Ideology of Chivalry*. Philadelphia: University of Pennsylvania Press, 2009.
———. "Literature as Essential Evidence for Understanding Chivalry." *The Journal of Medieval Military History* (2007): 1–15.
———. *Medieval Chivalry*. Cambridge: Cambridge University Press, 2016.
———. *War, Justice, and Public Order*. Oxford: Clarendon Press, 1988.
Kagan, Richard L. *Clio and the Crown: The Politics of History in Medieval and Early Modern Spain*. Baltimore, MD: The Johns Hopkins University Press, 2009.
Kagay, Donald J. and Vann, Theresa M., eds. *On the Social Origins of Medieval Institutions: Essays in Honor of Joseph F. O'Callaghan*. Leiden, Netherlands: Brill, 1998.
Kantorowicz, Ernst H. *The King's Two Bodies: A Study in Mediaeval Political Theology*. Princeton, NJ: Princeton University Press, 1957.
Keen, Maurice, *Chivalry*. New Haven, CT: Yale University Press, 1984.
Kollmann, Nancy Shields. *By Honor Bound: State and Society in Early Modern Russia*. Ithaca, NY: Cornell University Press, 1999.
Kuehn, Thomas. "Fama as legal status in Renaissance Florence." In *Fama: The Politics of Talk and Reputation in Medieval Europe*, ed. Thelma Fenster and Daniel Lord Smail, 27–46. Ithaca, NY: Cornell University Press, 2003.
Lacarra, María Eugenia. "Notes on Feminist Analysis of Medieval Spanish Literature and History." *La corónica*, no. 17.1 (Fall 1988): 14–22.
Ladero Quesada, Miguel Ángel. *Los señores de Andalucía: Investigaciones sobre nobles y señoríos en los siglos XIII a XV*. Cádiz, Spain: Universidad de Cádiz, 1998.
Lambert, T.B. and Rollason, David, eds. *Peace and Protection in the Middle Ages*. Durham, England: Centre for Medieval and Renaissance Studies, 2009.
Lewis, Laura A. "Between 'Casta' and 'Raza': The Example of Colonial Mexico." In *Race and Blood in the Iberian World*, ed. Max S. Hering Torres et al., 99–123. Zürich: Lit Verlag GmbH & Co., 2012
Liss, Peggy K. *Isabel the Queen*. Oxford: Oxford University Press, 1992.

Lozano-Renieblas, Isabel. *Novelas de aventuras medievales. Género y traducción en la Edad Media hispánica*. Kassel, Germany: Edition Reichenberger, 2003.

MacKay, Angus. "The ballad and the frontier in late mediaeval Spain." *Bulletin of Hispanic Studies*, LIII (1976): 15–33.

———. "Un Cid Ruy Díaz en el siglo XV: Rodrigo Ponce de León, Marques de Cádiz." In *El Cid en el valle del Jalón: Simposio Internacional*, 192–202. Calatayud, Spain: Centro de Estudios Bilbilitanos, 1991.

———. "Don Fernando de Antequera y la Virgen Santa María. In *Homenaje al profesor Juan Torres Fontes*, 949–958. Murcia: Universidad de Murcia, 1987.

———. "The Jews in Spain during the Middle Ages." In *Spain and the Jews*, ed. Elie Kedourie, 33–50. London: Thames and Hudson, Ltd., 1992.

———. "Religion, Culture, and Ideology on the Late Medieval Castilian-Granadan Frontier." In *Medieval Frontier Societies*, ed. Robert Bartlett and Angus MacKay, 217–243. Oxford: Clarendon Press, 1989.

———. "Ritual and Propaganda in Fifteenth-Century Castile." *Past and Present*, no. 107 (May 1985): 3–43.

———. *Spain in the Middle Ages: From Frontier to Empire, 1000–1500*. New York: Palgrave Macmillan, 1977.

Madden, Marie R. *Political Theory and Law in Medieval Spain*. New York: Fordham University Press, 1930.

Marino, Nancy. *Jorge Manrique's* Coplas por la muerte de su padre: *A History of the Poem and Its Reception*. Woodbridge: Tamesis, 2011.

Martínez Iniesta, Bautista. "Los romances fronterizos: Crónica poética de la Reconquista Granadina y Antología del Romancero fronterizo." *Lemir*, 7 (2003): np. http://parnaseo.uv.es/Lemir/Revista/Revista7/Romances.htm.

Mata Carriazo, Juan de. *En la frontera de Granada*. Granada, Spain: Universidad de Granada, 2002.

McLaughlin, Megan. "The Woman Warrior: Gender, Warfare, and Society in Medieval Europe." *Women's Studies*, vol. 17, no. 3–4 (1990): 193–209.

Menéndez Pidal, Ramón. *Los españoles en la Historia*. Madrid: Espase-Calpe, S.A., 1947.

Menéndez Pidal de Navascués, Faustino. "El linaje y sus signos de identidad." *En la España medieval*, Extra no. 1 (2006): 12–28.

Michael, Ian and Cardwell, Richard A., eds. *Medieval and Renaissance Studies in Honour of Robert Brian Tate*. Oxford: The Dolphin Book Co., 1986.

Miller, Townsend. *Henry IV of Castile, 1425–1474*. Philadelphia: J.B. Lippincott Company, 1972.

Miller, William Ian. *Humiliation, and Other Essays on Honor, Social Discomfort, and Violence*. Ithaca, NY: Cornell University Press, 1993.

Mirrer, Louise. *Women, Jews and Muslims in the Texts of Reconquest Castile*. Ann Arbor, MI: University of Michigan Press, 1996.

Mitre Fernández, Emilio. *La extension del regimen de corregidores en el reinado de Enrique III de castilla*. Valladolid, Spain: Gráf Andrés Martín, S.A., 1969.

Molina, Angel Luis. "Repercusiones de la guerra castellano-aragonesa en la economía murciana (1364–1365)." *Miscelánea Medieval Murciana*, no. 3 (1977), 119–160.

Montero Tejada, Rosa María. "Violencia y abusos en los señoríos del linaje Manrique a fines de la Edad Media." *En la España Medieval*, 20 (1997): 339–378.

Moore, R.I. *The Formation of a Persecuting Society: Power and Deviance in Western Europe, 950–1250*. Oxford: Basil Blackwell, 1987.

Morales Talero, Santiago de. "Don Fadrique de Castilla y Castro, Duque de Arjona." *Boletín del Instituto de Estudios Giennenses*, 40 (1964): 17–36.

Moreta, Salustiano. *Malhechores-Feudales: Violencia, antagonismos y alianzas de clases en Castilla, siglos XIII–XIV.* Madrid: Ediciones Cátedra, 1978.

Nader, Helen. *The Mendoza Family in the Spanish Renaissance, 1350–1550*. New Brunswick, NJ: Rutgers University Press, 1979.

Nakashian, Craig M. *Warrior Churchmen of Medieval England 1000–1250: Theory and Reality*. Woodbridge: Boydell Press, 2016.

Nirenberg, David. *Communities of Violence: Persecution of Minorities in the Middle Ages*. Princeton, NJ: Princeton University Press, 1996.

———. "Deviant Politics and Jewish Love: Alfonso VIII and the Jewess of Toledo." *Jewish History*, vol. 21 (2007): 15–41.

O'Callaghan, Joseph F. *Alfonso X, the Cortes, and Government in Medieval Spain*. Brookfield, VT: Ashgate Publishing Company, 1998.

———. *The Cortes of Castile-León 1188–1350*. Philadelphia: University of Pennsylvania Press, 1989.

———. *The Gibraltar Crusade*. Philadelphia: University of Pennsylvania Press, 2011.

———. *A History of Medieval Spain*. Ithaca, NY: Cornell University Press, 1975.

———. *The Last Crusade in the West: Castile and the Conquest of Granada*. Philadelphia: University of Pennsylvania Press, 2014.

———. *Reconquest and Crusade in Medieval Spain*. Philadelphia: University of Pennsylvania Press, 2004.

Ocaña, Antonio Cortijo et al., eds. *Estudios Galegos Medievais*. Santa Barbara, CA: Centro de Estudios Galegos, 2001.

Oosterwijk, Sophie and Knoell, Stefanie, eds. *Mixed Metaphors: The Danse Macabre in Medieval and Early Modern Europe*. Newcastle upon Tyne: Cambridge Scholars Publishing, 2011.

Owens, J.B. *"By My Absolute Royal Authority": Justice and the Castilian Commonwealth at the Beginning of the First Global Age*. Rochester, NY: University of Rochester Press, 2004.

Oxnes, Halvor. "Honor and Shame." *Biblical Theology Bulletin: A Journal of Bible and Theology*, vol. 23, no. 4 (Nov. 1993): 167–176.

Parsons, John Carmi. "The Queen's Intercession in Thirteenth-Century England." In *Power of the Weak: Studies on Medieval Women. A selection of papers presented at the annual conference of the Centre for Medieval Studies, University of Toronto, Feb. 1990*, ed. Jennifer Carpenter and Sally-Beth MacLean. Chicago: University of Illinois Press, 1995.

Paul, Nicholas. *To Follow in Their Footsteps: The Crusades and Family Memory in the High Middle Ages*. Ithaca, NY: Cornell University Press, 2012.

Peristiany, J.G. and Pitt-Rivers, Julian, eds. *Honor and Grace in Anthropology*. Cambridge: Cambridge University Press, 1992.

Phillips, Jr., William D. *Enrique IV and the Crisis of Fifteenth-Century Castile: 1425–1480*. Cambridge, MA: The Mediaeval Academy of America, 1978.

Piskorski, Wladimiro. *Las cortes de Castilla en el período de tránsito de la Edad Media a la Modern, 1188–1520*. Barcelona: Ediciones el Albir, S.A., 1977.

Pitt-Rivers, Julian. "Honour and Social Status." In *Honour and Shame: The Values of Mediterranean Society*, ed. Jean G. Peristiany. London: Weidenfeld and Nicolson, 1965.

Place, Edwin B. and Behm, Herbert C., trans. *Amadis of Gaul: A Novel of Chivalry of the 14th Century Presumably First Written in Spanish*. Lexington, KY: University Press of Kentucky, 1974.

Powers, James F. *A Society Organized for War: The Iberian Municipal Militias in the Central Middle Ages, 1000–1284*. Berkeley, CA: University of California Press, 1988.

Procter, Evelyn S. *Curia and Cortes in León and Castile, 1072–1295*. Cambridge: Cambridge University Press, 1980.

Quintanilla Raso, María Concepción. *Nobleza y caballería en la Edad Media*. Madrid: Arco Libros, 1996.

Ramos, Rafael. "A vueltas con la *Crónica del rey don Rodrigo*." *Tirant*, vol. 15 (2013): 353–368.

Ratcliffe, Marjorie. "Florinda la Cava: víctima histórica, víctima literaria: la Crónica sarracina en el Siglo de Oro." In *Memoria de la palabra: Actas del VI Congreso de la Asociación Siglo de Oro, Burgos-La Rioja 15–19 de julio 2002*, vol. 2, ed. Francisco Domínguez Matito and María Luisa Lobato López. Frankfurt: Iberoamericana Vervuert Verlagsgesellschaft, 2004.

Reilly, Bernard F. *The Medieval Spains*. Cambridge: Cambridge University Press, 1993.

Remensnyder, Amy. *La Conquistadora: The Virgin Mary at War and Peace in the Old and New Worlds*. Oxford: Oxford University Press, 2014.

Riley-Smith, Jonathan. *The Crusades: A History*. 2nd Edition. New Haven, CT: Yale University Press, 2005.

———. "Crusading as an Act of Love." *History*, vol. 65, no. 214 (Jun. 1980): 177–192.

Riley-Smith, Louise and Riley-Smith, Jonathan. *The Crusades: Idea and Reality, 1095–1274*. London: Edward Arnold Ltd., 1981.

Riquer, Martín de. *Caballeros andantes españoles*. Madrid: Espasa-Calpe, S.A., 1967.

Rodríguez Molina, José. *La vida de moros y cristianos en la frontera*. Jaén, Spain: Alcalá Grupo Editorial y Distribuidor de Libros, 2007.

Rodríguez-Picavea Matilla, Enrique. "Linaje y poder en la Castilla Trastámara. El ejemplo de la Orden de Calatrava." *Anuario de Estudios Medievales*, 35/1 (2005): 91–130.

Rodríguez-Velasco, Jesús. *El Debate Sobre la Caballería en el Siglo XV: La tratadística caballeresca castellana en su marco europeo*. Salamanca, Spain: Europa Artes Gráficas, S.A., 1996.

———. *Order and Chivalry: Knighthood and Citizenship in Late Medieval Castile*. Translated by Eunice Rodríguez Ferguson. Philadelphia: University of Pennsylvania Press, 2010.

Rosenwein, Barbara H. *Emotional Communities in the Early Middle Ages*. Ithaca, NY: Cornell University Press, 2006.

Round, Nicholas. *The Greatest Man Uncrowned, A Study of the Fall of Don Alvaro de Luna*. London: Tamesis Books Limited, 1986.

Ruiz, Teófilo F. *Crisis and Continuity: Land and Town in Late Medieval Castile*. Philadelphia: University of Pennsylvania Press, 1994.

———. *From Heaven to Earth: The Reordering of Castilian Society, 1150–1350*. Princeton, NJ: Princeton University Press, 2004.

———. *A King Travels: Festive Traditions in Late Medieval and Early Modern Spain*. Princeton, NJ: Princeton University Press, 2012.

———. "The Peasantries of Iberia, 1400–1800." In *The Peasantries of Europe*, ed. Tom Scott. London: Longman, 1998.

———. *Spain's Centuries of Crisis: 1300–1474*. Oxford: Blackwell Publishing Ltd, 2011.

———. *Spanish Society, 1400–1600*. Rochester, NY: University of Rochester Press, 2001.

Russell, P.E. *Portugal, Spain and the African Atlantic, 1343–1490: Chivalry and Crusade from John of Gaunt to Henry the Navigator*. Aldershot, England: Variorum, 1995.

Sánchez Albornoz, Claudio. *España, un enigma histórico*. Buenos Aires: Editorial Sudamericana, 1956.

Sánchez Saus, Rafael. "Aristocracia y frontera en la Andalucía Medieval." *Estudios de historia y de arqueología medievales*, vol. XI (1996): 191–215.

———. *Caballería y linaje en la Sevilla medieval: estudio genealogico y social*. Cádiz, Spain: Universidad de Cádiz, 1989.

Sancho de Sopranis, Hipólito. "Sobre Mosen Diego de Valera." *Hispania: Revista Española de historia*, 29, (1947): 531–553.

Serrano, Gloria Lora. "Los Muñíz de Godoy: Linaje y caballería en la Córdoba del siglo XIV." *Historia. Instituciones. Documentos*, no. 34 (2007): 159–187.

Smail, Daniel Lord. *The Consumption of Justice: Emotions, Publicity, and Legal Culture in Marseille, 1264–1423*. Ithaca, NY: Cornell University Press, 2003.

Stewart, Frank Henderson. *Honor*. Chicago: University of Chicago Press, 1994.

Strickland, Debra Higgs. *Saracens, Demons, and Jews: Making Monsters in Medieval Art*. Princeton, NJ: Princeton University Press, 2003.

Strickland, Matthew. *War and Chivalry: The Conduct and Perception of War in England and Normandy, 1066–1217*. Cambridge: Cambridge University Press, 1996.

Suárez Fernández, Luis. *Nobleza y Monarquía, Entendimiento y Rivalidad*. Madrid: La Esfera de los Libros, S.L., 2003.

Taylor, Craig. *Chivalry and the Ideals of Knighthood in France during the* Hundred Years' War. Cambridge: Cambridge University Press, 2013.

Throop, Susanna A. "Acts of Vengeance, Acts of Love: Crusading Violence in the Twelfth Century," in *War and Literature*, ed. Laura Ashe and Ian Patterson. Cambridge: D.S. Brewer, 2014.

———. *Crusading as an Act of Vengeance*. Burlington, VT: Ashgate Publishing, 2011.

———. "Zeal, Anger and Vengeance: The Emotional Rhetoric of Crusading." In *Vengeance in the Middle Ages: Emotion, Religion, and Feud*, ed. Susanna A. Throop and Paul Hyams. Burlington, VT: Ashgate Publishing, 2010.

Torres Fontes, Juan. "Las treguas con Granada de 1469 y 1472." *Hispania: Revista española de historia*, no. 90 (1963): 163–199.

Trigg, Stephanie. *Shame and Honor: A Vulgar History of the Order of the Garter*. Philadelphia: University of Pennsylvania Press, 2012.

Turner, J.P.W. "The Town Cellar, or the Church of the Monastery of St Clement's, and Other Buildings Supposed to be Connected Therewith, in the Town of Poole." *Proceedings of the Dorset Natural History and Antiquarian Field Club*, vol. IX (1888).

Tyerman, Christopher. *The Invention of the Crusades*. Toronto: University of Toronto Press, 1998.
Valdeón Baruque, Julio. "Enrique II, King of Castile." In *Medieval Iberia: An Encyclopedia*, ed. Michael E. Gerli. New York: Routledge, 2003.
———. *Pedro I el Cruel y Enrique de Trastámara: la primera guerra civil española?* Madrid: Santillana Ediciones Generales, S.L., 2002.
———. "La revolución Trastámara." In *Historia de España de la Edad Media*, ed. Vicente Ángel Álvarez Palenzuela. Barcelona: Editorial Ariel, S.A., 2002.
Valente, Claire. *The Theory and Practice of Revolt in Medieval England*. Burlington, VT: Ashgate Publishing Company, 2003.
Vaquero, Mercedes. "Cultura nobiliaria y biblioteca de Fernán Pérez de Guzmán." *Lemir: Revista de Literatura Española Medieval y del Rancimiento*, 7, (2003).
Villalon, L.J. Andrew. "'Cut Off Their Heads, or I'll Cut Off Yours': Castilian Strategy and Tactics in the War of the Two Pedros and the Supporting Evidence from Murcia," in *History of Warfare: The* Hundred Years' War *(part II):Different Vistas*, ed. L.J.A. Villalon and D.J. Kagay. Boston: Brill, 2008.
Vines, Amy N. *Women's Power in Late Medieval Romance*. Cambridge: D.S. Brewer, 2011.
Viroli, Maurizio. *From Politics to Reason of State: The Acquisition and Transformation of the Language of Politics*. Cambridge: Cambridge University Press, 1992.
Weiler, Björn. *Kingship, Rebellion and Political Culture: England and Germany, c. 1215–c. 1250*. New York: Palgrave Macmillan, 2007.
Weissberger, Barbara. *Isabel Rules: Constructing Queenship, Wielding Power*. Minneapolis: University of Minnesota Press, 2003.
———. "'¡A tierra, puto!': Alfonso de Palencia's Discourse of Effiminacy" in *Queer Iberia: Sexualities, Cultures, and Crossings from the Middle Ages to the Renaissance*, ed. Josiah Blackmore and Gregory S. Hutcheson. Durham, NC: Duke University Press, 1999.
West, Geoffrey. "King and Vassal in History and Poetry: A Contrast Between the 'Historica Roderici' and the 'Poema de Mio Cid'." In *"Mio Cid" Studies*, ed. A.D. Deyermond. London: Tamesis Books Limited, 1977.
Wilentz, Sean, ed. *Rites of Power: Symbolism, Ritual, and Politics Since the Middle Ages*. Philadelphia: University of Pennsylvania Press, 1999.
Wilkins, Constane L. *Pero López de Ayala*. Boston: G.K. Hall & Co., 1989.
Wilson, Peter H. *The Thirty Years War: Europe's Tragedy*. Cambridge, MA: Harvard University Press, 2009.
Wright, Nicholas. *Knights and Peasants: The* Hundred Years' War *in the French Countryside*. Woodbridge: Boydell Press, 1998.
Yeager, R.F. "Chaucer Translates the Matter of Spain." In *England and Iberia in the Middle Ages, 12th–15th Century: Cultural, Literary, and Political Exchanges*, ed. María Bullón- Fernández,189–202. New York: Palgrave Macmillan, 2007.

Index

Abu al–Hasan 'Ali, king of Granada 150
Alburquerque, Juan Alfonso de 33–5
Alemán, Rodrigo 204–5
Alexander II, Pope 109–10
Alfonso, prince of Asturias 63–6, 143, 148, 174
Alfonso V, king of Aragon 135
Alfonso VI, king of Castile 42, 47, 182–3
Alfonso VII, king of Castile 207
Alfonso X, king of Castile 66, 68
Alfonso XI, king of Castile 4, 10, 106
Almería, Siege of (1489) 206–7
Amadís de Gaula 123, 151–2, 185–6
Andalucían War (1471–1474) 143, 148–50, 153–4, 159–60, 167–8
anger 38, 130, 132, 156–7, 185
Antequera, Siege of (1410) 132–3

Barba, Juan de 193–5, 205–6
Barbastro Crusade 109
Basurto, Pedro de 189
Benedict XIII, Pope 90
Bernáldez, Andrés 195, 205
Blanche de Bourbon, queen of Castile 33–4
Book of the Knight Zifar, see *Libro del Cauallero Zifar*

caballero 14–16
Callixtus III, Pope 140
Cantar del Mio Cid 41–3, 47, 181–3
captives and capitivity 88, 113–15, 135
Carmona, Siege of (1371) 37–8
Carrillo de Huete, Pedro 58
Cartagena, Alfonso de, bishop of Burgos 13, 22, 168–70
Castilian Civil War (1351–1369) 4–5, 29–30, 33–5
Castro, Felipe de 35
Catalina of Lancaster, queen of Castile 5, 93, 129, 133
Charny, Geoffroi de 104–5, 189
chivalric elite
  definition of 13–17
  fluidity 16–17
chivalry
  chivalric animals 88–90, 205
  definition of 12–13

economic incentives 72–5, 101–2, 133, 153–4, 172
modern perceptions 1–3, 12, 69–70
prescriptive nature
  conduct toward Christians 168–72
  conduct toward commoners 73–4, 79–82
  conduct toward the Crown 43–7, 65–6
  conduct toward Muslims 104–5, 119–123
  conduct toward women 181–6
right to violence 86, 90
Chronicle of the Falconer of Juan II, see Carillo de Huete, Pedro
Claros Varones de Castilla, see Pulgar, Fernando del
Columbus, Christopher 3, 209
commoners, 7, 24–6, 69–71, 73–88, 94–102, 141, 208
  complaints about chivalric violence 7, 82–5
  knightly protection of 73–5
  knightly violence against 74–7, 79–82, 95, 141
  lack of honor 25, 70–1, 96–7
  lack of humanity 24, 75, 88
  petitions for reduction of violence 79–82
  rebellion 97–102
Consolatoria de Castilla, see Barba, Juan de
Coplas por la Muerte de su Padre, see Manrique, Jorge
Coronica del yllustre y muy magnifico cauallero don Alonso Pérez de Guzmán el Bueno 24, 154–5, 158–9
Corral, Pedro de 13, 116–23, 183–4
cortes 15, 16 n. 33, 49, 62, 78–83, 131 n.75, 135, 179–80,
Cots, Juan Vicens 2
Count Lozano 2
Crónica del Rey Don Rodrigo, see Corral, Pedro de
crusade theology 109–11
Cueva, Beltrán de la, Master of Santiago 25, 63–4
cultural community 16–17

Dance of Death, see Dança General de la Muerte
Dança General de la Muerte 83–5
Delacroix, Eugéne 69
Destruction of Spain, *see destruición*
destruición 115–24, 184–5, 193–4
Díaz de Vivar, Rodrigo 1, 21, 42–3, 46–9, 88, 152, 177, 181–3, 204
 coming of age 21, 177
 daughters attacked 181–3
 independent initiative 43, 47–9
 loyalty to king 42, 46–9
 national hero 1–2
 vengeance 2, 182–3
Díez de Games, Gutierre 14–15, 21, 36, 39–40, 46–7, 52–3, 56–7, 60, 73–6, 89–91
 active warrior 14–15
 idealistic chronicler 21, 46–7, 52–3, 73–6
Duke of Arjona 83–4, 180

El Cid *see* Díaz de Vivar, Rodrigo
El Victorial, see Díez de Games, Gutierre
Enrique II, king of Castile 4, 29–32, 34–41, 68, 79–80, 147
 claim to throne 31–2, 34–5, 68
 defeat of Pedro 4, 29–30, 34–5
 punishment of disloyalty 37–8
 rewards for loyalty 36–7
 vengeance 31–2, 34–5, 37–8
Enrique III, king of Castile 4, 127–8, 145
Enrique IV, king of Castile 5, 23, 51–2, 62–8, 82, 93–4, 138–44, 171, 174, 188, 192
 bad reputation 23, 141
 cautious approach to holy war 140–3, 192
 masculinity 64–66, 174, 192
 martial leadership 138–9
 rebellion against 5, 51–2, 63–7, 143–4
Enríquez del Castillo, Diego 23, 65–6, 139–42, 150, 154
executions 33–4, 37–9, 80, 87, 138, 159

Fadrique Alfonso de Castilla 29, 33–4
Farce of Ávila 64–7, 174
Fernando 'de Antequera' I, king of Aragon 5, 26, 77, 100, 128–34, 136, 139, 143, 187, 199
 Antequera campaign 132–3
 approach to holy war 26, 128–33
 use of religious imagery 131–2
 Fernando II, king of Aragon 6, 174, 193–5, 197–201, 205–6
 as savior of Castile 194–5
 reluctant holy warrior 199–201
Fernández de Velasco, Pedro, constable of Castile 198

Ferrandez de Cáceres, Matheos 36–8
Flórez, Darío Fernández 2–3
Foix, Bernal de 35
Franco, Francisco 2–3
Furtado de Mendoza, Juan 25, 56–8, 134

Gaiferos 114–15
García de Salazar, Lope 99–100
Generaciones y semblanzas, see Pérez de Guzmán, Fernán
Gibraltar, Siege of (1462) 143, 154–8
Golden Age 4, 210–11
González de Mendoza, Pedro, cardinal and archbishop of Toledo 204–5
Granada War (1482–1492) 193–5, 197–207
Gregory VII, Pope 109–10
Guesclin, Bertrand du 29, 35
Guzmán, Juan Alfonso de, Count of Niebla 36
Guzmán, Juan de, Duke of Medina Sidonia 143, 154–7, 161

Hechos del condestable Don Miguel Lucas de Iranzo 24, 65, 93–4, 113–14, 142–3, 161, 167, 170–1
 establishing Iranzo's nobility 93–4
 plea for holy war 113–14, 142–3
Herrara, Constanza de 188–9
hidalgo 13–15, 49
Historia de los hechos del marqués de Cádiz 1, 21, 24, 154, 157, 160, 168
Higueruela, Battle of (1431) 24, 164
homosexuality 65–6, 93, 177, 192
holy war 2–3, 5–6, 9, 26–7, 77–8, 92, 104–44, 146, 154–61, 166, 169–72, 187–8, 193–209
 cautious prosecution 138–41
 Christian captives 112–15
 crusade 9, 109–10
 historical imperative 26, 116–23, 169–70, 193–7
 historiography of 105–7
 political stability 5, 26, 108–109, 126–44
 political utility 108, 128, 135–6, 171–2
 relationship to non–holy war 5–6, 26–7, 146, 154–61
 spiritual reward 110–12, 119–21
 vigorous prosecution 92, 107, 121–2, 124–5, 129–33, 135–7, 199–204
honor 7, 17–20, 25–6, 30, 35, 37–8, 40, 42, 44, 49, 57, 67, 70–1, 74–5, 86–8, 90–7, 104–9, 110, 114, 122–5, 132–3, 141, 146, 151–61, 164–7, 172, 176–8, 181–3, 186–7, 189–90, 192, 194–8, 203–4, 208
 Castilian corporate honor 122–3, 141
 commoner lack thereof 25–6, 71, 86–8

INDEX

definition 17
feminine 178, 183, 186–7, 194–5
masculine 176–8, 196
public nature 18, 160–1
relationship to linaje 19–20, 26, 49,
  90–4, 124–5, 155–61, 166–7, 189–90
relationship to violence 18–19, 26,
  37–8, 40, 49, 70–1, 86, 151–4, 164–6,
  196–7
vengeance 18–19, 37–8, 74, 110, 182–3,
  192
Hundred Years' War 4–5, 27, 29, 73, 95,
  129, 134, 145, 196

Infantes of Aragon 53–4, 60–1, 134–5,
  137–8, 162–3
Iranzo, Miguel Lucas de, constable of
  Castile 24–5, 63, 65–6, 93–4, 113–14,
  142–3, 154, 161, 170–2
  holy war 25, 113–14, 142–3, 170–2
  linaje 93–4, 161, 172
  war against fellow Christians 161,
    170–2
Irmandiños Revolts 97–102, 208
Isabel I, queen of Castile 3, 5–6, 27, 174,
  178, 191–207
  as intercessor 191
  as martial leader 196–201, 204–7
  as mother 194–5
  as savior of Castile 193–5, 205–7
  demure femininity 192–5
  mastery of chivalric ideology 191–3,
    197–201, 204–7

Joan of Arc 196–9, 202–4
Joan II, king of Aragon 191–2
Juan I, king of Castile 4, 72, 80–1, 127,
  147, 179–80
Juan II, king of Castile 5, 26, 51, 53–62,
  76–8, 95, 99–100, 113, 128–9, 134–8,
  162–4, 169
  favoritism 5, 53–6, 59, 134, 137, 162–4
  holy war 26, 77–8, 113, 134–8, 164, 169
  internal wars 5, 51, 56–62, 95, 99–100
Juana 'la Beltraneja' 5, 64, 174
Julián, Visigothic count 116–19, 121, 183–4

knightly independence 5, 25, 30, 41, 43,
  48–50, 55–7, 80–2, 85, 127–8
  disruptions to public order 30, 80–2,
    85
  political power 25, 30, 43, 56–7
  warfare 30, 43, 48–9, 127–8

La Cava 116–17, 183–5
La Poncella de Francia 196–99, 202–4
la tala 76–7, 140, 199–201

effect on population 76
military strategy 77, 201
largesse 35, 202
law 43–4, 49, 79–80, 86–8, 182, 187–8
Libro de Rimado de Palacio, see López de
  Ayala, Pedro
Libro del Cauallero Zifar 44–5, 89, 96
linaje 7, 19–20, 26–7, 49, 86, 90–6, 107,
  121, 124–5, 153, 155–6, 158–9, 161, 166, 208
  definition of 19
  familial honor 19–20, 27, 49, 90–2,
    124, 153, 155–6, 161
  holy war 26, 92, 124–5, 155–6, 166
  individual honor 19–20, 90–6, 153
  memory 49, 124–5, 158–9, 166
  social status 19–20, 86, 90–4
López de Ayala, Pedro, Grand Chancellor
  of Castile 23–4, 34, 37–8, 112–13, 117,
  145, 147–8, 160
  active knight 23–4,
  chronicler 23–4, 38 145, 147–8, 160
  Libro de Rimado de Palacio 112
López de Córdoba, Martín, master of the
  Order of Calatrava 36–7
López de Mendoza, Iñigo 188
loyalty 25, 32, 40–7, 49–57, 59–62, 65–68
love (romantic) 22, 175–6, 178
Luna, Álvaro de, Constable of Castile 5,
  25, 53–6, 58–63, 76–7, 90–1, 137–8,
  162–4, 193
  holy warrior 164
  royal favorite 5, 25, 53–6, 162–3
  warrior, 25, 53–6, 60–1

Manrique, Juan 188–9
Manrique, Jorge 111–12, 124–5
masculinity 21, 27, 65, 158, 174–9, 189,
  193, 196, 207
  coming of age 21, 177–8
  domination 21, 176–8
  personal honor 65, 175–8, 189, 196
Matter of Spain 115–16, 123
Medina del Campo, Battle of (1441) 60–1,
  138
Medina Sidonia, Siege of 150, 159
Mendoza family 36, 91–2, 204
meritorious suffering 110–11, 162–3
Mocedades de Rodrigo 21, 46, 48–9, 88,
  152, 177
Moclín, Disaster of (1280) 205–6
Moclín, Siege of (1486) 205–7
Montemayor, Martín Alonso de 130
Montiel, Siege of (1369) 29
Muhammad VII, king of Granada 129
Muhammad VIII, king of Granada 113
Muhammad IX, king of Granada 113,
  135–6

Muhammad XII, king of Granada   206, 209

Nicholas V, Pope   140
Niño, Juan   39–40, 91
Niño, Pero, count of Buelna   13, 24, 46–7, 52–3, 56–7, 60, 73–6, 89–91, 101, 177
   effects of war on commoners   73–6
   fear   101
   his chivalric horse   89
   loyalty   46–7, 52–3, 56–7, 60
   upbringing   13, 90–91, 177
Niño, Pero Fernández   39

Olmedo, Battle of (1445)   60–1, 138, 162–4
Olmedo, Battle of (1467)   204

Pacheco, Juan, marquis de Villena   62–7, 174
   as favorite   62–3
   rebellion against the Crown   63–7
Palencia, Alfonso de   23–4, 66, 100–1, 141
Pedro 'the Cruel', king of Castile   4, 25, 29–30, 32–6, 39, 41, 68
   death of   29–30
   murders   29, 33–5
Pelayo, king of Asturias   120
Pere IV, king of Aragon   29
Pérez de Guzmán, Alonso 'el Bueno'   155, 158–9
Pérez de Guzmán, Fernán   23–4, 55–7, 76, 91–3, 100, 129, 132–3, 135–8, 166
   active knight   24
   chronicle of Juan II   55–7, 76, 100, 129, 132–3, 135–8,
   Generaciones y Semblanzas   91–3
   Mar de las estorias   166
petristas   36–40
Ponce de León, Juan, marques of Cádiz and count of Arcos   141, 148, 156–8
Ponce de León, Rodrigo, marques of Cádiz and count of Arcos   1, 149–50, 156–7, 159–60, 167–8
Poole, raiding of   73–5
prisoners of war   37, 73, 75, 95, 130
privado, see royal favorite
Pulgar, Fernando del   13, 91–2, 95, 197–8, 200, 202

Quiñones, Suero de   22–3, 165

rape   27, 116–17, 121, 150, 176, 179–81, 183–6
   chivalric scorn for   150, 176, 180–1, 185–6
   of La Cava   116–17, 121, 183–5
   proscription of   179–80
   shame   183–5
   vengeance for   185

rebellion   5, 33–4, 44–6, 51–2, 58–61, 64–8, 97–102, 133, 174, 191–2
   by commoners   97–102
   by nobles   5, 33–4, 52, 58–61, 64–8, 174
reconquista   3, 26, 105–7, 115–16, 120–5, 128–32, 136–44, 205–7
   Castilian failures   121–2, 128, 137–44, 205–7
   Castilian successes   123, 130, 132, 136, 205–7
   in modern historiography   3, 105–7
   vengeance for the Islamic conquest   26, 105, 115–16, 122–4
Rio Salado, Battle of (1340)   159
Roland   2, 21, 114, 157
royal favorite   5, 25, 33, 53, 62–3, 134
revenge, *see* vengeance
Rodrigo, king of Spain   116–22, 183–5

Saladin   166
Sanchez, Juana   188–9
Sancho, Visigothic prince   119
Sancho Alfonso de Castilla   35
Santa Hermandad   6, 97
Sevilla   37–8, 130, 149, 167
Siete Partidas   43–4, 86–7
Sixtus IV, Pope   113, 170, 172

Toledo Cathedral choir stalls   204–7
tournament   22–2, 104, 165
Trastámara, Enrique de, *see* Enrique II, king of Castile
treason   44–6, 65–6, 117, 184
Tristan   164–5

Urban II, Pope   109–10

Valera, Diego de   12, 23–4, 66, 94, 99, 139–41, 149–50, 154–7, 167, 180–1, 189–90
   active knight   24
   correspondence   99
   Memorial de diversas hazañas   66, 94, 139–41, 149–50, 154–7, 167, 180–1, 189–90
      Andalucian War   149–50, 154–7, 167, 180–1, 189–90
Vega, Leonor de la   187–8
vengeance   2, 18–19, 26, 32, 35, 37–8, 74–5, 97, 100, 106, 122–5, 144, 150–1, 157, 159–60, 182–6, 186, 192–3, 199, 202–3, 206
   against Islam   26, 106, 122–5, 144, 192, 202, 206
   for personal injury   37–8, 150, 192
   for familial injury   2, 35, 106, 124–5, 159–60, 182–4, 206
   of God   100, 209

Villandrando, Rodrigo de, count of Ribadeo 95
Villena, Enrique de, master of Calatrava 14
Visigoths 107, 115–19, 122, 184–5, 194, 202
Vox (political party) 3

War of the Castilian Succession 174
War of the Two Pedros 29
women 12, 27, 45, 73, 83, 88, 96, 114, 116, 150, 171, 174–6, 178–207
   as lords 187–9
   martial roles 188–9, 196, 204–7
   masculine protection of 12, 96, 114
   model motherhood 189–90, 194–5
   perpetrating violence 27, 187–91
   sexual purity 178
   shaming men 189–90
   submissiveness 178, 187, 191, 193–4
   violence against 12, 27, 83, 88, 96, 116, 150, 171, 179–86, *see also* rape

Yañez de Barbudo, Martín, master of Alcantara 127–8
Yusuf III, king of Granada 131–2
Yusuf IV, king of Granada 136

Warfare in History

The Battle of Hastings: Sources and Interpretations, *edited and introduced by Stephen Morillo*

Infantry Warfare in the Early Fourteenth Century: Discipline, Tactics, and Technology, *Kelly DeVries*

The Art of Warfare in Western Europe during the Middle Ages, from the Eighth Century to 1340 (second edition), *J.F. Verbruggen*

Knights and Peasants: The Hundred Years' War in the French Countryside, *Nicholas Wright*

Society at War: The Experience of England and France during the Hundred Years' War, *edited by Christopher Allmand*

The Circle of War in the Middle Ages: Essays on Medieval Military and Naval History, *edited by Donald J. Kagay and L.J. Andrew Villalon*

The Anglo-Scots Wars, 1513–1550: A Military History, *Gervase Phillips*

The Norwegian Invasion of England in 1066, *Kelly DeVries*

The Wars of Edward III: Sources and Interpretations, *edited by Clifford J. Rogers*

The Battle of Agincourt: Sources and Interpretations, *Anne Curry*

War Cruel and Sharp: English Strategy under Edward III, 1327–1360, *Clifford J. Rogers*

The Normans and their Adversaries at War: Essays in Memory of C. Warren Hollister, *edited by Richard P. Abels and Bernard S. Bachrach*

The Battle of the Golden Spurs (Courtrai, 11 July 1302): A Contribution to the History of Flanders' War of Liberation, 1297–1305, *J.F. Verbruggen*

War at Sea in the Middle Ages and the Renaissance, *edited by John B. Hattendorf and Richard W. Unger*

Swein Forkbeard's Invasions and the Danish Conquest of England, 991–1017, *Ian Howard*

Religion and the Conduct of War, c.300–1215, *David S. Bachrach*

Warfare in Medieval Brabant, 1356–1406, *Sergio Boffa*

Renaissance Military Memoirs: War, History and Identity, 1450–1600, *Yuval Noah Harari*

The Place of War in English History, 1066–1214, *J.O. Prestwich, edited by Michael Prestwich*

War and the Soldier in the Fourteenth Century, *Adrian R. Bell*

German War Planning, 1891–1914: Sources and Interpretations, *Terence Zuber*

The Battle of Crécy, 1346, *Andrew Ayton and Sir Philip Preston*

The Battle of Yorktown, 1781: A Reassessment, *John D. Grainger*

Special Operations in the Age of Chivalry, 1100–1550, *Yuval Noah Harari*

Women, Crusading and the Holy Land in Historical Narrative, *Natasha R. Hodgson*

The English Aristocracy at War: From the Welsh Wars of Edward I to the Battle of Bannockburn, *David Simpkin*

The Calais Garrison: War and Military Service in England, 1436–1558, *David Grummitt*

Renaissance France at War: Armies, Culture and Society, c. 1480–1560, *David Potter*

Bloodied Banners: Martial Display on the Medieval Battlefield, *Robert W. Jones*

Alfred's Wars: Sources and Interpretations of Anglo-Saxon Warfare in the Viking Age, *Ryan Lavelle*

The Dutch Army and the Military Revolutions, 1588–1688, *Olaf van Nimwegen*

In the Steps of the Black Prince: The Road to Poitiers, 1355–1356, *Peter Hoskins*

Norman Naval Operations in the Mediterranean, *Charles D. Stanton*

Shipping the Medieval Military: English Maritime Logistics in the Fourteenth Century, *Craig L. Lambert*

Edward III and the War at Sea: The English Navy, 1327–1377, *Graham Cushway*

The Soldier Experience in the Fourteenth Century, *edited by Adrian R. Bell, Anne Curry, Adam Chapman, Andy King and David Simpkin*

Warfare in Tenth-Century Germany, *David S. Bachrach*

Chivalry, Kingship and Crusade: The English Experience in the Fourteenth Century, *Timothy Guard*

The Norman Campaigns in the Balkans, 1081–1108, *Georgios Theotokis*

Welsh Soldiers in the Later Middle Ages, 1282–1422, *Adam Chapman*

Merchant Crusaders in the Aegean, 1291–1352, *Mike Carr*

Henry of Lancaster's Expedition to Aquitaine, 1345–1346: Military Service and Professionalism in the Hundred Years' War, *Nicholas A. Gribit*

Scotland's Second War of Independence, 1332–1357, *Iain A. MacInnes*

Military Communities in Late Medieval England: Essays in Honour of Andrew Ayton, *edited by Gary P. Baker, Craig L. Lambert and David Simpkin*

The Black Prince and the *Grande Chevauchée* of 1355, *Mollie M. Madden*

Military Society and the Court of Chivalry in the Age of the Hundred Years' War, *Philip J. Caudrey*

Warfare in the Norman Mediterranean, *edited by Georgios Theotokis*